International water security

# International water security: Domestic threats and opportunities

Edited by Nevelina I. Pachova, Mikiyasu Nakayama and Libor Jansky

**United Nations University Press**

TOKYO · NEW YORK · PARIS

The views expressed in this publication are those of the authors and do not necessarily reflect the views of the United Nations University.

United Nations University Press
United Nations University, 53–70, Jingumae 5-chome,
Shibuya-ku, Tokyo 150-8925, Japan
Tel: +81-3-3499-2811   Fax: +81-3-3406-7345
E-mail: sales@hq.unu.edu   general enquiries: press@hq.unu.edu
http://www.unu.edu

United Nations University Office at the United Nations, New York
2 United Nations Plaza, Room DC2-2062, New York, NY 10017, USA
Tel: +1-212-963-6387   Fax: +1-212-371-9454
E-mail: unuona@ony.unu.edu

United Nations University Press is the publishing division of the United Nations University.

Cover design by Mea Rhee

Printed in Hong Kong

ISBN 978-92-808-1150-6

Library of Congress Cataloging-in-Publication Data

International water security : domestic threats and opportunities / edited by Nevelina I. Pachova, Mikiyasu Nakayama and Libor Jansky.
    p.   cm.
  Includes index.
  ISBN 978-9280811506 (pbk.)
  1. Water-supply—Management—Political aspects. 2. Water resources development—International cooperation. 3. Integrated water development.
I. Pachova, Nevelina I. II. Nakayama, Mikiyasu. III. Jansky, Libor.
HD1691.I54   2008
333.91—dc22                                          2008003990

# Contents

# Figures

# Tables

# Contributors

**Bastien Affeltranger** is a researcher in Mekong hydropolitics, with a focus on hydrological data management. He graduated in Geography from Laval University, Quebec, Canada. A former UN consultant in natural disaster mitigation and now at the Institut National de l'environnement industriel et des risques (INERIS) in France, he is an Associate Researcher at the Institut Québécois des Hautes Études Internationales (IQHEI), Quebec.

**Anthi Dionissia Brouma** is finalizing her doctoral thesis at the School of Oriental and African Studies, University of London, UK, on the topic of Bi-Communal Water Policy Networks in Nicosia, Cyprus, while working at the same time with the Global Water Partnership – Mediterranean (GWP-Med) in the field of Integrated Water Resources Management in North Africa and the Middle East. Her research interests include the themes of water governance with an emphasis on policy networks, water policy and discourse analysis of national and transboundary watercourses.

**Mahmoud El Zain** is an Assistant Professor in the Department of Environment, Peace and Security at the United Nations-mandated University for Peace in Costa Rica. His research interests include issues of hydropolitics, environment and sustainable development, the political potential of environmental risks, conflict and conflict transformation, and socio-cultural displacement and the political potential of population movements.

**Mete Erdem** is an Edward Bramley research associate in public international law at the Centre for Law in its International Context in the University of Sheffield School of Law, UK, and was formerly an assistant legal adviser to the Turkish Ministry of Foreign Affairs. His area of interest lies in international environmental law, with a special emphasis on international watercourses.

**Libor Jansky** is currently a Senior Academic Programme Officer at the United Nations University Vice Rectorate in Europe. Prior to joining UNU in 1999, he was a Senior Lecturer in environmental science at the Comenius University in Bratislava, Slovakia. He is serving as a UNU Focal Point for the GEF project on Land Management in the High Pamir and Pamir-Alai Mountains in Central Asia and his research focus is in soil and water conservation, biodiversity and freshwater resources management.

**Marko Keskinen** is a researcher and PhD candidate at the Water Resources Laboratory of Helsinki University of Technology, Finland. His research focuses on the interactions between water and society as well as on multi- and interdisciplinary approaches to water management, with a specific focus on the Mekong region.

**Aysegül Kibaroglu** is an Associate Professor at the Department of International Relations, Middle East Technical University, Ankara, Turkey. Her areas of research include transboundary water politics, international water law, political ecology and environmental security. She has published extensively on the politics of water resources in the Euphrates Tigris river basin, including the volume *Building a Regime for the Waters of the Euphrates-Tigris River Basin* (Kluwer Academic Publishers, 2002).

**Katri Mehtonen** is a PhD candidate at the Water Resources Laboratory of

Helsinki University of Technology, Finland. Her research focuses on the management of international rivers, particularly on the viewpoints of the upstream countries. Her specific focus is China's role in relation to those international rivers that flow southwards from China.

**Richard Meissner** holds a D.Phil. in International Politics from the University of Pretoria, South Africa. His thesis focused on the transnational role and involvement of interest groups in water politics, with particular reference to the proposed Epupa Dam on the Kunene River and the Lesotho Highlands Water Project in the upper reaches of the Orange/Senqu River in Lesotho. His research interests include politics, international relations and leadership.

**Naho Mirumachi** is a PhD candidate at the Department of Geography, King's College London, UK. Her research interests include international transboundary relations and incentives for cooperation over shared water resources. For her PhD research, she is working on a conceptual approach – Transboundary Waters Interaction NexuS (TWINS) – to exemplify trajectories of different international transboundary relations.

**Mikiyasu Nakayama** is a Professor at the Graduate School of Frontier Science, University of Tokyo, Japan. His research interests include management of international water bodies, in particular the involvement of international organizations.

**Madiodio Niasse** is currently working with IRD (the French Institute for

Development Research) as Research Director. Since May 2004, he has been Chairman of the West Africa chapter of the Global Water Partnership (GWP/WA). Since June 2007, he has chaired the Roster of Experts of the newly established Independent Review Mechanism (IRM) of the African Development Bank. At the time of co-drafting his chapter in this volume, he was coordinator of IUCN's West Africa Regional Water and Wetlands Programme.

**Kayo Onishi** is a doctoral student in the Graduate School for Law and Politics, University of Tokyo, Japan, and the Department of Political Science, Indiana University, Bloomington, USA. Her research interests include water conflict and cooperation and resource politics.

**Nevelina I. Pachova** is a Programme Associate at the United Nations University Vice Rectorate in Europe, based in Bonn, Germany. She is involved in the development and implementation of sustainable land, water and forest resources management initiatives in transitional and developing countries in Central and Eastern Europe and Asia. Her academic background and interests lie in the fields of international development and environmental economics.

**Virpi Stucki** works currently as a Programme Officer at the Forest Conservation Programme of IUCN – The World Conservation Union. She has several years' work experience on water and forest issues mainly from Africa. Prior to joining IUCN, she worked as a Research Associate at the Helsinki

University of Technology's Water Resources Management laboratory, from where she has Master's and Licentiate's degrees.

**Olli Varis** is a Senior Researcher at the Water Resources Laboratory of Helsinki University of Technology, Finland, and has a broad and interdisciplinary experience in water, environment and development research and consultation. He is a frequently used expert by various international organizations, and the author of over 300 scientific papers.

**Jeroen Warner** is a Senior Researcher on participatory river planning at the Centre for the Sustainable Management of Resources, Radboud University Nijmegen, the Netherlands. He coordinated the "Multi-Stakeholder Platforms for Integrated Catchment Management" research projects for the Irrigation and Water Engineering group at Wageningen University (2001–2005). His research interests include water politics, conflict and participation, with special reference to flood management issues.

**Shuntaro Yamamoto** secured his BA from the Faculty of Law and his MA from the Graduate School of Public Policy of the University of Tokyo, Japan. When in the Graduate School he worked on the process of negotiation between India and Pakistan in the 1940s and 1950s over the shared water resources of the Indus River. He visited these countries and interviewed a number of relevant people for this study.

# 1

# Introduction: From domestic to international water security

*Libor Jansky, Mikiyasu Nakayama and Nevelina I. Pachova*

Water is essential for all aspects of life. Ensuring water security – i.e. adequate protection from water-related disasters and diseases and access to sufficient quantity and quality of water, at affordable cost, to meet the basic food, energy and other needs essential for leading a healthy and productive life without compromising the sustainability of vital ecosystems – has emerged as an overarching global goal over the past decade.

Integrated water resources management (IWRM), defined as the coordinated planning, development and management of water, land and related resources, through multi-level and multi-sectoral dynamic and interactive problem-solving approaches, has been proposed as a mechanism for maximizing the economic and social welfare benefits from water development and use in an equitable and sustainable manner. IWRM recognizes basins as the natural water management units and encourages the development of integrated basin-wide water use and management strategies, action plans and institutions.

Initially proposed in Chapter 18 of Agenda 21, the plan of action adopted at the United Nations Conference on Environment and Development in Rio de Janeiro in 1992, the concept of integrated water management has become a widespread national policy framework since then. Over the past decade, notable progress has been made in developing national IWRM strategies and action plans and integrating them in the broader development strategies of states aimed at achieving the Millennium Development Goals (MDGs), a time-bound set of goals agreed

*International water security: Domestic threats and opportunities, Pachova, Nakayama and Jansky (eds), United Nations University Press, 2008, ISBN 978-92-808-1150-6*

upon by world leaders in 2000. However, the application of the concept of IWRM to transboundary water resources, i.e. surface and groundwater resources shared by two or more states, has proved a challenging task.

Indeed, cooperation among riparian states over the use of shared waters has a long history. The numerous instances of and benefits from cooperation in the past have weakened fears of water wars, raised in the mid-1990s in light of the expected growth in water needs, particularly in developing states. Unresolved political tensions over the use of trans-boundary waters, however, continue to simmer and new ones continue to emerge along with changing water needs, values and governance structures in riparian states. These tensions constitute significant obstacles to undertaking the often much-needed development and utilization of international waters, on which the water security of more than half of the world's population depends.

The national sovereignty and security considerations of states have long been noted as critical causes of international water tensions and disputes. In the context of the processes of post–Cold War democratization and globalization, non-state domestic actors have come to play a much more prominent role in national decision-making on traditionally foreign policy debates. Furthermore, the definitions of the concepts of sovereignty and security have evolved. These changes entail new threats but also new opportunities for ensuring international water security.

This book explores some of them through a set of case studies analysing the multi-faceted and dynamic nature of the interplay between domestic and international water security. A range of past, ongoing and emerging international water disputes from the Middle East, Africa, Asia and Europe are examined. Well-known cases are revisited from new perspectives and new approaches are suggested as analytical frameworks and practical tools for understanding and coping with emerging security threats.

The book is divided into three parts. The first examines the impacts and implications of domestic security considerations for the negotiation and implementation of international water treaties and for the functioning of water management institutions in international basins. The second part highlights emerging water security threats in international basins driven by domestic security dynamics. The third proposes a range of new analytical frameworks and approaches for engaging domestic actors in the search for solutions to both long-standing water management disputes and emerging security threats.

Part I begins with three chapters that examine from a historical perspective the role that domestic factors, actors and processes have played in both facilitating and hindering the signature and subsequent implementation of important international water management agreements in

Asia, Africa and Europe. In Chapter 2 Yamamoto revisits the classic Indus water dispute and the agreement between India and Pakistan facilitated by the World Bank, highlighting the often overlooked role that communal divides, regional inequalities and national development policies in the two states have played in shaping their positions on international water management in the course of the negotiations.

In Chapter 3 Mirumachi brings out the role of domestic political leadership in a small landlocked country such as Lesotho in designing and negotiating a water management agreement with a large regional hegemon that was beneficial for the national economy. The author also highlights the importance of civil society activism in subsequently negotiating a more equitable sharing of the benefits from the international water management scheme.

In Chapter 4, Pachova and Jansky examine a case in which a civil society movement in a transitional context in Europe managed to forestall the implementation of an international treaty on water development in the Danube because of its expected environmental damage. Environmental activism coupled with political aspirations and ethnic minority concerns, however, triggered the escalation of an international dispute, whose alleviation has taken up significant efforts and resources.

In the last two chapters of Part I, the establishment and functioning of international water management institutions are examined from the viewpoint of domestic security challenges. Keskinen et al. (Chapter 5) analyse hindrances to the functioning of the Mekong Commission associated with domestic developments, priorities and capacities in China and Cambodia, the upstream and downstream riparian states. While noting the challenges, the authors also highlight the potential for strengthened regional cooperation in a broader development framework that the economic power and national priorities of the regional hegemon entail.

Stucki and Niasse (Chapter 6) follow up a similar line of research but take an extreme case, that of the Lake Chad Basin Commission, whose functioning has been severely constrained by the widespread civil strife and poverty affecting all of the riparian states. In the absence of an economically powerful regional hegemon, as in the case of the Mekong, the authors argue that international support is crucial for ensuring the functioning of the Commission.

In Part II of the book the domestic security lens is employed to identify emerging international water security threats. El Zain (Chapter 7) warns of an impending political conflict over the use of Nile waters owing to rapid population growth in riparian provinces in Sudan, as a result of refugee flows from regions disrupted by civil war, and to ill-conceived development policies deepening structural inequalities and socially constructed water scarcity.

In Chapter 8 Affeltranger pinpoints the Salween River Basin as an emerging hotspot of regional tensions in the Mekong region owing to a water development and transfer scheme between Myanmar and Thailand, aimed at alleviating growing domestic water demand in Thailand without incurring domestic opposition to the construction of new hydraulic infrastructure on the territory of the country. The author forewarns that the project, currently politically endorsed owing to the overlap of national and regional security and development objectives, entails hidden threats to the water security of the inhabitants of the Salween Basin as well as the Mekong region as a whole.

In Chapter 9 Nakayama proposes "virtual" water, i.e. water embedded in key water-intensive commodities, as an alternative approach for meeting water needs in the context of water scarcity, and argues that trade-offs between real and virtual water need to be examined before large-scale water transfer schemes in the Mekong Basin are undertaken. He also employs the concept of virtual water to highlight a looming water security threat in Central Asia, where the stabilization of Afghanistan is likely to lead to increased water demand for agricultural production, which is currently met through food imports and international aid.

Part III of the book introduces some new perspectives and practical tools for engaging domestic actors in the search for solutions to both domestic and international water security concerns. In Chapter 10 Onishi draws attention to the potential benefits from situating international water security debates in a broader framework of regional cooperation, which allows international water debates to become non-zero-sum games. The author suggests that, although domestic security considerations in China (including energy needs, regional inequalities and associated separatist threats) might make it difficult to reach a compromise on international water management in the Mekong, regional cooperation, motivated by the potential gains from trade and the growing importance of good reputation in the context of increasing economic and political interdependence globally, may provide an alternative avenue for meeting the water security and economic development needs of the downstream states.

For the benefits of regional cooperation to reach those who most need them, however, human security has to be situated at the centre of it according to Kibaroglu et al., who pursue the idea in Chapter 11. Taking up the case of the management of the Tigris and Euphrates river basins shared by Turkey, Syria and Iraq, the authors argue that, in contrast to negotiations focused narrowly on water, regional development cooperation could help address the pressing human security needs of the people inhabiting the basins in question, while fostering the capacities and potential for long-term partnership over transboundary water management through improved efficiency in water use and enhanced trust among the riparian states.

In Chapter 12, starting from the idea that perceptions of both water needs and security threats do matter in international water management disputes, Warner and Meissner propose a tool called security impact assessment (SIA) for analysing the redistribution of actual and perceived security as a result of water development interventions and projects among the key stakeholder groups involved. They employ SIA to examine water security trade-offs in the Okavango Basin, highlighting the positive role of information and knowledge exchange as a means for alleviating actual as well as perceived insecurity.

The authors of the individual chapters come from a range of disciplinary and professional backgrounds and approach the issue of water management from diverse theoretical perspectives. Their findings highlight the varied aspects of the multifaceted interplay between domestic and international water security. Furthermore, they bring to the fore the need to change the way we think of and deal with associated threats to international water security, which are discussed in more detail in the concluding chapter of the book.

# Part I

# Treaties and institutions

# 2

# The Indus water dispute and its relation with domestic policies

*Shuntaro Yamamoto*

## Introduction

The Indus water dispute was an international water issue originating in the independence of India and Pakistan. India and Pakistan had (and still have) a very complex international relationship and it was difficult to settle their issues, especially in the new era. Generally speaking, water issues involve so many difficulties to be resolved because they seem to be a zero-sum game. We therefore expect that the Indus case and its process of negotiation will give us some essential hints for resolving current international watercourse problems. It is well known that the World Bank played a very important role as a mediator and many researchers have undertaken studies from the viewpoint of third-party mediation. They offer many interesting facts and information for solving and preventing international water problems.

However, a third party such as the World Bank can always contribute to the settlement of international water issues. What researchers have paid less attention to is the domestic implications of this dispute. The World Bank's contribution had such a great impact that other aspects were less interesting. Thus, in this chapter, I focus on domestic issues in India and Pakistan and their relation to the negotiating process in the Indus case, a perspective that has been rather neglected.

For this purpose, domestic politics and the economic and international situation must be analysed and it is necessary to shed light on the detailed negotiations in the Indus case. *Keesing's Contemporary Archives* and newspapers in India and Pakistan (*Times of India* and *Dawn*) are

*International water security: Domestic threats and opportunities, Pachova, Nakayama and Jansky (eds), United Nations University Press, 2008, ISBN 978-92-808-1150-6*

very useful sources. *Keesing's Contemporary Archives* contain detailed information which tells us about the statements made by India and Pakistan and sometimes which minister was responsible for the statement. Newspapers have the same information but the number of articles dealing with the canal dispute will give clues to when the Indus issue was "hot". We can determine that the canal dispute was "hot" when a month or a year has a lot of articles about the issue and not when there are few articles. The memoirs of Jawaharlal Nehru (see Gopal 1987) and the diaries of David Lilienthal (1966), who were very important individuals in the Indus dispute, are also useful. Nehru's memoirs reveal how his and India's attitudes towards the canal dispute changed and Lilienthal's diaries enlighten us about the efforts of the World Bank. Interviews with people in India and Pakistan who are very knowledgeable about this dispute also have great value. I chose journalists who knew Nehru and the proceedings of the negotiations and administrators of the Indus. They provided important information from the viewpoint not only of history but also of technology.

Issues that had no direct link with the canal dispute are also included in this chapter; in particular, I refer to political, industrial and agricultural issues, making use of historical resources and articles about the economy. Because states face so many problems, it is impossible to focus on everything. This chapter concentrates on issues of economic development, unifying a multicultural society and security, which both newborn countries had to deal with. I also consider problems involving both countries, such as Kashmir. Immediately after independence, both India and Pakistan faced problems of state unity and development. Both countries had many ethnic groups in the areas at this time and language problems were fundamental to identity issues. At the same time, they had to develop their economies and improve national life and they were trying to promote industry and agriculture. However, their development plans did not work well. International problems between both countries were also critical. They had not agreed on the borders between Bengal and Punjab, or in Kashmir. The partition of British India's assets such as civil servants and armed forces led to other disputes. These problems were not resolved until 1960 and it is interesting to compare them with the Indus dispute, which was settled by a treaty.

Before I start to discuss the dispute, I need to provide general information about the problems in the Indus River Basin. The dispute had been a domestic issue in British India and became international after the partition of India and Pakistan following independence in 1947. A lot of people were killed during the partition process. Therefore this dispute was not just a competition over resources but also an emotional issue.

Prior to independence, there was an agricultural water utilization issue between the autonomous states of Sind and Punjab (Nakayama 1996: 78–

80). British India gave autonomous states rights to develop water resources in their region. In 1941, the Indus conference was established and chief engineers from both states who were responsible for water resource development held informal talks between 1943 and 1945, which resulted in a draft resolution. At the beginning of 1947 they asked the British government to mediate a final decision, but the mediation was unsuccessful. Before the water issue could be settled, independence was achieved and India and Pakistan were partitioned. The issue then became complicated. The former Punjab was divided into two parts: western Punjab became Pakistan and eastern Punjab became part of India.

The divided Punjab was important for both states, in different ways. For India, the Punjab region was one of its poorest and it recognized the necessity to develop the area, especially in terms of irrigation because no major irrigation system had been constructed in the eastern Punjab since 1917 (the Bhakra project had been prepared in 1919, but it was not authorized until 1945). On the other hand, Pakistan had no major industries apart from agriculture after independence and partition because the main products of the region had always been crops such as jute. Moreover, most capital flowed to India at that time. Thus, Pakistan had to depend on agriculture although it also tried to develop heavy industries just after independence. In these ways, both countries attached great importance to water from the Indus Basin. Negotiations between the two nations were destined to be difficult. It took more than a decade to resolve the problem in 1960, thanks to mediation by the World Bank.

Aside from water, India and Pakistan have had many complex problems, involving not only Kashmir but immigration, currency and trade issues. However, the Indus dispute was the only case in which they successfully resolved the conflicts between them. It is also important from the point of view of the World Bank's mediation. This was a leading case in which the World Bank tried to arbitrate an international water conflict. Paying attention to how the two countries treated this problem in relation to their other difficulties and how the World Bank effected political adjustment in both states will give us some clues to solving hydropolitical questions from both the domestic and the international security perspective.

## The Indus River Basin

### Geographical outline

The Indus is about 3,200 km (2,000 miles) in length and flows through north-west India and Pakistan. It has seven main tributaries. Two small ones, the Kabul River and the Kurram River, come from the west and together are over 1,100 km (700 miles) long. The five major tributaries are from the east – the Jhelum, the Chenab, the Ravi, the Beas and the Sutlej – and their total length is more than 2,800 km (1,800 miles). They begin in the Himalayan snow belt and discharge into the Arabian Sea, all the rivers conveying $90 \times 106$ acre-feet of water and covering a drainage area of 720,000 km$^2$ (450,000 square miles). The Indus and the Sutlej, its eastern-most tributary, have their origin in the Tibetan plateau; the western rivers, the Kabul and the Kurram, rise in Afghanistan. About 13 per cent of the total catchment area of the basin lies in Tibet and Afghanistan; the rest is in India and Pakistan.

The main Indus River and its major tributaries make up the Indus system. The main Indus starts north of the Himalayas, near Lake Mansarovar, and before it reaches south-eastern Kashmir it runs through Tibet for about 320 km (200 miles). Skirting Leh in Ladakh (India), the Indus runs south-west toward Gilgit and arrives in Pakistan after 56 km (35 miles). It then makes a long trip and appears out of the hills near Attock, where the waters of the Kabul and the Swat, another tributary, join the Indus. After this junction, it flows south-west and meets the Arabian Sea near Karachi.

Irrigation in the Indus system has had a long history since the beginning of civilization in this region. This does not mean that there were any large projects and, until the middle of the nineteenth century, people had a very limited irrigated area. Rapid population growth took off in the middle of the nineteenth century when the region was under the control of the United Kingdom. North-west British India, especially Punjab (which would be divided into east and west), played an important agricultural role owing to its fertile soil and it had not had other large industries because the United Kingdom located them in other parts of India. However, it has little rainfall; about half the area of the basin has 500–1,000 mm per year and the other half has 150–500 mm, except for an area between the Sutlej and the Ravi which has over 1,000 mm. In addition, because the land does not have great ups and downs, it costs a lot not only to develop but also to maintain an irrigation system. So it was all the more important to get enough water from the Indus system.

*The first phase of conflict and attempts at resolution, 1947–1951*

The progress of the negotiation between the two countries over the Indus River Basin was as follows. The Arbitral Commission, whose president was Lord Radcliffe, divided the state of Punjab into two parts in August 1947 and India took the upstream and Pakistan the downstream of five of the six rivers in the Indus system. Immediately after independence the two countries had not decided on their border, so they quarrelled over the distribution of the Indus River Basin (Hirsch 1956: 211). The first interim agreement was concluded on 20 December 1947; Pakistan was to pay fees for the water supply from the Ferozepore headworks, which is in East Punjab, to the Bari Doab Canal in West Punjab. The agreement was due to expire on 31 March 1948 and, before it ran out, both countries continued their discussions. India asserted exclusive rights over the eastern rivers but Pakistan demanded an equal share of the water of the Indus system. They made two Standstill Agreements in 1948 but failed to ratify them.

In the end Pakistan did not renew the interim agreement and the next day, 1 April 1948, India cut off the water supply to the canals, which posed a great threat to Pakistani livelihoods. This situation lasted for about two weeks and on 18 April the Simla agreement over the Central Bari Doab Canal and the Dialpur Canal was concluded, but Pakistan refused to confirm it. From 3 to 4 May, extensive discussions were held in an Inter-Dominion Conference in Delhi and the Delhi Agreement was concluded among India, Pakistan, East Punjab and West Punjab. This agreement covered two points: an interim water supply for Pakistan; and a compensation regime during the transitional period. East Punjab promised to keep on supplying water to West Punjab for irrigation until the latter state had had time to complete an alternative canal system. In return, West Punjab would pay the cost of water from the eastern rivers and deposit with the Reserve Bank of India an ad hoc sum to be specified by the Prime Minister of India; out of this sum, the Government of India would transfer to the East Punjab government an amount that would lead to no dispute.

Two months later, the next step had already begun: exchanges over a legal settlement and the utilization of water. Regarding the former issue, Pakistan began to refer to the need for legal settlement, that is, they had to solve the problem with the help of the International Court of Justice, but India refused and accused Pakistan of making unfounded allegations. India also claimed that cooperative work by both countries should come first and that a judicial tribunal would be better. India's proposal meant that a joint technical commission would be appointed to survey the total water resources of the Indus Basin. It was expected to achieve the equitable distribution of water if this worked well. Pakistan accepted this offer, which was the basis of later cooperative work.

What statements over the utilization of water had been exchanged? In this period, Pakistan repeatedly questioned India's intentions over water use and claimed that Indian actions had had ill effects. Whenever such claims were made, India contradicted them. In reply to a statement by Pakistan's Foreign Minister, Sir Zafarullah Khan, on 4 August 1948, India's UN delegate pointed out that Pakistan could utilize water more effectively and denied the Pakistani accusations about India's intention to threaten Pakistan. He noted that Pakistan failed to use most of the water in the Indus Basin and let it run wastefully into the sea; Pakistan would be able to achieve efficient utilization if it developed an independent irrigation system. On 17 September 1949, India claimed that it had an urgent need to develop East Punjab, and that it had no intention of harming Pakistan. In this statement, N. V. Gadgil, the Indian Minister for Works, said that East Punjab had not historically invested in irrigation and the people in the area had suffered poverty. So India urgently needed to develop relief projects for its inhabitants.

Pakistan's statement on 8 April 1950 claimed that India might deprive Pakistan of water and that India was trying to divert water out of the Indus Basin through large projects. India's rejection of Pakistan's allegation was announced in a communiqué from the External Affairs Ministry on 8 August 1951, which stated that diversion of Indus water was physically impossible; even if India controlled Kashmir, it would not be able to utilize the whole water supply of the rivers. Pakistan's Foreign Minister protested on 17 August that Indian projects in Kashmir threatened Pakistan's security, in terms of flood control, hydropower and water resources, and that giving India a free hand would put West Pakistan's whole economy at India's mercy. On 9 September 1951, in reply to Pakistan, India condemned Pakistan's statement as irrational. If Pakistan claimed Kashmir because the headworks of the Upper Jhelum Canal lay on the border of that state, on the same principle India could claim Kashmir because the headworks of the Upper Bari Doab Canal were on the border of Kashmir and East Punjab. Thus, it was hard for the two countries to find a breakthrough in this period.

## The second phase, 1951–1954: The World Bank starts mediation

February 1951 was the beginning of the next phase. At this time, David Lilienthal, former head of both the Tennessee Valley Authority and the Atomic Energy Commission, visited India and Pakistan and wrote an important article for *Collier's* magazine on the dispute. He noted that Pakistan's fears of deprivation should first be removed; that India should confirm Pakistan's current use of water; and that it was necessary to achieve effective water utilization by not letting it flow into the sea and allocating water cooperatively through engineering works and canals. To achieve this goal, joint works between India and Pakistan would be critical and also beneficial to India's future. They had to develop the whole Indus system as a unit. A jointly financed Indus Engineering Corporation, with representation from technical people in India, Pakistan and the World Bank, could easily work out an effective scheme.

Eugene R. Black, the president of the World Bank, read Lilienthal's article and consulted him about mediation. Black suggested on 11 November that the two countries establish a working group of engineers. On Lilienthal's recommendations, Black proposed that the problem of the Indus as a single unit would be treated in the group without taking into account any past negotiations or political considerations. On 10 March 1952, India and Pakistan welcomed the good offices of the World Bank and promised that, until mediation succeeded, they would each maintain the supply of water for the other's use.

Then Black proposed that, in order to fulfil the demand of their respective territories in the Indus Basin, India and Pakistan should cooperatively develop the storage ability of the basin and undertake other engineering works and should carry out a joint technical survey for this purpose. The World Bank was optimistic, presuming that an agreement on the distribution of water would be completed without excessive difficulty, but neither India nor Pakistan seemed willing to compromise their positions. The two countries and the World Bank held meetings in Karachi in November and in Delhi in January 1953, but a common approach to developing the waters of the Indus Basin was not achieved. The World Bank suggested that each country prepare its own plan. At the beginning of 1953, Pakistan repeatedly harangued India. On 26 January 1953, Abdus Sattar Pirzada, the Minister for Food and Agriculture, criticized India for restricting the water supply.

Replying to these successive accusations by Pakistan, Nehru expressed great surprise at "the new and intensive agitation started by Pakistan", and rejected it on 20 February. He also noted that the water shortage was caused by drought and stressed that India had continued to supply water under the Delhi Agreement. He explained that, as far as India was concerned, the Delhi Agreement was still in force and renewed the request to refer the matter to a joint tribunal. On 3 March, a statement by Sardar Abdur Rab Nishtar, the Pakistani Minister for Industries, claimed that this matter was under discussion with the mediation of the World Bank and that India should continue to supply water until joint exploitation ended. When India and Pakistan submitted their water use and allocation plans to the World Bank, it was recognized how difficult it would be to reconcile those plans because they differed significantly. Under the Indian plan, of the 119 million acre-feet (MAF) of total usable water, 29 MAF would be allocated to India and 90 MAF to Pakistan. But under the Pakistan plan, which estimated 118 MAF of total usable water, 15.5 MAF would be allocated to India and 102.5 MAF to Pakistan.

After some discussions and compromises from both parties, the plans were modified, but the modified plans also differed markedly. According to the modified Indian proposal, 7 per cent of the water of the western rivers and all the water of the eastern rivers was to be allocated to India, whereas 93 per cent of the water of the western rivers and no water from the eastern rivers was to be allocated to Pakistan. Pakistan's modified proposal allocated 30 per cent of the water of the eastern rivers and none of the western rivers to India, and 70 per cent of the eastern rivers and all of the western rivers to Pakistan. From these exchanges, the impossibility of realizing the joint management proposed by the World Bank was clearly acknowledged. In fact, the World Bank started to seek a new path to divide the water resources of the basin between the two countries on the basis of political boundaries.

On 5 February 1954, the World Bank proposed a new plan, which had three main points. First, the entire flow of the three western rivers of the Indus system (the Indus, Jhelum and Sutlej) would be available for the exclusive use of Pakistan, except for a small volume of water for Kashmir. Second, the entire flow of the three eastern rivers of the Indus system (the Ravi, Beas and Sutlej) would be available for the exclusive use of India, except that for a specified transitional period India would supply to Pakistan "her historic withdrawals from these rivers". In this period, estimated at five years, Pakistan would develop and complete the "link canals" needed to replace these supplies. Third, each country would construct and pay for the works located in its territory, but India would also bear the cost of link canals in Pakistan needed to replace supplies from India "to the extent of benefit derived by her therefrom".

On 22 March, India stated that it would accept the World Bank's proposal and emphasized India's sacrifice. However, Pakistan asked for a delay in making its decision in order to obtain an independent report on the proposals from a US firm of hydraulic engineers. The report announced that the plan was inadequate and would cause serious water shortages for irrigation developments. In May, the World Bank cautioned that if Pakistan did not accept or reject the proposals within a week India would be free to develop and utilize its own water resources. Then Pakistan demanded more information and the holding of a working party to undertake a detailed study. After that, the two countries kept negotiating, but without a big change in the World Bank's proposal, and final agreement could not be reached.

*The third phase, 1954–1960: No progress and the coup d'état*

On 21 June 1954, India stated that it recognized that Pakistan rejected the proposal and that the 1952 agreement was void. In addition, India conveyed its preparedness to formulate a new agreement. An official communiqué on 26 July 1954 showed India's desire to create an ad hoc agreement covering urgent projects and accused Pakistan of disrupting that desire. India also welcomed Pakistan's promotion of transitional projects, and approved the project that had already brought the Balloke–Suleimanke link into operation in April 1954.

On 8 June, India opened the Bhakra canal system. On the same day, President Nehru stated that India had no intention of harming Pakistan, that Pakistan should invest in water resource projects much more, and that India would wait for the completion of Pakistani development. In addition, he mentioned that Pakistan had "rejected" the World Bank's proposals and that India had the right to reduce its supply of water to Pakistan. However, he added: "We do not want to go by our legal right; we want to proceed in such a way that it does not harm the peasants and common people of Pakistan." It was clear from the Bank's proposals that there was no shortage of water and that Pakistan's difficulties were due to the lack of arrangements for diverting water.

The next day, the World Bank guaranteed that the opening of the Bhakra canal would cause no serious reduction in the supply to Pakistan and stressed the necessity for both countries to discuss withdrawals in September, although technical disagreement was quite a problem at this time. However, on 10 July, Pakistan protested against the opening of the canal and asked India to take immediate measures to restore a cooperative relationship. Pakistan persisted in making accusations against India. On 15 July, Prime Minister Mohammad Ali stated that India's action was likely to cause a Pakistani national emergency and a threat to the peace. In his statement, he mentioned that Pakistan was continuing to develop canal systems but India was ignoring this, and the survey by the World Bank proved insufficient, so it was necessary to carry out another survey.

Finally, on 5 August 1954, Prime Minister Mohammad Ali stated Pakistan's intention to accept the Bank's proposals "conditionally", adding that his government would "try the World Bank formula, accept it if it is workable, and guarantee proper usage of the waters". The World Bank immediately informed the Indian embassy in Washington that Pakistan was prepared to accept the proposals if certain clarifications could be realized, subject to a resumption of negotiations. India, in reply to the World Bank, expressed its willingness to discuss conditions with a view to evolving a clear basis for a new working party with the participation of the Bank. The World Bank sent US engineers to Pakistan to survey and report on the progress of the Marala–Ravi link canal.

Until the middle of 1958 the situation was static; in other words, negotiation by the two countries did not make any progress except for renewing ad hoc agreements. The situation was changed by the coup d'état on 8 October 1958 in Pakistan when General Ayub Khan seized power, and Pakistan became ready to have an agreement with India. On 1 September, H. M. Ibrahim, the Indian Minister for Irrigation and Power, stated that the new suggestion by William Iliff, the vice president of the World Bank, had failed to lead to any results. Moreover, on 2 December India rejected the Pakistani plan because of the cost involved. Pakistan was demanding not only the replacement of waters from the eastern rivers but the development of new resources, for which India could not be expected to pay. India put forward an alternative plan for the diversion of part of the waters of the Chenab through a tunnel under the Rohtang Pass, whence they would flow through the Indian rivers and canal system into Pakistan. India also offered to guarantee to supply to Pakistan exactly the same amount of water as it diverted into its rivers from the Chenab. Pakistan rejected this plan on the ground that it was contrary to the 1954 proposal.

On 17 March 1959, M. Shoaib, the Pakistani Finance Minister, claimed that a solution over the canal waters was being completed by the World Bank, and that the president of the Bank would visit India and Pakistan in May to discuss it. Mr Black and Mr Iliff visited Delhi on 12 May and Karachi on the 16th. On the 18th, Ayub Khan, the President of Pakistan, and Mr Black stated that Pakistan was "prepared to go ahead on the basis of the World Bank's plan for a settlement of the dispute". On 9 June, the Indian Ministry of Irrigation and Power exhibited a positive attitude towards settlement. Later an agreement between India and the World Bank was completed and the World Bank promised India that the Bank would contribute financially to the cost of construction works in India. India agreed to the length of the transitional period (approximately 10 years) and promised to complete all the engineering works required by the World Bank's proposal, which would be ready to withdraw water much before the end of this transitional period and to secure for India the necessary financial assistance to enable construction of storage on the Beas River.

In September, further discussions were held in London between India, Pakistan and the World Bank. A team of five engineers and financial experts from the World Bank visited Pakistan and began discussions on the implementation of the proposed scheme with the Pakistan Water and Power Development Authority. On 18 December, World Bank experts expressed that in their view the Pakistan Water Development Authority was competent technically, financially and organizationally to fulfil the scheme for the construction of replacement works under the proposed treaty. On 21 September 1960, the Indus Waters Treaty was finally completed.

## Politics in India

### Domestic controversy

In the post-independence period, India had two main domestic problems: national integration and economic development. Because of the legacy of the British administration, India faced three big obstacles to national integration: communalism, linguistic issues and the minority problem. As regards economic policy in the Nehru era, India had carried out five-year plans because the president was influenced by socialism, but these plans did not work as the leaders had expected. This section will cover these problems, together with diplomatic issues, except for its relations with Pakistan.

"Communalism" is Anglo-Indian and means attitudes and acts that give top priority to the interests of one's community, which is subjectivized by religion. Not only simple religious antagonism but interests based on non-spiritual relationships engender communalism. Religious groups started acting as social groups when the members became aware of problems with religious difference in terms of social class and their job. The problem came to the fore in the 1890s and Hindus and Muslims tended to be in conflict until independence. The British government took advantage of their differences to support its rule of British India, but was in difficulties by the Second World War (Karashima 2004: 413–418, 473–474).

The role of communal identity, including religious differences, was more important in north-west India, in Punjab, than in the south and Bombay. There are three major ethnic groups – Hindu, Muslim and Sikh – and each group had been involved in riots from the late nineteenth century to the early twentieth century. Assam and the north-east had demanded separation from the central government because of their opposition to the Hindus. Although each tribe in these regions had a different language, their spokesmen claimed that language and religion were not paramount in the demands for a split. The main motivation was that tribal peoples were simply not Indians.

Before independence, the linguistic conflict between Hindi and Urdu and the Devanagari script and Persian/Arabic was most prominent. After partition, in a great concession to Urdu and to Persian/Arabic, the two languages were given the status of official languages of India. Although no large-scale violence was experienced in Nehru period, the linguistic issue was one of the most conflictual. At the time, the central government pursued pluralist policies in relation to the major language and cultural movements, recognizing especially most of the large language groups among which major mobilizations had developed for the creation of separate linguistic states. At the same time, however, the central government sought to avoid direct involvement in regional conflicts between different ethnic and linguistic groups.

In 1950, the constitution was determined and it gives the state legislatures the right to decide the official language of the state regardless of whether the language is local, Hindi or English. In the meantime, people in the provinces had kept on speaking their own languages and the languages were recognized as "national". These languages were used in the examinations for entry into the Union public services. Language commissions were established as a constitutional compromise in 1955 and 1960 "to survey the progress of Hindi", but these concessions were accepted as "due regard" for the interests of people who did not speak Hindi and lived in the provinces mainly so that they would be able to get jobs in the public services. This implied that Hindi should not be the only language used in the entrance examinations because it would harm the interests of non-Hindi speakers.

In the early post-independence years, a succession of policies that aimed to promote tribal development and to protect the tribal people were chosen. However, the Indian government failed to achieve its goals in practice, as in so many policy areas. Tribes were banned from accessing the forests and their resources for conservation purposes, but the destruction of forests had continued because of the corrupt distribution of tracts of timber to contractors. Tribes had also been deprived of their lands to make way for steel plants and dams. These were intended to provide employment and improve irrigation systems in tribal regions, but the result was that the tribes lived in slums near the work sites, working as casual labourers for private construction companies.

*Agriculture*

The development policy of India resulted in failure and public discontent over the economy increased. The first Indian five-year plan (1950–1955) achieved certain results but the second one fell seriously short of its goal, so that Indian net gross national product did not increase. Moreover, rapid population growth reduced the efficacy of economic growth. India faced a balance of payments crisis. Before independence, India had a relatively healthy exchange reserve because of the Second World War and its value stood at US$1,550 million at the end of the first five-year plan. In the second plan, however, India lost US$1,250 million and faced a critical situation at the beginning of the third plan (Ishikawa 1963).

The persistence of regional imbalances should be mentioned first. In British-ruled India, considerable differences between areas were widespread. Urban areas had attracted most of the facilities of modern life, such as higher education and hospitals. At independence, regional divergence was substantial and the major urban cities such as Bombay, Madras and Calcutta enjoyed industrial growth and higher educational expansion. As time passed, capital was not invested broadly but was concentrated in particular places. Thus most states had remained in approximately the same position in relative terms. The poorer states were not able to achieve any important changes and the central government repeatedly urged that it was critical to develop regional balance in the nation.

However, India was unsuccessful in correcting the disparity or, in addition, in improving macroeconomic growth. Five-year plans aimed to achieve "balanced regional development" but had not been "in consonance with this national objective".

India had problems in food production. Its gross agricultural production grew rapidly after 1950, but, from the point of view of net product per person, output had increased only for a few years and had decreased after 1954. Moreover, the food production index per person fell below the pre-war level (Minami 1966: 37–39). India tried to deal with this question through the modernization of agriculture. The first five-year plan claimed that it was crucial for national policy makers to promote agricultural modernization. The leaders of India decided to achieve this object by abolishing the old social structure, the "zamindari system", and not by giving weight to technological innovation. Of course, there was a school of thought that promoted technological modernization but their views were not well received until the mid-1960s, when the "Green Revolution" was comprehensively implemented. Although several provincial states introduced "zamindari abolition acts" between 1949 and 1954, there were many difficulties in legislating them.

*Industry*

The modernization-cum-industrialization plan was drawn up by Nehru on the basis that a deliberate plan to make Indian industry strong and the economy self-reliant could achieve a self-reliant India. Nehru, who was influenced by socialism, sought to give the government a critical role in controlling important industrial infrastructures and strictly regulating all commodities from foreign countries in order to shut out products that might interfere with the expansion of industry. The Industrial Policy Resolution of 1948 blueprinted industrial development in the future and made clear the roles of the public and private sectors in the planned "mixed economy". The resolution recognized the exclusive rights of central and state governments to monopolize railroads, mining and the iron and steel industry. In March 1950, the Planning Commission, whose chairman was the president of India, was established.

However, implementation of the resolution encountered several difficulties, because the politics and economy of India simply did not have enough capacity and resources. Although the government kept on trying to execute the plans with modest bureaucracies, state leaders determined that there was little alternative to allowing private capital to participate in creating industrial infrastructure with public support. The "developmental alliance" between the state and the industrial and business classes was being established during the first five-year plan and continued to be consolidated in the period following the Industrial Policy Resolution of 1956 and the start of the second five-year plan.

The government's development strategy from 1956 was made clear in the Resolution and the second five-year plan, which was influenced by P. C. Maharanobis, who was Nehru's close confidant and the Planning Commission's statistical adviser. Heavy industry featured prominently in the plan and investment in industry was tripled in comparison with the first five-year plan. On the other hand, investment in agriculture was greatly reduced. The plan still carefully followed the "mixed economy" model, but the role of the private sector in development increased and extensive areas of the economy were opened up for private activity. Additionally, the government protected domestic markets from foreign competition to developing domestic capital. However, as mentioned before, the plan failed to achieve its goals.

## Politics in Pakistan

### Political controversy

Pakistan also had a diversity problem in its society. Like India, Pakistan has many languages, about 10, and they played critical roles in creating political identity. Pakistan had another big problem, the minority/refugee issue, to which deliberate attention had to be paid. Pakistan was constructed by those who had wanted to build a Muslim country and their goal was partially realized, as in Punjab and Bengal, but Muslims failed to be the majority in other districts. The *muhajir* (refugee) culture, which was different from the indigenous culture of Pakistan, originated in the Mutiny of 1857. Disputes between the two cultures were happening before independence.

The *muhajir* culture preferred secularism, liberal politics and a free economy whereas the indigenous culture wanted the establishment of an Islamic state and an economy under the control of the state. The first clash after independence was over the contents of a new constitution, which was discussed in the Constituent Assembly. The constitution's "basic problem" was debated for four years. Because the leaders wanted to build a new state on the basis of religion, they tried not to make an issue of the basic principle, but it became serious. The argument about the role of religion was connected to the question of the rights of the federating provinces, especially in East Pakistan where a sizeable Hindu minority remained.

During discussions on this question, the Muslim League was divided into three factions. The *muhajirs* under Muhammad Ali Jinnah controlled the most powerful faction while Jinnah (as Governor General) and Liaquat Ali Khan (as Prime Minister) were alive. Bengali Muslim Leaguers made up another faction but it was defeated in the 1954 elections, which reduced its power in national politics. Another faction was composed of landowners with feudal interests. The dominant faction had changed in the 1950s. From 1951 to about 1954, the Liaquat faction had the most power. After the defeat of the Bengali faction, from 1954 to 1958 the Liaquat faction and the Republican Party were in dispute over corruption at the national level. Until 1957, neither faction won absolute power but in 1958 the Republican Party beat the Liaquats and its representative, Malik Feroz Khan, became Prime Minister.

The three factions finally agreed on a solution to the constitutional problem in 1956 and the constitution's preamble stipulated Allah's sovereignty over man. Additionally, the constitution declared that all laws would conform to the Quran and Sunnah. Under this new constitution, which was framed by Prime Minister Chaudhri Muhammad Ali of the Muslim League, General Iskander Mirza became the first President. Ali was a *muhajir* who came from Jullundur in East Punjab and he did not favour *muhajirs* from urban cities in India. Ali had worked in the administrative structure of the new Pakistan as a prominent member of the civil bureaucracy and had seen Liaquat Ali Khan at close quarters. He was very suitable in the transition from a political system controlled by the *muhajirs* to one controlled by indigenous leaders.

However, there were many difficulties in promoting the transition to indigenization and it took a long time. In 1956, the Republican Party, whose patron was President Iskander Mirza, was established and it actively led the transition. It succeeded in bringing together a great many prominent politicians from West Pakistan and dissident Muslim Leaguers, and it beat the Muslim League. After this defeat, Chaudhri Muhammad Ali resigned and Malik Feroz Khan Noon became the new Prime Minister. However, because the process of change in political power was not smooth, political turmoil had ensued. This wasted Pakistan's national wealth and created the opportunity for General Ayub Khan to stage a coup d'état. This was the end of competitive parliamentary democracy and the beginning of military dictatorships.

*Agriculture*

Pakistan suffered stagnation in economic development in this period. Some large-scale plans, such as the Colombo Plan and the first five-year plan, were attempted but they failed to accomplish the expected results in terms of growth in national income, improvement in people's living conditions, or change in the structure of the economy. Pakistan had also implemented several agriculture plans but its productivity improved by only 0.3 per cent between 1955 and 1957 and by an estimated 3 per cent between 1957 and 1958. This was because Pakistan lagged behind in agricultural development in areas such as village growth, irrigation and water distribution (Yanagisawa 1961).

The agriculture sector was the most important for Pakistan because it had been the largest and it accounted for 53 per cent of gross domestic product when Pakistan achieved independence. Some serious land problems affected the crop-growing areas. There were 6,000 landlords, who were mainly political and/or religious leaders in their regions. They owned more land than the 3.5 million peasant households and they also had political power in the Muslim League. The *muhajirs* who shaped Pakistan's economic policy were from urban areas and they did not pay much attention to agriculture, which was very important for Pakistan in the early days. The political situation began to change in the middle of the 1950s. The landlords, who were indigenous to the country, returned to the political arena and brought government interest back to agriculture. General Ayub Khan moved the focus of political power from Karachi, a city influenced by industry and commerce, to Lahore and Rawalpindi, cities that were much more representative of indigenous and rural Pakistan. But the policy change was late considering the period between 1947 and 1960.

The direction of agricultural investment was also wrong. At the time of partition, Pakistan was an exporting country and the main products were cotton and jute. Export surplus from these two crops earned foreign currency and enabled the development of manufacturing industries, largely in the early phases of industrial development. Pakistan, in fact, invested mainly in irrigation projects, such as the construction of dams, intricate systems of canals and tube-wells, in its development strategy. On the other hand, Pakistan was unable to increase cereal production in line with the rapid population growth and soon became an importer of foods, particularly wheat. For the first 12 years after independence, Pakistan achieved agricultural growth of only 1.2 per cent annually.

Pakistan's dependence on agriculture indicated that it had little capital in industry, and the biggest industry, which had 41 per cent of factories, produced agricultural raw materials and operated seasonally. However, Pakistan chose to focus mainly on industrial growth. In the early 1950s, a few politicians and civil servants who had migrated from India were responsible for policy-making. These migrants from the cities of India understandably displayed a strong urban bias: they had little knowledge of or interest in agriculture. Accordingly, most of the government's attention and the bulk of public investment was directed to manufacturing.

*Industry*

The first development plan was set up in 1950 when the Colombo Plan was formulated, but it was not well structured and consisted merely of an accumulation of projects that seemed to be implemented in a hurry. The plan aimed to lay the foundations for development and develop the necessary infrastructure such as networks of modern communications, power and irrigation. Pakistan did not expect to achieve spectacular results, especially given the current national living standards, but it did hope to begin the modest lift-off of the economy, thus the budget was not enormous. However, the lack of planning machinery to handle development efficiently at that time led to failure. In fact, the undue emphasis that came to be laid on industrialization obstructed the working of the plan.

Pakistan, like India, first established a five-year plan in 1953 and it covered the period 1955–1960. Its objects were to raise the national income and living standards, achieve rapid growth in development, and reduce inequality between regions. For this plan, expenditure of more than three times that in the 1950 budget was fixed. At this time, Pakistan expected to receive about 30 per cent of the budget from external aid. The result was a great disappointment. Against its expectation of a modest 15 per cent increase in national income, the actual increase was about 11 per cent. Population growth was estimated to be 7 per cent but actually turned out to be 12 per cent. For the first three years of the plan, expenditure on the current account exceeded current revenues and the foreign exchange deficit increased alarmingly. Pakistan depended increasingly on foreign aid.

Although industrial production showed good progress, stagnation in other areas, mostly agricultural products, erased the results. In terms of per capita income, Pakistan's economy was practically static. In the five-year period from 1949/1950 to 1954/1955, Pakistan's gross national product increased by 14 per cent, which gives an annual average of 2.8 per cent. However, the per capita income in 1958/1959 was the same as in 1949/1950. Thus it could be said that there were high economic pressures on development.

## Relations between India and Pakistan

*India's foreign policy*

India's foreign policy in this period was clearly influenced by Jawaharlal Nehru, who was the Prime Minister and Minister for External Affairs. The active pursuit of non-alignment was the most typical feature of

India's foreign policy under Nehru. According to Nehru, non-alignment was simply an independent policy involving no political or military commitments to another state or group of states, limiting one's independence of policy and action. Specifically and negatively it meant the rejection of political or military alliances – bilateral or multilateral. Positively, it meant the taking of ad hoc decisions on international problems, as and when they came up, according to the merits of each case.

India's foreign policy consisted of three main goals. One was the maintenance of international peace and security. "Peace to us is not just a fervent hope; it is an emergent necessity," said Nehru. Peace was a necessity to India because without it India's multifaceted development would have been hampered. The second goal was encouraging self-determination for all colonial peoples. This was necessary because fundamental human rights ensure freedom for all peoples, irrespective of race, religion and state of economic development or even civilization. Opposition to racism and all its manifestations was the third important object of India's foreign policy. The justification for this was the same as for opposition to the continuance of colonialism. However, India's opposition to colonialism was modest and did not use violent methods.

In a world situation characterized by a Cold War in Europe and a developing colonial revolution in Asia and North Africa, the United States viewed "neutrality" as open hostility. In fact, Nehru promoted a policy of hostility to imperialism in the third world and therefore India had to pay attention to geopolitical issues. Although India did not reject resorting to force against Pakistan and European colonialism, Nehru was wise enough to realize India's lack of military strength to contend with its powerful neighbour to the north, the People's Republic of China. He therefore supported China's participation in the United Nations, refrained from criticism of the Chinese occupation of Tibet, and readily gave up India's inherited extraterritorial privileges in Tibet. Many gestures of goodwill led to a period of seeming amity in Sino-Indian relations in the mid-1950s. Shortly thereafter, however, efforts at longer-term accommodation were damaged by a series of Chinese territorial claims along the Himalayan border. Worse still, sharp border clashes took place in 1958 between the Chinese People's Liberation Army and Indian forces. Despite the mounting evidence of China's aggressive attitude, Nehru did not increase defence expenditures and continued his negotiations with the Chinese.

In a broader geopolitical context, Indian leaders at the time harboured no deep-seated anxieties that the United States or the Soviet Union would be directly aggressive to their country. To obviate any doubts that may have existed, Nehru announced a policy of opening détente with the Soviet Union and Western states simultaneously. While stating that "we intend cooperating with the United States of America and we intend cooperating fully with the Soviet Union", he also explained in parliament that, "in accepting economic help, or in getting political help, it is not a wise policy to put all your eggs in one basket". Indeed, the broader justification of what was later termed "Indian neutralism" had been enunciated by Nehru.

## Pakistan's foreign policy

Governor General Muhammad Ali Jinnah had indicated in a number of press statements that the foreign policy of Pakistan would be non-aligned, but this did not happen. After the Second World War, the power of the United Kingdom declined and the United States emerged as the dominant Western power. On the other hand, the Soviet Union and its brand of socialism expanded and created upheaval. Social movements under the leadership of communist parties arose all over the world and were a factor in destabilizing states. In this situation, Pakistan's first Prime Minister, Liaquat Ali Khan, chose to take the West's side; he rejected an invitation from Moscow and went to Washington instead.

The alliance was reinforced by two of Jinnah's successors. Ghulam Mohammad and Iskander Mirza, both bureaucrats, cemented the alliance because they needed US support to shore up their position in the government. US aid had already started in 1951. Pakistan got a fresh offer of aid from the United States in 1953 when a wheat crisis was caused artificially and Mohammad Ali Bogra, a former ambassador to the United States, became the new Prime Minister. US President Dulles acclaimed Pakistan as "a bulwark of freedom in Asia". The United States also sought to use Pakistan to promote US interests.

Pakistan's geopolitical role became important when India and Afghanistan refused to become members of the Western alliance. The army and the bureaucracy agreed to make the country a US base. In the autumn of 1953, the United States promised to give Pakistan military aid on conditions laid down by the United States. Pakistan's negotiator was General Ayub Khan. A Pakistan–Turkey alliance was agreed in April 1954 and Pakistan helped the United States to extend its sphere of influence along the Soviet frontiers and to isolate India. A month later the Mutual Aid and Security Agreement between the United States and Pakistan was signed in Karachi. In the mid-1950s, two Western military alliances, the North Atlantic Treaty Organization (NATO) and the Southeast Asia Treaty Organization (SEATO), were established. Both alliances assumed that Pakistan would play a role as a base of operations against any new social upheavals in the area.

However, opposition to the pro-US policy developed rapidly. Arab nationalism was in the ascendant and the turning point was the Anglo-French-Israeli invasion of Egypt in October 1956. Pakistan defended the invasion and backed the West. The Prime Minister at that time was H. S.

Suhrawardy, and this policy created huge protests and anger throughout Pakistan and split his party. In 1957, there was political turmoil between pro-US politicians and anti-US protesters. But in 1958 General Ayub Khan staged a successful coup and the military government reinforced the pro-Western policy again.

## Immediate problems arising from partition

The partition necessarily created several problems: the determination of the boundaries of the new states; the division of the army; and the equitable division of the sterling balances, public debt and other property or services that were previously handled or directed by India and Pakistan.

In accordance with the provisions of the statement by the UK government dated 3 June 1947, two Boundary Commissions, one for Bengal and the other for the Punjab, had been appointed on 30 June. Each consisted of two representatives from India and two from Pakistan; Sir Cyril Radcliffe was later appointed chairman of both Commissions. A Joint Defence Council, four partition councils and an Arbitral Tribunal were set up to deal with the other problems – the division between the new states of the armed forces and the civil services and of the assets and liabilities.

On the question of the civil services, the solution arrived at was simple. All government servants were given the option to choose the government they wished to serve, and six months from the date of partition they were also able to reconsider their decision. However, the division of the military supplies presented some difficulties. The Joint Defence Council agreed that one-third of military supplies be allocated to Pakistan. Pakistan complained that "India did not abide by the agreement arrived at and did not send us these armaments". Pakistan was further aggrieved by the fact that India insisted that the Supreme Command be ended on 30 November 1947.

The concrete contents of the division of assets and liabilities were: (a) the cash balances; (b) the functions of the Reserve Bank of India as the banker and currency authority for Pakistan as well; (c) physical assets; and (d) pre-partition debts. A Financial Agreement was reached with Pakistan on 12 December 1947 and this arrangement meant that those who held securities of the government of undivided India issued before 15 August 1947 would receive interest and the principal from the government of India. Pakistan would have to pay India its share in equal annual instalments spread over a period of 50 years. There were frequent disagreements over the interpretation of the agreement and then, on 22 August 1957, India's Finance Minister asserted in the Lok Sabha (the lower house of the parliament) that Pakistan had not paid anything and had been disputing the agreement. The Finance Ministers of the two countries met in August 1959 to consider the claims and counter-claims, but no agreement could be reached.

## The Kashmir problem

When in October 1947 a Pakistani-supported invasion of Kashmir happened, Nehru decided to provide military assistance to Maharaja Hari Singh, the last monarch of the princely state of Jammu and Kashmir. Nehru's commitment to non-alignment did not prevent the use of force when India's national security was threatened. India and Pakistan had armed clashes after the sending in of Indian forces. India's referral of the dispute to the United Nations and a subsequent UN-sponsored cease-fire halted the conflict on 1 January 1949. Despite the end of active hostilities, neither side showed any intention to compromise. India initially expressed a willingness to settle the dispute through a referendum, but the methods for a plebiscite became the subject of controversy. By the mid-1950s India had abandoned its policy to commit to a plebiscite.

Events in Kashmir in 1947–1949 provided a turning point both in Indo-Pakistan relations and in Pakistan's domestic priorities. Appalling killings in Jammu snuffed out any lingering hopes of the two dominions' economic or military interdependence. Although the military conflict between the two dominions was confined to Kashmir, it brought home the strategic dangers facing Pakistan, the weaker of the protagonists. Prime Minister Ali Khan said, in a broadcast to the nation on 8 October 1948, "The defence of the State is our foremost consideration ... and has dominated all other governmental activities. We will not grudge any amount on the defence of our country."

When the United States provided Pakistan with military and economic assistance in 1954, Pakistan inevitably became tied by the strings of membership of SEATO and the Baghdad Pact. In the wake of the Kashmir conflict, the Pakistan authorities came to take the side of the United States and tighten the relationship with the United States, while renouncing ties with the Muslim world that would have commanded popular support. The bureaucrats and their military allies were able to maintain their position at the centre because of US assistance.

## US military aid to Pakistan

There were various reasons for the Pakistan government seeking US military aid, but certainly the most important was to strengthen it militarily against India. Mohammad Ali Bogra, the Prime Minister in 1953–1954, publicly admitted that a defensive move against possible Indian aggression had led the military build-up. In an interview with a US periodical, the Prime Minister also said that US military aid to Pakistan would make it easier to resolve the Kashmir dispute. Ever since US military aid was received, Pakistani government leaders had repeatedly announced that it could be used in "self-defence" against a non-communist country, and this ambiguousness was suspicious in India's eyes. It was on the basis of "self-defence" that Pakistan had marched its troops into Kashmir in 1947–1948.

India had been opposed, in principle, to military pacts and alliances and the granting of foreign military aid, especially by the great powers. However, the Indian government and public opinion were not strongly against US military aid to Pakistan, unless Pakistan used the additional military equipment to threaten or even use actual force to settle any of their disputes. The aid was a "menace to India", said Nehru. Thus, the signing in 1954 of a mutual security treaty between the United States and Pakistan was an event that India could neither prevent nor ignore. Viewing the pact as bringing the Cold War to its doorstep, India attempted to discourage this reinforcing of Pakistan–US military relations.

US military aid to Pakistan introduced an incompatible and complicating element into Indo-Pakistani relations, in the sense that, henceforth, India and Pakistan had to deal with their relationship in light of US objectives and policies in the region. Pakistan came to have little desire to show any compromise or accommodation in the matter of the settlement of disputes with India, since it believed that the great and powerful United States was behind it and the US support would strengthen Pakistan in its demands on India. India was concerned that Indo-US relations immediately became worse than they had ever been because of US military aid to Pakistan and felt that it could no longer trust the US government and its leaders to take an independent, objective stand on Indo-Pakistani relations and disputes.

## Conclusion

Generally, countries in conflict need to achieve a sharing of interests, by compromising or confidence-building to create consensus. If the countries share interests, successful negotiation becomes much easier. Building confidence between the countries also helps them settle their issues. In the Indus water dispute, the two countries did have common interests and were able to compromise. Both countries wanted the eastern basin, which is better for agriculture, but Pakistan relinquished the basin and chose to develop the western basin, which was not so good for cultivation. India kept control of the upstream but allowed a decade for Pakistan's development. In fact, India needed to start to develop canals and other agricultural infrastructure in the eastern basin but decided to wait.

To make such compromises, it was necessary for both countries to have tolerance and to share interests. From this viewpoint, they both wanted to make peace in order to promote foreign investment. They needed not only agricultural and industrial infrastructure but also soft infrastructure such as education systems. India and Pakistan had difficult border disputes which sometimes led to armed conflict. Not many people or companies wanted to invest in an unstable region. India and Pakistan wanted to make a good impression so that foreign countries would invest in the region. India was in better financial shape than Pakistan but it needed a lot of foreign investment in order to develop the Indus Basin. Pakistan belonged to the Western bloc and it hoped for Western aid by accepting the mediation of the World Bank, which was in effect a Western organization.

Moreover, both countries tended to expect too much foreign aid. In developing their economic plans, they first set goals for a desirable economic growth rate and industrial structure and worked out the necessary resources to achieve their objectives. They then calculated the difference between what they needed and the resources that they could mobilize themselves and asked foreign society to cover this difference. For example, India took it for granted that developed countries would provide support (Ishikawa 1963). And these attitudes allowed for common interests. On the other hand, India and Pakistan did not intend to utilize the water of the Indus Basin as if there had been no boundary in the basin and this entailed double the investment for development compared with integrated resource management. They faced great difficulties, including emotional dislike, in achieving integrated management and they had no confidence in its worth.

Other incentives to agree could be found in this case from the point of view of security: to lessen the tension and avoid armed conflict. Although India once stopped the flow of water to Pakistan in the early stages of the dispute, for most of the period it demonstrated tolerance. This was connected with India's diplomatic policy, which tended to avoid armed conflict unless Indian security was threatened directly and militarily. The only case in which India resorted to force was the Kashmir dispute. This tolerance was explained not only by India's patience but also by the international environment. China existed as a direct threat and the United States was also important because it affected India's security through Pakistan. In terms of the bilateral relationship between India and Pakistan, India enjoyed supremacy but could not make use of it without carefully thinking about global politics. India preferred not to create tensions with the great powers and instead to reduce the triggers of conflict.

As already mentioned, India and Pakistan had failed to build confidence. Each saw the other as a real threat to security and they had not resolved other international issues. Emotional dislike did not disappear and because there was no confidence it took a long time for them to realize it would be better to settle the canal dispute. It could be said that Pakistan made rational use of a situation in which India could not use its geopolitical and military advantage in their direct relations to enlarge Pakistan's national interest. At the beginning of the conflict, Pakistan had to agree to pay the dues for the flow from India but it also succeeded in making India agree to make a financial contribution to development in Pakistan for a transitional period, in addition to extending the transitional period to 10 years. However, India was not a loser in this. In the Indus Waters Treaty, India not only got support from the World Bank but also ensured that India would be able to develop the eastern basin after the transitional period. Both countries protected their national interests in different ways. Pakistan's misunderstanding was also critical: Pakistan thought that it could solve the Kashmir dispute through the canal problem, but India completely denied Pakistan's purpose.

As regards the leaderships of the countries, leaders in both countries agreed to make peace especially to promote development. However, Kashmir and other issues involving emotional dislike prevented them from easily making compromises, which would have lost them their nation's support. It took time to cool emotions and increasing demands for development provided the opportunity. The World Bank's financial support gave the leaders a good reason to compromise. As far as Nehru was concerned, he probably did not particularly hate Pakistan. It is true that many Indians were killed just after the partition, but Nehru's real enemy was the United Kingdom. He wanted to create a good international environment with Pakistan. Pakistani Prime Ministers might have had the same attitude towards India but they did not have the great political power that Ayub Khan was to attain. There was, however, a sense in which the leaderships worked well. India and Pakistan were newborn countries: Nehru was the symbol of India's independence and no one tried to oppose him, and Ayub Khan was a dictator who could do anything he wanted.

According to Biswas (1992), the World Bank played a big role in the Indus water dispute because of the personal contribution of its president, Eugene R. Black. However, the historical background was also important. A sense of crisis and the Cold War were necessary for the World Bank's involvement. The World Bank wanted to prove the significance of its existence: India and Pakistan, which were supposed to be leading countries in the developing world, had failed to promote their development, so the World Bank aspired to help them advance. Furthermore, the World Bank could secure the cooperation of Western countries that were investors. The West needed to reduce military expenditure in South Asia, and the United States in particular wanted a stable South Asia because it wanted to focus on the Soviet Union and China. So they had a good incentive to support the World Bank as long as its activity was conducive to the stabilization of South Asia (Nakayama 1996: 81, 82, 85). Thus these opportunities let the World Bank suggest active support for both countries, and this was obviously acceptable to them. Salman and Uprety (2002: 59) point out that the World Bank promised India additional support if its finances were seriously damaged as a result of this resolution and this was essential to the success of the mediation.

It was not only in the financial aspect but also in the personal aspect that the World Bank played an essential role. The Bank asked Lilienthal to help its mediation of this canal dispute and Lilienthal was trusted by both countries. Lilienthal had access to A. N. Khosla, who was the Chief Engineer for the basin; he was an important adviser to Nehru and led the Indian delegation to the United Nations for the Indus water dispute. Lilienthal and Khosla had a good relationship and trusted each other. To have access to key individuals is as important as creating a reasonable solution. The World Bank did well in its choice of people to help. India, Pakistan and, of course, the World Bank exhibited great patience at that time. At the beginning of the Indus water dispute there were a lot of political difficulties but all three parties kept on trying to solve them. It was the great efforts made by these three parties that led to the settlement and the treaty.

## REFERENCES

Biswas, K. Asit (1992), 'Indus Water Treaty: The Negotiating Process', *Water International*, Vol. 17, pp. 201–209.

Gopal, S., ed. (1987), *Selected Works of Jawaharlal Nehru*, Jawaharlala Nehru Memorial Fund, Teen Murti House.

Hirsch, Abraham M. (1956), 'From the Indus to the Jordan: Characteristics of Middle East International River Disputes', *Political Science Quarterly*, Vol. 121, No. 2, pp. 203–222.

Ishikawa, Shigeru (1963), 'Mahalanobis Mokei no Mae to Ato [Pre and Post Mahalanobis Model]', *Asia Keizai*, Vol. 4, No. 2.

Karashima, Noboru, ed. (2004), *Minami Asia Shi* [History in South Asia], Yamakawa Shuppannsha.

*Keesing's Contemporary Archives* (1948–1960), Keesing's Publications.

Lilienthal, David E. (1966), *The Journals of David E. Lilienthal*, vols 3 and 4, New York: Harper & Row.

Minami, Ryouzaburo, ed. (1966), *Indo no Jinkou Zouka to Keizai Hatten* [Indian

Population Growth and Economic Development], Institute of Developing Economies.

Nakayama, Mikiyasu (1996), 'Indas Gawa Kyoutei no Koushou Katei ni Okeru Sekai Ginkouno Yakuwari ni Kansuru Kousatsu [Analysis of the World Bank's Role in the Negotiation Process of Indus Waters Treaty]', *Journal of Japan Society of Hydrology & Water Resources*, Vol. 9, No. 1, pp. 77–87.

Salman, M. A. and Kishor Uprety (2002), *Conflict and Cooperation on South Asia's International Rivers: A Legal Perspective*, Kluwer Law International.

Yanagisawa, Masakazu (1961), 'Pakisutan no Keizai Kaihatsu no Genjou to Mondaiten [The Present Condition and Problems of Pakistani Economic Development]', *Asia Keizai*, Vol. 2, No. 6.

# 3

# Domestic issues in developing international waters in Lesotho: Ensuring water security amidst political instability

*Naho Mirumachi*

## Introduction

Water can be converted into a multitude of benefits, in particular economic benefits from hydropower, agriculture or tourism. International river basins are where both conflict and cooperation occur among riparian states. International river development projects can cause tension owing to competing access to resources and can foster joint endeavours. The consequences of water development can bring about problems of water scarcity, water quality and environmental degradation. These problems can further challenge basin relations. The purpose of this chapter is to understand how the political and economic issues involved in developing international rivers within a state influence its water security. The analysis of this linkage is useful since the ideal form of river development would be to benefit all basin states, without compromising water security.

I first briefly address the concept of water security and how states frame water to ensure water security. I then use a case study to illustrate the evolution of domestic politics and state efforts towards water security. I use the case of Lesotho, a mountainous landlocked state with abundant water from the Senqu tributary in the Orange River Basin. Currently, Lesotho is developing a multi-phased water transfer project with South Africa. Despite the overwhelming political, economic and military power of the downstream state, a formal framework of cooperation has been established. However, according to the Basins At Risk (BAR) Project, a study that systematically ranks all events of water conflict and cooperation and then identifies which basins are likely to experience political

*International water security: Domestic threats and opportunities, Pachova, Nakayama and Jansky (eds), United Nations University Press, 2008, ISBN 978-92-808-1150-6*

stress in the future, the Orange Basin is considered to be "at risk" (Wolf et al. 2003). Furthermore, there has been an incidence of violence on a project site. Some claim this to be an example of "water war" in the basin. The domestic issues are analysed to see how water is treated in the political agenda. In other words, special attention is given to the objectives of harnessing water for Lesotho. The chapter shows how the domestic insecurity resulting from political instability does not necessarily threaten the development of bilateral water projects but it does weaken the state's capacity to ensure water security.

## Framing security

Water security has become a common agenda item for national and international waters. This is reflected in how international conferences such as the World Water Week (2000, 2001) and the World Water Forum have prioritized water security as their main theme. The Second World Water Forum produced the "Ministerial Declaration of The Hague on Water Security in the 21st Century", which recognized that providing water security involves "ensuring that freshwater, coastal and related ecosystems are protected and improved; that sustainable development and political stability are promoted, that every person has access to enough safe water at an affordable cost to lead a healthy and productive life and that the vulnerable are protected from the risks of water-related hazards" (*Ministerial Declaration of The Hague on Water Security in the 21st Century* 2000: 1). In this declaration, there is an underlying assumption that the threats to water resources hinder poverty alleviation. This assumption can also be observed in the Fourth World Water Forum summary, which emphasized how water security is essential for development (Martinez Austria and van Hofwegen 2006). Thus, water security touches upon many issues, including access to drinking water, food security and protecting ecological systems to provide a stable foundation for overcoming poverty. The Human Development Report published by the United Nations Development Programme (UNDP) in 2006 has the following definition of water security: "In broad terms water security is about ensuring that every person has reliable access to enough safe water at an affordable price to lead a healthy, dignified and productive life, while maintaining the ecological systems that provide water and also depend on water" (UNDP 2006: 3). Because the scope of threats is wide in the concept of water security, it requires not only the state to protect its people from threats but also the involvement of other actors such as international organizations, non-governmental organizations (NGOs) and local communities. Thus, water governance by various stakeholders is a crucial component of ensuring water security.

The concept of water security also recognizes how access to water can involve competition and conflict. As a result, water security is associated with peace. For example, UNESCO's From Potential Conflict to Co-operation Potential (PCCP) project focuses on water as a catalyst for peace, as represented in the synthesis document, *Water Security and Peace: A Synthesis of Studies Prepared under the PCCP–Water for Peace Process* (Cosgrove 2003).

In international river basins, the number and complexity of threats increase because there are more competing interests at the inter-state level and the domestic level. As indicated in the Hague Declaration, political stability is considered important. In international river basins, this would mean the stability of both the riparian states and the basin as a whole. This raises issues about the possibility of national security being endangered by international competition for water access (Brown 1977; Ullman 1983; Mathews 1989; Myers 1989). In this regard, the discourse on environmental security is also related to water security.

This chapter recognizes the importance of water security in relation to development and poverty. In particular, I focus on the effects of political instability. Political instability can be caused by water-induced problems and by problems that are unrelated to water. The effects are as diverse as the causes. In order to understand how political instability influences water security, it is first necessary to understand how the discourse around water is created. Domestic issues on political agendas provide the background to how the problem of water is framed. In an international basin, there will be different, and possibly contradictory, ways of framing water. For example, one state in a basin may consider water scarcity to be a threat to economic development if it is implementing infrastructure for resource capture. In the same basin, another state may consider water exploitation to be a threat to the ecology, especially if it is a downstream country being affected by less water flow. These different ways of framing water can add to the tension between riparian states over the development of a water project. By investigating political agendas and prioritized domestic issues, I identify (1) how Lesotho framed water through the negotiation and implementation process of an international water project and (2) the specific impacts of political instability on water security.

## Lesotho's bilateral water project

### Harnessing the Senqu River

Lesotho is located in Southern Africa, totally encompassed by South Africa. This small landlocked country of roughly 30,000 km$^2$ is mountainous, with the Drakensberg mountain range forming the eastern border.

This geographical feature has provided Lesotho with abundant water. Snowmelt from the mountains, which rise to over 3,000 metres, forms the Senqu River. This is the major tributary of the Orange River, together with the Vaal, which flows from South Africa. The Orange River flows west towards Namibia and empties into the Atlantic Ocean. The Senqu River contributes much of the total basin water flow because rainfall in this area is high and evaporation loss low compared with the downstream regions. This has made Lesotho an attractive source of water, especially for South Africa, because Lesotho is geographically close for transferring water. The largest water development project in Lesotho is undoubtedly the Lesotho Highlands Water Project (LHWP). This project transfers water from Lesotho to South Africa under a bilateral treaty. Currently, the first of four potential phases has been completed, allowing South Africa to receive 30.2 $m^3$/sec of water (Wallis 2000). If all phases are completed, 70 $m^3$/sec of water will be transferred (LHDA n.d.(b)). The LHWP has attracted much international attention for several reasons: the scale of the project, including Africa's highest dam, the Katse dam in Lesotho; the rare achievement of international water transfer; resettlement and environmental impact issues of dam creation; and, most recently, the exposure of corruption among international project contractors and LHWP authority personnel.

The transferred water is used to supply water to South Africa's urban area of Gauteng province. Supplies of both industrial water and drinking water are essential for this region because it generates roughly 40 per cent of South Africa's GDP (TCTA–LHDA 2003). For every cubic metre of water, Lesotho receives royalties of 16.33 cents in South African currency.[1] Lesotho also generates hydropower at the Muela Hydropower Plant using the dammed water. This plant generates 72 MW, supplying the country's off-peak electricity. Previously all electricity was bought from South Africa. Lesotho's dependence is now less, buying approximately 18 MW only during peak periods (Government of Lesotho 2004b).

Water allocation, especially in arid regions, can be problematic. This is because it involves changes in the volumetric share of water between upstream and downstream riparian states. Lesotho is the upper riparian vis-à-vis South Africa on the Senqu tributary. One reason why the water allocation aspect of the project has not been acutely conflictual is Lesotho's limited water use in the highlands. The highlands of Lesotho receive about 700–800 mm per annum of rainfall (LHDA n.d.(b)). According to the Food and Agriculture Organization of the United Nations (FAO 2005), there are wide disparities in irrigation potential. The area of irrigation land that can be developed on the Senqu is estimated to range from 3,500 to 7,000 hectares (ha) but there are other estimates of about 1,000 ha. Furthermore, only small-scale irrigation projects have been successful, despite a history of donor-led projects (FAO 2005). Because Lesotho cannot fully consume the waters, the royalty revenue from transferring water is a major appeal. In addition to the variable royalties for the quantity of transferred water, fixed royalties accrue within the framework of the project. It was calculated that, with the LHWP, South Africa saves 44 per cent of costs compared with an alternative domestic scheme, the Orange Vaal Transfer Scheme. The remaining 56 per cent of the difference in costs is paid to Lesotho as a fixed royalty. For Phase 1, US$55 million per annum is paid as fixed royalties. This represents 25 per cent of total annual export revenues, 14 per cent of public revenues and 3–5 per cent of GDP between 1990 and 2044 (LHDA 1995). During the financial year 2004/2005, it is reported that 693 million m$^3$ of water was delivered, which accounted for 226.08 million maloti in variable royalty payments (LHDA 2005).

## Domestic issues during the LHWP negotiations

Talks of water transfer had already begun when Lesotho became independent. In the early days of Lesotho as a sovereign state, there was fierce party competition for power. The strife can be said to have created a certain political propensity to political instability and party infighting that is seen even today: "politics in Lesotho have been marked by repression and intrigue on the part of the political elite, working within a highly polarised society, with weak political institutions and paltry economic resources" (Pherudi 2003: 360). The domestic power struggle was reflected in how economic and foreign policies were formed. This section examines the economic issues and diplomatic tactics that shaped the nature of the water negotiations and the significance of international water transfer for water-rich Lesotho.

### Water as an economic strategy

In 1966, Lesotho gained independence after being a British High Commission Territory called Basutoland since 1868. By this time, there had already been a decade of planning a water transfer scheme. The British administration showed some interest in a scheme that would supply water to South Africa and generate electricity. However, the British administration did not engage in the project because it had a passive attitude towards building the foundations of economic development for Basutoland's future independence (Matlosa 2000).

In preparation for independence, national elections took place in 1965. As a British protectorate, there had been discussion in the domestic political arena about the risk of incorporation into South Africa. However, the elections meant a new agenda for the parties: how would the independent state build its relationship with the powerful neighbour (Scott 1985)? The Basotho National Party (BNP) led by Chief Leabua Jonathan, claimed a majority by a slim margin in the simple plurality system. The BNP established a government that tended to have close ties with South Africa, which was implementing its controversial apartheid policies. In contrast to the major opposition party, the Basotho Congress Party (BCP), the BNP was regarded as more conservative and less aggressive towards South Africa. The South African government supported the new government and offered financial assistance (Scott 1985).

Since the former British administration had not implemented any economic policies, Lesotho was seeking ways to secure revenue for development. The new government sought pragmatic cooperation with South Africa to keep Lesotho economically afloat after the "notorious neglect" of the British (Lemon 1996: 265). Aware of the low level of the economy as well as its enclosed geographical location, the BNP focused on "bread-and-butter issues" (Weisfelder 1979: 250). It is likely that, in this context, Lesotho initially agreed to the water transfer project in 1968.

The economic policies of the early years of independence were reflected in Lesotho's five-year development plan. The first five-year plan started in 1970. It prioritized irrigation, water sales from the Malibamatso River to South Africa and the creation of hydroelectric plant (Central Planning and Development Office 1977; Lundahl et al. 2003). The LHWP was thus in line with Lesotho's development policy. In a mid-plan review of the second five-year plan, hydroelectricity plants were considered necessary despite the costs and, more generally, water was regarded as follows:

> A new urgency is felt in the wake of the political developments in Southern Africa [most notably, the increasingly powerful apartheid policy and consequent interstate conflict] which compel Government to put increased emphasis on those measures which hold forth promise of building the nation's capacity for self-reliance. There is a realistic hope that efforts in the natural resources sector can provide employment which will be both competitive with opportunities across the border and reduce imports. (Central Planning and Development Office 1977: WM-1)

This explains why Lesotho considered the inclusion of a hydroelectric plant in the LHWP from the beginning. The organization responsible for project implementation on behalf of Lesotho, the Lesotho Highlands Development Authority (LHDA), clearly states in a report how the existing Muela plant is a "strategic investment" to make the country less economically dependent on South Africa (LHDA n.d.(a): 15). Water has been framed as an economic strategy since independence.

## Power struggles and oppression

The elections of 1970 marked a significant change in Lesotho's domestic political climate. In January, the national elections brought victory to the BCP, the party that had been expected to win the previous 1965 elections had it not been for the BNP's surprise ascent to power. Jonathan's reaction to the BCP's victory was to declare a state of emergency. This resulted in the suspension of the constitution, the expulsion of the monarch, King Moshoeshoe II, and the arrest of BCP members. Jonathan's extreme action to retain power cemented the political structure of a dictatorial one-party rule for the next one and a half decades.

The reason for the BNP's electoral debacle was domestic protest against Jonathan's overt friendliness with South Africa. Despite criticism for being pro-South Africa and out of touch with its citizens (Gay et al. 1995), it is true that the BNP did have some disputes with its neighbour originating from two issues. First, Lesotho had been complaining about the return of "conquered territories", land lost during the wars of the 1860s to South Africa. Second, the apartheid policy had become increasingly oppressive, gradually causing tension within the whole of Southern Africa (Meissner and Turton 2003). Meissner and Turton (2003) note that there was concern about the influence of apartheid through joint water development. However, Jonathan's attitude towards South Africa was considered generally to be cordial, especially in comparison with the BCP. Weisfelder (1979) notes that the government had been oblivious to the domestic political costs of being close to apartheid South Africa. To regain support, Jonathan shifted from a cordial attitude to openly criticizing apartheid. This calculated and conscious decision was made to gain not only domestic but also international support. More and more black African countries were becoming opposed to South Africa's apartheid policy. In response, South Africa had made several diplomatic efforts at "détente" through dialogue initiatives and non-aggression pacts (Geldenhuys 1982). However, these attempts were not effective and so South Africa resorted to military means in pursuing its political demands. Against this backdrop, Lesotho sought to align itself with the Front Line States and strengthen its ties with the African National Congress (ANC), which was operating from many of the Front Line State regions. The ANC had gathered impetus for apartheid resistance because it was banned from conducting any activity in South Africa. Taking advantage of Lesotho's proximity to Pretoria, ANC members maintained safe houses there.

The BCP had been the first prominent political party to gain mass support before independence (Southall 2003). It had a "revived and more coherent nationalist movement", which criticized incorporation into

South Africa and promoted an independent Southern Africa (Gay et al. 1995: 17). In addition, it promoted democratic measures within the traditional chieftaincy. The BNP had formed merely to counter the BCP's specific agendas and its policies differed little from those of the BCP (Gay et al. 1995; Southall 2003). The unsatisfactory results of the elections for the BCP caused a failed coup in 1974, as a result of which the party leader and some supporters went into exile. Some of the exiled members created the Lesotho Liberation Army (LLA) to destabilize the government. Owing to its limited military capacity and resources and to internal dissension, the LLA eventually began cooperating with South Africa (Southall 2003). However, it is important to point out that the LLA did not accept the apartheid ideology. Rather, "both sides of the relationship regarded each other with distrust and distaste" (Southall 2003: 257).

The result of the power struggle between the BNP and the BCP was seen in the "perverse" outcome of Lesotho's relations with South Africa, which led to increased South African intervention (Mochizuki 1998: 134). Indeed, Lesotho was considered "an extremist state" (Barber and Baratt, as cited in Meissner and Turton 2003: 120) and accused of harbouring ANC "terrorists". As a result, the LHWP negotiations suffered from deep mutual mistrust between the two states, and no progress was made from 1976 to 1978.

During this negotiation period of the LHWP, politics in Lesotho was characterized by competition for power. This was especially apparent in the 1970s, after the BNP forcibly stayed in power after the elections, and political elites maintained power and state resources (Olaleye 2004). It is unclear whether the economic policies and the emphasis on assessing natural resource exploitation would have differed between the BNP and the BCP. Considering that the parties' policies were similar, perhaps there would not have been much difference even if the BCP had been in power. What is certain is that Lesotho, regardless of the party in power, would need ways to develop its economy after independence.

However, water issues, though important, did not gain special status in the economic policy such that the LHWP negotiations would be hurried. For example, although the second five-year plan recognized that the full economic potential of water and mineral resources was not being achieved, the government placed primary importance on identifying long-term domestic water needs and the economic feasibility of water development. The "thorough assessment" of natural resources was stressed during the time the bilateral negotiations were ongoing (Central Planning and Development Office 1977: WM-1). Therefore, for Lesotho, the LHWP was a "politicized" issue, an issue that involved state decisions and resource allocations (Buzan et al. 1998).

## Domestic issues and the LHWP Agreement

Bilateral relations deteriorated during the 1980s. South Africa and Lesotho accused each other of supporting guerrilla groups. In a situation
where ANC attacks were increasing (Jaster 1988), South Africa suspected Lesotho of allegedly harbouring ANC members. On the other
hand, Jonathan accused South Africa of supporting the LLA's destabili-
zation of his government. Geldenhuys expresses the repercussions of the
deep mutual suspicions of this time:

> Relations between South Africa and the black states are, on both sides, charac-
> terised by suspicion, fear and even a strong dose of paranoia. Each sees its se-
> curity and stability threatened by the other; each side, in other words, perceives
> itself the target of destabilisation by the other. (Geldenhuys 1983: 18)

### Donor games with the West and Soviet powers

Jonathan played a shrewd donor game, especially after becoming hostile
to South Africa. He portrayed Lesotho as a small poor country subject to
economic "strangulation" by South Africa (Libby 1987: 149). This would
lead to the overrepresentation of donors pursuing so-called development,
as analysed in Ferguson's (1990) well-known work *The Anti-Politics
Machine*. At the same time, Jonathan turned to communist countries for
foreign aid. Considering that the BNP had previously criticized the BCP
for its communist ties, this political inconsistency is significant. Libby
(1987) theorizes that the communist link was Jonathan's tactic for getting
Western donors more involved in Lesotho. It can be said that Jonathan's
tactics were effective in generating economic assistance. However, his
approach did not solve the fundamental problem of poverty. Rather, it
led to a further deterioration in bilateral relations, such that South Africa
began applying pressure on Lesotho through economic pressure.

South Africa exercised the "railway diplomacy" of applying economic
pressure: it offered infrastructure such as railways, ports and roads on
condition that military attacks were halted (Horovitz 1982; Jaster 1988).
This "reward" mechanism was applied to Lesotho in 1981, when South
Africa allegedly went to Lesotho with a deal to abate the LLA activities
if Lesotho expelled ANC members (Gutteridge 1983). Domestic dis-
approval of BNP rule had rapidly escalated while the LLA was operating
in the country. The guerrilla group had targeted infrastructure related
to water, such as small hydropower generators. According to Mochizuki
(1998: 135), this was effective in revealing the paralysis of Jonathan's rule
for two reasons. First, support for the BNP did not increase. Despite the
guerrilla activities influencing the daily lives of the people, the BCP,

which was linked to the LLA, retained strong support. Secondly, the attacks on the infrastructure led to increased dependence on South Africa, contrary to the government's efforts at self-reliance.

## The repercussions of economic pressure and political instability: Coup d'état

South Africa closed its border to Lesotho during the first weeks of January 1986 to further apply pressure. This was after a security pact to guarantee less hostility from Lesotho failed. South Africa accused Lesotho of allowing ANC members to operate from its territory and threatened that the LHWP would be abandoned unless Lesotho complied (*Rand Daily Mail*, 27 August 1984: 2). Lesotho regarded the security of Southern Africa as having little to do with the water transfer project (Pisto 1984; *Rand Daily Mail*, 30 August 1984: 6). Being landlocked, the border closure cut Lesotho off from all imports, causing a major economic standstill. Because Jonathan had not established a solid economic foundation to minimize dependence on South Africa, this was a severe blow.

This situation directly triggered a political crisis for Jonathan. A coup d'état took place and, on 20 January 1986, it was officially announced that a new military regime under the Lesotho Defence Force (LDF) leader, Major-General Justin Metsing Lekhanya, had been established. The military regime was initially popular in both Lesotho and South Africa (Cowell 1986; Mills 1992; Hayashi 1999). It was also reported that the Lesotho public was optimistic about the new government terminating the border closure (L'Ange 1986). Lekhanya was portrayed as a "pragmatic man who is likely to favour close economic and other ties with South Africa" (*The Star*, 20 January 1986: 1). To this can be attributed the fact that the LHWP treaty was signed in September of the same year.

It has been speculated that, considering the proximity of the timing, South Africa staged the coup d'état to facilitate the water agreement (Homer-Dixon 1999; Matlosa 2000; Furlong 2006). If South Africa orchestrated the coup d'état, it would also be possible to resolve the issues of security pacts and communist embassies. However, Lesotho's new government still insisted that security pacts were unnecessary and that it would not close the Eastern bloc embassies (Cornish 1986). Lekhanya did return "active" ANC members within Lesotho's territory to South Africa, though he is reported to have said that Lesotho could not do anything about South African refugees entering the country (Cornish 1986).

Furthermore, there are specific reasons to rebut South Africa's alleged motives. First, both states had appointed separate representative organizations to jointly compile a feasibility study of the LHWP during 1983–1985. The study recommended the realization of the project in early

1986. The study clarified the details of the project, including the royalty system and project governance between both Lesotho and South Africa (Laymeyer MacDonald Consortium and Olivier Shand Consortium 1986). The agreement was not the result of mere coercion without prior studies. The feasibility studies were the outcome of negotiations started nearly 30 years earlier.

Secondly, if South Africa wanted Lesotho's water, it would have been possible to force an agreement earlier. Considering the way the treaty is written, South Africa is concerned about Lesotho's failure to deliver water (Boadu 1998). It would seem unnecessary for such detailed treaty components if South Africa could simply coerce Lesotho into delivery. Boadu (1998) analyses why South Africa did not need an unequal treaty:

> There are no rational reasons for the RSA to engage in such a lengthy negotiation process, especially when it has the military and economic might to impose its will. The more rational inference is that RSA considered a relational treaty to be a cheaper alternative to a coerced and "unequal" treaty. The high cost of controlling violence and disruption of social life within its own borders during the period, could easily factor in RSA's calculus regarding its ability to cheaply police an extra-territorial water project. (Boadu 1998: 397)

Finally, Lesotho's new government was keen on economic development from the beginning. Considering that Lekhanya came to power after an event that displayed Lesotho's economic vulnerability, strengthening Lesotho's economy was always an obvious concern. The large-scale project had the potential to generate much-needed economic development. In other words, the project would secure long-term revenues that did not rely on international aid or remittances by Basotho migrant workers. Lekhanya's agreement to exchange permanent trade representatives in the following year also indicates that economic ties with South Africa were important.

Given that the military regime came into power after a coup d'état, it is possible to speculate that the politically volatile climate might pose a threat to implementation of the LHWP. However, the treaty had great significance in binding both Lesotho and South Africa to executing the project. The treaty shows how the costs and benefits of the project are shared, with South Africa responsible for infrastructure, except for the hydropower plant. By having a governance system composed of project authorities from both countries and a joint commission, the responsibility and ownership of the scheme are clear. More importantly, because Lesotho perceived the project to be an economic strategy, this strengthened its commitment; it is unlikely that a government would jeopardize its own assets in the midst of economic stagnation. Thus, the LHWP cannot be regarded as an impulsive decision by a military regime.

## Domestic issues during the LHWP implementation process

After the treaty signing, the first phase of the project began. This phase was divided into Phases 1A and 1B. Construction of Phase 1A started soon after the signing. The Katse dam was officially inaugurated for water delivery in 1998. The planning and construction of Phase 1B were also done in parallel with progress in Phase 1A. In 2004, the Mohale dam was inaugurated, marking the end of the first phase. These planning and implementation processes brought up a new set of issues for Lesotho to deal with. These issues were related to the socio-economic impacts of the project. As a report by NGOs put it, the LHWP "was conceived as a technical and engineering rather than a social challenge" (Archer 1996: 7). The project faced a lack of expertise and resources to solve socio-economic problems. These problems seem to have diluted the effect of the projected benefits. In addition, there was an incident of violence at the Katse dam, which some claimed was evidence of a "water war".

### Employment and economic potential of the LHWP

The agricultural sector in Lesotho does not require many workers because of limited arable land. Many Basotho have instead earned a living as migrant workers. In particular, the South African mines have been popular for job opportunities. During 1972–1978, Lesotho's GDP increased 12 per cent annually owing to migrant remittances, grants and customs union revenue (Lundahl et al. 2003). By 1980, 150,000 people were employed in South Africa, compared with 40,000 in the domestic wage sector (Maasdorp 1985). However, from the 1990s, South African mines started rationalizing their operations because of the decrease in gold prices. Furthermore, unemployment in South Africa had become an issue, having repercussions on the wages and recruitment of Basotho workers. The pace of recruitment in the mines became slower than the growth in the Lesotho labour force (Lemon 1996). Although the number of mineworkers in South Africa remained high until 1989 (Coplan 2001), it decreased from 126,264 in 1989 to 65,000 in 2000 (Conningarth Economists 2004).

The LHWP was seen as a way to generate employment opportunities for Lesotho workers. Unemployment and a decrease in remittances prompted Lesotho to stress that many of the jobs available through the LHWP should be given to its people rather than to foreign workers. It is reported that 7,500 jobs were created for Phase 1A and another 6,780 for Phase 1B (TCTA–LHDA 2003). The project aimed to employ many of the unemployed workers since they were skilled in construction activities from their experience working in the mines (TCTA–LHDA 2003:

27). Training programmes were also available for workers to encourage long-term skill development for job opportunities even after the completion of the construction. LHDA (2004) reports that roughly 45 per cent of the Basotho labour for Phase 1B was from the highlands.

By 1990, however, there were riots caused by civilians frustrated at Lesotho's depressed economic situation (Makoa 1990). Weisfelder (1992: 660) notes that the "greatest liability of the Military Council has been its abysmal failure to stem the deterioration of the economy and the quality of life in Lesotho". Makoa (1990) states that the military government lacked the political and administrative capacity to run a country. Members of the LDF showed *"noticeable signs* of dissatisfaction ... over salaries, terms of service and corruption amongst the leadership" (Mills 1992: 66, emphasis added). Lekhanya's control of the military gradually disintegrated, as he accused his own government members too for weakening and defaming the military government (SAPES Trust 2001). In addition, the relationship with the monarch became troubled because Lekhanya resented King Moshoeshoe II for allegedly attempting to implement feudal systems (Makoa 1990). Lekhanya exiled the king in 1990. In the end, there was a bloodless coup d'état, a mutiny by junior officers, in 1991. This reintroduced democratic practices after political activities had been banned under the military regime. In 1993, national elections resulted in the BCP finally gaining a majority.

However, even after the regime change, frustration with economic conditions persisted. This is highlighted in an incident in September 1996. Workers for the Lesotho Highlands Project contractors and the Muela Hydropower contractors were killed when Lesotho police opened fire. The details of the incident are unclear, with varying accounts of how the shooting occurred (Ambrose 1996). Workers had gone on strike earlier in the year, which resulted in 2,300 workers being fired. After the shootings, 1,700 workers were re-employed. However, further construction on the project was halted because of failure to reach agreement between the contractors and the retrenched 600 workers (Ambrose 1996). The unrest was caused by dissatisfaction at their low wages compared with those of foreign workers (Ambrose 1996; Pottinger 1996; Van Wyk 2000). Pottinger (1996) notes additional reasons: police harassment of workers and failure of negotiations between the contractors and the workers' union. Even though the LHWP was heralded as bringing economic development opportunities, this incident illustrates how the Basotho workers considered the project not to be achieving the goals of improving the economy.

Basotho workers are said to have earned an estimated 75 million maloti during Phase 1B, but the LHDA admits that job opportunities for local firms were fewer than expected (LHDA 2004). It is undeniable that the project contributed to the economy by providing jobs and bringing in foreign direct investment and customs union revenue from project-related imports during Phase 1. In 1998, the LHWP accounted for 14 per cent of Lesotho's GDP (TCTA–LHDA 2003). However, at the individual level, these benefits were less tangible, especially since on-site jobs were no longer available after the completion of the major construction.

## Social and environmental impacts

The treaty makes explicit in Article 7(18) that no one would be disadvantaged by the project implementation. The environmental action plans (EAPs) conducted by the LHDA were the core vehicle for assessing implementation and mitigation measures in terms of (1) compensation, resettlement and development, (2) public health and (3) natural environment and heritage. In short, despite the joint feasibility studies of 1986 reporting no major environmental and social issues deriving from the project, the scale of the mitigation measures worried the LHDA. There were fundamental problems in assessing the impacts. Criticisms that the project was being executed at the expense of the locals were made in Lesotho and by international organizations (Hoover 2001; Mwangi 2007; Thamae and Pottinger 2006).

Environmental impact assessments (EIAs) were conducted for both Phase 1A and Phase 1B. However, the EIA for Phase 1A commenced when construction had already started, thus making it difficult to assess possible impacts and appropriate mitigation measures. The construction of the Katse dam required resettlement in the highlands: 143 households had to be relocated owing to the flooding; another 110 households were relocated because of other project infrastructure or because the region would be potentially hazardous as a living location. All of the resettled people were offered housing in the highlands, close to their original location. For lost arable land (1,540 ha) and rangeland (2,800 ha), compensation was made in the form of crops and fodder, respectively. The total cash compensation payments for loss of garden land or arable land totalled 1.36 million maloti for Phase 1A (LHDA 1995). Mitigation measures for the environmental impact of the LHWP include two nature reserves in the highlands and one botanical garden to preserve the indigenous flora and fauna. The Katse botanical garden has plants from inundated sites as well as other indigenous species. Specific conservation programmes targeted at endangered species such as the spiral aloe and Maloti minnow have also been established.

There has been criticism that the EIA was unsatisfactory and the methods of compensating the resettled people inadequate. The scale of the resettlement, the loss of land and other negative impacts of the project were underestimated from the beginning. Hoover's (2001) analysis is that, despite the resettlement plan being funded well in comparison with other dam projects, underestimation of the resettlement impacts led to insufficient budget for compensation. The Rural Development Programme (RDP) was established to provide support for affected families in the highlands. This programme incorporated skills training, medical services, improvement in nutritional standards, expansion of water and sanitation services, and electricity provision. However, Horta and Pottinger (2006) suggest that the RDP should have been negotiated before the implementation process and avoided politicizing the responsibility for dividing the costs between Lesotho and South Africa.

The criticism of the project coincided with the "big dam debate" during which the negative social, economic and environmental impacts on communities of dams were widely discussed. The World Bank, which had provided funding for about 5 per cent of Phase 1A (LHDA n.d.(b)), has been criticized for accepting large-scale dam projects with major repercussions on local society and the environment (Hoover 2001; Horta 2006). This heightened attention to the soft issues of project implementation ultimately forced the LHDA to improve the EIA studies. The LHDA has commented that, although "[the EIA for Phase 1A] may not be fully compatible with the most recent methodologies of EIA's [sic], the process and outputs were at the time considered to be of high international standards" (LHDA 1995: 18). The Minister of Natural Resources went further and directly admitted the shortcomings of the EIA at a national workshop on the EIA for Phase 1B. The minister mentioned how, in Phase 1A, there were no baseline data as reference points for assessments and that the studies had limited influence in adjusting project design and implementation (Raditapole 1995). Phase 1B offered a choice of in-kind material compensation and cash compensation. It also offered people the choice of resettling close to their original location or in the lowlands. It emphasized community participation to assist understanding of the project. An Instream Flow Requirement Policy for considering downstream impacts was implemented for the first time in Phase 1B. The compensation for resettlement for Phase 1 is said to have been approximately US$13 million, or 1.3 per cent of the overall project budget (Hoover 2001).

Legum (1996) argues that, although the treaty emphasized commitment to assisting the resettled people, the project authorities did not give the locals adequate information and there was little organizational effort to assist in the enhancement of skills tailored to personalized methods of economic independence. Horta (1995) claims that the LHDA did not have the capacity to respond to the social impacts and that there was mistrust between the locals and LHDA staff. The Lesotho Highlands Water Revenue Development Fund, which operated until 1997 (and was replaced by the Lesotho Fund for Community Development in 2000), was suspected of political corruption by the public: "the *perception* that VDCs [Village Development Committees – committees that manage grants given by the Fund] and the Fund have been 'politicised' [to gain political support] is likely to sharpen antagonisms at village level and will weaken the Fund's capacity to make a long-term impact on poverty" (Archer 1996: 22, emphasis in original). Lesotho's ill preparedness to acknowledge specific project impacts and to respond in a suitable time contributed to domestic mistrust of the project. Political corruption in Lesotho had also influenced perceptions of how the benefits were going to be disseminated down to the local level.

## Unrest and intervention by the Southern African Development Community: Operation Boleas

The most violent incident the LHWP experienced was the heavy fighting between the South African National Defence Force (SANDF) and the Lesotho Defence Force (LDF) at the Katse dam. This happened during a military intervention called Operation Boleas by SANDF and the Botswana Defence Force (BDF) under the auspices of the Southern African Development Community (SADC) in 1998. The main objective of Operation Boleas (standing for BOtswana, LEsotho And South Africa) was to restore peace in Lesotho, which was on the brink of anarchy. In the capital there had been escalating protests by party supporters against the recent election results. Protesters hijacked cars and built blockades, causing turmoil. There had been casualties at the palace gates from a clash between demonstrators and the police. In addition, junior officers of the army had mutinied after rifts among factions (Africa Confidential 1998a; Ambrose 1998a). The mission objectives were announced in advance as "to create a safe environment by securing or controlling the Maseru Bridge Border post, the Lesotho Defence Force Military Bases, The Radio Broadcasting Station, Embassies and SA High Commission, Royal Palace, Airports, Government Buildings, power and water supply facilities" (Chief of Joint Operations Media Liaison 1998). On 22 September 1998, SANDF entered Lesotho first, followed by the BDF. The former attempted to secure the Katse dam. Shooting began when Basotho soldiers refused to hand over the garrison at the dam site and shot a member of SANDF (Ambrose 1998b).

Some have regarded this incident at the dam, which caused casualties of both Basotho and South Africans, as the manifestation of a resource war. For example, Likoti (2007) and Pherudi (2003) argue that the intervention was not an SADC peacekeeping mission but a way to protect the delivery of water for South Africa's own interests. The *International*

*Water Events Database: 1948–1999*[2] ranks this intervention as an event caused by South Africa's interest in securing water, and characterized by a high degree of conflict involving "extensive war acts causing deaths, dislocation or high strategic cost".[3] However, looking at the wider background against which this incident occurred, Operation Boleas cannot be considered to represent a "water war" caused by South Africa's greed for water. Rather, the incident reflects the fragility of Lesotho politics caused by ongoing power struggles.

Before the intervention, there had been elections in May 1998, which caused tension between the political parties to surface rapidly. The BCP was the ruling party after the return to democracy. Its belated succession to power was riven with internal conflict that was "not based upon any ideological or policy differences, but rather on leadership tussle involving the party bigwigs" (Matlosa and Shale 2006: 5). This resulted in BCP dissenters separating from the party in 1997 to form the Lesotho Congress for Democracy (LCD). Because the LCD had attracted many MPs from the BCP, the LCD held a majority of parliamentary seats and thus constitutionally became the ruling party. This caused the BCP to feel very hostile towards the LCD (Matlosa and Shale 2006). The tension between the parties escalated when the LCD won the 1998 election with 79 out of 80 seats in parliament. Opposition parties including the BCP, the BNP and the Marematlou Freedom Party considered the election had been rigged and refused to accept the results. They took the issue to the High Court and the SADC. The SADC Troika, consisting of Botswana, South Africa and Zimbabwe, formed the Langa Commission to investigate the election results. Meanwhile, election protests gradually became violent. Protests in the capital and in front of the royal palace resulted in casualties. The results of the Commission were delayed and, furthermore, they were inconclusive about the validity of the election and its results. This added to the frustration of the parties and aroused suspicion within the military about the reliability of the report (Santho 1999). Soon after the report was released, junior military officers mutinied. Violent protests and an army mutiny occurred at the same time. As a result, the LCD Prime Minister sent a written request to the SADC Troika for a military intervention to prevent a military coup d'état.

The 1998 crisis was the culmination of political instability in the new democratic system. There is much controversy and criticism about South Africa's intervention, because Article 5 of the SADC Protocol concerning the right of intervention was not yet ratified at that time. However, South Africa was in a situation where "Mandela was damned if he intervened and damned it he didn't" (Africa Confidential 1998b: 7). Yet intervention was not unprecedented. In early 1994, a faction within the army had mutinied after being dissatisfied with the military government's refusal of a pay rise. The Prime Minister requested military support from South Africa. Though not employing military means, South Africa, together with Botswana and Zimbabwe, made an attempt to resolve the situation diplomatically. Then, in August 1994, the King undertook a royal coup by deposing the Prime Minister. South Africa, Botswana and Zimbabwe once again diplomatically intervened by threatening economic sanctions. Khadiagala (2001: 143) notes how these interventions "established a diplomatic practice whereby core SADC states intervened without specific authorization from their regional allies". In Operation Boleas, the Katse dam was secured as part of the infrastructure to be protected. Van Nieuwkerk gives a mixed review of Operation Boleas, but contends "it succeeded in securing *Lesotho's strategic installations* such as fuel depots, the Highlands Water Project, and key buildings from being taken over or destroyed by the rebels" (1999: 15, emphasis added). Given that Lesotho has had a history of the LLA destroying water and power facilities, it is plausible that this experience would have made the SADC include the protection of LHWP infrastructure in its objectives and prioritize securing the biggest infrastructure at the beginning of the intervention.

In summary, the socio-economic issues surrounding the project, as well as the military intervention, show how the LHWP has had an impact on Lesotho. Though "macro" benefits to the state economy are being gained, the "micro" benefits – benefits that enhance the daily lives of the Basotho – are less tangible. Despite there being frustration and disappointment about the project benefits among the locals, these sentiments were not the main trigger of domestic turmoil. Rather, political instability caused by party competition, infighting and rocky relationships with the monarch was highlighted by the incapacity of the state to deal with the issues. In this regard, it would be hasty to analyse it as a water war by just taking a snapshot of the incident at the Katse dam and excluding the bigger picture. The causes of the intervention were unrelated to water. It is also noteworthy how the domestic turmoil did not change the relationship between Lesotho and South Africa over the usage of water; water delivery and royalty payments are still made.

## The LHWP and its effects on water security in Lesotho

The bigger picture of how to use revenues from the water transfer had been worked out but, initially, there was little understanding about the scale and scope of impacts on individuals and communities. For example, in 1991 the Lesotho Highlands Water Revenue Development Fund was established by the government of Lesotho to ensure income generation and improve infrastructure services within the country (LHDA n.d.(b)).

By 1996, the fund had accumulated US$42.7 million (LHDA n.d.(b)). This was used for creating infrastructure outside the highlands and consequently providing jobs. The infrastructure consisted of 784 km of rural roads, 125 small dams and 33 footbridges (LHDA 1995). However, this fund has been criticized for not being managed in an efficient manner (TCTA–LHDA 2003; Horta and Pottinger 2006). The overall goal of economic development was identified, but the methods of poverty alleviation were inappropriate. In 2000, the Lesotho Fund for Community Development was set up in an attempt to restructure the fund (Government of Lesotho 2001). It is expected that the new fund will be instrumental in accelerating poverty alleviation in the future (TCTA–LHDA 2003; Conningarth Economists 2004).

The government and the project authorities have gradually become aware of the need to increase its capacity for managing the socio-economic challenges if it is to pass on the benefits to the public. This can be seen in the introduction of the EIA policy and guidelines at the national level (TCTA–LHDA 2003). In 1999, NGOs and the LHDA signed a Memorandum of Understanding to establish cooperative relations. In 2003, an Ombudsman conducted an inquiry into complaints about the Phase 1B compensation. During this process, the LHDA admitted its failure to apply the compensation legislation and its misuse of the compensation policy (Office of the Ombudsman 2003).

This project has highlighted another aspect of water security for Lesotho. This is the issue of supplying water to the lowlands, which have faced water shortages. Whereas the treaty deals only with the provision of water to the project area, the need for a comprehensive water utilization plan for the whole of the state has been emphasized (National Environmental Secretariat 1999). The Lesotho Lowlands Water Supply Scheme has been investigated as a way to relieve water shortages in Maseru and the surrounding peri-urban areas (Government of Lesotho 2004a).

Since the LHWP has been implemented, there have been "unexpected" effects on water security. The government and the project authority had not considered these socio-economic issues thoroughly before implementation. Water is still currently framed as an economic strategy. However, how to use the benefits deriving from water is now attracting attention. It has been emphasized that the project should be governed in such a way that the benefits reach individuals.

## Conclusion

Developing water has been framed as an economic issue in Lesotho since its independence, irrespective of the regime or party in power. However, the emphasis was not on resource capture, as in the US or Spanish hydraulic missions where increased hydraulic infrastructure would signify development (Reisner 1993; Swyngedouw 2004). Rather, the emphasis was on the economic opportunities. Water was identified as a strong potential resource for developing the country. Because Lesotho faced increasing economic difficulties, the prospect of water transfer was a politicized issue. Ultimately, the way politics was structured in Lesotho allowed political elites to have the defining power of shaping agendas. However, these political elites were caught up in a power struggle, both between and within parties. Thus, the immediate interest was palpably to overpower opponents. Economics was a secondary issue; and water was a secondary issue. Even when the LHWP was being implemented, the LHWP was a peripheral issue and competition and acrimony between the parties was the dominant issue. The cause of the 1998 SADC intervention was not water per se but political vulnerability.

There was an institutional failure in dealing with the means to pass on the benefits of water development to the public; the LHWP was generally seen as the vehicle that would secure revenue but not as ensuring water security. At the same time, the public had little confidence that the government would maximize the opportunity for poverty alleviation. The political instability resulted in the government having little capacity to address the socio-economic challenges. Ensuring water security would mean reducing the threats to water resources and ecological systems. In addition, it would mean addressing the secondary impacts from utilizing water. In the case of the LHWP, there has been cooperation at the international level thus far, with Lesotho and South Africa upholding their responsibilities of water transfer and royalty payment. Because the LHWP is a big economic opportunity for Lesotho, the benefits and lessons have the potential to further ensure water security for Lesotho in the long term.

## Acknowledgements

The research carried out for this chapter was partly funded by the New Research Initiatives in Humanities and Social Sciences of the Japan Society for the Promotion of Science (JSPS) and the Core Research for Evolutional Science and Technology (CREST) of Japan. In addition, funding from the Sumitomo Foundation of Japan is gratefully acknowledged.

## Notes

1. See the website of the Trans-Caledon Tunnel Authority at ⟨http://www.tcta.co.za/article.jsp?menu_id=185⟩.

2. See ⟨http://www.transboundarywaters.orst.edu/projects/events/⟩.
3. ⟨http://www.transboundarywaters.orst.edu/projects/events/bar_scale.html⟩.


# REFERENCES

Africa Confidential (1998a), "Lesotho-Swaziland: Militants and Monarchs", *Africa Confidential*, Vol. 39, No. 19.

—— (1998b), "South Africa–Lesotho: To a Little Kingdom", *Africa Confidential*, Vol. 39, No. 20.

Ambrose, David (1996), "Police Action Resulting from Lesotho Highlands Strike Leads to Deaths", *Summary of Events in Lesotho*, Vol. 3, No. 3; available at ⟨http://www.trc.org.ls/events/events19.963.htm#Police%20Action%20 Resulting%20from%20Lesotho%20Highlands%20Strike%20Leads%20to%20 Deaths⟩ (accessed 29 October 2007).

—— (1998a), "Army Mutiny", *Summary of Events in Lesotho*, Vol. 5, No. 3; available at ⟨http://www.trc.org.ls/events/events19.983.htm#Army%20Mutiny⟩ (accessed 29 October 2007).

—— (1998b), "Intervention at Katse Becomes a Mass Slaughter and a Disaster for Public Relations", *Summary of Events in Lesotho*, Vol. 5, No. 3; available at ⟨http://www.trc.org.ls/events/events19.983.htm#Intervention%20at%20Katse %20becomes%20a%20Mass%20Slaughter%20and%20a%20Disaster%20for %20Public%20Relations⟩ (accessed 29 October 2007).

Archer, Robert (1996), *Trust in Construction? The Lesotho Highlands Water Project*, A Report of Christian Aid and the Christian Council of Lesotho, London: Christian Aid.

Boadu, Fred O. (1998), "Relational Characteristics of Transboundary Water Treaties: Lesotho's Water Transfer Treaty with the Republic of South Africa", *Natural Resources Journal*, Vol. 38, No. 3.

Brown, Lester R. (1977), "Redefining National Security", *Worldwatch Paper* 14, Washington: Worldwatch Institute.

Buzan, Barry, Ole Wæver and Jaap de Wilde (1998), *Security: A New Framework for Analysis*, Boulder, CO: Lynne Rienner.

Central Planning and Development Office (1977), *Kingdom of Lesotho: Donor Conference Papers September 1977*, Maseru: Government of Lesotho.

Chief of Joint Operations Media Liaison (1998), "SADC Launches Operation Boleas in Lesotho", Chief of Joint Operations Media Liaison, SANDF, 22 September; available at ⟨http://www.info.gov.za/speeches/1998/98a01_boleas 9811173.htm⟩ (accessed 29 October 2007).

Conningarth Economists (2004), *Lesotho Highlands Water Project: Phase 1B Economic Impact Study*, Maseru: LHDA.

Coplan, David B. (2001), "A River Runs Through It: The Meaning of the Lesotho–Free State Border", *African Affairs*, Vol. 100, No. 398.

Cornish, Jean-Jacques (1986), "Lekhanya Wants Negotiation – at Home and with South Africa", *The Star*, 29 January, p. 5.

Cosgrove, William J., comp. (2003), *Water Security and Peace: A Synthesis of Studies Prepared under the PCCP–Water for Peace Process*, IHP-VI, Technical Documents in Hydrology, PCCP series no. 20, UNESCO-IHP.

Cowell, Alan (1986), "Military Topples Lesotho Leader; Capital Jubilant", *New York Times*, 21 January, p. 3.

FAO [Food and Agriculture Organization] (2005), *Irrigation in Africa in Figures AQUASTAT Survey – 2005 Country Profile Lesotho*, Water Report No. 29, Rome: FAO.

Ferguson, James (1990), *The Anti-Politics Machine: "Development", Depoliticization, and Bureaucratic Power in Lesotho*, Cambridge and New York: Cambridge University Press.

Furlong, Kathryn (2006), "Hidden Theories, Troubled Waters: International Relations, the 'Territorial Trap', and the Southern African Development Community's Transboundary Waters", *Political Geography*, Vol. 25, No. 4.

Gay, John, Debby Gill and David Hall, eds (1995), *Lesotho's Long Journey: Hard Choices at the Crossroads: A Comprehensive Overview of Lesotho's Historical, Social, Economic, and Political Development with a View to the Future*, Maseru: Sechaba Consultants.

Geldenhuys, Deon (1982), "South Africa's Regional Policy", in Michael Clough, ed., *Changing Realities in Southern Africa: Implication for American Policy*, Berkeley: University of California, Institute of International Studies.

——— (1983), "The Destabilisation Controversy: An Analysis of a High-Risk Foreign Policy Option for South Africa", in Deon Geldenhuys and William Gutteridge, eds, *Instability and Conflict in Southern Africa: South Africa's Role in Regional Security*, Conflict Studies No. 148, London: Institute for the Study of Conflict.

Government of Lesotho (2001), "The Lesotho Fund for Community Development Operations in Full Swing", Government website article, 17 March; available at ⟨http://www.lesotho.gov.ls/articles/Lesotho%20Fund%20for%20Community.htm⟩ (accessed 29 October 2007).

——— (2004a), "The Lesotho Lowlands Water Supply Scheme", Government website article, 10 March; available at ⟨http://www.lesotho.gov.ls/articles/2004/LLW_Supply_Scheme.htm⟩ (accessed 29 October 2007).

——— (2004b), "Privatisation Act (Approved Privatisation Scheme for Lesotho Electricity Corporation) Notice 2004", Government website article, 31 March; available at ⟨http://www.lesotho.gov.ls/articles/2004/Ad_LEC_Privatization.htm⟩ (accessed 29 October 2007).

Gutteridge, William (1983), "South Africa's National Strategy: Implications for Regional Security", in Deon Geldenhuys and William Gutteridge, eds, *Instability and Conflict in Southern Africa: South Africa's Role in Regional Security*, Conflict Studies No. 148, London: Institute for the Study of Conflict.

Hayashi, Koji (1999), *Nanbu Afurica Seiji Keizai Ron*, Chiba: Institute of Developing Economies.

Homer-Dixon, Thomas F. (1999) *Environment, Scarcity, and Violence*, Princeton, NJ: Princeton University Press.

Hoover, Ryan (2001), *Pipe Dreams: The World Bank's Failed Efforts to Restore Lives and Livelihoods of Dam-Affected People in Lesotho*, Berkley, CA: IRN.

Horovitz, Richard A. (1982), "The Role of Donor Agencies in Southern Africa", in Gwendolen M. Carter and Patrick O'Meara, eds, *International Politics in Southern Africa*, Bloomington: Indiana University Press.

Horta, Korinna (1995), "The Mountain Kingdom's White Oil: The Lesotho Highlands Water Project", *Ecologist*, Vol. 25, No. 6.

────── (2006), "The World Bank's Decade for Africa: A New Dawn for Development Aid?", *Yale Journal of International Affairs*, Vol. 1, No. 2.

Horta, Korinna and Lori Pottinger (2006), "The Role of the World Bank: The Perspective of International NGOs", in Mabusetsa Lenka Thamae and Lori Pottinger, eds, *On the Wrong Side of Development: Lessons Learned from the Lesotho Highlands Water Project*, Maseru: Transformation Resource Center.

Jaster, Robert S. (1988), *The Defence of White Power: South African Foreign Policy under Pressure*. Basingstoke: Macmillan Press in association with the International Institute for Strategic Studies.

Khadiagala, Gilbert M. (2001), "Foreign Decisionmaking in Southern Africa's Fading Frontline", in Gilbert M. Khadiagala and Terrence Lyons, eds, *African Foreign Policies: Power and Process*, Boulder, CO: Lynne Rienner.

L'Ange, Gerald (1986), "Regime Acts in Key Areas", *The Star*, 21 January, p. 1.

Laymeyer MacDonald Consortium and Olivier Shand Consortium (1986), *Lesotho Highlands Water Project. Feasibility Study: Final Report*. Maseru: Ministry of Water, Energy and Mining.

Legum, Collin (1996), "Lesotho (1): Storm Clouds over the Malutis: Can the Ambitious Highlands Water Project Be Rescued?", *Third World Reports*, 30 September.

Lemon, Anthony (1996), "Lesotho and the New South Africa: The Question of Incorporation", *Geographical Journal*, Vol. 162, No. 3.

LHDA [Lesotho Highlands Development Authority] (1995), *Environmental and Social Aspects of the Lesotho Highlands Water Project Edition 1*, Maseru: LHDA.

────── (2004), *The Lesotho Highlands Water Project: Economic Impact of Phase 1B in Lesotho (Assessment of the Micro-Economic Impact of Phase 1B of LHWP: An Abridged Version)*, Maseru: LHDA; available at ⟨http://www.lhwp.org.ls/Reports/PDF/Executive%20Summary-microeconomic%20Impact-%20Ver3.pdf⟩ (accessed 29 October 2007).

────── (2005), *Annual Report 2004/2005*. Maseru: LHDA.

────── (n.d.(a)), *The Lesotho Highlands Development Authority: Muela Hydropower Plant Project*. Maseru: LHDA.

────── (n.d.(b)), *The Lesotho Highlands Water Project Commemorative Journal 1986–1996*, Maseru: LHDA.

Libby, Ronald T. (1987), *The Politics of Economic Power in Southern Africa*, Princeton, NJ: Princeton University Press.

Likoti, Fako Johnson (2007), "The 1998 Military Intervention in Lesotho: SADC Peace Mission or Resource War?", *International Peacekeeping*, Vol. 14, No. 2.

Lundahl, Mats, Colin McCarthy and Lennart Petersson (2003), *In the Shadow of South Africa: Lesotho's Economic Future*, Aldershot, Hants, and Burlington, VT: Ashgate.

Maasdorp, Gavin G. (1985), "Squaring up to Economic Dominance: Regional Patterns", in Robert I. Rotberg, Henry S. Bienen, Robert Legvold and Gavin G. Maasdorp, eds, *South Africa and Its Neighbors: Regional Security and Self-interest*, Lexington, MA: Lexington Books.

Makoa, Francis K. (1990), "The Military Kingdom: A Case for Restructuring the System of Government in Lesotho in the 1990s", in Sehoai Santho and Mafa Sejanamane, eds, *Southern Africa after Apartheid: Prospects for the Inner Periphery in the 1990s*, Mount Pleasant, Harare: Southern Africa Political Economy Series (SAPES) Trust.

Martinez Austria, Polioptro and Paul van Hofwegen, eds (2006), *Synthesis of the 4th World Water Forum, Mexico City, 2006*, Mexico D.F.: Comisión Nacional de Agua.

Mathews, Jennifer Tuchman (1989), "Redefining Security", *Foreign Affairs*, Vol. 68, No. 2.

Matlosa, Khabele (2000), "The Lesotho Highlands Water Project: Socio-Economic Impacts", in Daniel Tevera and Sam Moyo, eds, *Environmental Security in Southern Africa*, Harare: SAPES Books.

Matlosa, Khabele and Victor Shale (2006), "Impact of Floor Crossing on Party Systems and Representative Democracy: The Case of Lesotho", paper prepared for a Workshop on "Impact of Floor Crossing on Party Systems and Representative Democracy in Southern Africa", co-hosted by EISA and KAS, Cape Town, South Africa, 15 November.

Meissner, Richard and Anthony R. Turton (2003), "The Hydrosocial Contract Theory and the Lesotho Highlands Water Project", *Water Policy*, Vol. 5, No. 2.

Mills, Gregg (1992), "Lesotho: Between Independence and Incorporation", in Larry Benjamin and Christopher Gregory, eds, *Southern Africa at the Crossroads? Prospects for Stability and Development in the 1990s*, Rivona: Justified Press.

*Ministerial Declaration of The Hague on Water Security in the 21st Century* (2000); available at ⟨http://www.worldwatercouncil.org/fileadmin/wwc/Library/Official_Declarations/The_Hague_Declaration.pdf⟩ (accessed 29 October 2007).

Mochizuki, Katsuya (1998), "Lesotho Ga Komutta Nann – A Minshuka No Shougeki", in Katsumi Hirano, ed., *Minami Afurica No Shougeki: Post-Mandela Ki No Seijikeizai*, Chiba: Institute of Developing Economies.

Mwangi, Oscar (2007), "Hydropolitics, Ecocide and Human Security in Lesotho: A Case Study of the Lesotho Highlands Water Project", *Journal of Southern African Studies*, Vol. 33, No. 1.

Myers, Norman (1989), "Environment and Security", *Foreign Policy*, Vol. 74.

National Environmental Secretariat (1999), *State of the Environment in Lesotho 1997*, Maseru: National Environmental Secretariat, Ministry of Environment, Gender and Youth Affairs.

Office of the Ombudsman (2003), *Report on a Formal Inquiry on the LHDA Resettlement Programme*, Government of Lesotho; available at ⟨http://www.lesotho.gov.ls/articles/2003/Report-LHDA%20Resettlement.htm⟩ (accessed 29 October 2007).

Olaleye, Wole (2004), *Democratic Consolidation and Political Parties in Lesotho*, EISA Occasional Paper No. 15, The Electoral Institute of Southern Africa.

Pherudi, Mokete Lawrence (2003), "Lesotho: Political Conflict, Peace and Reconciliation in the Mountain Kingdom", in Erik Doxtader and Charles Villa-Vicencio, eds, *Through Fire with Water: The Roots of Division and the Potential for Reconciliation in Africa*, Trenton: Africa World Press.

Pisto, Mike (1984), "Lesotho–SA Links Likely to Get Worse", *Rand Daily Mail*, 28 August, p. 3.

Pottinger, Lori (1996), "Police Kill Striking Dam Workers in Lesotho", *World Rivers Review*, Vol. 11, No. 4.

Raditapole, Khauhelo Deborah (1995), "Welcome Address", *Proceedings of a National Workshop on Environmental Awareness and Public Participation in the Environmental Impact Assessment of Phase IB of the Lesotho Highlands Water Project: Including a Revised Outline of the EIA Document, Maseru Sun Hotel, Maseru, Lesotho, 11–12 October*, National Environment Secretariat, United Nations Educational, Scientific, and Cultural Organisation, United Nations Development Programme.

Reisner, Marc (1993), *Cadillac Desert: The American West and Its Disappearing Water*, revised edn, New York: Penguin Books.

Santho, Sehoai (1999), "Conflict Management and Post-Conflict Peacebuilding in Lesotho", in Kato Lambrechts, ed., *Crisis in Lesotho: The Challenge of Managing Conflict in Southern Africa*, FGD African Dialogue Series No. 2, Braamfontein: Foundation for Global Dialogue.

SAPES Trust (2001), *SAPES Trust: SADC Country Studies: Lesotho 2001*, Mount Pleasant, Harare: SAPES Trust.

Scott, Thomas M. (1985), "Lesotho: The Politics of Dependence", *Kurimoto Gakuen Souritsu Gojyushunen Kinen Nagoya Shouka Daigaku Ronshu*, Vol. 30.

Southall, Roger (2003), "Between Competing Paradigms: Post-Colonial Legitimacy in Lesotho", *Journal of Contemporary African Studies*, Vol. 21, No. 2.

Swyngedouw, Erik (2004), "Spain's Hydraulic Mission: Conflict, Power and Mastering of Water", in N. B. Harmancioglu, O. Fistikoglu, Y. Dalkilic and A. Gul, eds, *International Symposium on Water Resources Management: Risks and Challenges for the 21st Century, Izmir, 2–4 September 2004, Proceedings*, Izmir: Dokuz Eylul University.

TCTA–LHDA [Trans-Caledon Tunnel Authority and Lesotho Highlands Development Authority] (2003), *Sustainable Development: Lesotho Highlands Water Project*, Pretoria: TCTA-LHDA.

Thamae, Mabusetsa Lenka and Lori Pottinger, eds (2006), *On the Wrong Side of Development: Lessons Learned from the Lesotho Highlands Water Project*, Maseru: Transformation Resource Centre.

Ullman, Richard H. (1983), "Redefining Security", *International Security*, Vol. 8, No. 1.

UNDP [United Nations Development Programme] (2006), *Human Development Report 2006: Beyond Scarcity: Power, Poverty and the Global Water Crisis*, New York: Palgrave Macmillan.

Van Nieuwkerk, Anthoni (1999), "The Lesotho Crisis: Implications for South African Foreign Policy", in Kato Lambrechts, ed., *Crisis in Lesotho: The Challenge of Managing Conflict in Southern Africa*, FGD African Dialogue Series No. 2, Braamfontein: Foundation for Global Dialogue.

Van Wyk, Jo-Ansie K. (2000) "The International Politics of Dams with Specific Reference to Lesotho", *Strategic Review for Southern Africa*, Vol. 22, No. 1.

Wallis, Shani (2000), *Lesotho Highlands Water Project Volume 5*. Surrey: Laserline.

Weisfelder, Richard F. (1979), "Lesotho: Changing Patterns of Dependence", in Gwendolen M. Carter and Patrick O'Meara, eds, *Southern Africa: The Continuing Crisis*, Bloomington: Indiana University Press.

―――― (1992), "Lesotho and the Inner Periphery in the New South Africa", *Journal of Modern African Studies*, Vol. 30, No. 4.

Wolf, Aaron T., Shira B. Yoffe and Mark Giordano (2003), "International Waters: Identifying Basins at Risk", *Water Policy*, Vol. 5, No. 1.

# 4

# Domestic drivers of international water security on the Danube

*Nevelina I. Pachova and Libor Jansky*

## Introduction

International water security is a complex term that involves the multiple goals of ensuring peace, human security and environmental protection in the process of planning and implementation of water resources development and management of basins shared by two or more states (Second World Water Forum 2000). Empirical studies of water-related interactions between and among riparian states indicate that cooperation has prevailed over conflict, even when states have been in conflict over other issues in the past (Wolf 2003). Agreements over the joint use or management of shared freshwaters, however, have normally taken years, even decades, to negotiate. In the meantime, the water security of riparian populations and the integrity of vital ecosystems have often been compromised by unilateral developments of shared waters, prolonged maintenance of the status quo and delays of needed action. Furthermore, even once signed, water treaties have often proved difficult to implement in the context of changing water needs, societal values and government structures and goals.

The growing recognition of the fact that ensuring water security is a continuous process, rather than a one-time event, has brought home the importance of establishing adaptive water management mechanisms and structures (UNESCO 2006). Adaptation entails the ability to learn from the past, so as to enhance one's capacities to deal with uncertainties in the future (Folke et al. 2005). Future threats to international water security may not necessarily resemble those of the past (Wolf 2003). Indeed,

*International water security: Domestic threats and opportunities*, Pachova, Nakayama and Jansky (eds), United Nations University Press, 2008, ISBN 978-92-808-1150-6

over the past two decades, the processes of global climate change and globalization, accompanied by post–Cold War democratization and the associated evolution of the concepts of sovereignty, security and human rights, among other factors, have changed both the decision-making context as well as the composition and power balances of the different stakeholders involved in decisions on international water management. The increased leverage and capacities of domestic non-state actors to influence traditionally foreign policy debates and the growing importance of domestic security considerations in international security have been identified as critical features of that change (Green Cross International 2000; Second World Water Forum 2000). Understanding their implications for international water security is important for monitoring and forestalling emerging security threats and designing adaptive solutions that minimize not only political threats but also the human and environmental insecurities arising from past, ongoing and planned water use and management schemes or the lack thereof.

The collapse of the Soviet Union in the late 1980s, which triggered a wave of democratization across the former communist bloc states, has made the above-mentioned changes particularly potent in transitional states. The Gabčíkovo–Nagymaros water management case between Hungary and Slovakia illustrates some of the implications of the growing importance of domestic security considerations in international water security. In order to highlight these implications, the chapter analyses the evolution of the half-century-old water regulation project in the middle reaches of the Danube by tracing the key domestic political, social and economic factors, actors and processes in each of the involved riparian states that have played a critical role in navigating the direction of the water management discourse and actions related to the joint project through a set of turning points.

In the rest of the chapter the initial agreement on collaboration, its subsequent dissolution and the escalation of an international dispute, as well as the mitigation of the range of international water security threats it entailed, are examined in turn, following a brief technical summary of the case. The conclusion of the case study highlights the re-emergence of some of the critical factors that had brought about phase transitions in the water management dispute in the past but also draws attention to the changes in the international context in the framework of which their implications need to be interpreted.

## Case summary

In 1977 the governments of Hungary and former Czechoslovakia signed an agreement stipulating the joint construction of a multi-purpose system of locks for flood control, navigation extension and hydropower generation on a 205 km stretch of the Danube River that serves as a political border and connects the capitals of the two countries (UN Treaty Series 1978).

The project was designed to make use of declivities of 21 metres on 69 kilometres in its upper part at Gabčíkovo and of 7 metres on 136 kilometres in its lower part at Nagymaros. The two parts of the project were planned each to consist of a main reservoir, a weir, a hydropower station and navigation locks. The capacity of the Gabčíkovo and the Nagymaros hydropower stations was to be 720 MW and 157.8 MW, respectively, and the total volume of the main reservoirs 243 and 170 million $m^3$, respectively. A number of additional river regulation and protective measures, reconstruction of existing flood control dykes, sealing aprons, seepage canals, drains and pumping stations were also envisioned (Abaffy et al. 1995).

According to the treaty, the Gabčíkovo part of the project was to be completed by 1986 and the Nagymaros part by the end of 1989. Construction work started in 1978, continuing at a slower rate on the Hungarian side owing to mounting environmental concerns and financial constraints in the context of growing domestic pressure for political and economic transformation in the country. As a result, completion of the Nagymaros part of the project was postponed. In 1989 Hungary officially abandoned the project and in 1992 it unilaterally denounced the 1977 treaty. In the meantime, the Slovak side developed and subsequently constructed and put into operation an alternative Variant C, based on the original project. It involved damming the Danube, completed in October 1992, and construction of a central weir and auxiliary navigation locks and a hydropower plant at Čunovo on the territory of the Slovak Republic, which inherited the project following the disintegration of Czechoslovakia in January 1993 (Abaffy et al. 1995). Variant C was designed as a temporary solution intended to allow for the operationalization of the Gabčíkovo part of the project in the absence of the Nagymaros part of the originally designed system of locks. The operation of the unilaterally designed and implemented water management structures of Variant C, however, reduced the flow of water in the Danube and the Mosoni Danube, the old river bed flowing as a side arm to the main canal on Hungarian territory, thus threatening the vitality of important ecosystems along the river beds and on the Hungarian island of Szigetköz situated between them.

As a result, the water management dispute between the two countries escalated into a political dispute. In 1993 the governments of Hungary and the Slovak Republic agreed to submit the case to the International Court of Justice (ICJ) for arbitration (Plenipotentiary of the Slovak Republic for the Construction and Operation of the Gabčíkovo-Nagymaros

Hydropower Scheme 1993). Two years later, in 1995, an interim agreement was signed between the two countries, stipulating a minimum discharge into the Mosoni Danube that allowed for the partial restoration of the threatened ecosystems. In 1997 the court pronounced its judgment based on the United Nations Convention on the Law of the Non-Navigational Uses of International Watercourses, the major international agreement requiring the integrated use of water for human and environmental needs (United Nations 1997). The decision of the court found both countries at fault, Hungary for unilaterally terminating the 1977 agreement and Slovakia for unilaterally implementing Variant C. The court urged the governments of the two states to cooperate on reaching an agreement that takes into account the changed conditions since the signature of the 1977 Treaty (ICJ 1997). A bilateral agreement on its implementation, however, has not been reached yet.

Currently, negotiations are carried out within two main working groups dealing with the legal and technical aspects of the dispute separately. Input for negotiations on technical issues is provided by the joint environmental monitoring programme established in 1995 as a means for providing an unbiased basis for verifying the implementation of the 1995 agreement and for finding a long-term resolution to the case. Pressures for resolving the protracted dispute seem to be mounting in the context of the re-emergence of a set of factors that had led to phase transitions in the development of the Gabčíkovo–Nagymaros project in the past. Finding a sustainable and adaptive water management solution requires a reconsideration of the lessons from the past, as the history of the emergence of the Gabčíkovo–Nagymaros project itself and the escalation of the dispute surrounding it indicate.

## Cooperation: Domestic responses to water security needs

### Physical context: The origins of international water insecurities

Physical changes in the Danube river bed and in the flow characteristics in the middle reaches of the international river resulting from upstream water development works carried on in the past were among the key reasons for the emergence of the idea of the Gabčíkovo–Nagymaros water regulation project (GNP) in the mid-1950s.

The Danube River Basin, the largest international basin in Europe, flows from west to east through the territories of nine states and drains parts of the catchment areas of another six. Currently hosting an estimated 80 million inhabitants and spreading across an area totalling 817,000 km$^2$, the Danube Basin has long been a favourable location for human settlements and a major navigational channel in Europe. The use of the river for the satisfaction of basic human needs and economic development intensified significantly in the second half of the twentieth century, following the signature in 1948 of the Danube Convention, which provided a framework for regulating the navigational uses of the river. Between 1950 and 1980, the amount of goods transported and traded in ports on the Danube increased about 10 times. To ensure smooth navigation and to meet the growing electricity needs of urban centres and other settlements along the river, over the same period some 69 dams with a total volume exceeding 7,300 million m$^3$ and a number of more complex waterworks were constructed on the Danube (Secretariat of the United Nations Commission for Europe 1994; IWAC 2002). In the German and Austrian sectors of the river alone, between 1956 and 1997 some 40 water regulation structures and hydroelectric power projects were completed and put into operation (Mucha 1999).

In the middle reaches of the Danube, water regulation for flood control dates back to the thirteenth century. The earliest dykes in the middle Danube were constructed in 1426, systematic flood protection measures were instituted in the seventeenth century and river control, drainage channels and pumping stations were added at an increasing rate after 1850 (Fitzmaurice 1996). Regulations for navigation and hydroelectric power generation began later, in the nineteenth century, owing to their technically, politically and economically more demanding nature. Initial proposals for channelling the middle reaches of the Danube date back to the reign of Emperor Charlemagne and the dream of constructing a navigable waterway connecting the Rhine, the Main and the Danube, and thus the north and the Black Sea. Concrete construction and regulation plans were considered by the Austro-Hungarian monarchy as early as 1880 and some were undertaken and completed by 1915 (Lejon 1996).

As a result of early regulation works in the middle Danube and upstream at the beginning of the century, the once meandering system of shifting canals that connected Bratislava and Budapest turned into a straightened and heavily fortified channel, characterized by rapid water-level fluctuations, larger stream velocities, steeper and higher flood peaks and shorter but more frequent and devastating floods. Dam construction in the upper reaches of the river preventing the movement of sand and gravel resulted in increased flow velocity and erosion of the river bottom under Bratislava. The deepening of the water bed led to a sinking of the groundwater table, creating desertification and aggravating navigation conditions in the region, which became notorious as the second worst after the Iron Gate section of the river. Navigation at the time was possible on fewer than 160 days a year and, according to some sources, even much fewer.

At the same time, whereas before the intensive development of regulation works on the Danube serious flooding was recorded once or twice a century, the number increased significantly in the twentieth century, as demonstrated by historical records listing serious floods in 1929, 1947, 1954, 1963 and 1965. The 1954 and 1965 floods were particularly devastating. In 1954, the flood broke the dykes at four points on the Hungarian side in the Szigetköz region, and water completely or partially flooded an area of some 33,000 hectares (ha). During the flood of 1965, the dykes broke on the Czechoslovakian side at two places, near the villages of Patince and Čičov. Some 114,000 ha were flooded directly and at least 3,500 buildings were completely destroyed (Nominated Monitoring Agent of the Slovak Republic 2001). About 65,000 people had to be evacuated from the affected areas. The flow at Bratislava during the flood reached 9,170 m³/sec (Lejon 1996). Although Slovakia was most seriously affected by the 1965 flood, a great deal of damage was caused by it in Austria, Hungary and Yugoslavia as well.

The increased danger from floods and the deterioration in navigation conditions in the middle section of the Danube that had resulted from earlier water regulation works upstream exacted a response. Its nature and timing, however, were shaped by the political and socio-economic conditions in Hungary and Czechoslovakia at the time.

## Political context: Intra-state ambitions vs. regional cooperation

The domestic political environments in both countries in the first decades after the Second World War were characterized by the processes of establishment and consolidation of socialist political regimes under Soviet control. It was during this period that the initial idea for the joint water regulation project between Hungary and Czechoslovakia was developed in response to the deterioration of the physical conditions in the section of the Danube shared by the two countries, and in line with the broader goal of regional integration promoted by the Council for Mutual Economic Assistance among the socialist states (COMECON).

COMECON, which ratified the draft for the joint water management project between Hungary and Slovakia in 1963, conveniently channelled Soviet strategic interests in the extension of navigation along the Danube so as ensure access by the Soviet army fleet to the rebel Yugoslav state and to Austria and Western Europe, where the Soviets had lost military footing following the forced withdrawal of troops from Austria and Finland in 1955. Additional pressure also came from the Danube Commission, the implementing body of the Danube Convention that came into force in 1964, which was responsible for regulating the navigational regime of the international river and ensuring good navigable conditions

(Danube Commission 2004). Despite international pressure and the catastrophic floods of the 1950s and 1960s, however, it took some two and a half decades after the initial idea for a joint project was proposed by the Hungarian Academy of Sciences in the early 1950s before the two countries finally reached a joint agreement on its implementation. The delay was to a large extent due to the domestic political processes and transformations that took place in Hungary and Czechoslovakia in the aftermath of Stalin's death in 1953.

In Hungary, in the context of the liberalization of Moscow's centralized rule, which began in 1953, political opposition to the socialist regime strengthened and in 1956 seized political control. The Soviet military intervention in the same year thwarted political reforms but allowed for the establishment of a more liberal economic regime with a degree of cultural liberalization and communication with the West. In response, the Hungarian authorities agreed to honour their commitments to regional political and economic cooperation in the framework of COMECON. Thus, after a period of turmoil, the political environment in Hungary once again became favourable for undertaking the joint water regulation works.

In the meantime, in Czechoslovakia, a conflict of interest between Slovaks and Czechs, the main constituent nations of the country, hindered the finalization of the joint water management plan. The Czech-centred political authorities were not in favour of investing in the development of hydropower potential on the Slovak territory of the country. The project did not receive the necessary domestic political support until Slovak leadership was established in power, following the Prague Spring, a Czech-led reformist movement that was brought down by Soviet troops in 1968.

Even with domestic forces lined up in support of the project, however, it took another decade before economic factors provided the necessary incentive to go ahead with the joint water works.

In the context of state-controlled industrialization, which dominated the development objectives of the two states at the time, water regulation only for flood control was hard to justify. The extension of navigation and hydropower generation were therefore suggested as additional components to the original plan. Hydropower, however, was a costly energy option in the context of low-priced imports of fuels from the Soviet Union and cheap nuclear power energy (neither of which reflected the associated environmental costs). Thus it was not until the drastic rise in world oil prices in the early 1970s, and with them of the prices of Soviet fuel exports, that a strong economic incentive for undertaking the project emerged and helped resolve the conflict of interests among the water management and energy lobbies in the two countries that had developed in the course of planning the joint water regulation works. In 1977, close to three decades after the initiation of the idea of a joint water regulation project, an agreement between Hungary and Czechoslovakia regarding the project was finally reached and an international treaty stipulating the conditions of its construction, operation and financing was signed.

Limited awareness of and concern about the environmental implications of alternative energy, and broader economic development options in the two countries at the time, made the project's environmental costs acceptable. Indeed, according to Fitzmaurice (1996), over 400 studies of the potential environmental impacts of the project had been carried out before the signing of the treaty and many more after that. Some of those were developed and elaborated within the framework of a Bio-project initiated in 1976 and supplemented in 1982 and 1986 (Kocinger 1998). The 1977 treaty, however, included only three paragraphs on the protection of water quality, the fishing interests of Danubian states and the environment as a whole. The extent to which those paragraphs reflected and ensured the environmental security of the international river came under question and sparked the flame of an international water dispute as increased public concern about environmental quality in Hungary led to its politicization, which in turn gave rise to an actual environmental water security threat.

## Conflict: Changing domestic contexts and water security threats

Domestic socio-economic and political changes in Hungary in the early 1980s gave rise to public criticism of the GNP project shortly after its implementation started. The economic and cultural liberalization and reforms that had begun in the country following the 1956 uprising gave people more access to information available in the West and more freedom of association and expression than in other socialist states. Human rights, poverty and environmental quality became issues of public concern. Gradually, however, the freedom of expression and association with regard to such overtly non-political issues became an outlet for political criticism of the regime, and the common goal unified these movements. Although in 1983–1984 public criticism of the GNP arose based on concerns about its impacts on riverine ecosystems and the drinking water supply to Budapest, the project soon became a symbol of the political regime.

Financing constraints added to the growing political dangers of continuing with the implementation of the project in Hungary. Declining economic growth in the 1980s had made the government turn to Austria for financial support for the construction of the GNP. Growing pressure from environmental groups in the country and abroad, however, resulted in the discontinuation of Austrian financing (Bell and Jansky 2005). In the context of the broader political transformation from a socialist to a more open and democratic regime that began to accelerate in the country in the late 1980s, the Hungarian parliament was pressed to re-examine the GNP in 1988 and hold an open vote.

In 1989 Hungarian opposition to the GNP organized a massive petition with 140,000 signatures. In May 1989 the government suspended work on the project. Following the first democratic elections, the environmental activists, who had been protesting against the GNP, became members of the newly formed government. Their former position on the GNP and the high level of personalization of both the environmental movements and the first political parties formed during the collapse of the former regime constrained their ability to compromise (Fitzmaurice 1996).

Public feeling against the GNP in Hungary was intensified by the interposition of environmental and ethnic concerns. The quest for national identity on the part of Slovaks in the period of political transformations that led to the split-up of former Czechoslovakia into two countries – Czech Republic and Slovakia – in 1993 had fuelled discriminatory attitudes and treatment of the sizeable Hungarian minority living in Slovakia in response to its opposition to the dissolution of the former Czechoslovak state. The fact that a large part of the Hungarian minority inhabited settlements along the Danube, which were to be affected by the GNP, strengthened the link between the environmental and ethnic concerns.

In Slovakia, heightened nationalist sentiments and electoral politics shaped the response to Hungary's suspension of work on the GNP. The patchwork of minorities spread throughout the territory of Slovakia made the process of the establishment of the new country a challenging endeavour. A catch-all party representing the different minorities in Slovakia won seats in both the federal parliament and the Slovak National Council in the 1990 and 1992 elections. In addition, several Hungarian political parties founded at the beginning of the reforms accounted for about 10 per cent of the votes. These manifestations of political strength were accompanied by pan-Hungarian rhetoric from across the Danube and news of the mistreatment of Slovaks living in Hungary. In this context a public opinion survey carried out at that time indicated that 56 per cent of Slovaks included in the survey were in support of deporting the Hungarian minority. The ethnic polarization in Slovakia made nationalist politics a means for gaining political power and limited the scope of domestically acceptable responses to Hungary's suspension of work on the GNP. In this context the Slovak government initiated and implemented a unilateral diversion of the Danube under the alternative Variant C.

The diversion of the Danube led to a significant decrease in the water level of the main channel and of the groundwater level in parts of the adjacent plains. Although Variant C was implemented on Slovak territory, ecosystems on the Hungarian side of the river were affected. The patent damage turned an environmental into a political security threat to the international watercourse. Shortly after the diversion of the Danube, Hungary officially denounced the 1977 treaty and began dismantling the Nagymaros part of the GNP. Political tension between the two countries rose, but fell short of posing a military security threat.

Just as the conflict between the two states had escalated as a result of the interposition of water-related with broader social, economic and political factors, the environmental and political security threats in the middle reaches of the Danube were mitigated by broader incentives for cooperation beyond the scope of the water management case itself.

## Responses: Mechanisms for ensuring international water security

The collapse of the communist regimes throughout the former socialist bloc countries made integration with Western Europe the only viable option for Hungary and Slovakia in the context of accelerating post–Cold War integration and interdependence in the world. This provided the European Union with significant leverage with respect to the two Central European states and it used it to try to separate and channel through appropriate mechanisms for the resolution of the ethnic, legal and environmental aspects of the inter-state dispute.

### Political mediation of the ethnic dispute

In the framework of the post–Cold War increase in ethnic tensions and the disintegration of political entities of the former Soviet bloc in Europe and Asia, in 1993 the European Union (EU) launched an initiative known as the Stability Pact, which was meant to serve as a mechanism for wielding EU influence in border and minority disputes among potential member states.

In the framework of the Pact the European Union organized a series of bilateral meetings and roundtable discussions between the two countries, which led to the signature in 1995 of a bilateral agreement calling for border inviolability and guarantees of minority rights. The role of this agreement in mitigating ethnic tensions within and between Hungary and

Slovakia is a question of debate in view of the continued use of ethnic issues in domestic electoral politics throughout most of the 1990s. The agreement did, however, provide a framework for cooperation, which, combined with the dangers from an escalation in the ethnic disputes brought home by the disintegration of neighbouring Yugoslavia through a series of ethnic wars, prompted a number of bilateral efforts to keep dialogue on the minority and related issues open and successfully prevented them from escalating into a major crisis.

## Legal mediation of the political dispute

Under pressure from the European Union for a peaceful resolution of the GNP dispute, the governments of Hungary and Slovakia also agreed to submit the GNP case to the International Court of Justice (ICJ) for arbitration in 1993.

In 1997 the ICJ heard the case and pronounced its ruling on the legality of Hungary's suspension of work and termination of the 1977 treaty and of Slovakia's implementation of Variant C. The Court found both countries' actions illegal and urged them to reach an agreement on the implementation of the GNP as a joint investment project for energy generation, improvement of the navigability of the Danube and flood control, while ensuring the protection of the natural environment and taking into account other relevant international norms that had emerged since the signature of the original treaty.

The use of international law for the settlement of the GNP case set a precedent in the history of international water management. The ICJ had been suggested as a mechanism for settling conflicts over the non-navigational uses of international waters previously, but no two parties had ever agreed to submit a case for judgment to the ICJ before. Earlier attempts at using the ICJ had been constrained by the fact that the Court examines only cases between states and submission requires an agreement on the part of all parties involved to abide by the ICJ judgment. The implications of the Court's decision on the case thus go beyond the GNP dispute.

The fact that in its ruling the ICJ referred to the Convention on the Law of the Non-Navigational Uses of International Watercourses (United Nations 1997), despite the fact that it had not yet entered into force, underscored the importance of taking into account environmental considerations in the course of water management. The judgment, however, failed to provide practical guidelines for the legal scope of the concept of sustainable development, which it invoked (Sands 1998), and for its application to the settlement of bilateral international water management disputes or the GNP dispute in particular.

A decade after the pronouncement of the Court's decision, Hungary and Slovakia have not yet reached an agreement on its application. The ICJ verdict obliged the two parties to do so within six months of the pronouncement of its judgment, i.e. by March 1998. In light of the Court's decision, the then socialist government of Hungary annulled the parliamentary decision of 1992 to terminate the 1977 treaty and abandon the project and announced it would continue with the construction of the Nagymaros part. In March 1998, however, a demonstration by some 20,000 people demanding a presidential veto on the government's decision led to a postponement of the final decision in light of the up-coming elections. Nevertheless, the opposition party, which employed the GNP in its campaign, won the 1998 elections and abolished the plan to build the dam.

Alleged discrepancies in the technical aspects of the case led to the separation of the legal from the technical debate. In 2001, Joint Working Groups on Legal Matters and on Water Management, Ecology, Navigation, and Energy were established as forums for discussing the respective issues associated with the GNP dispute (Plenipotentiary of the Slovak Republic 2003). Although formal technical consultations and bilateral negotiations on a long-term solution to the dispute started only recently, the need for an intermediate response to mitigate the environmental consequences of the diversion of the Danube and to establish an unbiased factual basis for decision-making was agreed on as early as 1995.

## Technical mediation of the environmental dispute

Bilateral technical cooperation was undertaken within the legal framework provided by the "Agreement between the Government of the Slovak Republic and the Government of Hungary about Certain Temporary Technical Measures and Discharges to the Danube and Mosoni Danube", signed on 19 April 1995 (Plenipotentiary of the Slovak Republic 1995). The agreement was made possible by domestic political changes in Hungary and Slovakia in 1994 and provided a basis for further cooperation between the two states on the common goal of democratization and transition to an open market economy in the context of regional and European integration.

The 1995 agreement was intended as a temporary solution to some of the major environmental impacts of the construction and operation of the Gabčíkovo part of the project, namely the reduction in water quantity in the old river bed and the Mosoni Danube, the river arm situated on Hungarian territory. Initially the agreement was pending the judgment of the International Court of Justice in the case concerning the Gabčíkovo–

Nagymaros project. Following the pronouncement of the judgment in September 1997, the validity of the 1995 agreement was extended until an agreement on the implementation of the ICJ judgment was reached.

The technical stipulations of the agreement included an increase in the discharge of water into the old Danube river bed and into the Hungarian branch of the Danube, to make up for the decline in the river flow there as a result of the diversion of the Danube required for the operationalization of Variant C and the associated destruction of unique riverine ecosystems. The stipulated measures were implemented in 1995 and the associated increase in the level of the water supply in the old Danube river bed and its side arms on Hungarian territory allowed for the partial restoration of the endangered ecosystems along the river bank. This is demonstrated by the findings of the joint environmental monitoring system on the affected areas that was established as part of the 1995 agreement (Joint Annual Reports 1996–2001).

The joint environmental monitoring and data exchange obligation stipulated in the 1995 agreement are aimed at: (1) establishing compliance with the joint water management regime agreed in 1995; (2) observing, recording and jointly evaluating quantitative and qualitative changes in surface and groundwater bodies and the water-related natural environment in connection with the realized measure; and (3) providing joint evaluation of monitoring results and joint recommendations for monitoring improvement and environmental protection activities to the respective governments.

Building upon a range of monitoring activities initiated and financed by the governments of Hungary and Slovakia as a basis for generating scientific support for their respective claims in the ICJ, the joint monitoring continued to be financed and conducted separately by the two countries after 1995. However, the specific indicators included in the joint monitoring and the methodologies employed by the scientists in both states were jointly agreed. Technical cooperation was facilitated by the existence of relevant human resources and technical capacities in each of the two countries as well as by the long history of joint or coordinated research between various institutions in the two states (Jansky et al. 2004).

The joint monitoring has provided a basis for verifying compliance with the two countries' obligations under the 1995 agreement, which has been a key instrument for mitigating the environmental security threats from the international water dispute in the interim period until a longer-term solution is agreed. Given the intensity of the monitoring activities, the accumulated monitoring results could also help with modelling and assessing the implications of alternative water management regimes for the environment in the monitored territories. The scope of the joint monitoring activities, however, is insufficient as a basis for decision-making on water regulation schemes for the management of the middle reaches of the Danube, which are likely to have basin-wide implications.

## Pending closure: Opportunities and pitfalls

At the end of 2006 the Gabčíkovo–Nagymaros project was one of 13 cases pending resolution in line with rulings of the International Court of Justice. The temporary solution implemented in 1995 mitigated the impact of the unilateral diversion of the Danube on affected riverine ecosystems in Hungary. The pending closure of the case, however, makes it a source of uncertainty and political tensions between the two states.

The 2006 election results, which brought to power pro-GNP governments in both Hungary and Slovakia, constitute a window of opportunity for reaching an agreement on the ICJ ruling. Indeed, changes in the domestic political environments in both countries, combined with recent flooding in the middle Danube region and growing energy demands in Slovakia, in the context of reduced nuclear energy capacities and rapid economic growth associated with the country's recent entry into the European Union, have brought the GNP issue back on the table of intra- and inter-governmental as well as media discussions over the past year.

Furthermore, the scientific data accumulated over the past decade from the joint environmental monitoring and related research on the middle Danube, combined with the evolution of understanding and technologies for dealing with the environmental consequences of large water development projects, have already given rise to a range of alternative options for an environmentally friendly solution to the project that takes into account the value of the riverine ecosystems.

Indeed, the massive demonstration in Hungary against a possible resumption of construction of the Nagymaros dam in 1998 and the subsequent victory of the opposition indicate that the GNP case continues to be politically sensitive. In this regard, sluggish economic development in Hungary combined with the massive protests against the current socialist-led government at the end of 2006 may limit the government's capacities to tackle the GNP case.

At the same time, however, changing regional and international perceptions of human and environmental security threats in the framework of the growing manifestations of climate change and the search for more environmentally friendly and diverse energy sources than reliance on fuel from Russia might help raise the necessary public support and financing to complete the half-century-old project. For that purpose, however, all relevant domestic stakeholders would need to be involved in discussions of the available alternatives. The development over the past decade of democratic governance structures, including channels for expression of general public and minority interests and mechanisms for addressing them, in both countries provides a sound basis for undertaking such a broad-based public dialogue in the two riparian states.

In view of the international obligations of the two countries in the context of regional integration and interdependence, however, discussions on the future of the GNP would need to be broadened to take into account and abide by the latest EU water, flood control and related policies and directives. Furthermore, they would need to be informed by the basin-wide implications of water regulation schemes in the middle Danube in line with the current internationally accepted principles of integrated water management. The International Commission on the Protection of the Danube River Basin (ICPDR) and related basin-wide water management structures that have been established over the past decade could provide the necessary forums and data for discussions of the basin-wide implications of the project. To be truly sustainable, however, any agreement on the management of the middle Danube would also have to ensure the flexibility for adapting to potential changes in water conditions, needs and values in the future, in addition to taking into account current norms and views.

## Conclusion

The overview of the history of the GNP case indicates the complexity of interactions between domestic and international water security.

It illustrates how changing domestic political actors and power balances, economic conditions and needs, ethnic minorities and societal and state approaches towards them, as well as environmental preferences, come to play a role in shaping domestic decisions on international water management. Some of these factors may have been more important in the past, others today. The GNP case in particular highlights the increased leverage of domestic civil society groups over issues concerning international water security. New power, however, entails new responsibilities and the case raises the question of whether emerging civil societies have the capacity to recognize and cope with them.

The case also suggests that making the step from unilateral critiques to joint actions needed to alleviate a given international water security threat requires nuanced intermediate responses that take into account the multiple domestic factors involved in generating it. Separate mechanisms designed to tackle the diverse aspects of water management debates could help reduce political tensions and the harmful effects of delays in needed actions or unilateral measures arising from protracted conflicts over the use and management of shared watercourses. Arguably, they could also provide the basis for the reintegration of the diverse views and objectives of the different stakeholders involved in a given case, which is critical for designing and putting into place sustainable long-term solutions to water management disputes.

Complex configurations of dynamically changing factors within and between riparian states create the requisite windows of opportunity for policy action and change. In the GNP case, it is yet to be seen whether the civil societies in the two riparian states and the institutional channels and frameworks for communication and cooperation set up in the process of conflict mitigation are ready to take up the challenge of supporting the design of a broad-based solution to the protracted dispute and to live up to it when the opportunity comes.

## REFERENCES

Abaffy, D., M. Lukáč and M. Liška (1995), *Dams in Slovakia*, Bratislava: TRT Médium.

Bell, R. G. and L. Jansky (2005), "Public Participation in the Management of the Danube River: Necessary but Neglected", in C. Bruch, L. Jansky, M. Nakayama and K. A. Salewicz, eds, *Public Participation in the Governance of International Freshwater Resources*, Tokyo: United Nations University Press.

Danube Commission (2004), "Summary Information", December, available at ⟨www.danubecom-intern.org/English/Summary.htm⟩ (accessed 30 October 2007).

Fitzmaurice, J. (1996), *Damming the Danube*, Boulder, CO, and Oxford: Westview Press, a division of HarperCollins Publishers.

Folke, C., T. Hahn, P. Olsson and J. Norberg (2005), "Adaptive Governance of Social Ecological Systems", *Annual Review of Environment and Resources*, Vol. 30.

Green Cross International (2000), *National Sovereignty and International Watercourses*, Geneva, March.

ICJ [International Court of Justice] (1997), *Case Concerning Gabčíkovo-Nagymaros Project (Hungary/Slovakia). Summary of the Judgment of 25 September 1997*, available at ⟨http://www.icj-cij.org⟩.

IWAC [International Water Assessment Centre] (2002), *Assessment Practices and Environmental Status of Ten Transboundary Rivers in Europe*, IWAC, The Netherlands, January, available at ⟨http://www.iwac-riza.org/downloads/10_rivers_report.pdf⟩ (accessed 30 October 2007).

Jansky, L., M. Murakami and N. I. Pachova (2004), *The Danube: Environmental Monitoring of an International River*, Tokyo: United Nations University Press.

*Joint Annual Reports* (1996–2001), produced in accordance with the "Agreement between the Government of the Slovak Republic and the Government of Hungary about Certain Temporary Measures and Discharges to the Danube and Mosoni Danube, 19 April, 1995".

Kocinger, D. (1998), "The Gabčíkovo-Nagymaros Hydropower System and the Slovak Government", in A. Vlavianos-Arvanitis and J. Morovic, eds, *Biopolitics: Danube River Bonds; Bio-environment and Bio-culture*, Vol. VI, Athens: Biopolitics International Organization.

Lejon, E. (1996), *Gabčíkovo-Nagymaros. Old and New Sins*, Bratislava: H&H.

Mucha, I., ed. (1999), *Gabčíkovo Part of the Hydroelectric Power Project – Environmental Impact Review Based on Six Year Monitoring*, Faculty of Natural Sciences, Comenius University, Bratislava.

Nominated Monitoring Agent of the Slovak Republic (2001), *Gabčíkovo Part of the Gabčíkovo-Nagymaros Hydropower Project and Joint Slovak-Hungarian Monitoring of Environmental Impact*, Plenipotentiary of the Slovak Republic for the Construction and Operation of the Gabčíkovo-Nagymaros Hydropower Scheme, Bratislava, October.

Plenipotentiary of the Slovak Republic for the Construction and Operation of the Gabčíkovo-Nagymaros Hydropower Scheme (1993), "Special Agreement for Submission to the International Court of Justice of the Differences between the Republic of Hungary and the Slovak Republic Concerning the Gabčíkovo-Nagymaros Project – Jointly Notified to the Court on 2 July, 1993".

Plenipotentiary of the Slovak Republic for the Construction and Operation of the Gabčíkovo-Nagymaros Hydropower Scheme (1995), "Agreement between the Government of the Slovak Republic and the Government of Hungary about Certain Temporary Measures and Discharges to the Danube and Mosoni Danube signed on 19 April 1995".

Plenipotentiary of the Slovak Republic for the Construction and Operation of the Gabčíkovo-Nagymaros Hydropower Scheme (2003), Minutes from the Meetings of the Working Group on Legal Matters of the Delegations of the Government of the Slovak Republic and the Government of the Republic of Hungary on the Implementation of the Judgment of the International Court of Justice in the Case Concerning the Gabčíkovo-Nagymaros Project, available at ⟨http://www.gabcikovo.gov.sk/rokovania.htm⟩ (accessed 30 October 2007).

Sands, P. (1998), "Watercourses, Environment and the International Court of Justice: The Gabčíkovo-Nagymaros Case", in S. Salman and L. Chazournes, eds, *International Watercourses: Enhancing Cooperation and Managing Conflict. Proceedings of a World Bank Seminar*, World Bank Technical Paper No. 414, Washington, DC, World Bank.

Second World Water Forum (2000), *Ministerial Declaration of The Hague on Water Security in the 21st Century*, The Hague, 2000, available at ⟨http://www.waternunc.com/gb/secwwf12.htm⟩ (accessed 30 October 2007).

Secretariat of the United Nations Commission for Europe (1994), "Protection and Use of Transboundary Watercourses and International Lakes in Europe", *Natural Resources Forum*, Vol. 18, No. 3, pp. 171–180.

UNESCO (2006), "Sharing Water: Defining a Common Interest", in *UN World Water Development Report*, World Water Assessment Programme (WWAP), Paris and New York.

United Nations (1997), *Convention on the Law of the Non-Navigational Uses of International Watercourses*, New York: United Nations General Assembly.

UN Treaty Series (1978), "Treaty Concerning the Construction and Operation of the Gabčíkovo-Nagymaros System of Locks. Signed at Budapest on 16 September 1977 by Hungary and Czechoslovakia", No. 17134, in *Treaty Series: Treaties and International Agreements Registered or Filed and Recorded with the Secretariat of the United Nations*, Vol. 1109, I, Nos. 17124–17142.

Wolf, A. T. (2003) "Conflict and Cooperation: Survey of the Past and Reflections for the Future", PCCP Series Paper, Technical Documents in Hydrology, IHP-VI, UNESCO.

# 5

# Transboundary cooperation vs. internal ambitions: The role of China and Cambodia in the Mekong region

*Marko Keskinen, Katri Mehtonen and Olli Varis*

## Introduction

The Mekong River Basin offers a fascinating example of regional cooperation – and non-cooperation – in the development and management of an international river basin. The riparian countries have in recent decades experienced several internal and international conflicts that have seriously impaired regional political relations. This has also had its impacts on regional cooperation on water management, including the functioning of the Mekong River Commission (MRC) and its two predecessors.

Despite difficult circumstances, the Mekong River organizations have made important contributions to transboundary water management;[1] the Mekong cooperation has even been cited to be the most successful in the developing world (Phillips et al. 2006; Jacobs 2002). However, the functioning of the MRC and other regional organizations dealing with water – most importantly the Greater Mekong Subregion (GMS) Program – is still far from perfect, and they are often seen to be non-transparent and too detached from local realities.

This chapter examines water-related cooperation in the Mekong region through a review of the Mekong cooperation and two country-specific case studies focusing on China and Cambodia. In this way, we aim to illustrate the challenges of transboundary water cooperation, and in particular the specific role that the riparian countries have in its functioning. We show the effect that the past and present policies and internal

*International water security: Domestic threats and opportunities, Pachova, Nakayama and Jansky (eds), United Nations University Press, 2008, ISBN 978-92-808-1150-6*

developments of China and Cambodia have had on the management of the river and the regional cooperation in that context. Owing to the countries' different roles in the region, the China case study focuses on hydropower development, whereas the Cambodia case study concentrates on that country's tumultuous history and its current political setting.

The focus on China and Cambodia is for various reasons. Taken as a whole, China and Cambodia both have had a particular role in the Mekong region as well as in Mekong cooperation. For example, they both had a specific role in the way the Mekong Agreement – which established the MRC – was formulated. The countries also make an interesting pair for comparison: whereas China is the most upstream country, a regional superpower, a non-party of the MRC and the only riparian with dams in the Mekong mainstream, Cambodia is a downstream country and a member of the MRC and has potentially the most to lose from uncontrolled development of the river as a result of potentially destructive impacts on the country's floodplain and aquatic production.

It is important to note, however, that the focus on riparian states inevitably leaves out other important aspects of the Mekong cooperation. As highlighted by Sneddon and Fox (2006), Mekong cooperation should not be considered just as interaction between monolithic states, since there actually exists a variety of actors and processes at different scales that simultaneously support and challenge the riparian states.[2] The Mekong countries are also not particularly democratic, and implementing balanced water management and addressing possible water-related conflicts through transnational cooperation alone are therefore not the most viable options (Öjendal 2000). However, because a number of recent studies have focused on the above-mentioned topics (see e.g. Backer 2006; Hirsch et al. 2006; Lebel et al. 2006; Phillips et al. 2006; Sneddon and Fox 2006; Dore 2003; Öjendal 2000; Bakker 1999), we concentrate in this chapter on Cambodia and China and their specific roles in the Mekong cooperation.

## The Mekong River Basin

The Mekong River is one of the greatest rivers of the world: both its estimated length (4,909 km) and its mean annual volume (475 km$^3$) make it the tenth-largest in the world (Shaochuang et al. 2007; MRC 2005). It is also among the world's most pristine large rivers, supporting an exceptionally diverse and productive freshwater ecosystem and providing a source of livelihoods for millions of people. Six riparian countries share the river basin: Cambodia, China, Laos, Myanmar, Thailand and Viet Nam (Figure 5.1).

Figure 5.1 Map of the Mekong River Basin.
*Source*: Map by Matti Kummu.

The Mekong River Basin can be divided into the Upper and Lower Basins, with China and Myanmar forming the Upper Basin, which constitutes approximately 24 per cent of the total catchment area and 18 per cent of the total flow (MRC 2005, 2003). The river's runoff originates largely from the Lower Basin as less than one-fifth of the total flow is contributed by the Upper Mekong Basin (MRC 2003). The river's seasonal floods are vital for the basin's ecology and people's livelihoods because they support rice cultivation and diverse aquatic ecosystems and wetlands. Although the hydrology of the downstream Mekong is not that dependent on the Upper Basin, the latter contributes significantly to the river's dry season flow as well as to its sediments.

It is estimated that roughly half of the total sediment concentration of the river originates from the Upper Basin (Kummu and Varis 2007). Owing to sediment trapping by the dams, China's planned cascade of dams in the mainstream Mekong may therefore have a significant impact on the sediment balance and, consequently, on the aquatic productivity of the river system (Kummu and Varis 2007; Kummu et al. 2008). In addition, the dams' probable impact on raising dry season water levels poses a serious threat for the downstream floodplains, including the flooded forests of the Tonle Sap Lake.[3]

## The role of the Mekong in the riparian countries

All the Mekong countries are changing rapidly: population is growing and urbanizing, economies are developing and trade is increasing. At the same time, disparities are rising and natural resources are under increasing pressure. Although many consider the ongoing and planned water development projects – most notably the construction of large hydropower dams and irrigation projects – important for the countries' economic development, the negative impacts that they are likely to have on ecosystems as well as on the livelihoods of millions of people are also estimated to be remarkable.

The Mekong River and its tributaries have different hydrological, economic and social roles in different riparian countries. In the primarily rural economies of Cambodia, Laos and the Mekong Delta of Viet Nam, the river is the lifeline of the local people as it provides livelihoods for millions of fishers and farmers. Although not accessible for large-scale navigation, the Mekong River is an important navigation route, particularly for landlocked Laos and the Yunnan province of China. The river and its tributaries are also important sources of hydropower and, consequently, of energy and income for the riparian countries. The development of hydropower in the Mekong Basin has, however, faced severe criticism owing to its significant environmental and social impacts, which

Table 5.1 Some of the main functions, impacts and threats related to the Mekong River in five riparian countries

| Country | Main use/function | Major feared impacts caused by the country | Major threats to the country |
|---------|-------------------|---------------------------------------------|------------------------------|
| China | Hydropower, transportation route | Levelling out of the floods, trapping of sediments and nutrients | Lack of energy and transportation routes |
| Thailand | Water diversion for irrigation and other uses | Environmental degradation, flow changes | Lack of water for irrigation |
| Laos | Hydropower, navigation, aquatic resources | Levelling out of the floods, trapping of sediments and nutrients | Impacts on agriculture and fishing, river bank erosion |
| Cambodia | Aquatic resources, irrigation, possibly hydropower | Potential negative impacts owing to unsustainable fisheries management | Changes in floodplains, particularly in the Tonle Sap flood pulse → impact on fishing and agriculture |
| Viet Nam | Irrigation (delta), hydropower (Central Highlands) | Increasing environmental degradation and water quality problems in the delta owing to intensive agriculture and dense population | Decreased dry season water flows; increasing salt water intrusion and negative impacts on irrigation |

remain poorly analysed and recognized (see e.g. IUCN et al. 2007; Lamberts 2008). Moreover, the role of dams in shifting control of water resources from the local level towards provincial and central governments has been a serious concern, particularly when noting the existing governance challenges in practically all riparian countries (IUCN et al. 2007; Öjendal 2000; Bakker 1999).

Table 5.1 seeks to summarize the different ways in which the Mekong countries make use of the river and its resources.[4] The table also lists the major feared impacts that the national development plans may cause for the river as well as the foremost threats the countries face in relation to the river. Naturally, the majority of the impacts are caused by upstream countries, whereas the downstream countries are the ones threatened by them.

The diverse aspirations for the exploitation of the Mekong River's resources give rise to different, sometimes opposing, objectives in the riparian countries. For Cambodia, maintaining the seasonality of the river is seen as crucial in order to protect the productivity of its flood-plains and the exceptional ecosystem of the Tonle Sap Lake. Viet Nam too considers maintaining seasonality as important for the Mekong Delta, and sees the reduction of dry season flows as particularly unwanted. Thailand, by contrast, aspires to draw water from the river and its tribu-taries for irrigation, and has even planned to divert some of the Me-kong's water to other rivers within its area (Phillips et al. 2006). Thailand is also eager to get more hydropower from the Mekong, mainly through electricity-buying agreements with Laos and China. The most upstream country, China, wishes to improve the navigability of the upper parts of the river and – above all – has already built hydropower dams in the mainstream Mekong and has plans for several more.

The differing national interests in and needs for the Mekong form a po-tential source of conflict – but also cooperation – between the riparian countries. Overall, the riparian countries' governments seem to have rather similar aspirations for the development of the basin, including the development of hydropower and large-scale irrigation.[5] This is illustrated by the fact that there have recently emerged – or, rather, re-emerged – plans in Thailand, Laos and Cambodia to build dams in the mainstream Mekong.[6] If these plans materialize, it will be the first time that main-stream dams are built in the lower Mekong River, having potentially sig-nificant impacts in terms of both environment and livelihoods (see e.g. Baran and Ratner 2007). The planning and decision-making process re-lated to these plans can thus be seen to take regional cooperation, and particularly the functioning of the MRC, to a completely new level. Con-sequently, the success – or failure – of this cooperative process between the riparian countries will for its part show the way for the future of Me-kong cooperation.

## Regional cooperation

The Mekong region has changed a great deal during the past decade in terms of geopolitics. The riparian countries have developed rapidly, increased their cooperation, particularly in trade and economics, and re-oriented their policies towards more open international relations. Conse-quently, other modalities of regional cooperation increasingly determine Mekong cooperation and the role of the MRC in the region (Figure 5.2). The main institutions in this context are the Greater Mekong Sub-region (GMS) Program and the Association of Southeast Asian Nations (ASEAN), both of which are introduced briefly next. After that, the functioning of the MRC and its predecessors is discussed in more detail.

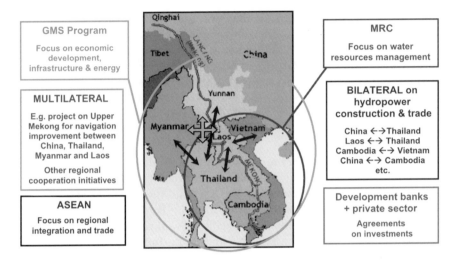

Figure 5.2  Different levels of cooperation in the Mekong region.

Together these two sections present the larger context of water-related cooperation in the Mekong region and discuss its possible future.

The GMS Program was initiated in 1992 with strong support from the Asian Development Bank and all six riparian countries are members.[7] The GMS Program focuses on economic and infrastructure development, but environmental issues too are listed on its agenda. However, the GMS Program's environmental initiatives focus mainly on land ecosystems,[8] and largely ignore the Mekong River and aquatic biodiversity aspects – undoubtedly the region's most important and controversial environmental issue. This would naturally offer a great opportunity for the GMS Program and the MRC to complement each other, but the interaction between the two remains limited. Part of the dilemma is that the MRC and the GMS Program are both dealing with somewhat similar issues but with a very different approach; it has even been indicated that the two organizations are in competition (Hirsch et al. 2006).

Another, geographically broader, economic cooperation organization in the region is ASEAN. Its 10 member countries include all the Mekong countries except China. However, ASEAN also has close connections with China through its dialogue processes. The development of the Mekong Basin is one of the five priority areas for ASEAN–China cooperation (ASEAN 2002), and the ASEAN–Mekong Basin Development Cooperation is one of the subregional cooperation frameworks in which ASEAN is involved. The framework was established in 1996, and its objective is to stimulate sustainable economic growth of the Mekong Basin and to encourage a process of dialogue and identification of common projects (ASEAN 1996). Again, these objectives could be easily linked with those of the MRC, but there is still little cooperation between ASEAN and the MRC. Part of the dilemma seems to be the different valuations and views of the river: whereas the MRC sees the Mekong River chiefly as a natural resource, the GMS Program and ASEAN seem to consider the river more as a symbol that defines the region in which they are promoting economic growth and cooperation (Weatherbee 1997).

There exist several other regional institutions and initiatives that have water-related issues on their agenda. These include the United Nations' Economic and Social Commission for Asia and the Pacific (ESCAP), the United Nations Development Programme's Regional Environmental Governance Programme for Asia-Pacific as well as the initiative by the World Conservation Union (IUCN) and its partners to make discussion about water development in the basin more transparent and participatory through a multi-stakeholder dialogue process (IUCN et al. 2007). Other multilateral cooperation processes include, for example, a navigation agreement for the upper Mekong River between China, Laos, Myanmar and Thailand and the Thai-initiated Ayeyawady–Chao Phraya–Mekong Economic Cooperation Strategy. In addition, the major financial institutions in the region – the World Bank and the Asian Development Bank (ADB) – are strongly involved in water issues through financing river development and related projects. The World Bank, together with the ADB, has also developed the Mekong Water Resources Assistance Strategy for the Mekong Basin.

Despite some interaction between all these different regional organizations, their cooperation remains limited, and some of them are actually seen more as rivals than as collaborators (Hirsch et al. 2006; Sokhem and Sunada 2006). Considering the limited capacity of the Mekong countries, the rapid pace of regional development and the tremendous possibilities and threats included in water development, this non-cooperation is unquestionably a remarkable opportunity wasted.

## The Mekong River Commission and its predecessors

In terms of water resources, the most central cooperation body for the Mekong countries is the Mekong River Commission (MRC). However, the functioning of the MRC and its predecessors (Figure 5.3) has often been limited for political reasons, particularly owing to differing national interests and domestic political challenges in the member countries. In addition, the organizations have operated in only the four Lower Me-

Figure 5.3 Three phases of the Mekong River organizations.
*Note*: The letters indicate the first letters of the names of the four member countries.

kong countries of Cambodia, Laos, Thailand and Viet Nam, which has left China out of the actual cooperation. A review of the functioning of the Mekong River organizations – the MRC and its two predecessors – therefore provides an interesting framework for analysing the roles of riparian states in regional water cooperation.

## The Mekong Committee and the Interim Mekong Committee

The Mekong Committee (MC), the first cooperative body between the four Lower Mekong countries, was established in 1957. The foundations of the MC were laid at the beginning of the 1950s, when the United Nations and the US Bureau of Reclamation carried out a series of studies that suggested great possibilities for irrigation and the development of hydropower, and aroused the interest of the four Lower Mekong countries (MRC 2002).

The Mekong Committee, headquartered in Bangkok, was set up only for the Lower Mekong Basin. China and Burma (now Myanmar) were not members: China was excluded mainly because it was not a UN member and was under a communist regime, and Burma was not interested in joining the cooperative body (Browder and Ortolano 2000). The formation of the Mekong Committee was also very much a product of the Cold War, because one of its objectives was to support the capitalist regimes in the region and in this way to prevent the spread of communism in the area (Phillips et al. 2006).

The mandate of the Mekong Committee was focused on planning, and throughout the 1960s the Committee was involved in a massive programme of water resources studies (Browder and Ortolano 2000). In 1970, the MC introduced the Indicative Basin Plan, which marked a shift from mere planning towards implementation. The plan presented a set of options for water resources projects, and included several large-scale dams to be constructed in the Mekong mainstream (MRC 1970).[9] These massive plans were, however, put together with few doubts about their actual desirability, guided by an optimistic view of the capitalist develop-ment of the basin (Phillips et al. 2006; Öjendal 2000).

The year 1975 proved to be one of the most important turning points for Mekong cooperation. During that year the MC issued a "Joint Decla-ration of Principles" in which the four member countries agreed that all mainstream, major tributary and inter-basin diversions require the un-animous approval of the Committee prior to implementation (Browder and Ortolano 2000). However, the Joint Declaration was not ratified nor were any of the projects defined in the Indicative Basin Plan imple-mented owing to the radical political changes emerging in the region in the very same year. Out of the four MC countries, Cambodia, Laos and Viet Nam acquired communist governments, and Thailand remained alone in the pro-Western, capitalist camp (Browder and Ortolano 2000).

In Cambodia, the extreme communist Khmer Rouge regime came to power in April 1975, and severed connections with the Mekong Commit-tee. The absence of Cambodia forced the remaining three member coun-tries to form the Interim Mekong Committee (IMC). The formation of the IMC was seen to be an important achievement in itself; after all, it brought socialist Viet Nam and Thailand to the same table, offering one of the very few opportunities for diplomatic negotiations between the countries during these turbulent years (Weatherbee 1997). However, the functions of the Interim Mekong Committee were much more limited than those of the Mekong Committee as the three remaining member countries concentrated on their internal water development projects. The region's tense geopolitical situation, along with Cambodia's continu-ing internal problems, transformed the IMC from a temporary coopera-tive body to a diplomatic battleground that was to operate for more than a decade. As a consequence, Mekong cooperation seemed to be slowly slipping into irrelevance during the 1980s (Browder and Ortolano 2000).

## The formation of the Mekong River Commission

The beginning of the 1990s marked the revitalization of Mekong cooper-ation and eventually led to the formation of the Mekong River Commis-sion (MRC). Soon after the signing of Cambodia's peace agreement in 1991, Cambodia's new government requested reactivation of the coun-try's membership in the former Mekong Committee. Although the IMC's statute declared that the Mekong Committee would succeed the IMC once Cambodia was ready to rejoin, things had changed dramatically. Although all the IMC members were willing to readmit Cambodia, Thai-land and Viet Nam in particular had serious disagreements over the constitutional structure of the new Mekong Committee. The idealistic and even euphoric atmosphere of joint interest that prevailed in the 1950s and 1960s was now absent (Phillips et al. 2006).

The disagreements between the countries resulted from the changed global and regional political environment. The ending of the Cold War era altered the geopolitical situation in Southeast Asia as well, and forced the riparian countries to rethink their domestic and foreign policies. In the new regional order China appeared as the region's most important power, with growing economic significance (Makim 2002). At the beginning of the 1990s, China also initiated an enormous hydropower development project for the upper Mekong River that caused concern in the Lower Basin countries and resulted in further disagreements about the focus and structure of Mekong cooperation. In addition to geopolitical changes, the regional socio-economic situation had changed as well. Whereas other Lower Mekong countries had suffered from poor economic growth throughout the 1980s, Thailand had developed significantly and was now clearly more developed than the other riparian countries. This was seen to give Thailand more bargaining power in the negotiations about the future of Mekong cooperation (Nakayama 1999).

Although all four Lower Mekong countries were ready to continue their cooperation, they disagreed over whether they should carry on under the old Mekong Committee framework or negotiate a totally new framework. In addition, Thailand was eager to incorporate China in the new Mekong organization, while the others were more hesitant (Radosevich 1995).[10] The impasse was solved in 1992 by the signing of a Memorandum of Understanding that returned Cambodia officially to Mekong cooperation and started negotiations for a new cooperation framework. After long and complex negotiations, the Mekong River Commission (MRC) was established in April 1995 by the four Lower Mekong countries with the signing of the "Agreement on the Cooperation for the Sustainable Development of the Mekong River Basin" (MRC 1995).

Despite China's prominent role and its massive plans for the development of its part of the Mekong River, it did not join the MRC. However, the 1995 Mekong Agreement includes an article that allows "any other riparian State" to become a member of the MRC with the consent of the other members (MRC 1995). In 1996, China and Myanmar became so-called dialogue members of the Commission. The MRC's cooperation with China was further improved in 2002 when China signed an agreement on the provision of hydrological information on the Mekong River (MRCS 2002).

The new Mekong Agreement started a new era of cooperation in the Lower Mekong Basin. Instead of the former emphasis on planning and construction, the Mekong Agreement focused on sustainable and comprehensive management of the Mekong River. Because of the prominence it gives to joint development, ecological protection and water allocation, the agreement has been praised as a milestone in international water resources management treaties (Radosevich and Olson 1999). However, the phrasing of the Mekong Agreement of 1995 emphasizes the territorial integrity and sovereignty of the signatory states, and rejects the enforcement power of the MRC. The Agreement is thus less binding than the 1975 Joint Declaration and leaves more freedom for national water utilization. The MRC can therefore be seen to be more a coordinator, rather than a controller, of the use of the Mekong's resources (Browder and Ortolano 2000). For this reason the Mekong Agreement has also been described as weak, allowing the member countries to interpret it as they like or even just to sideline it (Backer 2006).

## Way forward for Mekong cooperation?

It is obvious that the MRC and its predecessors have played an important role as a cooperation platform between the Mekong countries; the organizations have collected and shared information between the countries, made common plans for the basin development, and provided a dialogue forum for the governments. However, with the increase in unilateral and bilateral plans for water development – most notably hydropower construction – in the basin, there is a real danger that the MRC will be sidelined from the planning and decision-making processes.[11]

Despite the seemingly easy cooperation, the four member countries of the MRC seem not to be eager to carry out really comprehensive and coordinated development of the basin. We see two main reasons for this. First, the governments seem to be hesitant to give up even a small part of their national sovereignty. The different forms of regional cooperation – particularly those that involve agreements and limitations on countries' use of water and related resources – are subordinated to national interests, and the MRC therefore remains marginalized from the national decision-making processes (Dore 2003; Backer 2006; Hirsch et al. 2006).[12] The differing national interests are also related to the region's tumultuous history and the complex political relations between the riparian countries. Secondly, the member country governments seem to fear that cooperation in the MRC would considerably slow down and even prevent their plans for the utilization of the Mekong. Indeed, the countries seem to be reluctant to take steps towards a more regulatory role for the MRC, with greater emphasis on governance, as this would also mean compromising their national sovereignty and their plans for developing the river and its tributaries (Hirsch et al. 2006).

The MRC is also facing other, more general, challenges. The fairly weak institutional capacity of its member countries – Cambodia and

Laos in particular – is also reflected in the MRC, which still has plenty of room for improvement (Chenoweth et al. 2001). In addition, the very structure of the MRC as a cooperative body between the riparian states means that the MRC considers the entire basin mainly as a transnational space (Sneddon and Fox 2006). Many see that this state-centrism – particularly when combined with persisting governance challenges in the member countries – means that the MRC does not comprehensively address the different temporal and spatial scales of water use, does not involve the non-state actors properly in its work and fails to reflect the actual needs and concerns at the local level (IUCN et al. 2007; Sneddon and Fox 2006; Sokhem and Sunada 2006; Dore 2003; Öjendal 2000).

At the basin-wide level, the absence of two upstream countries – China and Myanmar – is perhaps the biggest deficiency of the MRC, seriously restricting comprehensive management of the entire basin. The fact that all three Mekong River organizations have had only Lower Mekong countries as members means that none of the organizations has complied with the most frequently highlighted prerequisite for basin-wide water management, i.e. that the river basin organization should coincide with the geographical extent of the watershed (Phillips et al. 2006). China thus has a very special role in Mekong cooperation and its actions – and non-actions – have a remarkable influence on the development and management of the entire basin; these are discussed more below, as well as in Chapter 10 on China.

A bit more than a decade after the Mekong Agreement was signed, the MRC is in many ways at a crossroads. Whereas the first 10 years of the MRC focused on building technical and management capacity, particularly for the MRC Secretariat, the long-formulated new strategic plan for 2006–2010 is moving towards an approach oriented more to development, investment and action (MRC 2006). This seems also to be what the member country governments and the CEO – unlike most of the donors – want (Backer 2006; Affeltranger 2005; Cogels 2005). This kind of approach is actually very close to that of the Greater Mekong Subregion Program and ASEAN, raising questions about overlaps. This approach has also attracted criticism owing to the lack of proper consideration of emerging conflict-prone issues, most importantly the ongoing construction of dams upstream and in the tributaries (Jensen 2005).

## Case study 1: China

China is a regional superpower with a history of non-cooperation in the management of its transboundary river basins.[13] This is also a reality in the Mekong Basin, where China is the uppermost riparian and has

Table 5.2 Proposed Mekong dam scheme in China

| Site | Dam height (metres) | Installed capacity (MW) | Current status | Estimated completion |
|------|------|------|------|------|
| Gonguoqiao | 130 | 750 | n.a. | n.a. |
| Xiaowan | 300 | 4,200 | Under construction | 2012 |
| Manwan | 126 | 1,500 | Completed | 1996 |
| Dachaoshan | 110 | 1,350 | Completed | 2003 |
| Nuozhadu | 254 | 5,850 | Under preparation | 2017 |
| Jinghong | 118 | 1,750 | Under construction | 2009 |
| Ganlanba | n.a. | 250 | n.a. | n.a. |
| Mengsong | n.a. | 600 | n.a. | n.a. |

*Sources*: Magee (2006), Dore and Yu (2004), Voigt (2004), IRN (2001), McCormack (2001), Plinston and He (1999).

expressed only limited interest in regional cooperation, at least when it comes to discussing its own plans for the exploitation of the river. This kind of self-centred approach has been easy for China: as the most upstream country it has control over the Upper Mekong Basin.

## Development in the upper Mekong

Despite the strong efforts towards integrated management of water resources, the international dimension and transboundary impacts have traditionally been to a large extent left out of China's water-related plans and activities. Best known of these activities is the plan to build a cascade of several large hydropower dams into the Mekong mainstream in Yunnan province (Table 5.2). The first dam, Manwan, was completed in 1996 without prior consultation with the downstream countries. The second one, the Dachaoshan dam, went into operation in 2003, and construction of the massive 300 metres high Xiaowan hydroelectric project began in 2002. The Xiaowan dam is China's second-largest dam project, smaller only than the Three Gorges project on the Yangtze River. The Jinghong dam is also under construction and the Nuozhadu dam is in preparation; the remaining projects are at the planning stage (Magee 2006; Dore and Yu 2004; Voigt 2004).

The dams in the upper Mekong – or Lancang as it is known in China – are mainly planned to provide energy. The dam cascade, concentrated close to China's southern borders, will have a maximum installed capacity of 15,000 MW. Yunnan province is one of the poorest in the country, and income from the power trade is therefore considered important for its economic development. At the national level, power shortages are becoming increasingly serious, and energy production is therefore high on the government's agenda. Hydropower is also considered to be a clean form of energy, particularly compared with the dominant coal-based energy production.

Besides national needs, the upper Mekong dams are expected to supply power to the growing markets in Southeast Asia, particularly to Thailand. The Chinese part of the Mekong has a remarkable total exploitable capacity of an estimated 23,480 MW (Chincold 2003). Nonetheless, the river forms only a minor part of the country's total hydropower potential, and is also situated far from the main industrial centres. However, considering the low level of development in Yunnan province as well as the energy needs of the other Mekong countries, there seems to be a growing demand for both local consumption and cross-border electricity trade.

The Mekong River also offers China access to the Southeast Asian markets. In order to improve the navigability of the river, China has initiated a navigation improvement project on the river together with Thailand, Laos and Myanmar. The plan included removal of several rapids and reefs in the upper reaches of the Mekong by dredging and blasting (Finlayson 2002). The navigation project has been criticized for poor impact assessments that did not properly assess the potential environmental impacts (Lazarus et al. 2006). Additionally, Cambodia and Viet Nam claim that they were not consulted or even properly informed about the agreement, although they are the two countries in many ways most dependent on the river and most affected by upstream development (Makkonen 2005).[14]

According to the official Chinese view, development in the upper Mekong will not have severe impacts. In fact, the Chinese view the impacts of dam construction as being mainly positive, because during the dry season the amount of water in the river could be increased and during the rainy season flood protection improved. With careful operation of the dams, the adverse effects could be minimized (Chapman and He 2000). China's statements have nevertheless been criticized for badly underestimating – and even neglecting – the negative downstream impacts. Many regional and international specialists maintain that the consequences of the Chinese dams will be considerable, and will have environmental and social impacts because the quality and quantity of the river flow will change remarkably (see e.g. IUCN et al. 2007; Lamberts 2008; Kummu and Varis 2007; Keskinen et al. 2007). In particular, the immense aquatic production, which is a major source of income and food in the basin, is likely to be endangered.

One of the main challenges in discussing the impacts of upstream dams is that there has not been a proper cumulative environmental assessment covering the entire river basin and the different development plans, at least not one that is publicly available. This is related to the problems with the availability of information; China has been hesitant to share detailed information on its plans or even on the hydrological measurements in its part of the Mekong River. On the other hand, comprehensive information about the different development plans and their impact assessments is usually very difficult to get in other riparian countries too.

## China's reluctance to cooperate regionally?

China's cooperation – or non-cooperation – in the Mekong Basin looks different depending on the viewpoint. The official Chinese version wants to give an impression of high-level cooperation as well as of mutual benefits from the Chinese projects. However, the alternative view reveals that the importance of the water projects, particularly those involving hydropower production, is so great that the possible negative impacts on downstream countries may simply not be taken seriously into account.

There are several reasons for China's relatively low cooperation in the management of the Mekong River, including:

- the structure of Chinese society and politics – a strong central administration;
- historical factors – turbulent relationships with the neighbouring countries;
- strong economic development, pressure to develop further and the need for energy – the necessity of the projects targeted at water resources development;
- challenges inside the country and the resources required to solve them – shortage of capacity and the low priority of international issues;
- lack of adequate benefits – what China would really achieve through increased Mekong cooperation.

All these factors should be taken into account when considering future actions to improve Mekong cooperation and in particular China's role in it. As can be seen, most of the factors are closely related to China's domestic issues. The structure of Chinese society remains highly centralized and relies on the one-party system. The process of maintaining this political system while aiming at a market economy and increased participation in the international community is a very special one. Adding the huge size of the country and the domestic challenges faced in many sectors, it is practically impossible to compare China with any other nation.

Based on the structures of Chinese society and politics, there is a tendency to keep internal matters – including the development of water resources – as the nation's own business. In addition, some of the working methods in the water sector clearly hamper the implementation of an integrated approach. Water-related responsibilities are divided among different ministries and bureaus, and there is hardly any information-sharing among them. To fulfil the aims set for them, the different agencies also compete with each other, which further reduces the motivation for information-sharing (Makkonen 2005). At the middle and lower levels of governance, contradictions exist in the position of the bureaus as they need to respond both to the next level in their own sector and to the general local governance. All these very basic governance challenges have their implications for international cooperation.

At the same time, China faces some substantial, high-level domestic challenges that demand priority over other issues. Environmental degradation, which has reached an alarming level, is one such challenge and is very difficult to curb. The same problems as are faced in many sectors – an inoperative management structure and a lack of funding – also occur in the environmental field. Owing to the scope of China's internal environmental problems, there may be little capacity for solving international matters related to the environment. China's national economy is another major challenge. The drive towards a Western idea of a developed country, a strong national economy and both economic and social balance are major factors in all decision-making. The importance of projects that support domestic development, such as energy and transportation sectors, must not be underestimated. Water resources have significant potential from both of these viewpoints. This provides strong justification too for the projects on transboundary rivers, even if the impacts on the other riparian countries are likely to be largely negative.

However, positive signs of China's willingness to cooperate more actively in the Mekong do exist. Local administrations and the non-governmental organizations seem to consider increased cooperation important, but rarely have real opportunities to work towards these aims because of bureaucratic challenges, problems with resources and lack of experience in real public participation (Makkonen 2005). At a higher level, China's economic opening, its drive for more transparency and its increasingly important position as a member of the international community encourage international cooperation. China is also becoming more and more dependent on the outside world, which seems to be giving increasing weight to relationships with its neighbouring countries as well.

## Future prospects for China's Mekong cooperation

Despite its history of weak regional cooperation, China is a major player in the Mekong region and has shown increasing interest in the region. China is keenly interested in more economically focused cooperation within the GMS Program and ASEAN, and it has substantially increased its bilateral cooperation with the other Mekong countries. Furthermore, even though China is not a member of the MRC, it meets regularly with the MRC because of its dialogue membership, and since 2002 it has also shared some hydrological information with the Commission (MRCS 2006, 2002).

As noted by Hirsch et al. (2006), the official Chinese position seems also to have shifted to be more favourable towards MRC membership. Although many see China's membership in the MRC as an important step forward in Mekong cooperation, there are fundamental challenges to China's membership from both sides. For the Chinese, the possible re-strictions that membership would entail – particularly on the building and operation of its dams – are difficult to accept. It also seems that China wants the Commission to cover more economic and trade issues in addition to environmental and water-related questions (Makkonen 2005). On the other hand, it is not clear if the MRC countries would actually accept China's membership, as the country could have a too dominant role in the Commission.

At the same time, China has become an increasingly important bilateral partner for the other Mekong countries. In Cambodia and Laos, China has become one of the largest foreign investors and trade partners, and it has also given significant donations and loans, particularly for infrastructure development, including hydropower (Sokha 2007; China Development Brief 2006).[15] This kind of increased bilateral cooperation could potentially lead also to increased multilateral cooperation. This requires, however, strong political will in the riparian countries for coordinated action; without this it seems likely that these kinds of bilateral partnerships will not strengthen more multilateral processes, but might even increasingly replace them.

## Case study 2: Cambodia

Cambodia is a centrally located downstream country that falls almost completely within the Mekong Basin. Tonle Sap Lake, which is the heart of the Mekong's aquatic production, an invaluable flood-leveller and an essential source of income for the region, is also situated in the country. Cambodia is hence deeply dependent on the Mekong River and concerned about the possible negative impacts of upstream development. Because of its central location and the vital role of the Tonle Sap for the entire Mekong system, Cambodia is also an important partner for the other Mekong countries.

The civil war and political unrest that have characterized Cambodia for much of recent decades have resulted in severe poverty, relatively poor infrastructure, a lack of technical, financial and human capacity and continuing governance challenges. Cambodia is one of the world's most aid-dependent countries, and donors and development banks are heavily involved in the country's development. Mekong cooperation is seen as important for bringing much-needed financial and technical assistance to the country. Although water resources management is high on the government's agenda (Chamroeun 2006), the governmental line agencies' weak capacity and a lack of coordination between the different ministries mean that Cambodia still lacks the means comprehensively to address the different aspects of the 1995 Mekong Agreement (Keskinen and Varis 2005; Sokhem and Sunada 2006).

At the same time, Cambodia has a history of exceptional internal problems and conflicts that have profoundly affected the regional geopolitics and have also seriously hindered Mekong cooperation. However, Cambodia's problems have by no means had only internal causes but have been greatly affected by the power struggles of both regional and global superpowers. Cambodia's strategic location between the two regional powers, Thailand and Viet Nam, means that it easily gets caught up in regional power battles. This situation has forced Cambodia either to favour one of the regional powers or to attempt to remain neutral by appealing to an outside power such as China or the United States (Chandler 1996).

*Internal turmoil in the 1970s and 1980s – Mekong cooperation ends*

Cambodia was, like Laos and Viet Nam, a French colony until it gained its independence and became a constitutional monarchy in 1953 under King Norodom Sihanouk. With the escalation of the Cold War in Southeast Asia, Sihanouk adopted a policy of neutrality that aimed to maintain Cambodia's internal stability and to keep the country out of the intensifying conflicts in neighbouring countries, particularly in Viet Nam (Kiernan 2007). The formation of the Mekong Committee in 1957 increased Cambodia's cooperation with its neighbours and provided possibilities and resources for the development of its water resources; it was also hoped that it would impede the spread of communism in Cambodia and in the region as a whole. However, towards the end of the 1960s the country was increasingly affected by the Viet Nam war, and Sihanouk's regime was unable to handle its increasing effects.

In 1970, Sihanouk was replaced by General Lon Nol in a bloodless coup d'état. Soon after that, the Cambodian communists, the Khmer Rouge, launched a civil war against the new right-wing and pro-US government (Chandler 1996). The civil war came to an end in 1975 with the takeover by the Khmer Rouge, which plunged the country into chaos and misrule that no one was able to predict. The Khmer Rouge regime, led by the infamous Pol Pot, adopted a policy of self-reliance, cutting practically all connections to the outside world (Browder and Ortolano 2000). The Khmer Rouge era also seriously affected Mekong cooperation because the Khmer Rouge regime had neither the capacity nor the will to be involved in regional cooperation. As a result, the regime ended Cambodia's participation in the Mekong Committee. As discussed earlier, this forced the remaining three member countries of Viet Nam, Laos and Thailand to form the Interim Mekong Committee (IMC).

The three-and-a-half-year misrule of the Khmer Rouge ended in 1979, when the Vietnamese Army occupied Cambodia and helped to form a new regime. Although the end of the Khmer Rouge regime was a positive step forward, the following decade involved foreign occupation, civil unrest and international isolation for the country (Kiernan 2007). In terms of Mekong cooperation, the Vietnamese presence in Cambodia weakened the relationship between Viet Nam and Thailand and made the operation of the IMC more troublesome. Although the Vietnamese-backed Cambodian government indicated its willingness to participate in the IMC, Thailand refused to recognize the government as legitimate because of the lack of international recognition (Phillips et al. 2006). Thus, Cambodia remained out of official Mekong cooperation for two decades.

*Stabilization in the 1990s – rejoining Mekong cooperation*

The 1990s brought considerable stabilization in Cambodia's political situation and also the reactivation of Cambodia's role in regional cooperation. The Vietnamese troops withdrew from Cambodia in 1989, and in 1991 the parties in the Cambodian civil war signed the Paris Peace Agreement, which calmed the hostilities in the country. Cambodia regarded the revitalization of Mekong cooperation as a key to breaking its long international isolation (Phillips et al. 2006), and the Mekong Committee was also seen as an important source of financial and technical assistance.

Accordingly, the newly formed coalition government requested re-admission to and reactivation of the Mekong Committee as soon as 1991. However, as was illustrated above, the region's political and economic situation had changed fundamentally, and the four Lower Mekong countries entered into long negotiations about the future of Mekong cooperation. The negotiations came to an end in 1995 with the establishment of the Mekong River Commission (MRC), which again had Cambodia as a member. Three years earlier, in 1992, Cambodia had already joined the other riparian countries and the Asian Development Bank to form the Greater Mekong Subregion (GMS) Program. The GMS Program was considered important in Cambodia to develop its poor infrastructure and promote its economic development (Krongkaew 2004). The formation of these major regional organizations meant that Cambodia was, after two decades, again an active and fully acknowledged member in Mekong cooperation.

The 1990s saw several remarkable changes in Cambodia's domestic politics too, many of which had impacts – both positive and negative – on its role in regional cooperation. The first notable step on Cambodia's path towards stability was the UN-led parliamentary elections of 1993, won by the royalist FUNCINPEC party. The party was, however, forced to form a coalition government with the Cambodian People's Party (CPP), which represented the earlier communist regime and had better connections at the provincial and commune levels (Roberts 2001). This coalition was characterized by mistrust, and ended in July 1997 when the tensions between the two parties led to an armed conflict. The CPP emerged as the winner, and the head of the party, Hun Sen, assumed the sole leadership of Cambodia as Prime Minister, a position he still holds today. The political crisis of 1997 – like most of the subsequent ones – negatively affected Cambodia's international relations. Cambodia's admittance to ASEAN was postponed and the majority of donors and foreign investors suspended their projects in the country.

New parliamentary elections were organized in July 1998. The CPP won the elections, although there were accusations of voter intimidation and vote buying, a lack of opposition access to the media and overall electoral fraud in favour of the ruling CPP (ICG 2000). After a four-month political deadlock, the CPP managed to form a coalition government with FUNCINPEC. Despite their unpromising history, the new coalition government proved to be relatively stable and it was able to initiate some economic reforms as well as to enhance international cooperation. The year 1998 was an important landmark for Cambodia in the newly started Mekong cooperation, as the MRC Secretariat was transferred from Bangkok to Phnom Penh during that year. This move marked considerable recognition of the fact that, throughout the 1990s, Cambodia had fought its way towards stability and an increased role in regional cooperation.

*Cambodia in the new millennium – progress with political problems*

Since the parliamentary elections of 1998, Cambodia has made progress towards stability and strengthened its links with its neighbours and the international community. Cambodia became a member of ASEAN in 1999 and of the World Trade Organization (WTO) in 2004, being only the second least developed country to be admitted to the organization through the full negotiation process. At the same time, however, the disparities between different parts of the country and particularly between urban and rural areas increased dramatically. Additionally, problems of corruption, mismanagement of the country's natural resources and continuous violations of human rights remain largely to be solved (Keskinen et al. 2007; ECOSOC 2006; Heder 2005; World Bank 2004).

Although the ruling CPP won the parliamentary elections of 2003, it failed to secure the majority to govern alone. Consequently, the political situation after the elections was again extremely difficult and was solved only a year later when a CPP–FUNCINPEC coalition government was formed. Because of the political stalemate, the functioning of the government was in practice paralysed for a full year, and most international donors postponed their funding for the country. In a country as deeply aid dependent as Cambodia, the postponement hampered the functioning of all ministries, including those in the water sector. Owing to the political stalemate, foreign investments were also deterred and the country's membership in the WTO was delayed. However, neither the strong financial incentives nor repeated requests from the international community for the formation of a new government had any noticeable effect on the political parties towards solving the political deadlock (Ten Kate 2004).

The anti-Thai riots that took place in Phnom Penh in January 2003 were another, unfortunate, example of how flammable Cambodia's political situation remains and how easily it affects regional cooperation. Although it remains unclear who the actual mastermind behind the riots was, it seems obvious that anti-Thai feelings were used only as a medium for the domestic political battle (Hinton 2006). Accordingly, the underlying reason for the riots had more to do with the upcoming parliamentary elections than with the troubles between Thailand and Cambodia as such.

Consequently, although Mekong cooperation is still highly regarded by the Cambodian government (Sen 2003a), the country's domestic political battles continue to hinder regional cooperation. Power struggles between the different parties and politicians also leave their mark on the country's foreign policy and, when necessary, regional cooperation is subordinated to domestic political purposes. In addition, the challenges to the sustainable management of the country's natural resources – fish in particular – have an impact on other Mekong countries owing to the enormous aquatic production in the Cambodian floodplains and particularly in the Tonle Sap Lake.

At the same time, ironically, the increasing economic dependence on other Mekong countries, particularly China, is a potential threat to the balanced management of Cambodia's water resources. Owing to fear of the political and economic consequences, Cambodia's politicians seem to be tempted to pay only limited attention to the possible negative impacts of the upstream development on the country's water resources.[16] There is therefore a danger that the melding of political and economic powers and Cambodia's increasing economic dependence on its neighbours will mean that the country will not use its position in the Mekong River Commission and other regional cooperation mechanisms to discuss openly the critical transboundary impacts on its water resources (Keskinen et al. 2007). Because of the crucial role of the country's floodplains and in particular of the Tonle Sap Lake in the entire Mekong River system, this would have unwanted consequences not only for Cambodia but also for the other riparian countries.

## Conclusion

### Challenges to regional cooperation

Mekong cooperation has existed in the Lower Mekong Basin for over five decades with the notable support and involvement of the United Nations, development banks and donors. Still, the Mekong River Commission and its predecessors have not been too successful in the comprehensive development and management of the water resources. The reasons for the weak performance of the MRC and its predecessors include the organizations' overambitious development plans with little connection to local-level realities, the lack of real commitment by the member countries to the Commission's work, and challenges to institutional capacity and transparency within the organizations as well as in the riparian countries. However, various internal governance problems and domestic political battles in the MRC member countries – including Cambodia – are at least as important. Finally, the absence of China and Myanmar seriously hinders the comprehensive and coordinated development of the basin.

Despite these challenges, the MRC offers an important platform for cooperation between the Mekong countries. After all, it is the only regional organization focused specifically on water resources management, a role that is increasingly important now that plans for water development are mushrooming in practically all parts of the basin. However, as discussed above, the growing number of bilateral and unilateral agreements – often including the private sector – in the riparian countries puts the MRC in a difficult position, and may potentially lead it to be sidelined from the actual planning processes on the development of the Mekong's water resources.

When considering the future of the MRC, it is important to note that both the Mekong Agreement and the internationally agreed principle of integrated water resources management (IWRM) require reasonable compromises between environmental sustainability, social equity and economic well-being. In addition, the MRC has set poverty reduction as its main goal. Because a significant proportion of the Mekong Basin's population gain their livelihood from the resources that the Mekong River and its tributaries offer, the health of the river ecosystems feeds directly back to the welfare of those people. The conflict is therefore not so much between the environment and wealth as between the modern and the more traditional sectors of society. As noted by Phillips et al. (2006): "The key development paradox of the region is that economic growth is necessary to bring many of the populations out of poverty, but the 'classical' route involving the subsidised construction of massive infrastructure is most unlikely to provide the optimal result in this respect for the poorer sections of the populations." Indeed, the existing decentralized utilization of the Mekong's resources – based on small-scale fishing, farming, the use of wetland and floodplain resources, etc. – is likely to form a more sustainable basis for poverty reduction than is the development of large-scale irrigation and hydropower.

Consequently, the MRC should get more actively and transparently involved in the discussion about development in the basin, including the potential impacts and trade-offs following development. Related to this, the MRC should acknowledge more clearly that coordinated water management between riparian countries is particularly conflict prone, and should increase its capacity for resolving disputes between its member states – and potentially with the other riparian countries.[17] Ultimately, the future of the MRC depends on the will for cooperation of member countries and their governments. Extended partnership with China, increased collaboration with other regional organizations and a more focused agenda would enable the MRC to concentrate on its original purpose – to serve the people of its member countries by recognizing the most sustainable ways to use the basin's water resources and by facilitating dialogue on the best possible paths for future development.

## Lessons learned from the China and Cambodia case studies

Besides an overall analysis of the Mekong River and its riparian countries, this chapter has analysed Mekong cooperation through two country-specific case studies. The first case study on China concentrated on the country's plans for hydropower and navigation development in the basin, and discussed the reasons for China's relatively low interest in regional cooperation. The Cambodia case study focused on the country's internal politics, and analysed their impact on Mekong cooperation during different periods.

The major differences between the two countries include their geographical location, geopolitical and economic might and development objectives for the river. Because China is the most upstream country in the basin, its decisions on the development of its part of the basin have significant impacts on the other riparian countries. In particular, the ongoing construction of a cascade of dams in the mainstream Mekong has raised concerns in the downstream countries. However, the benefits of Mekong cooperation in terms of economics, politics or water management do not currently seem to be strong enough to persuade China to join the MRC, because joining would simultaneously limit its plans for the upper Mekong. Although increasing regional cooperation through ASEAN and the GMS Program could potentially make multilateral water cooperation more attractive for China, it seems that it prefers, at least for the time being, to be more involved in bilateral arrangements with the downstream countries.

Whereas China seems to have more to lose than to gain from cooperation within the MRC, the situation for Cambodia is the opposite. Mekong cooperation gives Cambodia access to technical and financial assistance and offers a convenient forum in which to raise critical issues related to the development of the river basin and its impacts on Cambodia. However, Cambodia's internal political rivalries regularly override the needs of regional cooperation, and the country's government also appears to lack the capacity – and possibly the political will – to address comprehensively the potential transboundary impacts on its water resources.

As the case studies on China and Cambodia reveal, countries' internal problems can be so challenging that it may be unrealistic to expect international cooperation on water issues to be given a high priority. In addition, the development of water and related resources is both economically and socially so important for the riparian countries that national interests often override the need for closer regional coordination. The analysis of the domestic situation in China and Cambodia shows how significantly and differently the countries' internal problems and national interests have affected Mekong cooperation, in particular the functioning of the MRC and its predecessors. The analysis also illustrates that just having a regional cooperation institute in place is not enough; strong political commitment from the riparian countries is required for regional water cooperation to be really successful.

Despite the challenges, the different forms of regional cooperation still have a significant role in the development and management of the Mekong River Basin. Sustainable management of the basin's water resources requires that all these different forms of cooperation function transparently and take equal account of the different scales of water use. To achieve this, a truly open dialogue about future development plans, their impacts and their consequent trade-offs must be encouraged between the different actors and levels. In this, the riparian countries' governments have a key role to play.

## Acknowledgements

We are grateful to Matti Kummu, Mira Käkönen, Professor Pertti Vakkilainen, Zhou Bo and Henry Voigt for comments and assistance. Financial support from the Sven Hallin Research Foundation, the Academy of Finland (project 111672), the Foundation of Technology (TES) and Maa-ja vesitekniikan tuki ry. is acknowledged.

## Notes

1. The MRC and its predecessors, the Mekong Committee (MC) and the Interim Mekong Committee (IMC), are also referred to as the "Mekong River organizations" in this chapter.
2. For example, the private sector has played a remarkable role in the development of the basin's water resources – particularly in the construction of hydropower dams and large-scale irrigation projects – and its role seems to be only strengthening.
3. It has been estimated that a 30 cm increase in the dry season water level would permanently submerge – in essence destroy – around one-third of the remaining large canopy forests in the Tonle Sap floodplain (Keskinen et al. 2007; Kummu 2007).
4. Myanmar is excluded from the table owing to the lack of reliable information and the relatively small significance of the Mekong River for the country.
5. Consequently, it has been suggested that it is more probable that serious conflicts over water development will occur *within* the countries rather than *between* them (Keskinen et al. 2007).
6. Interestingly, the feasibility study for Cambodia's planned dam on the mainstream Mekong will be carried out by a Chinese company (Sisovann 2007).
7. China as a whole is not in fact a member of GMS, but the Yunnan province is. The Guangxi Zhuang Autonomous Region also has been involved in the programme (Qin 2005).
8. Environmental issues are addressed particularly through the GMS Program's Sub-regional Working Group on the Environment as well as through the Core Environment Programme and the Biodiversity Conservation Corridors Initiative.
9. The Mekong is thus relatively unique for a river of its size, because a regional master plan for its development was completed – although not applied – before any major projects were initiated (Bakker 1999).
10. China and Myanmar actually took part in a planning meeting on Mekong cooperation organized by Thailand – and boycotted by Viet Nam – in March 1992. The two upstream countries, however, did not attend the subsequent meetings (Browder 2000).
11. It could even be claimed that this has already happened, and that as a result the MRC has been turned from a regional cooperation body into a kind of smokescreen: in theory the MRC coordinates the sustainable and balanced development of the basin, but in reality it has practically no influence in the planning of water projects that will have trans-

boundary impacts. This has led to a situation where the development of the basin looks to be relatively well coordinated, when in reality it is not. This, in turn, can mislead researchers, non-governmental organizations and even donors to "over-focus" on the MRC and other regional cooperation mechanisms, instead of on more relevant planning processes within national governments and – increasingly – within the private sector.

12. Indeed, it has been suggested that the member countries actually prefer the MRC to be a toothless organization focusing on planning, capacity-building and attracting external funding, while control of the development of the basin remains with the countries themselves (Backer 2006).

13. The only known significant transboundary river treaty that China has signed is the Tumen River Agreement, which concerns mostly economic aspects.

14. Related to this it is interesting to note that neither Thailand nor Laos – despite being MRC member countries – involved the MRC in the actual negotiation of the project (Dore 2003).

15. China is even considered to be "the main engine for Cambodia's hydropower development" (Sokha 2007). Unlike Western donors, China does not impose conditions on its aid – at least publicly. As stated by the Cambodian Minister of Commerce: "Others say, 'You have to do this with human rights, you have to do that with democratic reforms.' China doesn't do that" (Lee 2006).

16. Cambodian Prime Minister Hun Sen said in a speech in 2003 that "the Upstream countries' projects in the Mekong River, namely the continued dam constructions and commercial navigation plan, have become a major concern for the downstream countries including Cambodia", being particularly concerned about the impacts on the Tonle Sap Lake (Sen 2003b). Two years later, just before leaving for the second GMS Summit organized in China, Hun Sen was quoted in a Chinese newspaper as saying that he believed hydropower dams built by the Mekong's upstream countries would pose "no problems" to Cambodia, and he also criticized people wanting to undermine the unity among the riparian countries by claiming otherwise (*People's Daily Online* 2005).

17. Although the MRC's role as a commonly agreed cooperation framework, together with its ability to provide scientific information on possible development impacts, naturally facilitates discussion and prevents some misunderstandings between the member countries, the capacity for actual resolution of disputes and conflicts is still predominantly lacking within the Commission.

## REFERENCES

Affeltranger, B. (2005), "Intra-Basin Conflict Resolution in the Mekong Basin: Is a Reconciliation of Water Values Possible?", *Papers and Abstracts of International Workshop Value of Water – Different Approaches in Transboundary Water Management*, Koblenz, Germany.

ASEAN [Association of Southeast Asian Nations] (1996), *Basic Framework of ASEAN–Mekong Basin Development Cooperation*, Kuala Lumpur, 17 June.

——— (2002), *Framework Agreement on Comprehensive Economic Co-Operation Between ASEAN and the People's Republic of China*, Phnom Penh, 5 November.

Backer, E. B. (2006), *Paper Tiger Meets White Elephant? An Analysis of the Effectiveness of the Mekong River Regime*, Lysaker, Norway: Fridtjof Nansen Institute.

Bakker, K. (1999), "The Politics of Hydropower: Developing the Mekong", *Political Geography*, Vol. 18, No. 2, pp. 209–232.

Baran, E. and B. Ratner (2007), "The Don Sahong Dam and Mekong Fisheries", a science brief, WorldFish Center, Penang, Malaysia.

Browder, G. (2000), "An Analysis of the Negotiations for the 1995 Mekong Agreement", *International Negotiation*, Vol. 5, No. 2, pp. 237–261.

Browder, G. and L. Ortolano (2000), "The Evolution of an International Water Resources Management Regime in the Mekong River Basin", *Natural Resources Journal*, Vol. 40, pp. 499–531.

Chamroeun, S. (2006), "Scoping Study of Existing Frameworks Related to the World Commission on Dams Strategic Framework – Cambodia", in R. A. R. Oliver, P. Moore and K. Lazarus, eds, *Mekong Region Water Resources Decision-making: National Policy and Legal Frameworks vis-à-vis World Commission on Dams Strategic Priorities*, Bangkok, Thailand, and Gland, Switzerland: IUCN.

Chandler, D. (1996), *A History of Cambodia*, 2nd updated edn, Boulder, CO: Westview Press.

Chapman, E. C. and D. He (2000), "Downstream Implications of China's Dams on the Lancang Jiang (Upper Mekong) and Their Potential Significance for Greater Regional Cooperation, Basin-Wide", Australian National University, Canberra.

Chenoweth, J., H. M. Malano and J. F. Bird (2001), "Integrated River Basin Management in the Multi-Jurisdictional River Basins: The Case of the Mekong River Basin", *Water Resources Development*, Vol. 17, No. 3, pp. 365–377.

China Development Brief (2006), "Communist Capital Flows Downstream: China's Aid to Laos", *China Development Brief*, February, available at ⟨http://www.chinadevelopmentbrief.com/node/454⟩ (accessed 31 October 2007).

Chincold (2003), web pages of Chinese National Committee on Large Dams; at ⟨http://www.icold-cigb.org.cn⟩ (accessed 1 October 2003).

Cogels, O. (2005), "River Commission Takes on Development Role in the Lower Mekong Basin", *Mekong Update and Dialogue*, Vol. 8, No. 2, Australian Mekong Resource Centre, Sydney.

Dore, J. (2003), "The Governance of Increasing Mekong Regionalism", in M. Kaosa-ard and J. Dore, eds, *Social Challenges for the Mekong Region*, Bangkok: White Lotus.

Dore, J. and X. Yu (2004), "Yunnan Hydropower Expansion – Update on China's Energy Industry Reforms and the Nu, Lancang and Jinsha Hydropower Dams", Chiang Mai University, Chiang Mai, and Green Watershed, Kunming.

ECOSOC [Economic and Social Council] (2006), *Report of the Special Representative of the Secretary-General for Human Rights in Cambodia, Yash Ghai*, Commission on Human Rights, E/CN.4/2006/110.

Finlayson, B. (2002), *Report to the Mekong River Commission on the "Report on Environmental Impact Assessment: The Navigation Improvement Project of the Lancang-Mekong River from China-Myanmar Boundary Marker 243 to Ban Houei Sai of Laos"*. Joint Expert Groups on EIA of China, Laos, Myanmar and Thailand.

Heder, S. (2005), "Hun Sen's Consolidation – Death or Beginning of Reform?", in *Southeast Asian Affairs*, Institute of Southeast Asian Studies, Singapore.

Hinton, A. (2006), "Khmerness and the Thai 'Other': Violence, Discourse and Symbolism in the 2003 anti-Thai Riots in Cambodia", *Journal of Southeast Asian Studies*, Vol. 37, No. 3, pp. 445–468.

Hirsch, P. and K. M. Jensen, with B. Boer, N. Carrard, S. FitzGerald and R. Lyster (2006), *National Interests and Transboundary Water Governance in the Mekong*, Australian Mekong Resource Centre at the University of Sydney in collaboration with Danish International Development Assistance.

ICG [International Crisis Group] (2000), *Cambodia: The Elusive Peace Dividend*, ICG Asia Report No. 8, Phnom Penh/Brussels: International Crisis Group.

IRN [International Rivers Network] (2001), "Proposed Mekong Dam Scheme in China Threatens Millions in Downstream Countries", *World Rivers Review*, June.

IUCN [World Conservation Union], TEI [Thailand Environment Institute], IWMI [International Water Management Institute], and M-POWER [Mekong Program on Water, Environment and Resilience] (2007), *Exploring Water Futures Together: Mekong Region Waters Dialogue. Report from Regional Dialogue*, Vientiane, Lao PDR.

Jacobs, J. W. (2002), "The Mekong River Commission: Transboundary Water Resources Planning and Regional Security", *Geographical Journal*, Vol. 168, No. 4, pp. 354–364.

Jensen, K. M. (2005), "Response 1", *Mekong Update and Dialogue*, Vol. 8, No. 2, Australian Mekong Resource Centre, Sydney.

Keskinen, M. and O. Varis (2005), "Transboundary Agreement and Local Realities – Case from the Tonle Sap Lake, Cambodia", *Proceedings of the IWRA's XII World Water Congress*, New Delhi, India.

Keskinen, M., M. Käkönen, P. Tola and O. Varis (2007), "The Tonle Sap Lake, Cambodia; Water-Related Conflicts with Abundance of Water", *Economics of Peace and Security Journal*, Vol. 2, No. 2, pp. 49–59.

Kiernan, B. (2007), "Conflict in Cambodia, 1945–2006", in B. Kiernan and C. Hughes, eds, *Conflict and Change in Cambodia*, London: Routledge.

Krongkaew, M. (2004), "The Development of the Greater Mekong Subregion (GMS): Real Promise or False Hope?", *Journal of Asian Economics*, Vol. 15, No. 5, pp. 977–998.

Kummu, M. (2007), personal communication, 26 February, Helsinki University of Technology, Espoo.

Kummu, M. and O. Varis (2007), "Sediment-Related Impacts Due to Upstream Reservoir Trapping in the Lower Mekong River", *Geomorphology*, Vol. 85, pp. 275–293.

Kummu, M., D. Penny, J. Sarkkula and J. Koponen (2008), "Sediment – Curse or Blessing for Tonle Sap Lake?", in O. Varis, M. Keskinen and M. Kummu, eds, *Modern Myths of the Mekong*, in press.

Lamberts, D. (2008), "Little Impact, Much Damage: The Consequences of Mekong River Flow Alterations for the Tonle Sap Ecosystem", in O. Varis, M. Keskinen and M. Kummu, eds, *Modern Myths of the Mekong*, in press.

Lazarus, K., P. Dubeau, C. Bambaradeniya, R. Friend and L. Sylavong (2006), *An Uncertain Future: Biodiversity and Livelihoods along the Mekong River in Northern Lao PDR*, Bangkok, Thailand, and Gland, Switzerland: IUCN.

Lebel, L., P. Garden and M. Imamura (2006), "The Politics of Scale, Position, and Place in the Governance of Water Resources in the Mekong Region", *Ecology and Society*, Vol. 10, No. 2.

Lee, Don (2006), "Cambodia Greets a Cash Invasion", *Los Angeles Times*, 17 September.

McCormack, G. (2001), "Water Margins: Competing Paradigms in China", *Critical Asian Studies*, Vol. 33, No. 1, pp. 5–30.

Magee, D. (2006), "Powershed Politics: Yunnan Hydropower under Great Western Development", *The China Quarterly*, Vol. 185, pp. 23–41.

Makim, A. (2002), "The Changing Face of Mekong Resource Politics in the Post-Cold War Era: Re-negotiating Arrangements for Water Resources Management in the Lower Mekong Basin (1991–1995)", Working Paper No. 6, Australian Mekong Resource Centre, University of Sydney.

Makkonen, K. (2005), "Integrated Water Resources Management in China", in A. K. Biswas, O. Varis and C. Tortajada, eds, *Integrated Water Resources Management in South and Southeast Asia*, New Delhi: Oxford University Press.

MRC [Mekong River Commission] (1970), *Report on Indicative Basin Plan. A Proposed Framework for the Development of Water and Related Resources of the Lower Mekong Basin. Committee for the Coordination of Investigations of the Lower Mekong Basin*, Khmer Republic, Laos, Thailand and Republic of Viet-Nam.

——— (1995), *Agreement on the Cooperation for the Sustainable Development of the Mekong River Basin, 5 April 1995*, Mekong River Commission, Bangkok.

——— (2002), *The Story of Mekong Cooperation*, Mekong River Commission, Phnom Penh.

——— (2003), *State of the Basin Report 2003*, Mekong River Commission, Phnom Penh.

——— (2005), *Overview of the Hydrology of the Mekong Basin*, Mekong River Commission, Vientiane.

——— (2006), *Strategic Plan 2006–2010*, Mekong River Commission, Vientiane.

MRCS [Mekong River Commission Secretariat] (2002), "China Signs Data-Sharing Agreement", *Mekong News – the Newsletter of the Mekong River Commission*, October–December, Issue 2002/2.

——— (2006), "Strategic Plan Ready to Go into Operation", *Mekong News – the Newsletter of the Mekong River Commission*, October–December, Issue 2006/4.

Nakayama, M. (1999), "Aspects behind Differences in the Agreements Adopted by Riparian Countries of the Lower Mekong River Basin", *Journal of Comparative Policy Analysis: Research and Practice*, Vol. 1, pp. 293–308.

Öjendal, J. (2000), "Sharing the Good: Modes of Managing Water Resources in the Lower Mekong River Basin", PhD dissertation, Department of Peace and Development Research, Göteborg University, Sweden.

*People's Daily Online* (2005), "Cambodian PM Dismisses Impact of Mekong's Upstream Dams", 30 June; available at ⟨http://english.people.com.cn/200506/30/eng20050630_193155.html⟩ (accessed 31 October 2007).

Phillips, D., M. Daoudy, S. McCaffrey, J. Öjendal and A. Turton (2006), *Transboundary Water Co-operation as a Tool for Conflict Prevention and for Broader Benefit-sharing*, Windhoek, Namibia: Phillips Robinson and Associates, available at ⟨http://www.egdi.gov.se/pdf/44699_om_web.pdf⟩ (accessed 31 October 2007).

Plinston, D. and He, D. (1999), *Water Resources and Hydropower*, Manila: Asian Development Bank.

Qin, J. (2005), "Summit to Enhance Co-ops along Mekong", *China Daily*, 5 July; available at ⟨http://www2.chinadaily.com.cn/english/doc/2005-07/05/content_457021.htm⟩ (accessed 31 October 2007).

Radosevich, G. E. (1995), "Agreement on the Cooperation for the Sustainable Development of the Mekong River Basin – Commentary and History of the Agreement", draft.

Radosevich, G. E. and D. C. Olson (1999), "Existing and Emerging Basin Arrangements in Asia: Mekong River Commission Case Study", Third Workshop on River Basin Institution Development, 24 June, World Bank, Washington DC.

Roberts, D. W. (2001), *Political Transition in Cambodia 1991–99 – Power, Elitism and Democracy*, London: Curzon Press.

Sen, Hun (2003a), "Addressing the MRC's Council Meeting", speech by Prime Minister Hun Sen, *Cambodia New Vision*, Issue 70, November; available at ⟨http://www.cnv.org.kh/cnv_html_pdf/cnv_70_November_03.pdf⟩ (accessed 31 October 2007).

——— (2003b), "Addressing the Management of Large Rivers Symposium", speech by Prime Minister Hun Sen, *Cambodia New Vision*, Issue 61, February; available at ⟨http://www.cnv.org.kh/cnv_html_pdf/cnv_61.pdf⟩ (accessed 31 October 2007).

Shaochuang, L., L. Pingli, L. Donghui and J. Peidong (2007), "Pinpointing Source of Mekong and Measuring Its Length through Analysis of Satellite Imagery and Field Investigations", *Geo-Spatial Information Science*, Vol. 10, No. 1, pp. 51–56.

Sisovann, Pin (2007), "Chinese Firm to Study Possible Mekong Dam Site", *Cambodia Daily*, 5–6 May, p. 3.

Sneddon, C. and C. Fox (2006), "Rethinking Transboundary Waters: A Critical Hydropolitics of the Mekong Basin", *Political Geography*, Vol. 25, No. 2, pp. 181–202.

Sokha, Cheang (2007), "China Transforms Cambodia's Electricity", *Phnom Penh Post*, Issue 16/05, 9–22 March, Phnom Penh, Cambodia.

Sokhem, P. and K. Sunada (2006), "The Governance of the Tonle Sap Lake, Cambodia: Integration of Local, National and International Levels", *International Journal for Water Resources Development*, Vol. 22, No. 3, pp. 399–416.

Ten Kate, Daniel (2004), "Ministries Discuss Requests for Aid Money", *Cambodia Daily*, 11 May.

Voigt, H. (2004), personal communication, Yunnan Environmental Protection Bureau, Kunming, China.

Weatherbee, D. E. (1997), "Cooperation and Conflict in the Mekong River Basin", *Studies in Conflict and Terrorism*, Vol. 20, No. 2, pp. 167–184.

World Bank (2004), *Cambodia at the Crossroads: Strengthening Accountability to Reduce Poverty*, Report No. 30636-KH, Word Bank Group.

# 6

# The role of domestic security in the functioning of the Lake Chad Basin Commission

*Virpi Stucki and Madiodio Niasse*

## Introduction

The performance of river basin organizations is very uneven. In West and Central Africa the Senegal River Basin Authority (Organisation pour la Mise en Valeur du Fleuve Sénégal, OMVS) has been relatively active since its establishment in 1972, whereas many other basin organizations in the region, sometimes older than the OMVS, continue to be lacklustre. That is the case for the Gambia River Basin Development Organization (OMVG) and to a lesser extent for the Niger Basin Authority (NBA) and the Lake Chad Basin Commission (LCBC).

There have been many attempts to justify these differences in performance. One explanation often given is that the basin countries did not devote enough effort to defining the exact mandate of these basin organizations. It is certainly on the basis of such an implicit assumption that the World Bank has supported vision exercises in the LCBC, and more recently in the NBA, in order to help these organizations better figure out their raison d'être and mandate.

Another explanation has more to do with geographical determinism, and uses the differences in the geographical configuration of river basins to explain the difference in performance of the basin organizations. Niasse (2003) points out that, in West Africa, boundary rivers such as the Senegal River – the boundary between Mali and Senegal and between Senegal and Mauritania – lend themselves more easily to international cooperation than transboundary rivers such as the Niger River or the Gambia River. Riparian states in transboundary river basins often

*International water security: Domestic threats and opportunities, Pachova, Nakayama and Jansky (eds), United Nations University Press, 2008, ISBN 978-92-808-1150-6*

have scarcely reconcilable interests as far as the management of these rivers is concerned. This makes it very difficult for basin organizations in charge of such rivers to craft a strategy around which riparian countries would coalesce as a result of clear perceptions that their respective aspirations and national interests are properly taken into account.

A third way of analysing the uneven level of performance of the basin organizations is through the quality of the relationships between basin countries, and especially between the countries that make up the basin organization. It seems evident that a deterioration in diplomatic relationships and/or the start of conflicts between two or more of the basin countries negatively affect the performance of the basin organization.

Another avenue worth exploring in order to understand the performance of basin organizations is the internal security and socio-political and economic situation of the member states. In this chapter we use the case of Lake Chad to examine the extent to which internal problems within basin countries affect the performance of the basin organization, the LCBC, and the condition of the Lake Chad ecosystem.

## Background to the Lake Chad Basin

### Geographical setting

The Lake Chad Basin is situated in the Sudano-Sahelian zone in Western and Central Africa and covers an area of 2,381,635 km$^2$. The basin spreads across a total of seven countries: Algeria, Niger, Nigeria, Chad, Cameroon, Central African Republic (CAR) and Sudan. Traditionally, part of the basin has been called the Conventional Basin, which includes the states of Niger, Nigeria, Chad, Cameroon and CAR and has an area of about 96,000 km$^2$. This Conventional Basin is under the mandate of the Lake Chad Basin Commission.

Lake Chad is the main body of water in the basin. It crosses three different climatic zones: humid tropical, semi-arid Sahelian and arid Saharan. Annual rainfall varies from 1,500 mm in the southern parts of the basin to under 100 mm in the northern parts. This inland freshwater lake gets its water from three main river systems: Chari–Logone–El-Beïd, Komadugu–Yobe and Yeseram–Ngadda (Figure 6.1).

The size of the lake has undergone an extreme change (Figure 6.2) since the 1960s when its surface area was 25,000 km$^2$ in average years to its present size of about 2,000 km$^2$ (Jauro 2000a). This shrinking of the lake has raised concerns at the subregional and especially at the international level, where the lake is classified as one of the world's ecological hotspots and areas that need urgent attention (GSFC 2001). Whether the shrinking of the lake is caused by the highly variable and unpredictable

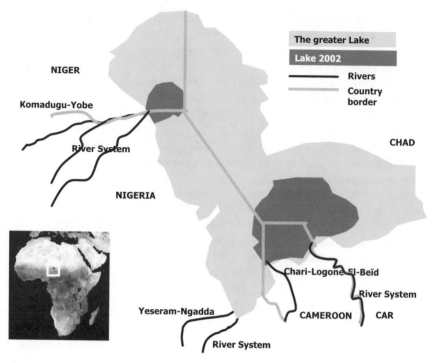

Figure 6.1  The Lake Chad Basin.

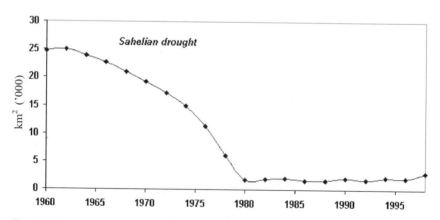

Figure 6.2  The surface area of Lake Chad.
*Source*: Jauro (2000a), modified from the original source.

Table 6.1 Information on the Lake Chad Basin countries

| Country | Total area of the country ('000 km$^2$)$^a$ | Area of the country within the basin ('000 km$^2$)$^a$ | As % of total area of basin$^a$ | As % of total area of country$^a$ | Contribution to the LCBC budget (%)$^b$ |
|---|---|---|---|---|---|
| Algeria | 2,382 | 93.5 | 3.9 | 3.9 | – |
| Cameroon | 475 | 50.8 | 2.1 | 10.7 | 26 |
| CAR | 623 | 219.0 | 9.2 | 35.2 | 4 |
| Chad | 1,284 | 1,046.0 | 43.9 | 81.5 | 11 |
| Niger | 1,267 | 691.0 | 29.0 | 54.6 | 7 |
| Nigeria | 924 | 179.0 | 7.5 | 19.4 | 52 |
| Sudan | – | 101.0 | 4.2 | 4.0 | – |

*Sources*: $^a$FAO (1997), $^b$IMF (1999).

climate or by human actions (such as irrigation and upstream dam construction) is often argued about. A study by Coe and Foley (2001) shows that, in the period 1966–1975, 5 per cent of the 30 per cent decrease in the size of the lake was caused by irrigation. This figure has risen to 50 per cent since the 1960s and 1970s. However, the same study concludes that climate variability is still the controlling factor of the lake inflow's inter-annual fluctuations.

According to the Food and Agriculture Organization (FAO 1997), the area under irrigation around the lake is about 113,000 hectares (ha), and the irrigation potential is estimated at 396,000 ha within the Conventional Basin and 1,163,200 ha within the whole basin. Given the results of Coe and Foley (2001), one could advise prudence in further irrigation schemes.

Africa's fourth-largest lake by surface area, Lake Chad is an important water source for its riparian states. The biggest share of the basin's area is under the territory of Chad (Table 6.1), whereas most of the lake's inflow (95 per cent) originates in Cameroon and CAR, from where the Chari and Logone rivers bring approximately 38.5 km$^3$ a year to the lake (the volume of the lake has varied between 20 km$^3$ and 100 km$^3$ in recent history). Another important inflow originates on the border of Niger and Nigeria where the Komadugu–Yobe river system drains approximately 0.5 km$^3$ a year into the lake. Algeria in the very northern part of the basin does not have rivers flowing into the lake and Sudan in the east could, in theory, deliver about 0.08 km$^3$ a year to the lake through its alluvial aquifers (FAO 1997).

## The people

The socio-economic situation in the basin area is rather challenging. The total population in the basin countries in 2001 was 219 million, of whom about 10 per cent (22 million people) live in the basin area; the total population in 2015 is estimated to be 295 million. Gross domestic product (GDP) in the lake countries varies from 850 (PPP$) in Nigeria to 6,090 (PPP$) in Algeria. The countries range in rank from 174 (Niger) to 107 (Algeria) in human development (in the Human Development Index of the United Nations Development Programme, the total number of countries is 175). Life expectancy at birth is on average 51 years and the adult literacy rate is 53 per cent. The percentages of underweight for age (under age 5) vary from 40 per cent in Niger to 6 per cent in Algeria. The Gini index measures inequality over the entire distribution of income or consumption, a value of 0 representing perfect equality and a value of 100 perfect inequality. The index varies from 61 in CAR to 35 in Algeria (data from Sudan and Chad are not available) (UNDP 2003).

## Politics

A history of political instability has characterized the basin countries since their independence from their colonial powers around the beginning of the 1960s. All of the basin countries have gone through a civil war of some degree and some of them are still in a rather unstable condition. Disputes and tensions among the basin countries include those between Nigeria and Cameroon over the Bakassi peninsula, Nigeria and Chad on exploiting oil reserves (Collelo 1998), Niger and Nigeria on the lower Niger River, the re-demarcation of the boundary in the Lake Chad region (CIA 2002), as well as the recent political crisis between CAR and Chad.

Changes of regimes, coups d'état and unrest between different ethnic groups have been more the rule than the exception in the Lake Chad Basin countries. A total of some 26 coups and 16 occasions of civil unrest have occurred in the Lake Chad Basin area since the beginning of the 1960s (Table 6.2). Even though nowadays the basin countries are relatively calm, the possibility of sudden change is prevalent and the security situation in some of the countries is still weak.

## Domestic security and transboundary watersheds: Problem definition

This study concentrates on analysing the role of two macro-level stakeholders: the Lake Chad Basin countries and the Lake Chad Basin Commission (LCBC). Their interconnections with the "silent stakeholder", Lake Chad, are examined.

These actors have a two-way relationship – they partly influence and partly are influenced by the other. Some of the linkages are fairly easy to determine and predict on the basis of information available from inter-

Table 6.2  Political instability in the Lake Chad Basin countries

| Country | Coups and coup attempts | Civil unrest | External disputes |
|---------|-------------------------|--------------|-------------------|
| Algeria | 1965<br>1992 | Throughout 1980s: riots<br>Throughout 1990s: civil unrest<br>2001: clashes between police and the Berbers | |
| Cameroon | 1984 | Early 1990s: violent protests | 1990s: tension between Cameroon and Nigeria over the Bakassi peninsula |
| CAR | 1965<br>1979<br>1981 | Late 1970s: government-ordered massacre<br>1996: ethnic feuding<br>1997: army mutinies | |
| Chad | 1975<br>1987<br>1990 | 1966–1973: guerrilla war<br>1990s: armed rebel groups, especially in the north | 1970s and 1980s: dispute with Libya |
| Niger | 1974<br>1983<br>1996<br>1999 | Early 1960s: rebel warfare<br>Early 1980s: civil unrest<br>Early 1990s: conflict between government and the Tuareg | |
| Nigeria | Jan. 1966<br>Jul. 1966<br>1975<br>1976<br>1983<br>1985<br>1993<br>1995 | Early 1960s: conflicts between regions<br>Late 1960s: war between Biafra and Nigeria<br>Late 1990s: riots, violence in the north | 1990s: tension between Nigeria and Cameroon over the Bakassi peninsula |
| Sudan | 1958<br>1969<br>Early 1980s: numerous attempts<br>1985<br>1989 | Since independence (1956): civil war, except in the period 1972–1982 | 1998: US missiles destroyed a pharmaceutical plant in Khartoum |

*Sources*: CIA (2002) and *Encyclopedia Columbia* (2003).

national databases, whereas some of them are very difficult or impossible to define.

One example of the latter is domestic security and its influence on a water basin. This aspect has received little attention until now, even though it can have a tremendous influence on the functioning of a water basin organization and on the state of a shared water basin.

Domestic security may be affected by factors external to the watershed such as coups, where the situation of a country is unbalanced by a factor that is not connected with the water resource but that will have consequences for the water resource. Or the water resource itself may be the impetus for jeopardizing the domestic security situation. This case is often linked to the question of water allocation, for example, when competition for access to a watershed occurs between different ethnic groups, such as herders and farmers. The latter case is more well known and studied, whereas the first case has received rather little attention among water professionals, in spite of the fact that a crisis inside one of the water basin countries may seriously hinder the development plans of the water basin organization.

In this chapter, we shall scrutinize the threats inside the basin countries that originate outside the water resource but influence the functioning of the Basin Commission.

Figure 6.3 illustrates the definition of the problems. The interactions are divided into three: Lake Chad with the basin countries; Lake Chad

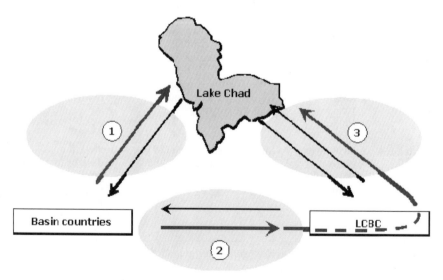

Figure 6.3 Definition of the problems.
*Note*: The bold arrows indicate the problems investigated in this study.

with the LCBC; and the basin countries with the LCBC. Among these, the study concentrates on three main questions (marked with bold arrows in Figure 6.3):
• What are the effects on Lake Chad's ecology if domestic security in a basin country deteriorates?
• What are the effects on the functioning of the LCBC if domestic security in a basin country deteriorates?
• What are the indirect effects of the previous point on Lake Chad?
The following analysis is carried out for the Conventional Basin area, thus covering Cameroon, CAR, Chad, Niger and Nigeria.

## The stakeholders

### Lake Chad Basin countries

The following gives an overview of the political and economic situation in the Conventional Basin member states.

Central African Republic (CAR) is a country with seven major ethnic groups. It had a parliamentary government until the end of 1965, after which various military regimes controlled the country until 1993 when the country had its first multi-party elections. However, army mutinies and fighting have characterized the country ever since, resulting in a large number of victims. A pan-African peacekeeping force has been present in CAR since 1999.

In economic terms, CAR faces constraints owing to its landlocked position, weak transportation system, unskilled labour and poor macroeconomic policies. Its economy is based on subsistence agriculture and forestry, the former accounting for 50 per cent of GDP. The major export products are timber and diamonds. The economy has been seriously affected by the civil unrest (Encyclopedia Columbia 2003).

Cameroon, with some six major ethnic groups, has experienced relatively peaceful development since the unification of the French and British parts of the country in 1961. This has allowed the country to develop a fairly functional system of transportation, as well as a petroleum industry. Despite attempts to form a democratic regime, there is a perception that political power is increasingly controlled by an ethnic oligarchy.

Cameroon's economy is classified as one of the best performing in sub-Saharan Africa because of its oil resources and favourable climatic conditions for agricultural production. However, the economy is greatly affected by fluctuations in world oil prices as well as by corruption (CIA 2002).

Chad has some 200 distinct ethnic groups and a history of ethnic war-fare that has lasted three decades since the country's independence in 1960. Even though the government drafted a democratic constitution in 1990 and multi-party elections were subsequently held, power remains in the hands of a northern ethnic oligarchy. In 1998 ethnic rebellion broke out again and a peace agreement between the government and the rebels was signed only in 2002 (CIA 2002). The security situation in the country remains rather unstable.

In economic terms, Chad struggles owing to its landlocked position and mainly agricultural economy, which is vulnerable to climate conditions and also relies on only a few agricultural export products (cotton) that are very susceptible to fluctuations in world market prices. Instability and high energy costs add to the unfavourable situation. Oilfield and pipeline projects planned to boost the country's economic situation are under development, but are highly controversial (CIA 2002).

In 1993, 33 years after its independence from France, Niger made the transition to civilian rule. The country has eight major ethnic groups and has experienced much rebel warfare; most recently, a five-year insur-gency between the government and the Tuareg ended in 1995.

Niger's economy is very weak, being mainly reliant on agriculture and to a small extent on uranium. The country is landlocked and suffers strongly from unfavourable climatic conditions; the country was pro-foundly affected by the Sahelian drought in 1968–1975. Niger has long been among the very least developed countries in terms of human devel-opment and remains highly dependent on foreign aid (CIA 2002).

Nigeria is no exception among the African countries in having a long history of military rule. After 16 years of military rule, the biggest coun-try in Africa in terms of population, with more than 250 different ethnic groups, adopted a new constitution and moved to civilian government in 1999.

Nigeria's economy is among the five biggest in Africa. Yet its heavy dependence on the oil industry makes it extremely vulnerable to world price fluctuations. Massive corruption,[1] money-laundering, drug-trafficking and poor macroeconomic management, as well as a rapidly growing population, are factors negatively affecting the nation's eco-nomic development (CIA 2002).

## Lake Chad Basin Commission

The Lake Chad Basin Commission (LCBC) was created in 1964 between Cameroon, Chad, Niger and Nigeria in a situation where the member states' activities were seen as alarming in terms of water utilization and possibilities for conflict (Lambert 2002). Other agreements include the

Mondou Accord, signed between Chad and Cameroon in 1970 in order to fix the water level in the Logone such as to allow both countries to develop hydro-agricultural activities in a sustainable way. In addition, the Enugu Accord was signed in Nigeria in 1977 with the aim of conserving all natural resources in the subregion.

The original mandate of the LCBC was to:

- have common regulations so as to allow the effective application of the Statute and the Convention of the LCBC;
- collect and distribute information on projects under development by the member states in order to encourage joint planning as well as research activities in the Lake Chad Basin;
- maintain liaison between the high-level signatories to enable the most efficient water utilization in the basin;
- monitor studies and other activities in the Lake Chad Basin, taking into account the current Convention and inform member states about them;
- devise common rules in relation to navigation;
- establish rules for its personnel and ensure their application;
- examine complaints and contribute to their solution;
- ensure that the prescriptions of the Statute and the Convention are applied (Lambert 2002, translated from the French).

The Sahelian drought at the beginning of the 1970s motivated the LCBC to take urgent action in the fields of agriculture, livestock breeding, fishing, forestry and water resources, as well as civil engineering and telecommunications. However, in 1985 the member states realized that, instead of being proactive and developing the basin in an integrated and sustainable way, it had been rather reactive and had concentrated on national – instead of regional – activities. During the 35th Meeting of the Commission, the LCBC was given a mandate to approach international organizations for technical assistance and to study the possibilities for restructuring the Commission. In 1990 changes at the level of the executive secretary were made, since when the LCBC has been undertaking activities with a regional approach.

The period 1984–1992 has been considered especially successful in terms of the conflict resolution activities of the LCBC and has reinforced the role of the Commission as a conflict resolution body in the basin. In 1994 the Central African Republic joined the Commission as a fifth member. Sudan was accepted as an observer in 2000 and it will become a member after ratifying the Convention and Statute of the Commission.

Today the LCBC's aims include regulating and controlling the utilization of water and other natural resources in the basin; initiating, promoting and coordinating natural resource development projects and research within the basin area; and examining complaints and encouraging the settlement of disputes, thereby promoting regional cooperation.

The LCBC structure comprises the following permanent bodies (IMF 1999): the Summit of heads of state, which is the highest authority and is held once a year; the annual Commissioners' Meeting (also called "Session"); and the Executive Secretariat, which has an executive secretary, an assistant executive secretary, a financial controller and three departments (Administration and Finance, Planning and Project Execution, and Documentation, Information, Remote Sensing and Advanced Technologies).

The LCBC's yearly budget of around CFA 600–950 million (about US$1.0–1.5 million) (GEF 2000) is divided as follows: Nigeria 52 per cent, Cameroon 26 per cent, Chad 11 per cent, Niger 7 per cent and CAR 4 per cent (IMF 1999). However, for many years, member states have accumulated substantial arrears in the payment of their contributions (Rangeley et al. 1994, and resolutions of the 47th, 48th, 49th and 50th sessions of the LCBC Council of Ministers between 2000 and 2002). The LCBC is collaborating on technical and financial matters with the United Nations Development Programme (UNDP), the United Nations Sudano-Sahelian Office, the United Nations Environment Programme (UNEP), the World Conservation Union (IUCN), the Food and Agriculture Organization of the United Nations (FAO), France and the Islamic Development Bank as well as with some other donors.

## The challenges facing Lake Chad and the LCBC's actions

Lake Chad faces many problems of ecological, socio-economic, institutional and political origins. A variable and unreliable rainfall pattern, a highly interlinked water balance, considerable variability of soil types, a proneness to droughts and desertification, and human-caused environmental degradation (i.e. deforestation, dam construction) are listed as the biggest environmental problems in the basin (LCBC 2000).

High population growth – with an estimated 36 million inhabitants in the basin by 2025 in comparison with about 22 million today – is one of the strongest socio-economic driving forces in the future development of the basin. Migration, poverty and conflicts over resource use between different ethnic groups add to the list. The last factor should be especially recognized in future basin development activities. The session on "Water and Conflict" during the Second World Water Forum (2000) in The Hague recommended, among others things, that more attention should be paid to local groups and non-governmental organizations, which have a definite role to play in local and subregional water disputes.

The LCBC *Vision for 2025* (LCBC 2000) lists today's challenges facing the lake as:

- climatic changes
- poor decision-making
- lack of policies
- weak coordination
- weak economic situation

According to Jauro (2000b), the challenges facing the Lake Chad Basin area are conservation of limited water resources, restoration of the lake level and its ecosystems, halting of desert encroachment, the development of data collection, collation, storage and dissemination systems, as well as regional cooperation.

To meet these challenges, the LCBC has undertaken various development exercises (Jauro 2000a). First, a Master Plan for the Development and Environmentally Sound Management of the natural resources of the basin was prepared with the assistance of the FAO, UNEP and the United Nations Sudano-Sahelian Office (UNSO). Then a Strategic Action Plan (SAP) for the basin was developed between 1996 and 1998 and approved by the Council of Ministers in 1998. This document was the basis for the Lake Chad Basin Vision for 2025 and a Framework for Action that was developed soon after approval of the SAP.

The Vision for 2025 includes a short-term action plan (eight years) with the following components:

- create dynamism in the management of shared water resources with intra- and inter-country cooperation and integration mechanisms;
- put in place viable basic information collection networks for better knowledge about water resources, ecosystems and their exploitation, and its follow-up;
- carry out basic sectoral activities to meet the demand for water and to control desertification and biodiversity loss.
- start feasibility studies on intra- and inter-basin water transfer and environmental impacts;
- prevent and control contaminants, as well as preserve fishery resources;
- improve methods for tapping aquatic aquifer ecosystems and protect floodplains in relation to regional development.

The long-term action plan (20 years) divides the basin into four geographical entities and it envisages developing the region in a sustainable way.

Until recently, the LCBC has mainly relied on its own financial resources to fund and implement the identified development activities. The investment budget being very small (about 40 per cent of the LCBC budget of US$1.0–1.5 million) and not always actually used owing to accumulated arrears, the LCBC's achievements between 1964 (the date of its establishment) and 1990 have been considered "disappointing"

(Rangeley et al. 1994), and the level of implementation of the 1992 Master Plan is so far very low. There are better prospects for the future as a US$13 million Global Environmental Facility (GEF) project aimed at implementing the 1998 Strategic Action Plan was launched in 2003.

## Analysis

*What are the effects on Lake Chad's ecology if domestic security in a basin country deteriorates?*

One way to answer this question is to look back at the history. Nigeria, Chad, CAR and, to a lesser extent, Cameroon and Niger have been embroiled in political instability and ethnic and religious warfare to the extent that development concerns have tended to be secondary. The fate of Lake Chad as well as of the Lake Chad Basin Commission has seldom been a priority for the ruling governments of the basin countries, leading to the contemporary degraded state of the lake.

*What are the effects on the functioning of the LCBC if domestic security in a basin country deteriorates?*

According to the LCBC's mandate, the Commission is to promote regional cooperation, and therefore promoting the settlement of a dispute within one of the member states can be considered to be outside the Commission's mandate. Civil wars have been prevalent in the Lake Chad Basin countries and the situation is still rather unstable in some of them. A dispute in one of the countries will therefore continue to jeopardize the functioning of the Commission in a situation where it does not have a mandate to promote peace in individual states.

The headquarters of the LCBC has been located in the capital of Chad, N'Djamena, except for 1979–1987, when it was transferred to Maroua in Cameroon owing to the civil war in Chad (Tam 2003). This is clearly understandable given the constraints that a country seriously affected by a war imposes on the functioning of an international organization. The level of security in N'Djamena continues to restrict the full-scale operational functioning of the LCBC and one can speculate whether it would have made a significant difference if the headquarters had been sited in a different country and if relocating now to a basin country with a better security situation could boost the Commission's functioning.

Further, war-torn countries also suffer from financial shortcomings. The LCBC member states have to provide yearly disbursements to the

Commission (see Table 6.1) according to a distribution scale agreed on in 1997. The basin countries are all facing difficult economic situations and, consequently, have not been able to fulfil their financial contributions to the Commission to varying degrees for a while now. For this reason the Commission faces recurrent financial difficulties, which affect its overall performance. The LCBC can be said to be fully dependent on outside donor financing and this naturally influences its ability to work in a pro-active way.

### What are the indirect effects of the previous point on Lake Chad?

Among the aims that the LCBC endeavours to fulfil, "settling disputes" is perhaps the most crucial one in the light of basin development. A country involved in a war has little means to protect or develop a natural resource – be it as vital as Lake Chad. The LCBC has taken initiatives to solve problems between its member states, yet the success of these attempts can be debated.

However, the LCBC can be considered fairly successful when it comes to its aim to initiate and promote natural resources development projects in the basin. Various large-scale projects are currently under development (e.g. a GEF grant for the reversal of land and water degradation trends in the Lake Chad Basin ecosystem) and, if successfully implemented, they could significantly improve the situation in the basin. Moreover, the Lake Chad Basin Vision for 2025 can be considered a great piece of work. A lot depends naturally on the completion of the planned activities.

## Conclusion

Lake Chad is an example of a transboundary watershed where the basin states have varying – and sometimes conflicting – interests in the development of the lake. It is also an example of a watershed whose countries have historically experienced diplomatic conflict, the situation remaining to some extent similar nowadays.

These factors alone make the management of Lake Chad a challenging task. Yet there is another one to add, namely political instability inside the basin countries.

A nation with internal political, socio-political and economic stresses has little means to extend its energy into long-term natural resources management plans. The financial capital and political will needed for such activities are simply non-existent.

Lake Chad in Sahel is an example of an ecosystem that for a long time has been a victim of its basin countries' unstable political situation. The ecological shrinking and deterioration of the lake are widely acknowledged in international forums. A drying climate and high agricultural demand for water are often blamed for these negative changes. Similarly, the unstable political situation and devastating civil wars of the basin countries have commonly been recognized. Yet these two phenomena – the ecological deterioration and the civil unrest – have seldom been linked in the discussions.

This chapter suggests that weak domestic security in the Lake Chad Basin countries has had a notable effect on the functioning of the Lake Chad Basin Commission. This is seen in a lack of political will, the location of the headquarters in a war-damaged country and the inability of the member states to pay their membership fees.

However, despite all the constraints, a comprehensive management plan for the basin has been developed and a number of projects identified in this plan are being implemented as part of the newly launched GEF Lake Chad project (GEF 2000). Given the particularly difficult sociopolitical context in the basin countries, this can be seen as a notable achievement for the Basin Commission.

Yet the ecological challenges facing Lake Chad remain high. It is crucial that the current, politically fairly calm state of the basin countries prevails or further stabilizes in order to save one of the greatest oases of the Sahel.

## Note

1. Nigeria's Corruption Perceptions Index is 1.6 – a Corruption Perceptions Index of 0 indicates extremely corrupt whereas 10 indicates not at all corrupt (Transparency International 2003).

## REFERENCES

CIA [Central Intelligence Agency] (2002), *The World Factbook*, online version, available at ⟨http://www.cia.gov/cia/publications/factbook/index.html⟩ (accessed 31 October 2007).

Coe, M. T. and J. A. Foley (2001), "Human and Natural Impacts on the Water Resources of the Lake Chad Basin", *Journal of Geophysical Research* (Atmospheres), Vol. 106, No. D4, pp. 3349–3356.

Collelo, Thomas, ed. (1998), *Chad: A Country Study*, Country Studies/Area Handbook Series, Washington, DC: GPO for the Library of Congress; published online at ⟨http://countrystudies.us/chad/⟩ (accessed 31 October 2007).

*Encyclopedia Columbia* (2003), ⟨http://www.bartleby.com/65/⟩ (accessed 31 October 2007).

FAO [Food and Agriculture Organization] (1997), "Irrigation Potential in Africa: A Basin Approach", *FAO Land and Water Bulletin 4*, FAO Land and Water Development Division.

GEF [Global Environmental Facility] (2000), "Reversal of Land and Water Degradation Trends in the Lake Chad Basin Ecosystem", project document.

GSFC [Goddard Space Flight Center] (2001), "A Shadow of a Lake: Africa's Disappearing Lake Chad", *GSFC on-line News Releases*, available at ⟨http://www.gsfc.nasa.gov/gsfc/earth/environ/lakechad/chad.htm⟩ (accessed 31 October 2007).

IMF [International Monetary Fund] (1999), *Directory of Economic, Commodity and Development Organizations*, available at ⟨http://www.imf.org/external/np/sec/decdo/contents.htm⟩ (accessed 31 October 2007).

Jauro, A. B. (2000a), "The Lake Chad Basin Vision for 2025", Second World Water Forum, The Hague.

——— (2000b), "Problems and Challenges on Integrated River Basin Management in the Lake Chad Basin", Second World Water Forum, The Hague.

Lambert, T. (2002), "Le modèle de la commission du bassin du Lac Tchad (CBLT)", Atelier Régional sur la Gouvernance de l'Eau, Ouagadougou, 25–27 September, IUCN/BRAO.

LCBC [Lake Chad Basin Commission] (2000), "Integrated River Basin Management. Challenges of the Lake Chad Basin", *Vision for 2025*.

Niasse, M. (2003), "Défis et opportunités de la gestion durable et équitable des cours d'eau transfrontaliers d'Afrique de l'Ouest", paper presented at the Forum Régional Praiai+9: Foncier rural et développement durable au Sahel et en Afrique de l'ouest, CILSS, Bamako, 17–21 November.

Tam, L. (2003), "Adjoint au Secretaire Executif", LCBC, personal discussions, 19 December.

Rangeley, R., M. T. Bocar, R. A. Andersen and C. A. Lyle (1994), "International River Basin Organizations in Sub-Saharan Africa", World Bank Technical Paper No. 250, Washington, DC.

Second World Water Forum (2000), Session "Water and Conflict" note, 17.3.

Transparency International (2003), *Global Corruption Report 2003*, available at ⟨http://www.transparency.org/publications/gcr/download_gcr/download_gcr_2003⟩ (accessed 31 October 2007)

UNDP [United Nations Development Programme] (2003), *Human Development Report 2003*, New York: Oxford University Press.

# Part II

# Emerging security threats

7

# People's encroachment onto Sudan's Nile banks and its impact on Egypt

*Mahmoud El Zain*

## Introduction

The dispersed population distribution in Sudan observed in the 1970s is increasingly tending towards concentration, leading to a range of impacts on resources at the domestic level in Sudan and on water, in particular, in relation to neighbouring Egypt. As a result of increased environmental scarcity[1] and protracted civil wars in Sudan, large numbers of people have been displaced, and they have largely targeted and settled along the banks of the Nile and its tributaries. Although the trend of population concentrating along the Nile and its tributaries in Sudan can be traced back to the 1920s, it has certainly gained added momentum in the past three decades. The rapid population concentration indicates that more people whose livelihoods had been dependent on rain in ecological zones far from the Nile will be clustering along the banks of this river and its tributaries, therefore taking more water from them, and this is precisely what is endangering the Nile waters. The main premise of this chapter is that it is the impact of environmental scarcity on livelihoods that is the immediate cause of Sudan's current increase in demand for Nile water. Thus, rather than rapid economic development, to which high water abstraction is often attributed and which has always aggravated Egypt's fears, it is the very failure of such development in Sudan that is actually now increasing Sudan's demand for Nile water. Thus, as a corollary, it is the pressing questions of livelihood – not of

*International water security: Domestic threats and opportunities, Pachova, Nakayama and Jansky (eds), United Nations University Press, 2008, ISBN 978-92-808-1150-6*

"extravagant" development – that will affect water flowing downstream and therefore strain and/or reshape current and future relations between Sudan and Egypt.

Thus, by highlighting the incidence of population concentration along the banks of the Nile and its tributaries in Sudan, my first aim is to show its magnitude, its causes and whether it will continue. My second aim is to work out some possible impacts on water flowing to Egypt and the likely effects on relations between Egypt and Sudan. I essentially explore the potential of the new population contours in Sudan by viewing them as population–political contours – portraying the pressures they exert at the domestic level and questioning whether they are affecting the historical ties between (northern) Sudan and Egypt. Thus, the chapter is divided into three main sections. The first elaborates on the incidence of population concentration both on a regional scale and in the urban areas along the banks of the Nile and its tributaries in contrast to areas away from these rivers. The second section details the responses of governments in Sudan to population concentration and whether this, in connection with the food security discourse, would lead to increasing abstraction of Nile water and how this affects the flow of Nile water downstream to Egypt. The third section explores the impact of population concentration on the political weight of groups that had developed special ties with Egypt and aspired for unity with it. I question whether the new population contours will intensify identity politics in Sudan and whether this will endanger Egypt's anticipated benefits from the Jonglei Canal.

In order to determine empirically whether or not there is population concentration along the Nile and its tributaries, I shall divide the larger landscape of Sudan into two areas. The first is the area covered by the Nile River system, which I shall refer to as the riverine zone (RZ); the second comprises the remaining parts of Sudan's national territory, which I shall refer to as non-riverine zones (NRZ). As the Nile system extends into all nine regions of Sudan,[2] the division into RZ and NRZ is based on whether a region's inhabited territory predominantly lies in one or the other zone. Accordingly, the RZ embraces the three arid and semi-arid administrative regions of Northern region, Khartoum and Central region, the bulk of whose populations dwell on the banks of the Nile or in the vicinity of the Nile, the Atbara, the Blue Nile and the White Nile. The RZ also includes the three wetter regions of southern Sudan (Bahr al Ghazal, Upper Nile and Equatoria), where rivers and streams pouring into the Nile system cross the largest part of the territories of these regions. The NRZ comprises the regions of Kurdufan, Darfur and Eastern region, which have about 1 per cent, 8 per cent and 18 per cent of their territories, respectively, lying inside the RZ.[3]

## Population concentration in Sudan[4]

Contrary to the thesis that natural population increase causes water scarcity, I argue here that, in relation to the Nile water in Sudan, it is the forces that led to population migration and displacement that seem to be the major cause of this scarcity. This is because the banks of the Nile in Sudan had for centuries not been subject to population pressure – any "extra" population had always moved onto the open plains to the west and the east. In recent history, for about a century between 1820 and the early 1920s, the RZ in northern Sudan experienced large population out-migrations. This characterization of the RZ had, in fact, reinforced a pattern that had prevailed since the seventh century AD. In the second half of the seventh century, the Arab nomadic tribes infiltrating into Nubia in northern Sudan had first settled along the banks of the Nile and then drifted onto the plains to the east and the west of this river. These non-riverine plains were both climatically suitable for pastoralists and remote from the riverine Nubian towns and their restrictive centralized political systems (Awad 1987: 37). The Turkish invasion of Sudan in 1820 marked the beginning of a large movement of population out of the riverine zone into remote areas in the west and the south. Hundreds of thousands were repeatedly on the move from the RZ, escaping the regime of terror that the Turks installed, and they settled permanently in those remote regions (see Warburg 1992; Ibrahim and Ogot 1990). Both the Mahdist nationalist rule (1885–1898) and the British colonial administration from 1898 had their headquarters in the RZ, and had replicated the measures that prevailed during the Turkish rule; as a result, large groups of people escaped to the west and the south (see Mohamed Salih 1999).

### Population concentration in the RZ (the regional scale)

Since the 1910s the millennial pattern of out-migration from the RZ to the NRZ has been permanently reversed and the RZ has become the focus for labour immigrants, who eventually became settlers in this area. The immigrants included West Africans, who, by the mid-1950s, accounted for about 10 per cent of the total population of Sudan (Galal al-Din and Elmustafa 1979: 97), where most of them were engaged as labourers in irrigation schemes (Duffield 1979). By the early 1930s, in addition to the continuing immigration of West Africans, the RZ received large groups of people from within Sudan – descendants or members of groups driven from the RZ by the three regimes mentioned above. Since the early 1970s the RZ has become the refuge of drought- and famine-hit

Table 7.1 The population in the riverine and non-riverine zones in northern Sudan, 1922–2000

| Year | Total population | RZ | % RZ | Average annual change (%) | Central RZ | % Central RZ | Average annual change (%) |
|------|-----------------|-----|------|---------------------------|------------|--------------|---------------------------|
| 1922 | 2,638,000 | 1,113,700 | 42.22 | | 749,800 | 28.42 | |
| 1931 | 4,010,500 | 1,900,400 | 47.39 | 0.57 | 1,521,800 | 37.95 | 1.06 |
| 1956 | 7,479,400 | 3,447,628 | 46.09 | −0.05 | 2,574,569 | 34.42 | −0.14 |
| 1973 | 11,308,765 | 5,636,578 | 49.84 | 0.22 | 4,718,855 | 41.72 | 0.43 |
| 1983 | 15,328,124 | 6,917,525 | 45.12 | −0.47 | 5,834,514 | 38.06 | −0.37 |
| 1993 | 21,266,641 | 10,238,544 | 48.14 | 0.30 | 8,945,268 | 42.06 | 0.40 |
| 2000 | 26,030,908 | 12,850,271 | 49.37 | 0.17 | 11,367,876 | 43.67 | 0.23 |

*Sources*: Aggregate population figures for sub-regions in northern Sudan are calculated for 1922 and 1931 from estimates compiled by Lahmeyer (2002); for 1956 from Department of Statistics (1983); and for 1973, 1983, 1993 and 2000 from Central Bureau of Statistics (2000).

internally displaced persons (IDPs) and since the mid-1980s it has continued to be a refuge for IDPs from war-torn southern Sudan.

My calculations from different population estimates and census data show a substantial increase in the population of the RZ of northern Sudan in general and Central RZ in particular.[5] The riverine population of northern Sudan increased from 42 per cent of northern Sudan's total population in 1922 to 49 per cent in 2000, and that of Central RZ increased from 28 per cent in 1922 to 44 per cent in 2000 (Table 7.1).

Table 7.1 suggests that between 1922 and 2000 the RZ had a fluctuating population, whose relative size increased in four of the periods and decreased in the remaining two. However, if we look at these dynamics over longer time intervals, sufficient to see the trends (i.e. 1922–1956, 1956–1983 and 1983–2000), we may note different dynamics. Thus, the RZ's percentage of the total population had increased by 3.87 points by the end of the first interval (1922–1956) and by 4.25 points at the end of the third (1983–2000), whereas it witnessed a relatively slight decrease (0.97 points) between 1956 and 1983. Yet, the Central RZ's share in the total population increased steadily for all the three intervals. In the first it increased by 6.0 points, in the second by 3.64 points and in the third by 5.61 points. Calculations from Table 7.1 also suggest that the average annual change in the post-1983 period was higher than that of previous periods. Thus, whereas the average annual change in the RZ's share of the total population for the period 1922–1956 was 0.11 per cent, it was 0.25 per cent between 1983 and 2000. In Central RZ it was naturally higher – in the period 1922–1956 the average annual change was 0.18 per cent, and between 1983 and 2000 it reached 0.33 per cent.

*Population concentration in urban areas of Sudan*

According to recorded history, towns appeared in the Nile Valley, i.e. in the riverine zone, in the form of ancient Nubian capitals or royal seats and of trade and religious centres in the period from the sixteenth century to the nineteenth century. However, from the 1820s towns began to increase dramatically on the plains of the rich savannah zone – away from the Nile and its tributaries – and their population size started to compete with that of existing RZ towns – in some cases even overtaking them. In fact, by the late nineteenth century the NRZ (western Sudan) could be considered more "urbanized" than RZ central and northern Sudan. The largest town in Sudan in the early 1880s was El Obeid, the capital of the western region of Kurdufan in the NRZ, with 100,000 inhabitants (Moorhead 1960: 209). El Obeid was thus almost three times bigger than the RZ's Khartoum, the capital of Turkish Sudan, which at the time had 34,000 inhabitants, of whom 8,000 were soldiers (Moorhead 1960: 234).

Since the mid-twentieth century, in contrast, there has been a return to the old pattern of growth of towns along the river banks. Estimates compiled by Lahmeyer (2001) and census data (Department of Statistics 1996) paint a picture of fluctuation in the ranking of towns in Sudan. Between the late 1930s and late 1940s, the NRZ's large towns of El Obeid, Port Sudan, Kassala and Fasher had risen up the rankings, but in the following decades they started to fall back. RZ towns, on the other hand, are increasingly elevated. Besides Omdurman and Khartoum, which now occupy rank 1 and 2 respectively, Khartoum North, which ranked 8 in the early 1920s and 10 in the early 1940s, has been at rank 3 since 1973. Medani, which ranked 6 in 1955 and 1964, is now at rank 4. Wau, which ranked 12 in 1955, entered the club of the 10 largest cities in 1973 and rose to rank 6 in 1983, where it remains. Juba, the capital city of southern Sudan, moved from rank 10 in 1955 to rank 9 in 1973 and maintained its elevation when it ranked 8 in 1983 and 7 in 1993 (for population figures before 1955 see Lahmeyer 2001).

The urban population in Sudan dramatically increased from 0.9 million (8.3 per cent of the total population) in 1956 to 7.5 million (29.2 per cent of the total population) in 1993 and the number of urban areas increased from 68 in 1956 to 143 in 1983. Both the number of new towns and their populations are increasing faster in the RZ than in the NRZ. For instance, out of 14 new towns joining the category of urban areas with more than 10,000 inhabitants, the RZ acquired 10 (6 in the Central region alone, the rest in the Southern region), and the NRZ hosted 4.

Of the 10 largest cities in Sudan, 6 are in the RZ (Table 7.2). The population of these 6 towns increased from 318,400 in 1956 to 4,595,900 in 1993, out of the 10 largest towns' population of 471,700 and 5,869,700

Table 7.2 Population of the top 20 towns in Sudan (riverine and non-riverine) and their percentage increases, 1956–1993

| Rank in 1993 | Town | Location | Population ('000) | | | | Percentage increases | | | | | |
|---|---|---|---|---|---|---|---|---|---|---|---|---|
| | | | 1956 | 1973 | 1983 | 1993 | 1956–73 | 1973–83 | 1983–93 | 1956–83 | 1973–93 | 1956–93 |
| 1 | Khartoum | RZ | 93.1 | 349.1 | 760.7 | 1,063.2 | 274.97 | 117.90 | 39.77 | 717.08 | 204.55 | 1,042.00 |
| 2 | Omdurman | RZ | 113.6 | 309.5 | 513.5 | 1,361.8 | 172.45 | 65.91 | 165.20 | 352.02 | 340.00 | 1,098.77 |
| 3 | Khartoum North | RZ | 45.7 | 150.2 | 301.1 | 988.7 | 228.67 | 100.47 | 228.36 | 558.86 | 558.26 | 2,063.46 |
| 4 | Wad Medani | RZ | 47.7 | 118.0 | 243.3 | 465.0 | 147.38 | 106.19 | 91.12 | 410.06 | 294.07 | 874.84 |
| 5 | Port Sudan | NRZ | 47.6 | 135.1 | 246.5 | 450.0 | 183.82 | 82.46 | 82.56 | 417.86 | 233.09 | 845.38 |
| 6 | Wau (US) | RZ | 8.0 | 53.4 | 177.0 | 383.1 | 567.50 | 231.46 | 116.44 | 2,112.50 | 617.42 | 4,688.75 |
| 7 | Juba (US) | RZ | 10.7 | 56.7 | 155.1 | 334.1 | 429.91 | 173.54 | 115.41 | 1,349.53 | 489.24 | 3,022.43 |
| 8 | Nyala | NRZ | 12.3 | 63.3 | 152.6 | 329.5 | 414.63 | 141.07 | 115.92 | 1,140.65 | 420.54 | 2,578.86 |
| 9 | Kassala | NRZ | 40.6 | 100.5 | 158.6 | 257.9 | 147.54 | 57.81 | 62.61 | 290.64 | 156.62 | 535.22 |
| 10 | El Obeid | NRZ | 52.4 | 92.2 | 145.1 | 236.4 | 75.95 | 57.38 | 62.92 | 176.91 | 156.40 | 351.15 |
| 11 | Kosti | RZ | 22.7 | 60.6 | 102.3 | 173.2 | 166.96 | 68.81 | 69.31 | 350.66 | 185.81 | 663.00 |
| 12 | Jineina | NRZ | 11.8 | 38.6 | 77.3 | 165.9 | 227.12 | 100.26 | 114.62 | 555.08 | 329.79 | 1,305.93 |
| 13 | Gedaref | NRZ | 17.5 | 66.2 | 101.1 | 156.2 | 278.29 | 52.72 | 54.50 | 477.71 | 135.95 | 792.57 |
| 14 | Aweil (US) | RZ | 2.4 | 17.8 | 51.9 | 151.3 | 641.67 | 191.57 | 191.52 | 2,062.50 | 750.00 | 6,204.17 |
| 15 | Yei (US) | RZ | – | 12.0 | 41.4 | 144.0 | – | 245.00 | 247.83 | – | 1,100.00 | – |
| 16 | Malakal (US) | RZ | 9.7 | 37.1 | 76.1 | 136.3 | 282.47 | 105.12 | 79.11 | 684.54 | 267.39 | 1,305.15 |
| 17 | Fasher | NRZ | 26.2 | 54.5 | 80.7 | 131.5 | 108.02 | 48.07 | 62.95 | 208.02 | 141.28 | 401.91 |
| 18 | Sinnar/Madina | RZ | 8.1 | 32.6 | 64.6 | 128.5 | 302.47 | 98.16 | 98.92 | 697.53 | 294.17 | 1,486.42 |
| 19 | Atbara | RZ | 36.3 | 64.3 | 87.6 | 122.4 | 77.13 | 36.24 | 39.73 | 141.32 | 90.36 | 237.19 |
| 20 | Yarol (US) | RZ | – | 14.7 | 40.2 | 110.1 | – | 173.47 | 173.88 | – | 648.98 | – |
| | Top 20 towns[a] | RZ+NRZ | 606.4 | 1,826.4 | 3,576.7 | 7,289.1 | 201.19 | 95.83 | 103.79 | 489.83 | 299.10 | 1,102.03 |
| | 13 RZ towns[a] | RZ | 398.0 | 1,276.0 | 2,614.8 | 5,561.7 | 220.60 | 104.92 | 112.70 | 556.98 | 335.87 | 1,297.41 |
| | 7 NRZ towns[a] | NRZ | 208.4 | 550.4 | 961.9 | 1,727.4 | 164.11 | 74.76 | 79.58 | 361.56 | 213.84 | 728.89 |
| | 7 downstream towns[a] | DS-RZ | 367.2 | 1,084.3 | 2,073.1 | 4,302.8 | 195.29 | 91.19 | 107.55 | 464.57 | 296.83 | 1,071.79 |
| | 6 upstream towns[a] | US-RZ | 30.8 | 191.7 | 541.7 | 1,258.9 | 522.40 | 182.58 | 132.40 | 1,658.77 | 556.70 | 3,987.34 |

*Sources*: 1956 population figures – Department of Statistics (1983); 1973, 1983 and 1993 population figures – Department of Statistics (1996: 160–161); percentage increases are computed.

*Notes*: US = upstream, which coincides with the territory of southern Sudan; DS = downstream.

[a]Computed.

for the two periods, respectively. The relative size of the 6 RZ towns therefore increased from 67.58 per cent in 1956 to 78.30 per cent in 1993. Of the 26 medium and small towns (with a population of more than 50,000 in 1993; see Department of Statistics 1996), 16 are in the RZ. This means that more than 61 per cent of urban areas of this size are in the RZ, and, more importantly, they are growing faster than those in the NRZ (Table 7.2).

## Reasons behind the population concentration in the RZ

The colonial administration and post-independence governments had seized large tracts of RZ lands from traditional farmers and pastoralists, who as a result became landless and moved to and settled in marginal lands (Hassaballa and Eltigani 1995: 29) in the NRZ. Regions that once had subsistence economies have now been taken over by cotton plantations, whose revenues are confined to those directly associated with the state's apparatus – the riverine elite.

Besides making those who had land into landless people, the colonial administration and post-independence governments encouraged traditional farmers to engage in cash-crop production and wage labour, which meant that they would pay taxes (Hassaballa and Eltigani 1995; Mohamed Salih 1999). Thus, marginal lands have been not only overwhelmed by groups whose primary lands had been captured by the state, but also made to produce cash crops and, therefore, have been gradually degraded. Labour migration has increasingly acquired momentum owing to the growing economic disparities between the modern and traditional sectors generated by the expansion of large-scale agricultural schemes and the great anomalies in production systems created by this expansion as well as the environmental hazards it has generated (Abu Sin 1995: 13). Continuing throughout the post-independence era, "voluntary" migration to the RZ has been overtaken since the early 1970s by much higher waves of "involuntary" migration, which have characterized the period since then.

The 1980s marked the beginning of a more rapid and relentless flow of population into the RZ. In fact, since the mid-1960s, "resource capture" by the state has become very intense and larger groups have been ecologically marginalized within a short time span that did not allow for their readjustment. From the mid-1920s until 1970 the total land seized for large-scale irrigated agriculture did not exceed 1.4 million hectares (see Waterbury 1979: 178) and that for large-scale rain-fed mechanized farming was within the order of half a million hectares (Suliman 2000: 124–125). By the late 1980s the aggregate area of large-scale agriculture increased five-fold, generating wide inequalities, especially in connection with mechanized farming. According to Suliman (2000: 131), the licensed area of mechanized farming reached 8 million hectares in 1989 and there was a similar area of unlicensed cultivation. Suliman (2000: 137) points out that more than 7 million hectares are licensed for 8,000 families, whereas traditional rain-fed agriculture accounts for 4 million hectares, which supports 4 million poor farmers. Moreover, since the late 1980s, even more primary land has been seized from traditional farmers and pastoralists. As I shall detail later, by the early 1990s the irrigated area had more than doubled and the area of mechanized rain-fed farming reached 17 million hectares.

The droughts of the 1970s and 1980s, in combination with the economic policies of a socially and ecologically insensitive state, led to the collapse of subsistence economies and left the population of the marginal lands with no option but to move *en masse* towards the river (see Markakis 1998: 90; Abu Sin 1995: 14). "During the drought of 1983–85, the rural societies that had been pushed into fragile ecosystems were the first to starve. As quickly as possible, they moved to the national capital seeking food and shelter and trying to draw attention to their plight" (Hassaballa and Eltigani 1995: 33). Since the early 1980s Sudan has been plagued by persistent famine (Eltigani 1995: 1), accompanied by tense conflicts over resources (see Duany and Duany 2000; Harir 1993). Thus, although the displacement of large groups originated in the early 1970s, it certainly took a much more dramatic course in the mid-1980s when the country faced one of its most severe famines in its post-independence history and when its government failed to deliver food during crisis situations (Cheru 1989: 112). The number of people who died as a result of the 1984–1985 famine rose to 250,000 (Haug 2000: 12; also see Al-Mahal and Omer 2001: 14).

In addition to the impacts of the droughts, the resumption of the civil war in southern Sudan has caused severe famines in which the majority of the 1.5 million who died were victims of war-induced famine (Mohamed Salih 1999: 152). Large groups of people moved from the war zones in southern Sudan into the RZ of northern Sudan. Deepening economic disparities and the impacts of environmental scarcity have resulted in disputes at different levels – local, regional and national. It is these domestic disputes that will trigger yet larger waves of population movement.

As a consequence, in the 1980s and 1990s Sudan had the highest number of IDPs in the world (Suliman 2000: 393). Available statistics show that in 1988 the total number of IDPs had reached approximately 6.8 million. This figure represented 29.1 per cent of the total population of Sudan (Mahran 1995: 64), a very high proportion by any standard. The two main causes of this mass displacement are recurrent droughts and insecurity caused by civil wars and tribal conflicts. Out of the total population in Sudan, those displaced by drought represent 11.2 per cent, and those displaced for security reasons represent 17.6 per cent (Mahran 1995: 64) – i.e. over 38 per cent and over 60 per cent, respectively, of the 6.8 million IDPs mentioned above, leaving only 1 per cent displaced by all other possible causes. The displacement trend continued in the 1990s: "The number of people affected by war and war-induced famine in 1994/95 was some 4.5 million (about 15 per cent of Sudan's population)" (Mohamed Salih 1999: 65). The current civil war in Darfur, raging since 2003, has caused the displacement of 1.8 million people, of whom 90 per cent had lost their livestock (UNEP 2007), which were one of their principal sources of livelihood. Some of these IDPs have already arrived in the RZ towns, and the continuation of the war will mean larger numbers will aim for this zone to escape destruction and seek sources of livelihood.

## Responses to population concentration and Sudan's increasing demand for Nile water

Many researchers have pointed out that population growth reduces water availability or causes water stress and scarcity (Postel 1993: 60; Falkenmark and Lindh 1993: 90). Referring to the Nile waters, in particular, Dickinson and Wedgewood (1984: 35) observed that "[p]opulation growth has led to increasing demand for water for agriculture". The expected effect on the waters of the Nile of the inhabitants of the NRZ has raised concerns before their arrival on the banks of this river, particularly in terms of their increasing numbers. "Periodic drought has affected the Sudan down the ages, but today the *new dimension is a much larger rural population on the desert margins* than ever before; the use of the Nile waters to their capacity merely caused the river to *present new challenges to the riveraine peoples*" (Davies 1984: 152, emphasis added). The failure of subsistence economies and the recent concentration of population in the RZ have made these challenges more acute. This is precisely because large numbers of farming and herding communities from the margins of the desert as well as from other ecological zones have now clustered on the RZ's irrigable lands.

However, it is to be noted that the state has persistently set up restrictive measures to block immigrants/IDPs from reaching favourable areas of the RZ. For instance, post-independence governments reduced the influx of NRZ western Sudanese into the Managil Extension scheme (Shaw 1987: 154), whereas the British encouraged them as labourers and tenancy holders in the Gezira scheme established in 1925. In the late 1970s and early 1980s, the Khartoum municipality authorities adopted what came to be known as the *kasha* – the close observation of rural immigrants, and their capture and "repatriation" to their areas of origin or removal to the so-called "production areas" (for further details on the *kasha*, see Shazali 2000; Suliman 2000: 410–411; Salih 1999). Relocation or eviction and the demolition of IDPs' homes (El-Kheir 1991: 158) and exclusion from urban services (Bannaga 2001: 52) are among the government's restrictive regulations in cities.

Despite these restrictions, the IDPs have prevailed. By the mid-1980s it had become clear that population concentration was continuing and that the IDPs were unlikely to return to their areas of origin. During the Third Democracy (1986–1989), the Umma Party recognized the plight of the IDPs. Out of the official estimate for June 1985 of 1.35 million IDPs, some 600,000 (45 per cent) were located in Khartoum province (El-Bushra and Hijazi 1991: 254). These IDPs "are settled in 23 sites recognised as settlements by the government" (El-Bushra and Hijazi 1991: 254). Following its coup d'état, the National Islamic Front (NIF) government launched a brutal campaign to destroy IDPs' homes (Mohamed Salih 1999: 66) and some IDPs were killed in the process of resettling them (Ahmed 1993: 117). However, the NIF government also resorted to resettling IDPs along lines similar to the policies of the Umma Party. Accordingly, in Khartoum province alone, the number of permanent settlement sites for IDPs reached 38 (Ahmed and El-Batthani 1995: 205).

Some researchers who are known as active NIF cadres and government officials have done extensive research into the IDP subject and have increasingly adopted a political economy approach to the causes of displacement, thus refuting their party's attribution of this phenomenon to God. The causes of displacement were clearly spelled out as being human induced (Bannaga 2001: 31) and, as a corollary, solutions that are not religiously formulated were considered (see Mohammed 2001). These researchers/officials endorsed policies for the rehabilitation and resettlement of IDPs. Al-Mahal and Omer (2001: 79–80), in particular, suggested medium- and long-term solutions to the IDP problem that have direct connections to our discussion. For the medium term, they suggested the construction of agricultural schemes that depend on permanent irrigation, with the aim of absorbing IDP labour. They also suggested that in these schemes, which were to be modelled on the Rahad and New Halfa irrigation schemes, basic services should be provided so that the IDPs would finally settle down and their misfortune would not be repeated every time a new drought occurs. Al-Mahal and Omer proposed, for instance, that a canal could be constructed in a north-westerly direction from the Jebel Awlia dam in order to irrigate 1 million feddan,[6] where diverse farms could be established for animal and plant production and for resettling the nomads. They also recommended the construction of similar schemes in different valleys in western, eastern and southern Sudan.

Recognizing the plight of the IDPs and resettling them have raised some new concerns, important among which is effective engagement in a food security discourse that seems to have placed great emphasis on an "irrigated grains policy".

## Food security: Expanding areas of wheat and irrigated sorghum

Sudan, which was once viewed as the breadbasket of Africa and the Middle East (Shazali 2000; Mohamed Salih 1999), has actually experienced persistent food shortages in recent decades. Viewed in the context of its neighbours, Sudan is actually a late-comer to the club of countries that suffer from hunger and food shortages. Sudan escaped the ravages of the famines that devastated the Sahelian countries in the 1960s and 1970s because its leading economic sector had produced food for internal markets rather than for export (O'Brien 1985: 23–24). "Generally, the Sudan used to have surplus most of the years of sorghum, exporting more than 500 thousand tons annually" (Faki et al. 1995: 458). Subsistence economies have for some time operated productively in the shadow of the dominant mechanized farming subsector, and farmers have maintained their own food surpluses, which they store against short-term food shortages (O'Brien 1985: 26–27; Markakis 1998). Sudan also used to have "more or less a balance in millet", although during this same period it had faced a large deficit in wheat (Faki et al. 1995: 458). It was probably because of this balance in sorghum and millet that Sudan maintained relatively dispersed population settlements, as Waterbury (1979: 9) described it, in contrast to Egypt's concentrated settlements along the banks of the Nile.

Since then, the balance in grains and the concomitant population distribution have changed. "Frequent years of drought during the 1980s have jeopardized the dependable supplies of sorghum and millet from rainfed areas" (Faki et al. 1995: 458). They even caused the 1984/1985 famine and loss of life, as mentioned earlier, and since then Sudan has been haunted by the spectre of famine. "Wheat imports, amounting to three quarters of the annual needs, have exerted a heavy burden on Sudan's meager and deteriorating foreign exchange resources, and involved a worsening of its negative trade balance" (Faki et al. 1995: 458).

Thus, despite the fact that droughts have occurred in Sudan since the 1960s (Markakis 1998), those of the 1980s caused a dramatic decline in crop productivity (Mahran 1995: 67; GAPS 2000; see also Eltigani 1995: 1–2) as well as in livestock numbers (Al-Mahal and Omer 2001: 13–14).

Questions of livelihood started to haunt governments in Sudan from the early 1980s and effected a change in agricultural policies in terms of the expansion of both the area to be irrigated and the crops to be cultivated. These pressures prompted an expansion in wheat production and necessitated resort to the cultivation of irrigated sorghum in addition to expanding the area of rain-fed sorghum.

Until the end of the 1950s the area cultivated with wheat did not exceed 15,000 hectares, and the crop was sufficient to meet needs in northern Sudan as well as in towns. The other parts of the country had been dependent on sorghum, millet and cassava (Abdalla and Nour 2001). Whereas wheat is cultivated through irrigation along the banks of the Nile, all other grains (sorghum in central and eastern Sudan, millet in western Sudan and cassava in southern Sudan) are rain-fed (Abdalla and Nour 2001). "However, with the *expansion of the urban communities* in the last 50 years, food consumption habits have changed, and *wheat consumption has soared* to about a million tons annually. The wheat area expanded from about 75,000 hectares in 1989, to 415,000 hectares in 1992" (Abdalla and Nour 2001, emphasis added). Policies driven by a food security discourse led directly to this expansion. The high proportion of imported wheat, together with the effect of drought on the production of sorghum and millet, "has provided large incentives to expand the utilization of domestic resources in wheat production, although wheat requirements are also intended to be reduced through a promotion of bread-making technology with composite flour" (Faki et al. 1995: 458). The rapid urbanization I described above implies big increases in the area cultivated with wheat.

The area cultivated with sorghum, on the other hand, had witnessed dramatic expansion in the 1940s, when mechanized farming was first introduced to "provide food for the troops during the Second World War and later to feed the growing urban population" (Ahmed and El-Batthani 1995: 195). Its largest expansion, however, followed in the post-independence era, as I pointed out above. An interesting thing with sorghum was that demand for it increased not because of changes in lifestyle per se, but rather because of the very process of expansion in its production. To be precise, payment for the labour involved in sorghum production was partly made in kind (O'Brien 1985: 24) – sacks of sorghum were exchanged for labour, which in this case involved tens of thousands of immigrants. Mohamed Salih (1987: 112) points to a figure of 100,000 labourers who annually participated in the processes of weeding and harvesting in large-scale mechanized schemes. A labour population of this size has certainly contributed to making sorghum the staple food for large groups of people who previously depended on either millet or cassava. In other words, people in western and southern Sudan whose subsistence economies are failing have now become dependent on sorghum. This led to another transformation, the production of sorghum under irrigation, because rain-fed cultivation (both mechanized and traditional) turned out for climatic reasons not to produce enough to meet increasing demand. "With the uncertain situation of sorghum and millet production under rainfed conditions, *irrigated sorghum* has also gained increasing importance" (Faki et al. 1995: 458, emphasis added). One significant change, which enhanced this trend, was that farmers abandoned the cultivation of millet because it is too labour intensive and is vulnerable to birds, and thus is not profitable under market integration (O'Brien 1985: 28). Sharp rises in the prices of cash crops led to diversification away from millet (Umbadda 1981: 110).

Grain production has increasingly taken priority over cotton and groundnuts in the irrigated sector. This becomes more apparent if we compare the average area cultivated with grains to that of cotton and groundnuts in the Gezira scheme for two periods of 10 years, i.e. 1974/1975–1983/1984 and 1984/1985–1993/1994. In the second period, the areas cultivated with sorghum and wheat in the Gezira scheme had increased by 81.2 per cent and 129.7 per cent, respectively, whereas the areas cultivated with cotton and groundnuts decreased by 32.9 per cent and 35.9 per cent, respectively (GAPS 2000: 5). Accompanying this was an expansion in the cultivated area under mechanized and traditional rain-fed farming, yet without attaining food security. The failure to attain food security was attributed to declining productivity in all crops, except for wheat, and to increasing instability and population displacement – the social effects of environmental scarcity. It would appear that the contribution of rural subsistence economies has fallen dramatically or in some areas has stopped altogether. Certainly, displacement has led to a decrease in cultivable areas and livestock production (see Al-Mahal and Omer 2001: 45) and of course has added to the demand for the towns' staple food, i.e. wheat or a combination of wheat and sorghum. The paradox is that in Sudan there are now relatively more food consumers than there were food producers.

## The National Comprehensive Strategy and prioritizing food security in Sudan

In 1992 Sudan adopted the National Comprehensive Strategy (NCS), which was further reinforced in 1994. Associated with the NCS, the food security discourse peaked in the 1990s, being part of a broad mobilization campaign for meeting really pressing needs as well as for gaining support for an authoritarian regime that was unusual in operating against the current of globally espoused democratization. The leaders of the military coup, which was inspired and backed by the National Islamic Front (NIF), had to respond swiftly to the looming food crisis. The NIF officers had coined the slogan "we shall eat from what we cultivate and shall clothe from what we fabricate" (El Zain 2006: 143; 2002), which was to become cherished by them (see Suliman 2000: 411–412). The slogan accurately captured the worries about food insecurity and, as a corollary, appealed to those in the areas of hunger surrounding the big cities in the country, particularly the Tripartite Capital (Khartoum). Khartoum, where popular uprisings had contributed to the toppling of the two previous military regimes, is swollen with the slums of destitute IDPs and its urban poor are increasing rapidly (see Ahmed and El-Batthani 1995: 205). The dangers that Khartoum now poses are inherent in the size of its population, which increased from 1 million in the early 1980s (Davies 1984: 133) to 6.9 million by the end of the twentieth century (Mohammed 2001: 21). Assuming a growth rate of 6.8 per cent (the figure for 1993) (Department of Statistics 1996: 161), Khartoum will have 10.7 million people by 2010.

Khartoum is not the only case of a sprawling town along the river banks in the now entrenched wheat and sorghum zones. As Table 7.2 suggests, all RZ towns, except for Atbara, witnessed dramatic population increases between 1973 and 1993 – increasing their population by between 186 per cent and 1,100 per cent, whereas NRZ towns showed increases between 136 per cent and 420 per cent over the same time span. The 13 RZ towns (in the top 20 category) increased their relative population share from 65.63 per cent in 1956 to 76.30 per cent in 1993, at the expense of the NRZ towns (calculated from Table 7.2).

It was in this situation of town sprawl and population concentration in rural areas in the RZ that the Sudanese felt the need for more water from the Nile to achieve food security. Having the highest number of IDPs in the world, Sudan certainly faces serious food insecurity. Pressures on food security are particularly high in northern and central RZ towns, especially Khartoum, because they are not included in food aid, which is distributed in some parts of Sudan (see Bannaga 2001). In the early 1990s, the Sudanese put their demand for Nile water at 24.5 million $m^3$ (Owda 1999: 58), only to increase this, a couple of years later, to double their current legal share of Nile water of 18.5 billion $m^3$.

In response, the Sudanese government has designed a national strategy for upgrading existing water storage facilities, whose current capacity is around 30 per cent of Sudan's share of Nile water (HCENR 2003). In line with this strategy, the Roseires reservoir is to be expanded from 3 billion $m^3$ to 7.2 billion $m^3$ (Elsheikh 2000: 258–259; HCENR 2003), which means that it alone accounts for 45 per cent of Sudan's current share (HCENR 2003). This strategy also involved the building of other dams such as El Satit and El Remila on the Atbara River and Hammadab and Kajbar on the main Nile (MOCI 1998; see also Muindi 2002).

Table 7.3 Increase in cultivated area by sector and types of crop, 1994/1995–2001/2002

| Subsector | Area (million ha) | | Main crops | % increase |
|---|---|---|---|---|
| | 1994/1995 | 2001/2002 | | |
| Irrigated farming | 1.63 | 3.78 | Sorghum, wheat, cotton, sunflower, groundnuts, vegetables, fruit trees, alfalfa, forage sorghum | 131.90 |
| Traditional farming | 8.21 | 9.12 | Sorghum, millet, sesame, groundnuts, water melon, roselle, cowpea | 11.08 |
| Mechanized farming | 7.93 | 12.60 | Sorghum, sesame, cotton, sugar | 58.89 |

*Source*: Zaroug (2000).

The strategy will take advantage of the currently unused 4.5 billion $m^3$ of Sudan's share of Nile water, in addition to the water "lost" in the Sudd region in southern Sudan (Sudan News Agency 1999).

The anticipated area of cultivation in the 1990s is huge by any standards. "According to the Comprehensive National Strategy 1994/95–2001/2002, the area for grains will increase by 15 million feddans, i.e., 78% more than the area grown in 1992–93" (Abdalla and Nour 2001). As can be seen in Table 7.3, sorghum is the main crop in all agricultural subsectors, followed by wheat in the irrigated subsector. Table 7.3 also reveals that in 1994 the area under irrigation was planned to increase by 132 per cent in the 2001/2002 season, whereas the areas of traditional and mechanized rain-fed farming were planned to increase by 11 per cent and 59 per cent, respectively. The 3.78 million hectares of irrigated crops will need at the minimum 36.7 billion $m^3$ of water – double Sudan's current legal share of Nile water.[7] According to the Food and Agriculture Organization of the United Nations (FAO), there are plans "to increase irrigation to about 2.8 million hectares by the year 2000, almost all to be irrigated by Nile water" (FAO 1997). Even though this area is significantly less than that planned in the National Comprehensive Strategy, it still requires more than 27 billion $m^3$ of water, which is much higher than Sudan's legal share of Nile water.

The planning had been followed by some action on the ground. The 1990s witnessed the launching of two projects, the Great Kenana project and the Rahad project (Phase II). The full implementation of these two projects, in which 1 million feddan and 500,000 feddan, respectively, were to be brought into cultivation in order to achieve food security as well as to increase export revenues, depended on increasing the height of the Roseires dam (Elsheikh 2000: 259). Work on the two canals that were planned to feed the two projects had stopped (Horn of Africa Bulletin 1995) owing to economic hardship and the inadequate international assistance the government receives, which also rendered the dam heightening process very slow (HCENR 2003). The government perceives that the two canals, which were anticipated to be completed in 1997, "would have guaranteed the country's *food security* irrespective of *climatic changes and drought*" (Horn of Africa Bulletin 1995).

Faced with financial difficulties, the government resorted to involving the private sector in small and medium irrigation schemes, which brought a total area of 627,000 feddans under irrigation. This increased the total cultivated area under irrigation from 2,286,000 feddans in the 1988/1989 season to 3,132,000 in the 1991/1992 season, an increase of 37 per cent (Elsheikh 2000: 260–261). Certainly, this is no mean achievement within a period of three years. Some of the small and medium projects that were implemented are clearly identified as food security projects, such as the Atbara Food Security Scheme with an area of 8,000 feddans and the Wadi Halfa Food Security Project with an area of 3,000 feddans (MOCI 1998: 129).

More recently, expansion in the irrigated area started to pick up owing to the facilitation of funds by the Arab Fund, China (Muindi 2002), the Organization of the Petroleum Exporting Countries (Ministry of Finance 2001: 19) and the Islamic Development Bank (MOCI 1998: 131). In 1998, the Northern state's Ministry of Agriculture financed a number of selected projects with an area of 4,000 feddans, and the Programme for Instituting Wheat Farming in this state started in 1999 with the cultivation of 160,000 feddans, which was planned to increase to 400,000 feddans by 2001 (Salih 1999: 15–17). The Northern state "aims at increasing the area cultivated in wheat to 800,000 feddans in the long run. The objective of that increase is to *satisfy 50% of the national need of wheat*" (Salih 1999: 16, emphasis added).

Increases in the area of wheat and sorghum should not be viewed as merely taking over areas earmarked for cotton and groundnuts. The area under irrigation will expand further owing to the desire to increase sugar production (Muindi 2002) and recent campaigns to expand the area under cotton in the major irrigation schemes (FAO 2002; MOCI 1998: 120).

## The aggravation of identity politics: The fate of the Jonglei Canal and decreasing Egypt's prospective water share

If the population contours are as I described above, how will they affect internal politics in Sudan and, therefore, Sudan's relations with one of its most strategic neighbours, Egypt? Based on what I have discussed so far, we can say that the magnitude of recent population concentration is considerable and could effect some significant changes both nationally and internationally in terms of the Nile waters. Elsewhere I have detailed how population displacement/concentration has been used by active urban agents in pushing their own political agendas and how it has effected a shift in the state discourse from development to a religious/ethnic discourse (El Zain 1996, 2002). In the 1980s and 1990s the political party that capitalized most on the presence of IDPs in Khartoum was the National Islamic Front (NIF), which was in alliance with the previous military dictatorship between 1978 and 1985 and has consolidated the current dictatorship since 1989.

With political Islam as its ideology, the NIF was successful in the early 1980s in mobilizing the IDPs in the slums around Khartoum to pressurize President Nimeiri to implement Islamic (*sharia*) laws. After this agenda was met in 1983 the NIF had mobilized the same groups to support the then crumbling regime. The short-lived democracy following the collapse of Nimeiri's dictatorship was not able to consolidate an order that appealed to all citizens regardless of their ethnic/religious background and, as a result, a full-fledged ethnic/religious regime was installed in Sudan in 1989, after the NIF-backed military coup. Pitting the Muslim/Arab north against the largely animist/Christian/African south, the NIF's *sharia* laws have transformed the nature of conflict in Sudan. "The fundamentalist *coup d'etat* of June 1989 did not make economic promises. In fact, what made it possible to rule up to now, despite severe economic difficulties, is its ability to shift the public focus from secular development to religious and ethnic concerns" (El Zain 1996: 528).

The assertion of ethnicity and religion as the NIF regime's source of legitimacy paved the way for strict identity polarization, further fuelled the civil war and prolonged the destruction of southern Sudan and made it too difficult for southern Sudan and northern Sudan to stay together as one country. Recently, most southern Sudanese have come to embrace the view that "[n]othing short of partition will bring an end to the conflict in the Sudan" (Majak 2000: 52). The link to be made here is that southern Sudan, which is likely to secede from northern Sudan, has all the water that northern Sudan and Egypt sought to develop in order to overcome anticipated water shortages. As stated above, Sudan aims to carry out its strategy for food security by using more Nile water, including developing the swamps. The latter was part of a joint deal between Sudan and Egypt in what is known as the Jonglei Canal project for draining the swamp water into the White Nile. In fact, since its inception in 1974, the Jonglei Canal has triggered opposition by southern Sudanese for the economic and environmental disasters it has generated (see de Jong-Boon

1990). However, the most important aspect in relation to identity politics is that the Jonglei Canal has led to mobilization among southern Sudanese because its implementation was seen as an Egyptian re-colonization measure or as an Arab colonization (by both northern Sudan and Egypt). It was therefore incorporated as a component in the ethnic issue that contributed to fuelling civil war in southern Sudan (Hultin 1995: 47).

The scenarios for conflict resolution in Sudan that have been debated so far are a confederal state and, in the extreme case, the splitting of Sudan into northern and southern states. Both scenarios have now become acceptable to the current regime and the opposition. Whereas the second scenario would mean the rejection by southern Sudan of any past agreements signed by "colonial" northern Sudan, the first scenario is likely to give some rights to southern Sudan to benefit from its water resources for its own rehabilitation (El Zain 2006). Over two decades ago, John Waterbury wrote:

> Although southern Sudan is not a sovereign state, it is possible in a *de facto* sense that it might try to lay claim to water in its territory that might otherwise be siphoned off to northern Sudan and Egypt, even though at the present time it may not be able to use that water effectively. (Waterbury 1984: 173)

The civil war, which lasted for 22 years, established the Sudan People's Liberation Army/Movement (SPLA/SPLM) as the de facto power in the largest part of southern Sudan's territory. The Jonglei Canal project came to a stop in 1984 when the SPLA attacked it as one of its earliest targets (Mohamed Salih 1999; Goldsmith et al. 2002), thus bringing to a halt the plans of northern Sudan and Egypt to utilize the waters of the vast swamp region.

## *The changing landscape in southern Sudan and possible water abstraction for resettlement and rehabilitation*

Water utilization in southern Sudan should not be viewed as mere leverage – irrigation was planned for southern Sudan from the early 1970s, when the Jonglei Canal was due to be implemented (see Holt and Daly 1979: 212; Ahmed 1993: 120). Today, more than any time before, the southern Sudanese require water for rehabilitating their devastated region. Besides the damage to subsistence economies caused by the civil war, two other significant changes imply the need to use water for irrigation in southern Sudan. Firstly, drought, which usually affects the regions of northern Sudan, has recently affected even the wetter zones of southern Sudan (Mageed 1994) and, secondly, urbanization in southern Sudan is much faster than in northern Sudan. If urbanization in northern Sudan necessitated the irrigation of thousands more hectares for food production, southern Sudan must be in dire need of irrigation too, and probably more so. Whereas the population of towns in the downstream RZ (northern Sudan) increased between 1956 and 1993 by 1,072 per cent, the population in the upstream RZ (southern Sudan) increased by 3,987 per cent (Table 7.2).

In 1993, around 48 out of a total 170 towns for the whole country were located in southern Sudan.[8] Of the 20 largest towns in the country, the upstream RZ has 6 towns (Table 7.2). In the period 1973–1993 it was this upstream RZ that recorded the highest growth rates, with three of its towns (Aweil, Yarol and Yei) joining the top 20 club. In the period 1973–1993, 4 of these 6 upstream RZ towns (Yei, Aweil, Yarol and Wau) were the fastest-growing towns of this size ever known in the history of Sudan. It is clear that the return of refugees after the Addis Ababa Accord in 1972 and internal displacement following the resumption of civil war in 1983 induced this unprecedented "urbanization".

Thus, at a minimum, resuming the development of the Jonglei Canal implies technical changes to cater for new needs in southern Sudan. Thus, the 1970s deal between Sudan and Egypt will certainly be affected. The chances for Egypt to work out a more beneficial deal are getting fewer and fewer, not only because of the pressing water needs in Sudan, but mainly because Egypt's allies in Sudan are not likely to continue to have the same political influence and commitment.

## Sudan and Egypt: From historical alliance to serious conflict over Nile water

North Sudan and Egypt had for a long time entertained an aspiration for unity. This was manifested ideologically in the "unity of the Nile Valley", hydropolitically in concerted efforts in the face of water demands by upstream Nile riparians, politically and economically in integration in these two spheres (Dellapenna 1997: 132), and militarily in a common defence treaty reached in 1976 (Woodward 1984: 159). Egypt's influence in Sudan continued for quite a long time, and contributed to the generation of the "unity of the Nile Valley" ideology. "In modern times an ideology arose, inspired by the Egyptians but eventually adopted by the Sudanese as their own, that all the peoples of the Nile Valley (but not the Christian populations of the Ethiopian highlands) are one and only the nefarious designs of outside forces have kept them apart" (Waterbury 1979: 43). Yet, not fully controlled by this ideology, Sudan has independence forces driving it towards the south, in contrast to those opting for union with Egypt – the unionist forces – driving Sudan towards the Mediterranean (Haj Hamad 1980; see also Waterbury 1979: 49). At the core of the independence forces is the Umma Party, which is historically "premised on an anti-Egyptian stance" (Mohamed Salih 2001: 80) and stands as the main rival to the unionists.

The driving force towards the Mediterranean has historically shaped and maintained fraternal relations with Egypt. As I understand it, the implicit ideology that underlies the call for "unity of the Nile Valley" stems from the common peasantry of the Nile Valley in Egypt and north Sudan. This relationship is not necessarily the outcome of colonization. Not least, the Nile has created an "imagined community", making its living from the same source and developing similar means of production. The Nile Valley has generated a compatible world view in both north Sudan and Egypt, which makes the aspiration for unity a natural outcome (El Zain 2006). Moreover, "Egyptian and Sudanese enjoy a common ancestry, since the migration of Egyptian traders ( *jallaba*) and tribesmen across the non-visible frontier, started long before Islam came into the region. The coming of Islam in the seventh century A.D. gave an added impetus to that migration" (Warburg 2000: 75). The creation of "Sudan's *new riverain elite*" (Tvedt 1993: 185, emphasis added) during the Condominium rule (1898–1956), in which Egypt was the colonial partner to Britain, sowed the seeds that would make this elite in almost permanent alliance with Egypt. This is basically because the creation of the new Sudan (Tvedt 1993: 185) placed the riverine Sudanese within a larger geography, many times larger than their narrow Valley, in which they were exposed to cultural groups with which they had little in common.

Thus, being imbued with a feeling of a minority, this riverine elite has very often sought the backing of Egypt to maintain its rule, in part against its main political rival, the Umma Party, and in part against other communities it failed to subdue. At the core of the Umma Party is the Mahdist Ansar religious sect, although this party is largely backed by NRZ western Sudanese.[9] The riverine elite also appealed to a wider solidarity with the Arab region and largely contributed to constructing a new identity and divide between an Arab/Muslim northern Sudan and an African/Christian/animist southern Sudan. Thus, the dominance of the riverine elite over power in Sudan has been largely attributed, rightly or wrongly, to the backing of Egypt, which at another level is the leading Arab state. Two incidents that exemplify Egypt's intervention in backing the riverine elite could be mentioned here by way of example. The first was when Egypt helped crush the Mahdists who rebelled at Jazeera Aba in 1970 against President Nimeiri's dictatorship; and the second was when it helped re-install Nimeiri in power after Khartoum was conquered by the troops of the National Front in 1976.[10] In both cases Egypt intervened militarily (Swain 1997: 681), clearly pursuing well-specified ends. "In return for helping [Nimeiri] stay in power, Sudan agreed to construct the Jonglei Canal, which was to begin in 1978" (Swain 2002: 296–297).

President Nimeiri not only agreed to "seize" the lands through which the Jonglei Canal was to be constructed, but also to boost rain-fed cultivation, which Egypt stressed was Sudan's great agricultural potential (see Waterbury 2002: 43). Thus, the "unity of the Nile Valley" is conceivable, probably, only for riverine Sudanese – those who inhabit the arid region of the main Nile (north of and including Khartoum) – whose interests are served by advocating it. Certainly, and more vocally, southern Sudanese who, in the face of injustice maintained by the riverine elite, carried guns for 39 years out of Sudan's 51 years of independent rule are against such unity.

A significant change, which I attribute to the change in the population–political contours boosting the NIF party, took place in the relationship between Sudan and Egypt in the 1990s over Nile water. After the NIF regime assumed power in 1989, protection of Sudan's fair share of Nile water became a foreign policy priority (Ahmed 2001: 7), perhaps the first official assertion of its kind since the 1959 agreement (El Zain 2006). Sudan signed an agreement with Ethiopia in 1991, committing the two countries to the principle of equitable utilization of the waters of the Blue Nile and Atbara rivers. The two countries established a technical joint committee to exchange data and to explore cooperation (Dellapenna 1997: 132–133). By so doing, Sudan jeopardized its strategic relations with Egypt. The significance of the agreement with Ethiopia in changing the old formula for the Nile water is seen in the strengthening of Ethiopia's appeal to equitable entitlement as the guiding principle in the international law of shared rivers (Shapland 1997: 82) in its dispute with Egypt. Thus the stage was set for conflict between Sudan and Egypt.

Sudan's actions in the 1990s increased Egypt's fears. Abdelmalik Owda (1999: 64) observes that Sudan had the idea of building an alliance with Ethiopia for mutually benefiting from water and that this alliance was expected to involve the states of East Africa. Foreign comments on the agreement between Sudan and Ethiopia, in his view, indicate that should these agreements be implemented they would threaten what was achieved in the 1959 agreement (Owda 1999: 58). The assassination attempt on President Mubarak's life in Addis Ababa in June 1995 triggered a fierce war of words between Egypt and Sudan, with the real issue being radical Islamism, which was behind the plot (Warburg 2000: 73). A few days after the attempted assassination, President Mubarak accused Sudan's NIF leader, Turabi, of involvement in the plot and warned of a sharp response if Sudan continued to provoke Egypt (Ali-Dinar 1995; Warburg 2000: 73). The following day, an aide to Turabi told a Lebanese newspaper "that any Egyptian attack on Sudan would become a massacre for Egypt" (Ali-Dinar 1995). A tense atmosphere aggressively loomed. According to Bleier (1997: 117),

Egyptian Foreign Minister Amr Moussa bluntly warned Sudan's Islamic leader Hassan al-Turabi not "to play with fire" after reports quoted him as threatening to cut Egypt's water quota. Information Minister Safwat el-Sherif said Egypt "rejects the hollow threats [on water] from the Sudanese regime. Any [Sudanese] wrongdoing or infringement will be met with full force and firmness". (Square brackets in the original; also see Warburg 2000: 73)

Events on the ground were no less dramatic. In July 1995, military patrols from the two countries clashed in the Halayib Triangle and several Sudanese lost their lives (Warburg 2000: 74). Thus, the sanctity of the blood of "brothers" that was evident in the late 1950s when the two countries were about to clash is now risked and the "sons of the Valley" are at loggerheads. This is very much in contrast to the rhetoric of sisterhood and unity between the two nations.

Given that Sudan has maintained "strategic relations" with Egypt for three decades without interruption, despite periods of serious conflict, the signing of an agreement with Ethiopia without the involvement of Egypt could be seen as the first significant departure from the norms governing the relationship between the two countries. The internal conditions in Sudan that gave rise to this move are severe enough to jeopardize the historical alliance with Egypt. Thus, structural inequality and environmental scarcity, which led to the change in population contours, have contributed, in addition to what I have discussed above, to lessening Egypt's influence in Sudan.

Certainly, the new population contours described in the first section have made the Nile Valley more heterogeneous, demographically and culturally, than ever before. Modern history has opened the boundaries of the historical imagined community to the expansion of empires and the appearance of nation-states. Large territories of the "non-Valley" were annexed to the Nile Valley to create the Republic of Sudan. The populations of the annexed NRZ and upstream wetter RZ, who have been subjected to severe processes of impoverishment caused by persistent "resource capture" and "ecological marginalization" and prompted by drought and civil war, have now moved into the Nile Valley (the arid RZ) on the basis of citizenship offered by the nation-state. Environmental scarcity and civil war have brought into the Valley those who are not included in the historical Valley's imagined community and its advocated unity; they are not only culturally different, but also new contenders for the scarce resources of the Valley. Large segments of these newcomers have now become established dwellers in riverine cities, altering their ethnic demographic balance, and are unlikely to return to their areas of origin. But, most importantly, they exert pressure and make additional demands for Nile water.

The seeds of change in the population contours were present much earlier and probably it was during the 1980s that they came out more aggressively.

> The 1980s were truly a decade of political turmoil and deepening political conflicts. Increasing foreign dependence, food crisis, and social disintegration during the first half of the decade sharpened conflicts and led to collapse of the ruling alliance and a reorganization of the power bloc after 1985. (El-Mekki, cited in El Zain 1996).

Yet, if we look closely at the new population–political contours, we see that the power bloc is not only undergoing reorganization; it is in fact experiencing a significant transformation. Whereas politics in Sudan since independence had been predominantly a game of reshuffling positions among the riverine elite (Harir 1993: 22), it is now clear, given the overwhelming identity politics, that under a fairly representative system of rule the chances of the riverine elite maintaining a monopoly on power are decreasing. In other words, the new population–political contours mean the shrinking of the influence of certain regions within Sudan. In this case, Egypt, which almost exclusively enjoyed the political support of a big group of the population represented by the second-largest political party in Sudan – the Democratic Unionist Party (DUP)[11] – will be affected.

In light of this, the tensions between Sudan and Egypt in recent years could be attributed largely to Egypt's significant loss of sympathizers in decision-making positions in Sudan. The current situation, by bringing people from western Sudan (the electoral base for the Umma Party, which historically maintained an anti-Egypt position) and people from southern Sudan (who always looked suspiciously on north Sudan's relationship with Egypt) to the RZ, gives more weight to the southward-driving forces. Whereas people from southern Sudan have their own tensions with Egypt, those from western Sudan were effectively mobilized by the NIF in the 1980s and 1990s. Sidahmed Khalifa, the editor of *Alwatan* newspaper, observes that the NIF "had built its popular glory, in the past and after it has seized power, on the educated descendants of the Ansar and supporters of the Umma Party in western Sudan" (cited in El Zain 2006: 142). These people were mobilized not only to achieve the NIF's fundamentalist ambitions at the national level, but also to export its revolution to Egypt. In the words of Turabi, ideologue of the NIF regime, "Egypt is today experiencing a drought in faith and religion ..., [but] Allah want Islam to be revived from Sudan and flow along with the waters of the Nile to purge Egypt from obscenity" (cited in Warburg 2000: 74). As I understand it, the emphasis on religion in itself shows the upheaval that the institutions (national and local) had undergone; for, despite the prevalence of "pre-modern" forms of organization, the state institutions in Sudan for quite some time had aspired to adopt and use a "development discourse truth".

Bearing in mind the dramatic population increases in all towns mentioned above, let us examine the ethnic demographic change in Khartoum – the seat of the ruling elite and the laboratory of national politics. According to Mohammed (2001: 20–21), Khartoum is witnessing a dramatic change in its ethnic diversity: the city has rapidly moved towards an African entity from its previous Arab outlook. He states: "Out of the 545,933 population of the 1955 census, about 372,596 were people of an Arabic and Nubian origin, mainly coming from the Northern part of the country, forming approximately 70% of the population." Referring to the same census, he cites the number of people from western Sudan and probably West Africa at 14,935, and people from southern Sudan numbered only 10,833. The percentages of western and southern Sudanese were respectively 3 per cent and 2 per cent of the total population of Khartoum in 1955. Now, the number of people from western and southern Sudan has reached 4 million out of Khartoum's 6.9 million (Mohammed 2001: 21), accounting for 58 per cent of the city's total population. This indicates, according to Mohammed (2001: 21), "that the city has within 46 years, witnessed a great diversion to an African [outlook] and entity". The question now is whether these new population trends will persist, namely that the increase in numbers will continue and that there will be no prospect of return of these groups to their areas of origin.

Figure 7.1 suggests a persistent increase in the population of the Central RZ (Central region and Khartoum) in the decade ahead. Moreover, it is now clear, as one author observes in relation to the Nuba Mountains, "that most of the old migrants and the displaced changed into settlers in Greater Khartoum like most of the displaced from Western Sudan drought-ridden areas" (Al-Karsani 2000: 47).

There is consensus among scholars that the great majority of IDPs will not return to their areas of origin, an indication of the increasing failure of the state to alter the original causes of displacement. Six reasons can be provided to support this view. First, environmental scarcity remains the same – the "conditions that turn drought into famine have not improved; indeed, they have worsened" (Markakis 1998: 91). Civil war, armed banditry and tribal clashes, which all contributed to displacement, are still raging in different regions of the country. Secondly, because of the collapse of local institutions, namely the communal "welfare" system, and the loss of assets of those who migrated, these assets are more likely to have been utilized by those who stay behind or by other IDPs who

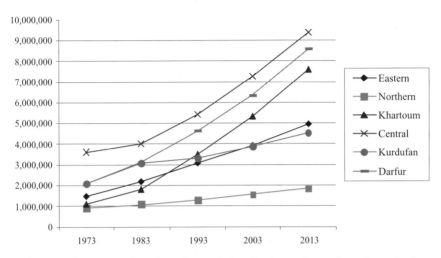

Figure 7.1 Current and projected population in the regions of northern Sudan, 1973–2013.
*Sources*: population figures for 1973, 1983 and 1993 – Central Bureau of Statistics (2000: Table 2); figures for 2003 and 2013 – calculated from Central Bureau of Statistics (2000: Table 18).

settled there. The new users might have effected some significant changes, which complicates property rights issues (Bannaga 2001: 50–51), especially if we consider the communal nature of land tenure systems in large parts of rural Sudan. Thirdly, some of the IDPs have already found their own ways of eking out a living and settling in towns (see Al-Karsani 2000: 39), with new generations being born and brought up in recipient areas. Fourthly, structural inequality is increasing – the original "pull factors" have stayed the same, and development is increasingly being concentrated in the Central RZ (see Abdel Ati 1991: 170). Fifthly, the return of IDPs to their areas of origin is seen as voluntary, as was clearly emphasized in the peace agreement between the government and the SPLA/Nuba Mountains Sector (Ibrahim 2002: 183). Finally, and most importantly, the IDPs are unlikely to return because the government is engaged in programmes for resettling them in the RZ.

## Conclusion

Egypt's historical experience of high population concentration along the banks of its river is rapidly being replicated in Sudan, at least in the north (downstream and central RZ) and to some extent in the form of urbanization in southern Sudan (the upstream RZ). Population concentration along the banks of the Nile and its tributaries in Sudan increases demand for their water, to meet the food needs of the erstwhile producers of millet and cassava in the rain-fed agricultural sector as well as to proceed with economic development in general. The increase in demand for water in the short and medium term might not exceed Sudan's legal share, but it will certainly result in impounding 4.5 billion $m^3$ of water that used to flow freely downstream to Egypt. In the long term, given that the trends of population concentration will continue, Sudan will certainly abstract more water from the Nile by draining the swamp water in southern Sudan for its own use. Even before such further abstraction takes place, tensions between Sudan and Egypt reached a stage little short of direct military engagement.

Ill-conceived economic development policies in Sudan, which deepened structural inequality and caused environmental scarcity, have largely been behind the currently observed water scarcity induced by population concentration. As the last waves of displacement are attributed largely to the persisting civil war, armed banditry and tribal conflicts, it becomes evident that internal conflicts have a serious impact on international rivers. Egypt's role in supporting the riverine elite in northern Sudan had certainly, at least historically, contributed to deepening these regimes of structural inequality and environmental scarcity. As my analysis has shown, this undertaking has clearly proved to be counterproductive. It needs to be reversed for the benefit of the two countries and, particularly, for the benefit of population groups in Sudan.

The scarcity of Nile water caused by the concentration of the NRZ population inside the RZ in reality entails the loss of rainwater in the ecological zones that have for millennia nourished their inhabitants. In this respect, population concentration creates water scarcity through the concealing of rainwater in the NRZ population-sending regions. Within the evolving atmosphere of geo-economic modalities of the post–Cold War era, Sudan and Egypt should work together to alter the old geopolitical modalities in order to regain the lost rainwater. This certainly applies to all the Nile Basin countries and necessitates catering for the needs of different groups in different regions and simultaneously catering for the needs of the wider Nile Basin's ecosystem.

## Notes

1. "Environmental scarcity" will be used here in accordance with Homer-Dixon's (1998: 205) definition, to refer to three forms of scarcity. These are supply-side scarcity (a decrease in the resource supply owing to depletion), demand-side scarcity (owing to an increase in the number of consumers) and structural scarcity (an imbalance in the distri-

bution of wealth and power whereby a few groups get larger slices of a resource through "resource capture" whereas others get smaller slices and undergo "ecological marginalization").

2. Four political regimes have ruled over Sudan since 1820: the Turkish colonization (1820–1885), the Mahdist nationalist regime (1885–1898), the Anglo-Egyptian Condominium (1898–1956) and post-independence governments since 1956. Under these regimes, Sudan's territory has been subject to constant administrative restructuring, with administrative units differing in number from one period to another and being given different names such as province, region, state. In this chapter I shall refer to the administrative units as regions and confine myself to the nine regions existing in the early 1980s.

3. These proportions are based on my own rough estimation from different maps, including the *National Atlas of Sudan*. The 1 per cent and 8 per cent being riverine in Kurdufan and Darfur regions is in connection with the Nile tributary of Bahr al Arab, which crosses part of the southern areas of these two regions. The 18 per cent in the Eastern region is in connection with the Atbara River, which crosses this region. Non-Nilotic rivers and streams are excluded.

4. Elsewhere I have extensively elaborated on the subject of population concentration in Sudan in connection with water scarcity (see El Zain 2003).

5. By Central RZ I refer to the region bounded by the Blue Nile and the White Nile, namely Khartoum province (now Khartoum state) and the Central region (now redivided into four states: Blue Nile, El Gezira, Sinnar and White Nile).

6. 1 feddan = 0.42 hectare.

7. The figure of 36.7 billion $m^3$ is calculated by multiplying the irrigated area by the lowest average water delivery per hectare to the command area of state-run schemes, as reported by the FAO. The lowest average was 9,700 $m^3$/ha and the highest was 12,600 $m^3$/ha. This figure is very conservative if we compare it with actual water usage in 1990, which was 14,000 $m^3$/ha (FAO 1997).

8. No complete figure for towns is available for 1993 owing to civil war. However, given a rate of increase of around 3 towns every year between 1956 and 1983, the total number of towns in 1993 must have exceeded 170.

9. According to Waterbury (1979: 48), the unionists led by Al-Azhari and leaders of the Khatmia religious order were "joined only by their hope that Egypt could aid their respective causes: Sudanese independence on the one hand, and the diminution of the Mahdist Ansar on the other".

10. The majority of both officers and rank and file troops of the National Front, which infiltrated Khartoum from Libya and pushed Nimeiri into hiding for three days, were western Sudanese followers of the Umma Party.

11. The DUP predominates in the whole main Nile region north of Khartoum and in Khartoum province (both share a world view with the Egyptians), as well as in eastern Sudan. Whereas the populations of the main Nile and eastern Sudan are relatively small, in Khartoum, with its large population, the DUP has twice as many adversaries as supporters.

## REFERENCES

Abdalla, A. and Hassan O. A. Nour (2001), "The Agricultural Potential of Sudan", *Executive Intelligence Review*, Vol. 28, No. 8.

Abdel Ati, Hassan A. (1991), "Child Vagrancy in the National Capital: A Growing Social Problem", in H. R. J Davies and M.-E. Abu Sin, eds, *The Future of Sudan's Capital Region: A Study in Change and Development*, Khartoum: Khartoum University Press.

Abu Sin, Mohamed E. (1995), "Environmental Causes and Implications of Population Displacement in Sudan", in E. Eltigani, ed., *War and Drought in Sudan: Essays on Population Displacement*, Gainesville: University Press of Florida.

Ahmed, Abdel G. M. (1993), "The Human and Ecological Impact of the Civil War in the Sudan", in Terje Tvedt, ed., *Conflict in the Horn of Africa: Human and Ecological Consequences of Warfare*, Uppsala: EPOS – Uppsala University.

Ahmed, Adil M. and Atta E. El-Batthani (1995), "Poverty in Khartoum", *Environment and Urbanisation*, Vol. 7, No. 2.

Ahmed, Hassan H. A. (2001), "Determinants, Constraints and Prospects of Sudan–UK Foreign Relations", paper presented to the Sudanese-British Relations Conference, Khartoum, February, unpublished.

Ali-Dinar, A. B. (1995), "Mubarak Assassination Attempt", *Sudan Update*, Vol. 6, No. 11; available at ⟨http://www.sas.upenn.edu/African_Studies/Newsletters/SDate611.html⟩ (accessed 20 November 2007).

Al-Karsani, Awad A. (2000), "The Nuba and the Identity Crisis", *Dirasat Ifriqiyya*, Issue No. 24, pp. 29–54.

Al-Mahal, Abdelazim S. and Amin H. Omer (2001), *Escaping to the Periphery: Issues of Displacement and IDPs in the Sudan*, Khartoum: Research and Publication Department, Research and Translation Institute, International University of Africa.

Awad, Mohamed H. (1987), "The Evolution of Landownership in the Sudan", in El-Fatih Shaaeldin, ed., *The Evolution of Agrarian Relations in the Sudan*, London: Ithaca Press.

Bannaga, Sheref Al-Din I. (2001), *The Displaced and Opportunities for Peace*, Khartoum: Research and African Studies Centre, International University of Africa, Issue No. 39.

Bleier, Ronald (1997), "Will Nile Water Go to Israel? North Sinai Pipelines and the Politics of Scarcity", *Middle East Policy*, Vol. 5, No. 3, pp. 113–124, available at ⟨http://desip.igc.org/WillNile1.html⟩ (accessed 20 November 2007).

Central Bureau of Statistics/Ministry of Finance and Economy, Republic of Sudan (2000), *Statistical Yearbook*, Khartoum.

Cheru, Fentu (1989), *The Silent Revolution in Africa: Debt, Development and Democracy*, London: Zed Books.

Davies, H. R. J. (1984), "Continuity and Change in the Nile Valley: A Geographical Viewpoint", in M. O. Beshir, ed., *The Nile Valley Countries: Continuity and Change*, Vol. 2, Khartoum: Institute of African and Asian Studies/University of Khartoum.

De Jong-Boon, Caroline (1990), *Environmental Problems in the Sudan*, Khartoum and The Hague: Development Studies and Research Centre, University of Khartoum; Institute of Social Studies.

Dellapenna, Joseph W. (1997), "The Nile as a Legal and Political Structure", in Edward H. P. Brans et al., eds, *The Scarcity of Water: Emerging Legal and Policy Responses*, The Hague: Kluwer Law International.

Department of Statistics, Republic of Sudan (1983), *1983 Population Census*, Khartoum.

——— (1996), *Fourth Population Census of Sudan 1993: Analytical Report*, Khartoum.

Dickinson, H. and K. F. Wedgewood (1984), "Nile Waters: The Sudan's Critical Resource", in M. O. Beshir, ed., *The Nile Valley Countries: Continuity and Change*, Vol. 1, Khartoum: Institute of African and Asian Studies, University of Khartoum.

Duany, W. and J. Duany (2000), "Genesis of the Crisis in the Sudan", in J. Spaulding and S. Beswick, eds, *White Nile Black Blood: War, Leadership, and Ethnicity from Khartoum to Kampala*, Asmara: Red Sea Press.

Duffield, Mark R. (1979), "Observations on the Demography of Settlements of the Nigerians in Northern Sudan", in Mohamed A. Galal al-Din and Mohamed Y. A. Elmustafa, eds, *Immigration and Migration in the Sudan*, Khartoum: Economic and Social Research Council, National Research Council.

El-Bushra, Sayed and Nayla B. Hijazi (1991), "The Impact of Greater Khartoum on the Rest of the Sudan", in H. R. J. Davies and M.-E. Abu Sin, eds, *The Future of Sudan's Capital Region: A Study in Change and Development*, Khartoum: Khartoum University Press.

El-Kheir, Osman M. (1991), "Unauthorized Settlements in Greater Khartoum", in H. R. J. Davies and Mohamed E. Abu Sin, eds, *The Future of Sudan's Capital Region: A Study in Change and Development*, Khartoum: Khartoum University Press.

Elsheikh, Abdalla (2000), *Evaluating the Performance and Gain of the National Salvation Revolution in Ten Years 1989–1999*, Khartoum: n.p.

Eltigani, E., ed. (1995), *War and Drought in Sudan: Essays on Population Displacement*, Gainesville: University Press of Florida.

El Zain, Mahmoud (1996), "Tribe and Religion in the Sudan", *Review of African Political Economy*, Vol. 23, No. 70.

——— (2002), "The Passing of Development Discourse and Its Successors: The Case of the Sudan", paper presented at the 50th ISS Anniversary Conference: Globalisation, Conflict and Poverty, Institute of Social Studies, The Hague, 7–9 October, unpublished.

——— (2003), "Population Concentration and Water Scarcity in the Nile Basin: The Imperatives of International Co-operation and Sustainability", paper presented at the 3rd World Water Forum, Session EN&F-06, Kyoto, 16–23 March, unpublished.

——— (2006), "Reshaping the 'Political': The Nile Waters of the Sudan", in T. Tvedt and R. Coopey, eds, *A History of Water: Vol. II The Political Economy of Water*, London: I. B. Tauris.

Faki, Hamid H. M., Yousif T. Gumaa and Mohamed A. Ismail (1995), "Potential of the Sudan's Irrigated Sector in Cereal Grains Production: Analysis of Various Policy Options", *Agricultural Systems*, Vol. 48.

Falkenmark, Malin and Gunnar Lindh (1993), "Water and Economic Development", in Peter H. Gleick, ed., *Water in Crisis: A Guide to the World's Fresh Water Resources*, New York and Oxford: Oxford University Press.

FAO [Food and Agriculture Organization] (1997), "Irrigation Potential in Africa: A Basin Approach", FAO Land and Water Bulletin 4, FAO Land and Water Development Division, available at ⟨http://www.fao.org/docrep/W4347E/w4347e0k.htm⟩ (accessed 20 November 2007).

——— (2002), "Special Report FAO/WFP Crop and Food Supply Assessment Mission to Sudan", 24 December, available at ⟨http://www.fao.org/WAICENT/faoinfo/economic/giews/english/alertes/2002/SRSUD120.htm⟩ (accessed 20 November 2007).

Galal al-Din, Mohamed A. and Mohamed Y. A. Elmustafa, eds (1979), *Immigration and Migration in the Sudan*, Khartoum: Economic and Social Research Council, National Research Council.

GAPS [Group for Alternative Policies for Sudan] (2000), "Towards a Strategic Framework for Sustainable Agricultural Development in the Sudan", paper presented to the Agricultural Policies Workshop, Cairo, 21–25 January.

Goldsmith, Paul, Lydia A. Abura and Jason Switzer (2002), "Oil and Water in Sudan", in Jeremy Lind and Kathryn Sturman, eds, *Scarcity and Surfeit: The Ecology of Africa's Conflicts*, Pretoria, South Africa: Institute for Security Studies, available at ⟨http://www.iss.co.za/PUBS/BOOKS/Scarcity+Surfeit/Main.html⟩ (accessed 20 November 2007).

Haj Hamad, Mohamed A. G. (1980), *Sudan: The Historical Predicament and the Future Horizons*, Beirut: Dar El Kalima for Publication.

Harir, Sharif (1993), "Marginalization of Conflict, Displacement and the Legitimacy of the State: A Case from Dar Fur, Western Sudan", in Terje Tvedt, ed., *Conflict in the Horn of Africa: Human and Ecological Consequences of Warfare*, Uppsala: EPOS – Uppsala University.

Hassaballa, O. and E. Eltigani (1995), "Displacement and Migration as a Consequence of Development Policies in Sudan", in E. Eltigani, ed., *War and Drought in Sudan: Essays on Population Displacement*, Gainesville: University Press of Florida.

Haug, R. (2000), "Livelihood Security among Pastoralists in Northern Sudan: Post-Hunger Development in a Country at War", Noragric Working Paper No. 19, Noragric Centre for International Environment and Development Studies, NLH Agricultural University of Norway, available at ⟨http://www.nlh.no/noragric/publications/workingpapers/noragric-wp-19.pdf⟩ (accessed 20 November 2007).

HCENR [Higher Council for Environment and Natural Resources], Republic of Sudan Ministry of Environment and Physical Development (2003), *Sudan's First National Communications under the United Nations Framework Convention on Climate Change*.

Holt, P. M. and M. W. Daly (1979), *The History of the Sudan: From the Coming of Islam to the Present Day*, London: Weidenfeld & Nicolson.

Homer-Dixon, T. F. (1998), "Environmental Scarcity and Mass Violence", in Gearoid O'Tuathail et al., eds, *The Geopolitics Reader*, London and New York: Routledge.

Horn of Africa Bulletin (1995), "Sudan's Irrigation Plans Blocked by Cash Crunch", 10 August; available at ⟨http://www.sas.upenn.edu/African_Studies/Newsletters/HB7895_SUD.html⟩ (accessed 20 November 2007).

Hultin, Jan (1995), "The Nile: Source of Life, Source of Conflict", in Leif Ohlsson, *Hydropolitics: Conflicts over Water as Development Constraint*, London and New Jersey: University Press, Dhaka, and Zed Books.

Ibrahim, Hamid E. (2002), *In Search of the Absent Wisdom and Lost Conscience: An Attempt at Understanding Tribal Relationships and the Dynamics of War and Peace in the Nuba Mountains*, Khartoum: n.p.

Ibrahim, Hassan A. and B. A. Ogot (1990), "The Sudan in the Nineteenth Century", in Ade J.F. Ajayi, ed., *General History of Africa, Vol. VI: The Nineteenth Century until 1880*, California: Heinemann, UNESCO.

Lahmeyer, Jan (2001), "Sudan Historical Demographical Data of the Urban Centers", available at ⟨http://www.populstat.info/⟩, updated 8 March 2004.

———— (2002), "Sudan Historical Demographical Data of the Administrative Division", available at ⟨http://www.populstat.info/⟩, updated 8 March 2004.

Mageed, Yahya A. (1994), "The Nile Basin: Lessons from the Past", in Asit K. Biswas, ed., *International Waters of the Middle East: From Euphrates-Tigris to Nile*, Bombay, Delhi, Calcutta, Madras: Oxford University Press.

Mahran, Hatim A. (1995), "The Displaced, Food Production, and Food Aid", in E. Eltigani, ed., *War and Drought in Sudan: Essays on Population Displacement*, Gainesville: University Press of Florida.

Majak, Damazo D. (2000), "Rape of Nature: Environmental Destruction and Ethnic Cleansing in the White Nile Basin", in J. Spaulding and S. Beswick, eds, *White Nile Black Blood: War, Leadership, and Ethnicity from Khartoum to Kampala*, Asmara: Red Sea Press.

Markakis, John (1998), *Resource Conflict in the Horn of Africa*, Thousand Oaks, CA: Sage Publications.

Ministry of Finance (2001), "Irrigated Agricultural Schemes", *Al-Iqtisaadi*, No. 48.

MOCI [Ministry of Culture and Information] (1998), "Sudan 1998", Khartoum: External Information Secretariat General, Ministry of Culture and Information.

Mohamed Salih, Mohamed A. (1987), "The Tractor and Plough: The Sociological Dimension", in M. A. Mohamed Salih, ed., *Agrarian Change in the Central Rainland: Sudan*, Uppsala: Scandinavian Institute of African Studies.

———— (1999), *Environmental Politics and Liberation in Contemporary Africa*, Dordrecht: Kluwer Academic Publishers.

———— (2001), *African Democracies and African Politics*, London: Pluto Press.

Mohammed, Hassan M. (2001), "The Refugees and Displaced Issue and the Changing Character of Khartoum", *Dirasat Ifriqiyya*, No. 25.

Moorhead, Alan (1960), *The White Nile*, London: Hamish Hamilton.

Muindi, Matthias (2002), "Sudan: Dam Could Provoke Water Wars", *AFRICA-NEWS*, January, available at ⟨http://web.peacelink.it/afrinews/70_issue/p8.html⟩ (accessed 20 November 2007).

O'Brien, Jay (1985), "Sowing the Seeds of Famine: The Political Economy of Food Deficits in Sudan", *Review of African Political Economy*, Vol. 12, No. 33.

Owda, Abdelmalik (1999), *Egyptian Policy and the Nile Waters in the Twentieth Century*, Cairo: Centre for Political and Strategic Studies.

Postel, Sandra (1993), "Water and Agriculture", in P. H. Gleick, ed., *Water in Crisis: A Guide to the World's Fresh Water Resources*, New York: Oxford University Press.

Salih, Halima A. A. (1999), "Troubled Waters", *Sudanow*, Vol. 23, No. 7.

Shapland, Greg (1997), *Rivers of Discord: International Water Disputes in the Middle East*, London: Hurst & Company.

Shaw, D. J. (1987), "The Managil South-Western Extension: An Extension to the Gezira Area", in El-Fatih Shaaeldin, ed., *The Evolution of Agrarian Relations in Sudan*, London: Ithaca Press.

Shazali, Salah (2000), "Effecting Development: Reflections on the Transformation of Agro-Pastoral Production Systems in Eastern Sudan", in L. Leif Manger and Abdel Ghaffar M. Ahmed, eds, *Pastoralists and Environment: Experiences from the Greater Horn of Africa*, Addis Ababa: OSSREA.

Sudan News Agency (1999), "News Report", Khartoum, 6 November.

Suliman, Mohamed (2000), *Sudan's Civil Wars: New Perspective*, Cambridge: Cambridge Academic Press.

Swain, A. (1997), "Ethiopia, the Sudan, and Egypt: The Nile River Dispute", *Journal of Modern African Studies*, Vol. 35, No. 4, pp. 675–694.

—— (2002), "The Nile River Basin Initiative: Too Many Cooks, Too Little Broth", *SAIS Review*, Vol. 22, No. 2, pp. 293–308.

Tvedt, Terje (1993), "The River Nile as Stick and Carrot: Changing Water Policies in the Aftermath of World War I", in Terje Tvedt, ed., *Conflict in the Horn of Africa: Human and Ecological Consequences of Warfare*, Uppsala: EPOS – Uppsala University.

Umbadda, Siddig (1981), "Socio-economic Aspects of Environmental Deterioration in Northern Kordofan (Sudan)", *Sudan Journal of Development Research*, Khartoum: Economic and Social Research Council.

UNEP [United Nations Environment Programme] (2007), *Sudan: Post-Conflict Environmental Assessment*, Nairobi: UNEP Publications.

Warburg, Gabriel R. (1992), *Historical Discord in the Nile Valley*, London: Hurst.

—— (2000), "The Nile Waters, Border Issues and Radical Islam in Egyptian–Sudanese Relations, 1956–1995", in J. Spaulding and S. Beswick, eds, *White Nile Black Blood: War, Leadership, and Ethnicity from Khartoum to Kampala*, Asmara: Red Sea Press.

Waterbury, John (1979), *Hydropolitics of the Nile Valley*, Syracuse: Syracuse University Press.

—— (1984), "The Near-Term Challenge of Managing Resources in the Nile Basin", in Mohamed O. Beshir, ed., *The Nile Valley Countries: Continuity and Change*, Vol. 1, Khartoum: Institute of African and Asian Studies, University of Khartoum.

—— (2002), *The Nile Basin: National Determinants of Collective Action*, New Haven, CT: Yale University Press.

Woodward, Peter (1984), "Some Dimensions of Neighbour-State Relations in the Nile Valley", in M. O. Beshir, ed., *The Nile Valley Countries: Continuity and Change*, Vol. 1, Khartoum: Institute of African and Asian Studies, University of Khartoum.

Zaroug, Mahgoub G. (2000), "Country Pasture/Forage Resource Profiles (Sudan)", FAO, Grassland and Pasture Crops, May, available at ⟨http://www.fao.org/ag/AGP/AGPC/doc/Counprof/sudan.htm⟩ (accessed 20 November 2007).

# 8

# Inter-basin water transfers as a technico-political option: Thai–Burmese projects on the Salween River

*Bastien Affeltranger*

## Introduction

For several years now, Thailand has been confronted with chronic pressures on water that threaten irrigation, the filling of dams and reservoirs, as well as the usual discharge of some rivers. This situation, exacerbated by drought episodes, has induced localized water shortages on several occasions. Water scarcity is accompanied by rising tensions among users – in both urban and rural areas – as well as among provinces (Postel and Wolf 2001; OEPP 1997; *Bangkok Post* 2000). Technical, economic and political factors converge to limit the number of options available to the Thai government.

In order to increase the water supply, the authorities have been considering – or in some cases have implemented – inter-basin water transfers. In some cases, these resources involve a transboundary basin – the Mekong. In doing so, Thailand seeks to externalize its water supply and to avoid the domestic reluctance to build new hydraulic infrastructure. In addition, Thailand also aims at strengthening its position as a key regional player in the regional power grid. The Salween River, which originates in China and flows down through Myanmar and Thailand, offers a good illustration of how tapping a transboundary river basin can help a government cope with its domestic public opinion.

The chapter is organized as follows. First, I explain the reasons for, and the structure of, Thailand's water scarcity. Secondly, I describe the (scarce) means and resources available to the authorities to address the

*International water security: Domestic threats and opportunities, Pachova, Nakayama and Jansky (eds), United Nations University Press, 2008, ISBN 978-92-808-1150-6*

situation. Thirdly, I introduce the hydraulic projects on the Salween as an example.


# Why is Thailand facing a situation of water scarcity?

Ohlsson and Turton (1999) distinguish a *first-order* type of water scarcity (where the available water does not match needs) from a *second-order* type (where the available water does meet needs in theory, but where conditions of water sharing do not allow universal access to water). Thailand is confronted with situations of both first- and second-order water scarcity. There are few options for solving these problems, as explained in the following sub-sections.

## *Geographical background*

Located between 12° and 20° North, the Kingdom of Thailand covers 513,115 km². The country has a vast central plain, drained by the Chao Phraya River. The north-eastern region is composed of the Khorat Plateau. In the north there are hills; in the west, a mountain range; in the south, an isthmus between the Gulf of Thailand and the Andaman Sea. The country shares borders with Myanmar (1,800 km), the Kingdom of Cambodia (803 km), the Kingdom of Laos (1,754 km) and Malaysia (506 km).

The climate of Thailand is tropical, warm and humid, with three seasons: dry (March to April), rainy (May to October) and cool (November to February). Everywhere but in the south, some 85 per cent of precipitation occurs in the rainy season; rainfall patterns exhibit strong sub-regional contrasts – between 1,000 and 6,000 mm/year (Bogardi 1997). Thailand has some 25 major river basins (Shivakoti 2000; Yaowalert 2002), and shares several transboundary basins (Salween, Mekong).

## *Drought characteristics*

Thailand relies on an annual total of 110 km³ of renewable freshwater. The per capita available volume is 1,854 m³/year[1] – though ranging between 1,256 m³ and 5,109 m³ (World Bank 2001). In comparison, neighbouring Myanmar relies on, respectively, 1,082 km³ and 22,719 m³/capita/year.

Official Thai climate statistics reveal a decrease in precipitation over the past 40 years (OEPP 1996), and drought has become chronic in the dry season (Royal Irrigation Department 2003; Krairapanond and Atkinson 1998). Deforestation and the type of soil are aggravating factors (Krairapanond and Atkinson 1998). The north-eastern region of Khorat illustrates this accumulation of factors: with 40 per cent of the national available area for agriculture, this region accounts for less than 25 per cent of total agricultural production. According to the government, in 1997, 63 provinces (over 75 per cent) were affected by drought. The water level in major dams has also decreased (Kongrut 1999).

On several occasions, droughts forced the authorities to restrict public access to water – sometimes running the risk of jeopardizing the rice harvest. Also in 1997, farmers were encouraged to grow corn or soy instead of rice, in order to reduce water consumption.[2] In Bangkok, the domestic water supply was interrupted – triggering complaints about the huge water demand of the tourism sector. Also in response to water scarcity, the state authorities decided to pump groundwater, causing localized subsidence – for instance in the vicinity of Bangkok (OEPP 1996; Inchukul 1999). The number of privately owned tubewells also rose.

## Why water demand keeps growing

A first factor in the increase in the demand for water is export-oriented agriculture (rice). The absence of water pricing means there is no incentive for farmers to reduce their consumption and improve irrigation efficiency (Kumar and Young 1996). According to the Food and Agriculture Organization (FAO), irrigation accounts for more than 80 per cent of water abstraction (FAO-Aquastat 1997).

A second factor is population growth. According to the United Nations Development Programme (UNDP 1999), the population of Thailand was 62 million in 1999, compared with 41.1 million in 1975. Consequently, water demand is growing. The ageing supply network is also a cause of major losses in the distribution of water (Janchitfah 2000).

The rise of industrial and tourism activities is another factor. In 1987–1997, the so-called "Golden Age" of the Thai economy (mean annual growth rate of around 9 per cent) witnessed a transition in the structure of the economy and wealth production from agriculture to industry. The industrial sector is responsible for rising demand – and rising pollution, as is for instance the case in the lower reaches of the Chao Phraya (World Bank 2001).[3]

## The energy market: A key factor

Both national and regional demand for electricity in Thailand have played a role in increasing the demand for water. Historically, the key factor in hydroelectricity development in the Mekong subregion was Thai demand for electricity.[4]

In the years before the 1997 financial crisis, Thailand had been experiencing a period of strong economic growth. Consequently, demand for electricity also rose, by 13 per cent in 1987 and 15 per cent in 1988–1989 (JBIC 2000). Because the Thai energy sector could not meet the demand (Oxfam 1998; Pataud-Celeriez 1999), neighbouring countries considered that investing in power production capacities would be a wise move. However, the Thai financial crisis of 1997 was accompanied by a decrease in Thai demand for electricity, thus revealing overcapacities in the country – and in the region. In many cases, analysts and managers had to temper their expectations in terms of returns on investment for newly built hydropower dams or infrastructure. In this relatively weakened economic context, the Thai energy sector experienced a period of deregulation. In addition, the national electricity company EGAT lost market share to private producers of electricity – often coal-burning facilities with operating costs lower than those of hydropower dams (Oxfam 1998).

Overcapacities in power production exposed countries in the region – especially Laos – to a semi-monopoly situation to the advantage of EGAT, which was both a producer and a purchaser of electricity. With such bargaining clout, EGAT was able to renegotiate electricity prices (Oxfam 1998), and much more.[5] In addition, hydropower developments in neighbouring countries helped EGAT reduce its financial commitment to new hydraulic infrastructure (Khampa 2002).

EGAT's strategy has direct consequences for new hydropower infrastructure construction programmes in the region. As explained later in the text, EGAT's strategy is driven not only by power grid considerations, but also by political considerations. In short, the government authorities in Bangkok want to avoid confrontation with a growing civil society that is increasingly active in the field of water resources management. Indeed, according to some observers, EGAT's hydropower strategy could be related to the water scarcity situation in the country. In 1998 for instance, an analysis published in the *Bangkok Post* newspaper (Noikorn 1998) asserted that overproduction of electricity had led to the unnecessary release of water from reservoirs, thus threatening the water supply to the agricultural and urban sectors.

## Thailand: A strong political influence

Addressing the domestic growth in water demand is not the only reason the Thai authorities want to see hydropower infrastructure develop in *other* countries of the region. As a diligent follower of the Southeast Asian "dragon" economic model, it is clear that Thailand can be proud of its achievements in terms of economic development. The country was however severely hit by the 1997 financial crisis, ranking second in the greater region (after Indonesia) in terms of socio-economic damage. Although gross domestic product (GDP) quadrupled between 1986 and 1997, the financial crisis caused a "breach in the social fabric, in a society well-known for having always been strongly inegalitarian" (Golub 2001).

Despite these weaknesses, Thailand remains an influential player in the subregion (Selth 2001). This has triggered resentful feelings, and the perception that this influence might well turn into domination. Laos is a clear example of this influence. Indeed, half of imports in Laos and a large share of foreign investment come from Thai sources. "Thailand is the China of the Lower Mekong", as an observer of the subregion has commented.[6] Nam Theun 2 dam (681 MW) was built by a consortium of five international companies, of which three are Thai (Pataud-Celeriez 1999). The Thai influence also penetrates language, television, music and other cultural dimensions of Laotian society. The authorities in Vientiane fear that national identity might be in jeopardy, and have tried to react by reactivating figures of the country's history (Ehrlich 2003). Hostility against Thai influence is also noticeable in Cambodia, with riots and the burning of the Thai embassy.

## Addressing water demand: Options available to the Thai government

Although it is not clear whether government agencies in charge of water issues always act in a coordinated way (Krairapanond and Atkinson 1998), the overall approach to meeting water demand is basically a supply-side one. I explain below how the lack of technical options *within* the country is forcing the Thai authorities to rely increasingly on transboundary water resources.

### Is building new dams an option?

In technical terms, it appears that the best sites for building dams and reservoirs on Thai national territory have already been utilized. Moreover, in economic and financial terms, it is unlikely that Thailand will still be willing to undertake new programmes for the construction of hydropower facilities. The return on investment in such new infrastructure appears doubtful. Despite population growth and an expected rise in agricultural demand, this sector of activity now represents less than 10 per cent of GDP.[7] According to the Thai government, the increasing Thai demand for water resources will be driven less by irrigation than by industry, urbanization and services (Royal Irrigation Department 2003).

Politically, the situation is not easy for the Thai government. Political ecology in the country is increasingly similar to what can be found in the rest of the world, where hydropower dams generate increasing public dissent (Postel 1999: 81–82). Opponents of the building of new hydraulic infrastructure tend to be radical (Pataud-Celeriez 1999). The lack of public debate and participatory processes is also criticized (Inchukul 1997). The Thai state actually acknowledges that it has long privileged supply-side options for addressing water demand: "the State has emphasised supply management and engineering solutions. Other instruments such as demand side management tools are yet to be developed" (OEPP 1997).

Environmental advocacy movements are barely tolerated by the state, when not simply excluded from political debate – in spite of apparently progressive environmental legislation (East 2001). In fact, environmental advocacy is seldom – if ever – disconnected from broader political considerations. The discourse on environmental protection and sustainable development is usually accompanied by criticism of existing structures of political power. "Environmental NGOs [non-governmental organizations] and civil society movements play a major role in changing power structure, decentralize natural resources management and acknowledge the rights of communities to choose a development path outside neoliberalism" (Boonchai 2001).

The political ecology elements described above are fuelling a negative representation of the social acceptability of hydropower-related infrastructure. Consequently, the Thai authorities are reluctant to build new dams or reservoirs *within* the country. Maintaining power and limiting social instability are at the top of the authorities' agenda (Ryder 1996).

## Is water pricing an option?

Water pricing has been developing in Thailand since the end of the 1990s, in a context of the strong indebtedness of the agriculture sector. Academics and environmental activists were the first to urge the government to set or raise water prices, so that the value of water can be assessed and environmental costs can be internalized (Noikorn 1997). Until that time, water supply was based on the irrigated surface area (5 *baht/ rai*[8]) and billed regardless of the volume provided.

In 1999, the Asian Development Bank (ADB) and the International Monetary Fund (IMF) agreed on a US$600 million loan to the Thai agricultural sector. As part of the conditionalities related to this loan, the Bangkok government drafted a Law on Water Resources, which introduced an irrigation tax (Arunmas 1999). According to the text of this law, the state would invest in infrastructure and only exports would be taxed. This conditionality was clearly perceived as a threat by the agricultural sector and the NGO sector. This prompted the Thai government to renegotiate the conditions of the loan (*Bangkok Post* 1999).

The ADB reviewed its conditions and the objective of water pricing was reframed in softer terms as "cost recovery" for new infrastructure (Noikorn and Arunmas 1999). In addition, poorer users of the resource would be exempt from taxation. A pilot implementation in the Mae Klong Basin, however, triggered public dissent (Hongthong and Tangwisutijit 2000), although some farmers welcomed the government decision to price water supply (Junturasima 2000; Hongthong and Tangwisutijit 2000).

*Participation: Making changes in water demand more acceptable?*

Although Thai law gives the state ownership of water resources, environmental advocacy movements have been asking since the late 1990s for a more participatory approach to the management of the resource (Noikorn 1997).

Historically, water resources management has been successfully operated at the local level in Thai villages (Yaowalert 2002). Since the "green" agricultural revolution, new ways of managing irrigation have been developed, in which the state plays an increasing role, for instance in building dams and reservoirs and managing the supply of fertilizers. The approach then was to consider dams and similar infrastructure as assets for socio-economic development and necessary to the modernization of the country (Sneddon 1998). This paradigm has dominated Thai bureaucratic thought ever since (Sretthauchau 2000). For environmental activists, dams are a source of tension and conflict in Thai society (Boonchai 2001). Elites (in the bureaucracy, in politics and in the economy or financial sector) are under NGO scrutiny for having marketed natural resources (teck forests, land, etc.) at the expense of the rest of society (Boonchai 2001). It is a fact that the 1997 crisis was an incentive for the Thai state to privatize the management of much of national natural resources.

In this context of strong distrust between the state and civil society, the few initiatives to develop participatory (user-based) management of water resources have received little if any public opinion support (Shivakoti 2000; RMAP 2003).

# The Salween River: A hydropolitical escape route?

Confronted with increasing demand for water and water scarcity, in the late 1990s the Thai government reactivated a project to divert part of the flow of the Salween River. A study of the hydraulic potential of the river had also been conducted in 1991 and 1993 (Onta et al. 1994). The project had been abandoned for financial reasons.

## The Salween River

The Salween River originates in the Tibetan plateau in the People's Republic of China (see Figure 8.1), where other major rivers (the Mekong, the Yangtze, the Huanghe) also originate.

The Salween River travels through Yunnan province (in China) and Shan and Kayah states in Myanmar, forms the Thai–Burmese border, and eventually drains Kachin state (Myanmar), emptying into the Gulf of Moattama (Martaban) in the Andaman Sea. The 244,100 km$^2$ river basin of the Salween (Wolf et al. 1999)[9] is shared by China (52.43 per cent), Myanmar (43.85 per cent) and Thailand (3.71 per cent).

Land cover is mainly vegetal, with some 91.7 per cent in forests and grassland (WRI 2001). The length of the Salween is 2,400 km, and it has an average discharge of 3,784 m$^3$/sec and an annual volume of 124 km$^3$. Depending on the season (wet or dry), discharge can vary between 1,730 and 5,831 m$^3$/sec (ORST 2003). The Salween Basin has some 5 million inhabitants (ORST 2003), so the population density is very low (22/ km$^2$). This figure is to be compared with the 122/km$^2$ density of the Chao Phraya Basin in Thailand. Consequently, the per capita amount of water available on the Salween is very high, at some 23,796 m$^3$ per year.

The basin climate is influenced by the south-west monsoon (May to October) and the north-east monsoon (November to April). Mean precipitation is 2,000 mm in the upstream reaches, 1,200 mm in the middle reaches and 4,000–5,000 mm in the downstream reaches). Until recently the Salween regime was not well known, as only two measuring stations had been installed on the river's main stem – one in Myanmar and one in Thailand. In Thailand, however, several tributaries of the Salween have received hydrometric networks or equipment (Pai, Mae Rit, Lamao, Ngao, Yuam, Moei).

## Hydroelectric and water transfer projects on the Salween

Since the late 1970s, the governments of Thailand and Myanmar, along with national academics and international consultants, have conducted several studies to assess the hydraulic potential of the Salween River.

Both the water transfer and the hydropower capacities of the Salween have been assessed. In theory, the loss in altitude (1,600 metres over the whole length of the river) does indeed offer promising prospects for

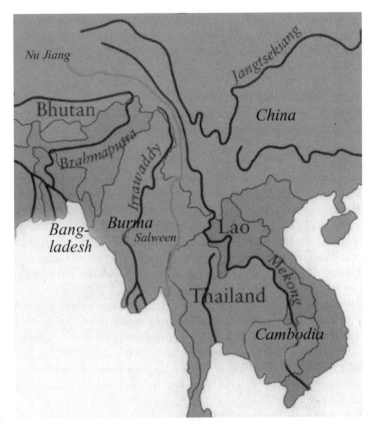

Figure 8.1 Location map of the Salween River, continental Southeast Asia.
*Source*: Salween Watch website (⟨http://www.salweenwatch.org/maps.html⟩, accessed 21 November 2007).

hydropower production. It has been estimated that a total of 12,000 megawatts (MW) could be developed on the Salween.

*Hydropower projects on the Salween*

Two hydropower dams are planned for construction on the Salween. Both will be linked by a high-voltage line with the domestic Thai power grid (the power stations of Thaton and Tak 2 in Thailand).[10]

One dam is located at Hutgyi (Myanmar). This run-of-the-river infrastructure is planned 33 km downstream of the meeting point between the Salween and the Moei River. Another dam is located at Ta Sang in the south of Shan state (Myanmar). Other infrastructure might be needed downstream of these dams in order to moderate the outflow of the turbines (SEARIN 1999). Electricity generated by these facilities is of interest to the Thai national electricity company EGAT, because its cost would be lower than that produced at Bhumibol dam in Thailand (Khampa 2002).

Rangoon and Bangkok will have dams located in Myanmar, while the hydropower production units will be built in Thailand. This decision could be interpreted as a way of politically easing the Thai search for international funding to build these facilities (Khampa 2002).

*Water transfer: A strategic goal*

The development of the above-mentioned infrastructure was also planned to make inter-basin water transfer possible from the Salween River Basin to Thai territory. In practice this water transfer project aims at diverting water from the Salween and from the Moei and Yuam rivers (tributaries of the Salween) to the reservoir of the Bhumibol dam (Tak province, Thailand).[11] The principle is that hydropower dams built by Thailand and Myanmar will generate the energy needed for pumping water out of the Salween Basin into Thai territory.

This water transfer is meant to address the water scarcity situation in the Chao Phraya River Basin. The current water deficit of 2,440 million $m^3$ is expected to rise to some 6,164 million $m^3$ by 2020. According to the director of the Thai Energy Department, only 3,700 million $m^3$ of water would be diverted annually – a contribution that would "cover the needs of several regions in Thailand, for the next twenty years" (Wangvipula and Changyawa 2002).

Four routes have been considered for operating the transfer of water: two from the Salween and two from the Moei:
Route 1: Salween – Upper Yuam – Bhumibol reservoir
Route 2: Salween – Mae Lama Luang – Bhumibol reservoir
Route 3: Moei – Huai Khanaeng dam – Bhumibol reservoir
Route 4: Moei – Mae Song dam – Bhumibol reservoir
Tables 8.1 and 8.2 indicate the technical characteristics of these water transfer projects.

Although the Salween projects were validated by the energy ministers of the countries of the Association of Southeast Asian Nations (ASEAN), these projects did not develop without conflict. In March 2002, for instance, the press (anonymously) quoted an official of the Myanmar Ministry of Foreign Affairs, who rejected Thailand's claims to receive a share of Salween water equal to the percentage of the Salween River Basin located on Thai territory. According to this official, "if Thailand wants water, it might have to pay for it" (Wangvipula and Changyawa 2002). However, the situation has progressively improved. In November 2002, EGAT officially invited China and Myanmar to join the

Table 8.1  Water transfers to Thailand: Technical details, Routes 1 and 2

| Technical characteristics | Unit | Route 1 | | Route 2 | |
|---|---|---|---|---|---|
| | | Salween – Upper Yuam | Upper Yuam – Bhumibol | Salween – Mae Lama Luang | Mae Lama Luang – Bhumibol |
| Watershed | km$^2$ | 295,668 | 4,860 | 295,000 | 6,030 |
| Annual discharge | million m$^3$ | 112,629 | 1,371 | 112,399 | 2,790 |
| Storage capacity | million m$^3$ | | 15.3 | | 344.0 |
| Maximum transfer | m$^3$/sec | 100 | 100 | 100 | 100 |
| Annual transfer | million m$^3$ | 1,512.1 | 2,459.1 | 1,184.0 | 2,448.9 |
| Pumping period | | Jan–Dec | Jun–Nov | Jan–Dec | Jun–Nov |
| Difference in altitude | metres | 136.5 | 184.5 | 141.1 | 188.0 |
| Pumping capacity | kW | 2 × 75,500 | 2 × 102,000 | 2 × 78,000 | 2 × 104,000 |
| Energy requirements for pumping (per year) | GWh | 634.2 | 1,393.5 | 513.1 | 1,414.9 |
| Additional energy needs | GWh | | 645.4 | 225.1 | 867.7 |
| Transfer tunnel | km | 21.2 | 67.4 | 14.5 | 67.4 |

project (Khampa 2002). The Ta Sang project was then officially signed in Rangoon on 20 December 2002 by the Myanmar Ministry of Electricity and the Thai MDX Consortium (TNLM 2002). The Salween projects appear to be a new piece in the regional power grid puzzle developed under the auspices of and/or with support from ASEAN, the World Bank and the Asian Development Bank (Rajesh 2003).

## Environmental, social and political impacts

Thai–Burmese political disagreement over water sharing is not the only tension triggered by the Salween projects. In particular, both non-governmental organizations (NGOs) and political movements active in several states of Myanmar have voiced concerns about the environmental, social and political impacts of the Salween projects. In 2002, for instance, a coalition of 69 environmental NGOs co-signed an official letter of dissent that was sent to the Thai Senate Commission for Foreign Affairs (SHAN 2002). Some of the consultants working on the Salween projects do not deny the environmental and social impacts of the dams. Increased salinity in the Salween delta, for instance, is identified as a possible risk generated by dam-building upstream on the river.

Table 8.2 Water transfers to Thailand: Technical details, Routes 3 and 4

| Technical characteristics | Unit | Route 3 | | Route 4 | | |
|---|---|---|---|---|---|---|
| | | Moei – Huai Khanaeng | Huai Khanaeng – Bhumibol | Moei – Mae Song weir | Mae Song weir – Mae Song dam | Mae Song dam – Bhumibol |
| Watershed | km² | 6,261.0 | 84.3 | 7,395.0 | 401.0 | 393.0 |
| Annual discharge | million m³ | 4,261.0 | 43.1 | 6,480.5 | 433.1 | 425.2 |
| Storage capacity | million m³ | 100 | 10.8 | | 3.3 | 33.7 |
| Maximum transfer | m³/sec | 100 | 100 | 140 | 140 | 157 |
| Annual transfer | million m³ | 1,079.6 | 1,091.4 | 2,068.1 | 2,068.1 | 2,392.5 |
| Pumping period | | Jun–Nov | Jun–Nov | Jun–Dec | Jun–Dec | Jun–Dec |
| Difference in altitude | metres | 43.4 | 146.5 | 15.4 | 54.1 | 126.5 |
| Pumping capacity | kW | 2 × 24,000 | 2 × 81,000 | 3 × 7,850 | 3 × 27,540 | 2 × 72,180 |
| Energy requirements for pumping (per year) | GWh | 144.0 | 491.1 | 89.2 | 335.0 | 839.5 |
| Additional energy needs | GWh | | 284.3 | | | 915.0 |
| Transfer tunnel | km | | 15.9 | | | 52.6 |

It is, however, difficult to distinguish the environmental message from a more "political" discourse (e.g. autonomy for the Shan states and pro-democracy demands). In 2000, for instance, the International Day against Dams was an opportunity for the Salween Watch organization to claim that the Internet-only nature of its campaign was a direct consequence of the lack of political freedom in Myanmar.

The military dimension of the Salween dams should also be recognized. According to the Shan Herald Agency for News, technical studies on the Salween were conducted under the protection of the Myanmar regular (central state) army (SHAN 2002). Needless to say, given the political context of the subregion, the neutrality of the Shan Agency could certainly be debated.

It is no wonder, then, that several military movements active in the boundary area between Myanmar and Thailand have viewed the growing presence of the Myanmar army in the area as a by-product of the dam-building developments on the Salween. According to these stakeholders, the dam projects offer an opportunity to both the Myanmar and Thai governments to increase their military presence in the basin – hence cutting "rebellion forces" and other political movements off from their bases and resources. Likewise, a growing number of civilian refugees (already some 300,000 people) may be a direct consequence of this military presence in the area (*The Irrawady* 1999).

## Thailand and Myanmar: Similar goals?

"Complex" is certainly the best description of intergovernmental relations between Myanmar and Thailand – a strategic and political mix concerning territorial claims, drugs and refugees (Lasserre and Gonon 2001). In 1988, however, some three months after the military coup in Rangoon, the first high-ranking official seconded by Thailand to visit its neighbour was General Chavalit Yongchaiyudh, then Commander-in-Chief of the Thai army. The press interpreted this visit as a first step in establishing a long-term relationship of well-understood mutual interests between the two countries (Zaw 2001). This early (and official) recognition of the new regime in Rangoon was also understood as a way of facilitating Thai access to Myanmar's natural resources and of reducing Rangoon's political isolation. Boucaud and Boucaud (2000) see Thailand as Myanmar's "Trojan horse" in the international arena.

The dam projects on the Salween can thus be seen as directly following on a strategy that General Chavalit called "transboundary development". Last but not least, Thailand would certainly welcome a pacified situation in the vicinity of its border with Myanmar, with less active or better-controlled autonomous movements and other politico-military forces.

## The Salween: A sign of regional integration

A broader regional picture emerges from the water infrastructure described above. Hydropower generation on the Salween seems to exemplify the hydraulic destiny of the entire region. In short, turning the Salween into a source of (hydro)power makes particular sense when considering railroad developments in continental Southeast Asia. The Greater Mekong Subregion (GMS) initiative, for instance, has been persistently supported by the Asian Development Bank (ADB) since 1992. With a clear mandate to develop the economies of the region and of its countries, the GMS initiative has materialized as a clear choice for overall infrastructural development in the subregion. The SKRL railroad project (Singapore–Kunming Rail Link) is an illustration – and one of the symbols – of the GMS dynamics.

The SKRL initiative aims to develop a 5,500 km railroad grid, based on the extension of existing Singaporean and Thai railway networks and linking Kunming (Yunnan province in China) with the rest of the subregion. This project (costing some US$2.5 billion) is funded mostly by Malaysia, South Korea, Japan and the ADB.[12] The availability of a judiciously distributed power grid is seen as crucial to the feasibility of the SKRL project. Developing hydropower is therefore essential to ensure a power supply to the railways of the region. No wonder, then, that promoters of the Salween projects have elaborated an official discourse whereby developing the Salween River Basin is a condition of successful hydropower development in the region and is essential to achieving regional integration: "the dream of the ASEAN Power Grid cannot be realised without the Upper and Lower Salween dams" (cited by Rajesh 2003: 30).

## Conclusion

There are several reasons the Salween River could, in the future, be a new source of hydropolitical tension and threat in the subregion.

First, promoters of the Salween projects would do well to learn from Laos. In this country, hydropower development has absorbed up to 66 per cent of foreign direct investment (Pataud-Celeriez 1999). In this case, experience has shown how foreign-owned hydropower development has the potential to threaten national sovereignty over water resources, for instance when choosing between hydropower and irrigation. This could have a disastrous impact on a country where more than half of the economy remains driven by agriculture (56 per cent in 1999). Although the population density of the Salween River Basin remains quite low, there is a risk that hydropower development might one day jeopardize agriculture-based human development in the area.

Second, China has been significantly absent from the Salween water development projects – at least until recently.[13] Considering hydropower projects in Myanmar and Thailand, Postel and Wolf have warned that no sustainable hydropolitical solution can be achieved in the basin without involving the upstream neighbour: "without a treaty in place, or even regular dialogue between the nations about their respective plans, there is little institutional capacity to buffer the inevitable shock as construction [or projects] begins" (Postel and Wolf 2001: 1). Water-sharing tensions can be expected in the years to come when dams start being built in Yunnan province: 13 of them are planned for the Upper Salween (Samabuddhi and Praiwan 2002).[14]

Third, growing requests for access to Salween water should also be expected from the authorities in Bangkok. It already appears to observers that the planned water transfers will not be sufficient to meet water demand in Thailand, while the Thai authorities consider long-term water shortages or scarcity not to be an acceptable scenario for urban users, particularly in Bangkok (Wangvipula 2002). Similarly predatory behaviour by Thailand in relation to transboundary waters can be observed in the Mekong River Basin (Miller 2001).

## Notes

1. Water scarcity is generally agreed as 1,000 $m^3$ per capita per year (FAO 2003).
2. FAO's Global Information and Early Warning System.
3. According to the FAO (FAO-Aquastat n.d.), Thailand produced 0.83 $km^3$ of wastewater, of which it treated only 0.04 $km^3$ (in 1995).
4. The Mekong subregion is defined here as comprising all Mekong riparian countries.
5. According to various sources contacted during my PhD fieldwork, Thailand has made its purchase of Laotian electricity conditional on Thai companies being able to install a high-voltage network across the country in order to connect with the Yunnan power grid.
6. Cited in Affeltranger (2007).
7. Online CIA *World Factbook*, accessed second semester of 2006.
8. 1 *rai* = 1,600 $m^2$.
9. There are other estimates: 276,000 $km^2$ according to Neiff (1996); 271,914 $km^2$ according to the World Resources Institute (WRI 2001).
10. Because this chapter focuses on water transfer issues, technical details of the hydropower facilities (height, surface and volume of reservoir, discharge, etc.) are not provided here.

11. For technical details of these water transfer projects, see Rajesh (2003: 33).
12. China has requested financial support to extend the SKRL network to Beijing (*The Irrawady* 2002).
13. Nu Jian is the Chinese name of the Salween River. Planned dams on the upper Nu Jian have triggered protests from environmental NGOs, both in Yunnan and abroad, with direct political impacts on the Beijing authorities.
14. This project is becoming a reality, as shown by the recent creation of the Chinese-owned Yunnan Huadian Nu River Hydropower Development Co.

# REFERENCES

Affeltranger, B. (2007), "The Politics of Hydrological Data", PhD dissertation (Geography), Laval University, Quebec, Canada.

Arunmas, P. (1999), "Water Fee to Be Charged for Agricultural Purposes", *Bangkok Post*, 15 January.

*Bangkok Post* (1999), "Challenge to Terms of $600 m Farm Loan", 16 February.

———— (2000), "City Profligacy Costs Farmers Dearly", 25 June.

Bogardi, J. (1997), "Report on the Review Mission of the Mekong Hydrology Programme", unpublished report, UNESCO Division of Water Sciences, Paris, 13–30 January.

Boonchai, K. (2001), "Political Ecology Movement in Thailand", 10th Northeast Asian Conference on Environmental Cooperation (NEAC), Incheon City, Republic of Korea, 16–19 October.

Boucaud, A. and L. Boucaud (2000), "La Thaïlande, cheval de Troie de la Birmanie", *Le Monde Diplomatique*, January.

East, J. (2001), "More Activists Getting Killed in Thailand's 'Green Wars'", *Straits Times Interactive*, Thailand Bureau, 4 July.

Ehrlich, R. S. (2003), "Laos: Le régime communiste réhabilite un ancien roi", *Courrier International*, No. 637, 16–22 January, p. 24.

FAO [Food and Agriculture Organization] (2003), "Review of World Water Resources by Country", at ⟨ftp://ftp.fao.org/agl/aglw/docs/wr23e.pdf⟩ (accessed 21 November 2007).

FAO-Aquastat (1997), "Thailand", at ⟨http://www.fao.org/nr/water/aquastat/countries/thailand/index.stm⟩ (accessed 21 November 2007).

———— (n.d.), "General Summary Asia: Water Withdrawal", at ⟨http://www.fao.org/nr/water/aquastat/regions/asia/index4.stm⟩ (accessed 21 November 2007).

Golub, P. S. (2001), "Paysages d'après-crise en Thaïlande", *Le Monde Diplomatique*, June, pp. 18–19.

Hongthong, P. and N. Tangwisutijit (2000), "Water-Pricing Test Project to Start Soon – Burden on Small Farmers a Concern", *The Nation*, Bangkok, 23 April.

Inchukul, K. (1997), "Ministry Upbraided over Seminar – Parallel Meeting to be Staged in Bangkok", *Bangkok Post*, 10 April.

———— (1999), "B5bn Sought to Stem Land Subsidence", *Bangkok Post*, 24 January.

Janchitfah, S. (2000), "The Case of the Disappearing Water", *Bangkok Post*, 25 June.

JBIC (2000), "Bhumibol Hydro Power Renovation Project", Ex-post Evaluation for ODA Loan Projects (Summary), Japan Bank for International Cooperation.

Junturasima, M. (2000), "Farmers Not Opposed to Water Charge", *Bangkok Post*, 1 July.

Khampa, P. (2002), "Thailand's EGAT Wants China and Burma to Join in Huge Hydropower Project", *Bangkok Post*, 20 November.

Kongrut, A. (1999), "Bangkok to Get Taste of Water Crisis", *Bangkok Post*, 9 January.

Krairapanond, N. and A. Atkinson (1998), "Watershed Management in Thailand: Concepts, Problems and Implementation", *Regulated Rivers: Research and Management*, Vol. 14, pp. 485–498.

Kumar, R. and C. Young (1996), "Economic Policies for Sustainable Water Use in Thailand", CREED Working Paper Series No. 4, International Institute for Environment and Development, London, and Institute for Environmental Studies, Amsterdam, June.

Lasserre, F. and E. Gonon (2001), *Espaces et enjeux: Méthodes d'une géopolitique critique*, Montreal and Paris: collection Raoul-Dandurand and éditions l'Harmattant.

Miller, F. (2001), "Adaptation/Control: Perceptions and Responses to Environmental Risks in Water Resources Management in the Mekong Delta, Viet Nam", IWHA Conference, Bergen, Norway, August.

Molle, F. (2001), "Water Pricing in Thailand – Theory and Practice", Kasetsart University, Thailand, DORAS Center, Research Report No. 7.

Neiff, G. (1996), "Large Rivers of the World", in S. M. Mandaville, *Rivers – The Cradle of Civilization!*, Soil & Water Conservation Society of Metro Halifax.

Noikorn, U. (1997), "Call for Water Price Increase to Ease Water Shortages", *Bangkok Post*, 12 October.

——— (1998), "EGAT Produces Too Much Power, Causing Country to Suffer from Drought", *Bangkok Post*, 21 November.

Noikorn, U. and P. Arunmas (1999), "Farmers Won't Be Charged for Water", *Bangkok Post*, 19 February.

OEPP [Office of Environmental Policy and Planning] (1996), "Thailand – State of the Environment Report, 1995–1996", Government of Thailand.

——— (1997), "Thailand – State of the Environment Report, 1997", Government of Thailand.

Ohlsson, L. and A. R. Turton (1999), "The Turning of a Screw", in *Urban Stability through Integrated Water-Related Management*, 9th Stockholm Water Symposium.

Onta, P. R., R. Loof, A. D. Gupta and R. Harboe (1994), "Study of Potential Development of Water Resources in the Salawin River Basin", AIT Research Report No. 273, Submitted to National Economic and Social Development Board, Royal Thai Government.

ORST (2003), "Transboundary Freshwater Database", at ⟨http://www.transboundarywaters.orst.edu⟩ (accessed 21 November 2007).

Oxfam (1998), "Hydrodevelopment on the Mekong", Briefing Paper No. 22, December.

Pataud-Celeriez, P. (1999), "Le Laos, un pays plein d'énergie en quête de devises", *Le Monde Diplomatique*, July.

Postel, S. L. (1999), *Pillar of Sand – Can the Irrigation Miracle Last?*, New York and London: WorldWatch Norton.

Postel, S. L. and A. T. Wolf (2001), "Dehydrating Conflict", *Foreign Policy*, September/October.

Rajesh, N. (2003), "Thailand's Salween Dams to Fuel Southeast Asian Regional Power Grid at the Cost to Ethnic Communities, Forests and Rivers", *Watershed*, Vol. 9, No. 1, pp. 30–33.

RMAP (2003), "Indigenous Hydrological Knowledge and Dry-Season Agriculture in Upland Catchments of Northern Thailand", Resource Management in Asia-Pacific Program, Research School of Pacific and Asian Studies, Australian National University.

Royal Irrigation Department (2003), "Information on Water Resources Management in Thailand", Government of the Kingdom of Thailand website, ⟨http://www.rid.go.th⟩.

Ryder, G. (1996), "The Political Ecology of Hydropower Development in the Lao People's Democratic Republic", Mekong campaign, 13 December, Probe International.

Samabuddhi, K. and Y. Praiwan (2002), "China Plans 13 Dams on Salween", *Bangkok Post*, 18 December.

SEARIN [Southeast Asia Rivers Network] (1999), "Ta Sang Dam Project in Southern Shan State", April, at ⟨http://www.searin.org/Th/SWD/SWD_TSDinfoE1.htm⟩ (accessed 21 November 2007).

Selth, A. (2001), "Burma: A Strategic Perspective", Strategic and Defense Studies Center, Australian National University, Working Paper No. 13, Asia Foundation Working Paper Series, May; article prepared for the conference Strategic Rivalries on the Bay of Bengal: The Burma/Myanmar Nexus, Washington, DC, 1 February.

SHAN (2002), "Petition to Stop Dam on the Salween to Thai Senate", *Shan Herald Agency for News*, 3 December.

Shivakoti, Ganesh P. (2000), "Participatory Interventions in Farmer-Managed Irrigation Systems in Northern Thailand: Dynamism in Resource Mobilization", in *Constituting the Commons: Crafting Sustainable Commons in the New Millenium*, Eighth Conference of the International Association for the Study of Common Property, Bloomington, Indiana, 31 May–4 June.

Sneddon, C. (1998), "The River Basin as Common Pool Resource: Opportunities for Co-Management and 'Scaling Up' in Northeast Thailand", paper presented at "Crossing Boundaries", the seventh annual conference of the International Association for the Study of Common Property, Vancouver, British Columbia, Canada, 10–14 June.

Sretthauchau, C. (2000), "Political Ecology of Large Dam Scheme in Thailand – A Case Study of Kae Sua Ten Dam Project", Abstract, MA thesis, Graduate School, Chiang Mai University, Thailand.

*The Irrawady* (1999), "Dam Study Underway", Vol. 7, No. 2.

——— (2002), "Railway to Connect Asia", Vol. 10, No. 10, December.

TNLM (2002), "Agreement on Construction of Hydel Power Plant Signed", *The New Light of Myanmar*, 21 December, at ⟨http://www3.itu.int/MISSIONS/Myanmar/02nlm/n021221.htm⟩ (accessed 21 November 2007).

UNDP [United Nations Development Programme] (1999), *Human Development Report of Thailand 1999*, Bangkok: UNDP.

Wangvipula, R. (2002), "Seminar Discusses Diversion Schemes", *Bangkok Post*, 8 May.

Wangvipula, R. and P. Changyawa (2002), "Rangoon May Seek Payment to Supply Dam", *Bangkok Post*, 24 March.

Wolf, A. T., et al. (1999), "International River Basins of the World", *Water Resources Development*, Vol. 15, No. 4, pp. 387–427.

World Bank (2001), "Thailand Environment Monitor 2000", *Water Quality Overview*, June.

WRI [World Resources Institute] (2001), "Major Watersheds of the World", in *World Resources 2000–2001*, World Resources Institute.

Yaowalert, H. (2002), "Water Management in Thailand", Mekong Dialogue Workshop "International Transfer of River Basin Development Experience – Australia and the Mekong Region", 2 September.

Zaw, A. (2001), "Chavalit Looking Forward to Returning to the Past", *The Irrawady*, 11 April.

# 9

# The implications of domestic security policy for international water issues in the context of "virtual" and "real" water: The Aral Sea and Mekong River basins

*Mikiyasu Nakayama*

## Introduction

Water scarcity has been observed in many parts of the world. In some regions it has become a major political agenda item, in particular where water resources are shared among countries as in international water bodies. Scarcity in one country has in many cases caused conflicts among basin countries, mainly owing to attempts within a country to increase water security for various reasons and purposes, as illustrated in the following cases.

Put very simply, two possible solutions exist to alleviate water scarcity in a country, by importing either "real" water or "virtual" water. A seemingly simple solution is to transfer "real" water to water-poor regions from water-rich areas. In this context, the transboundary transfer of water resources has been planned in many places. The "Interbasin Water Transfer" session at the Second World Water Forum in 2000 concluded that, in regions where water demand is still growing, transboundary water transfer will continue to be a viable option for meeting increasing needs (World Water Forum 2000). However, water resources have been transferred from one international river or lake basin to another in only a limited number of cases. The Lesotho Highlands Water Project (LHWP) is one of the few exceptions, and transboundary water transfer has taken place between Lesotho and South Africa since 1998.

Transferring "real" water has been proposed in many parts of the world at least since the eighteenth century. The former Soviet Union,

*International water security: Domestic threats and opportunities, Pachova, Nakayama and Jansky (eds), United Nations University Press, 2008, ISBN 978-92-808-1150-6*

for example, once suggested transferring water from water-rich Siberia to water-poor Central Asia by constructing a canal of several thousand kilometres. In Southern Africa, transferring water from the Zambezi River to surrounding water-poor regions has been planned for more than a century. None of these plans has materialized, which implies that transferring water from one basin to another is both technically and politically very difficult.

It should be noted that water resources are mostly used for agriculture even in water-poor regions. Water scarcity may thus be alleviated by importing agricultural products from other water-rich areas. Allan (1998) has pointed out that such "virtual" water transfers explain why countries in the Middle East have not fought over water, despite the fact that some countries in the Middle East can no longer produce enough food to meet domestic demand owing to water scarcity.

The concept of "virtual" water, most broadly defined as "water embedded in key water-intensive commodities", is fairly new, appearing first in academia in the late 1990s. However, being an intuitively easily understandable and practical concept (rather than a theoretical model), it has been attracting increasing attention as an analytical tool for re-thinking the issue of water scarcity and water conflict.

Trade in water resources, whether real or virtual, should have an impact on relations between basin countries in an international water system. "International water system" in this context implies both traditional international river or lake systems and a system involving trade in virtual water. The latter suggests that even a country that does not share any international river or lake with another country (Japan, for example) may be a stakeholder in debates about "real" water in international water bodies.

The concept of virtual water is still too new to have accumulated case studies by researchers. The following case studies, which deal with the virtual water concept, were carried out under the auspices of the United Nations University, in collaboration with other research institutes. This chapter summarizes the findings from these case studies.

## The Aral Sea Basin

### The Amu Darya Basin: The presence of Afghanistan as a basin country

The Aral Sea Basin covers over 690,000 km$^2$, including Kazakhstan, Kyrgyzstan, Tajikistan, Turkmenistan and Uzbekistan. A small proportion of its headwaters is located in Afghanistan, Iran and China. The basin is formed by two of the largest rivers of Central Asia – the Amu Darya and the Syr Darya – both of which are fed by snowmelt and glaciers in the mountains. The sources of the Amu Darya are mostly located in Tajikistan, with some watercourses originating in north-eastern Afghanistan. The Syr Darya originates mainly in Kyrgyzstan. It travels across a small area of Tajikistan and Uzbekistan and through the Kazakh provinces of Chimkent and Kzyl-Orda.

In 1960, the Aral Sea was the fourth-largest inland lake in the world. Since then, however, it has shrunk significantly because of the nearly total cut-off of the river inflow from the Amu Darya and Syr Darya as a result of heavy withdrawals for irrigation. By 1989 the sea level had fallen by 14.3 metres and the surface area had shrunk from 68,000 km$^2$ to 37,000 km$^2$. The salinity of the sea had increased to 2.8 times its 1960 level. The main issues relating to the Aral Sea Basin area are: the shrinking of the Sea, the destruction of its aquatic ecosystem, the reduction in soil quality in the Aral Sea Basin, pollution of the surface water and groundwater of the delta draining into the Aral Sea, a depressed economy, and adverse health impacts on the population owing to a lack of potable water and inadequate sanitation.

Of eight basin countries, five former Soviet Union countries have been considered to be major stakeholders. These nations have a mechanism, in the form of a river basin organization, for discussing the shared water resources. The mechanism does not, however, seem to be functioning well. In terms of tackling the environmental disaster of the basin, which stems from the Soviet Union's policy of large-scale irrigation development in the 1950s–1980s, few measures have been taken by these five countries to reduce water consumption for irrigation.

The new challenge these countries now face is political stabilization in Afghanistan and the subsequent increase in consumption of water resources to enhance agricultural production in the northern part of the country. The water in the Aral Sea is replenished by two major rivers. One of these, the Amu Darya, has its source in high mountains in Tajikistan and Afghanistan. Any increase in water consumption within Afghanistan will lead to a decrease in water availability in the downstream region. This implies that reconstruction of the agricultural production system in Afghanistan may create tensions among the basin countries of the Amu Darya, in particular between those in downstream and upstream regions. It should be recalled that the Amu Darya River and its tributaries are also a crucial source of water for the extensive irrigated areas in Afghanistan's northern fertile plains. About 40 per cent of the country's irrigated lands lie in this northern region (UNEP 2003).

*The role of food aid in regional security*

The World Food Programme (WFP) defines the role of food aid for Afghanistan as follows (WFP 2005: 7):

21. Food aid through food for work (FFW) and food for training (FFT) will provide an income transfer and safety net for extremely poor people, while rehabilitating and creating physical assets and imparting marketable skills.
22. Food will address short-term hunger and provide incentives for increasing enrolment and attendance, with a special focus on girls and teachers (particularly women), and for imparting literacy and life skills to targeted participants.
23. Food aid will encourage tuberculosis patients and their families to seek and continue treatment while enhancing their nutritional status.
24. Food aid will improve the capacity of vulnerable households to manage shocks and meet food needs during and after disasters. Emphasis will be placed on building the capacities of communities and counterparts and on linkages with national strategies.

These roles are mostly concerned with human security. It should be noted that food aid may also have an important role in terms of regional security in diminishing or mitigating potential conflicts over water resources among the basin countries of an international water system. This role is achieved by the introduction of virtual water into the basin from outside the region. It is exactly the same as the role of food imports (by nominal trade not by food aid) in some international river systems in the Middle East, in that conflicts among riparian states have been diminished or mitigated thanks to the "imported" virtual water from outside (Allan 1998).

*The implications of an improving production system in Afghanistan*

Food production in Afghanistan in the early 2000s was nearly half that in the late 1970s, as shown in Figure 9.1. Depending on the yield of a particular year, Afghanistan thus requires as much as 2 million tons of cereal imports (see Figure 9.2). As a consequence, a lot of virtual water has been brought into Afghanistan either through food imports or through food aid operations by the donor community.

If Afghanistan consumes more water in the Amu Darya Basin to achieve food self-sufficiency, there will be much less water in the river available to downstream countries. Producing 2 million tons of cereals requires, very roughly speaking, about 2 km$^3$ of water. As shown in Table 9.1, the contribution by runoff from snowmelt in the high mountains of Afghanistan to the river flow of the Amu Darya is thought to be 10.8

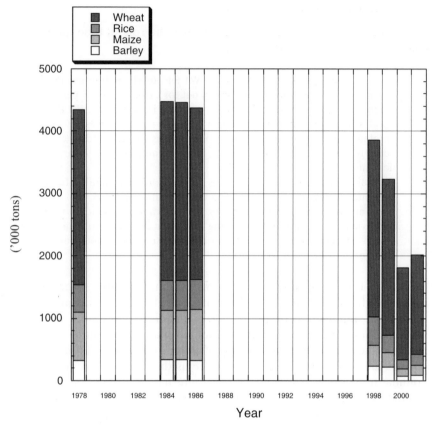

Figure 9.1  Food production in Afghanistan, 1978–2001.
*Source*:  JSCE (2002).


km$^3$. This implies that a substantial proportion of the water that currently flows from Afghanistan to the Amu Darya may in future be used by Afghanistan for its expanding irrigated agriculture.

What is worse, the population of Afghanistan is expected to increase dramatically in the coming decades. This too implies a drastic decrease in flow in the downstream reaches of the Amu Darya, assuming that Afghanistan aims at food self-sufficiency for its increasing population.

These trends of increasing water consumption in Afghanistan may lead to conflicts among basin countries. Some measures may need to be taken to mitigate the impacts of the expansion of agricultural production in Afghanistan. Such measures might include improvements in water-use effi-

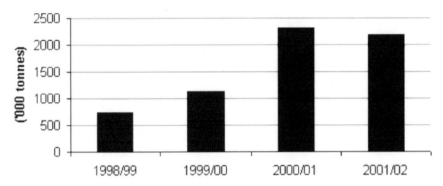

Figure 9.2  Food import requirements in Afghanistan, 1998/1999–2001/2002. *Source*: FAO (2001).

ciency in the downstream area and changes in the economic structure of both upstream and downstream countries. A new river basin organization, with the participation of all the basin countries, should be established and made functional as a mechanism to address issues concerning their shared water resources. Above all, trade-offs between "real" water consumption (food production within the country) and "virtual" water consumption (imports of food from abroad) in Afghanistan should be addressed from the viewpoint of security among basin countries.

### The Syr Darya Basin: A trade-off between energy and agriculture

The other river that flows into the Aral Sea is the Syr Darya. As is the case with the Amu Darya, water in this river comes from snowmelt in high mountains in Kyrgyzstan and China. Although water consumption has not led to a major conflict among the basin countries, the way in which water should be released from dams in upstream countries to the downstream areas has been a matter of dispute between Kyrgyzstan, Uzbekistan and Kazakhstan.

A few dams were constructed on the Syr Darya within Kyrgyzstan during the former Soviet Union days in order to maintain irrigation during the summer in the downstream regions of Uzbekistan and Kazakhstan. At that time, the energy-resource-poor country of Kyrgyzstan received gas and oil from the energy-resource-rich downstream countries (Lange 2001). This trade between water and energy sources was maintained when these countries (then "republics") were under the umbrella of the Soviet Union.

Table 9.1 Afghanistan's contribution to the flow of the Amu Darya: Natural surface flow in the Amu Darya River Basin (mean annual runoff, km³/year)

| River basin | River flow generated within the countries | | | | | | Total Amu Darya Basin |
| | Kyrgyzstan | Tajikistan | Uzbekistan | Turkmenistan | Afghanistan and Iran | |
| --- | --- | --- | --- | --- | --- | --- |
| Pyandj | – | 30.081 | – | – | 3.300 | 33.381 |
| Vakhsh | 1.654 | 18.400 | – | – | – | 20.054 |
| Kafirnigan | – | 5.575 | – | – | – | 5.535 |
| Surkhandar | – | – | 4.841 | – | – | 4.841 |
| Sherabad | – | – | 0.228 | – | – | 0.228 |
| Kashkadary | – | – | 1.222 | – | – | 1.222 |
| Murgab | – | – | – | 0.771 | 0.771 | 1.542 |
| Tedjen | – | – | – | 0.488 | 0.489 | 0.977 |
| Atrek | – | – | – | 0.136 | 0.137 | 0.273 |
| Rivers of Afghanistan | – | – | – | – | 6.167 | 6.167 |
| Total (km³) | 1.654 | 54.056 | 6.291 | 1.405 | 10.814 | 74.220 |
| Amu Darya Basin (%) | 2.2 | 72.8 | 8.5 | 1.9 | 14.6 | 100.0 |

*Source:* ⟨http://www.cawater-info.net/amudarya/water_e.htm⟩, cited in Katsurai (2005).

The situation dramatically changed shortly after the independence of these nations from the Soviet Union. Kazakhstan and Uzbekistan started charging for supplying gas and oil to Kyrgyzstan. Kyrgyzstan then opted to use the water in the reservoirs for hydropower generation in winter, when energy was needed for heating. The surge of water in winter from the reservoirs caused massive flooding in the downstream countries and led to conflicts among the basin countries (Lange 2001).

The problem in the Syr Darya River Basin may be seen from the viewpoint of both "real" and "virtual" water. In terms of "real" water, the total annual amount of water flowing from upstream to downstream is unchanged. The issue is the timing of the water release from upstream to downstream. For Uzbekistan and Kazakhstan, securing "real" water in summer is the only solution. Water scarcity in summer in these countries cannot be alleviated by "virtual" water, simply because the huge amount of agricultural production (mainly cotton and rice) in these nations cannot be sustained by importing "virtual" water. On the other hand, Kyrgyzstan's need for "real" water in winter may be reduced by importing energy, as was the case under the Soviet Union.

Importing energy sources (i.e. gas and oil) is not defined as the transfer of "virtual" water per se, because the "virtual" water concept concerns only the import of foods. However, energy sources in this case are nothing but substitutes for "real" water. Expanding the concept of "virtual" water to include energy sources seems appropriate to express the situation in the Syr Darya River Basin.

Not surprisingly, the basin counties of the Syr Darya came round to the idea of barter agreements over water and energy resources between the upstream and downstream countries. However, recent events suggest that the barter agreement system has collapsed. For example, efforts to collaborate between basin countries have stagnated after the failures of annual agreements in 2003 and 2004 (Kitamura 2005). Consequently, two downstream countries (namely Kazakhstan and Uzbekistan) are taking measures (a) to absorb floods caused by the discharge of water for power production in winter by Kyrgyzstan and (b) to avoid shortages of irrigation water in the summer. Uzbekistan has decided to construct a series of regulating reservoirs (five in total). These dams will provide additional storage capacity of about 2.5 billion $m^3$. Kazakhstan plans to build a regulating dam that will provide capacity of about 3.0 billion $m^3$.

The prevailing situation in the Syr Darya suggests that the concept of trade between "real" and "virtual" water is theoretically possible, but it may not be feasible in a region where distrust among the basin countries prevails. Constructing huge control reservoirs would appear not to be the best solution, not least in terms of the economy.

## The Mekong River Basin

The Mekong River rises in Tibet and flows for about 2,000 km through high mountain ranges and valleys in China and Myanmar. It then enters the Lower Mekong Basin in Laos, forms the border between Laos and Thailand, and then flows through Cambodia and Viet Nam before discharging into the South China Sea. The Lower Mekong Basin covers 609,000 km$^2$ (about 77 per cent of the Mekong's total catchment) and includes almost all of Laos and Cambodia and large parts of Thailand and Viet Nam. The Mekong's potential for hydropower, irrigation, flood control, navigation and fishery development is immense (Kirmani and Le Moigne 1997).

In 1952, the Bureau of Flood Control of the Economic Commission for Asia and the Far East (ECAFE) of the United Nations published an initial report on flood control and water resources development of the Mekong River Basin. A further study was carried out by ECAFE in 1956 of the basin's potentialities in hydropower, irrigation and flood control. The results of the study, published in 1957, provided a conceptual framework for developing the Mekong River Basin as an integrated system through close collaboration among the riparian countries. Representatives of the four countries (Cambodia, Laos, Thailand and Viet Nam) met in May 1957 to follow up on the ECAFE report. They recommended the creation of a coordination committee. Another meeting was held in September 1957, and the Statutes were unanimously adopted by the representatives of the four basin countries. The Mekong Committee thus came into being.

The Mekong Committee was established to promote, coordinate, supervise and control the planning and investigation of a water resources development project in the Lower Mekong Basin. Leading industrialized countries supported the idea of the comprehensive international development of the Mekong River Basin. Various studies were launched concerning hydropower, irrigation, navigation, fisheries and flood control within the framework of the Mekong Committee (Hori 1993). The Mekong Committee thus served as a focal point for donors in the region. The strong and persistent desire of the basin countries to collaborate, known as the "Mekong spirit", has been much admired, to the extent that the Ramon Magsaysay Award was given to the Mekong Committee in 1966 (Mekong Secretariat 1989).

The Agreement on the Cooperation for the Sustainable Development of the Mekong River Basin was signed by plenipotentiaries from Cambodia, Laos, Thailand and Viet Nam at Chiang Rai, Thailand, in April 1995. It provides principles for the sustainable development, utilization, management and conservation of the water and related resources of the Mekong River Basin and institutional, financial and management issues relating to the mechanism of coordination between the member countries (Mekong River Commission 1996). The Agreement immediately established the Mekong River Commission, which replaced the Mekong Committee established in 1957 by the same set of four riparian countries.

This new mechanism for the basin countries was the outcome of numerous discussions held among basin countries in the early 1990s, stemming from conflicts between Thailand and Viet Nam. In January 1975 the Mekong Committee adopted the Joint Declaration of Principles for Utilization of the Waters of the Lower Mekong Basin (Mekong Committee 1975a). This Joint Declaration, which comprised 35 articles, defined the water resources of the mainstream as "a resources of common interest not subject to major unilateral appropriation by any riparian State without prior approval by the other Basin States" (Mekong Committee 1975b: Article 10). Article 20 noted: "Extra-Basin diversion of mainstream waters by a riparian State shall require the agreement of all Basin States." Each basin country was thus in practice given "veto power" over the conduct of another country regarding diversion of mainstream waters, regardless of the use, whether within the basin or outside the catchment.

In a workshop held by the Interim Mekong Committee in March 1991, a representative from Thailand noted that "the principles enshrined in the 1975 Joint Declaration have been taken as the guidelines in the mutual co-operation between interested riparian states for already 16 years. It is high time now to review this Declaration in order to identify problems that it entails in practice" (Danvivathana 1991). Thailand clearly wanted to replace the Joint Declaration with a new framework. The reason Thailand disliked the 1975 Joint Declaration was because it had a plan (the Kong-Chi-Moon project) to direct water from the mainstream of the Mekong River into its north-eastern region. Thailand thus wanted to circumvent the veto power given to other basin countries through the Joint Declaration.

The command area for irrigation under the Kong-Chi-Moon project was estimated to be 1,277,700 hectares. The project included a pumping scheme to transfer water from the Mekong River into the project area to supplement dry-season irrigation shortages (Tingsanchali and Singh 1996). The government of Thailand approved the Kong-Chi-Moon project in April 1989. Phase I of the project, which was to last for nine years (1991–2000), aimed at irrigating 260 million hectares of farmland. The project was expected (1) to help at least 750,000 people in north-eastern Thailand avoid water shortages in the dry season, (2) to encourage agro-industry, and (3) to improve the standard of living of the region to reduce migration to the cities (*Bangkok Post* 1993). The north-east part of Thailand, the command area of the planned Kong-Chi-Moon project, is a poor hinterland within Thailand. The government of Thailand thus sought to reduce the sense of relative deprivation that was widely felt in the north-east by speeding up the process of regional development. This initiative included improving agricultural production through its Accelerated Rural Development Programme, which promoted green revolution-type intensification and also the extension of farming into hitherto unutilized upland areas (Parnwell 2005). The Kong-Chi-Moon project was one element of these efforts.

Viet Nam objected to the Kong-Chi-Moon project because it might reduce the flow of the river in the dry season and might cause intrusion of saline water into the Mekong Delta, the "rice bowl" of Viet Nam. The position of Thailand was uncompromising. Thailand claimed to reserve the right to abstract from the mainstream waters an amount equivalent to the contribution of the tributaries in Thailand, which Thailand believed to be 12–16 per cent of the total flow (Weatherbee 1997). This conflict was resolved after nearly five years of negotiations among the basin countries with mediation by the United Nations Development Programme (Nakayama 1999).

This case too should be examined from the viewpoint of virtual water, so that the following questions may be answered:

(a) To what extent does the export of virtual water by Thailand and Viet Nam, in the form of the export of agricultural products, affect the relations of these countries in sharing the water resources of the Mekong River?

(b) How may the economic structure of these countries be changed in future to reduce exports of "virtual" water?

(c) Is getting "real" water from the Mekong River the only viable solution for the economic development of Thailand's north-east region?

No single and obvious answer may be obtained for each of these questions, because the issues are extremely complex and political. However, looking at the issues from the viewpoint of a trade-off between "real" and "virtual" water may provide us with new insights. This viewpoint is particularly important nowadays, because both Thailand and Viet Nam are socio-economically in transition, from a traditional agriculture-driven society into one based on small and medium-scale industries. It needs to be asked whether a traditional agriculture-based economic development scheme, such as the Accelerated Rural Development Programme of Thailand, is still the best possible way forward. The demand for water may be reduced significantly through such changes in society, as was the case in Japan in recent decades. The concept of virtual water may thus shed light on the relationship between Thailand and Viet Nam over their shared water resources in the Mekong River Basin.

# Conclusion

More than 200 international water systems exist in the world. About 50–60 per cent of the global population resides within international water systems. The security issue of international water systems is thus of great importance for many people. This issue should be seen from both the "real" and the "virtual" water viewpoints – the latter may give the basin countries a clue to alleviating tensions among them owing to a scarcity of "real" water within one country.

Some existing policies should be re-examined. Attaining or improving food self-sufficiency by a basin country may lead to a conflict with other nations sharing in an international water system. Reliance on food aid from foreign countries, i.e. importing free virtual water, may be seen as a mechanism to reduce conflicts among basin countries. Trade-offs between "real" water and "virtual" water should thus be examined before carrying out any large-scale transboundary water transfer scheme. The concept of virtual water may also be expanded, so that trading in other "substitutes" for water (e.g. energy sources) may be regarded as the transfer of virtual water.

# Acknowledgements

The research for this chapter was partly funded by the New Research Initiatives in Humanities and Social Sciences of the Japan Society for the Promotion of Science (JSPS) and by the Core Research for Evolutional Science and Technology (CREST) of the Japan Science and Technology Agency (JST).

# Note

This paper is based on my presentation "Implications of Virtual Water Concept on Management of International Water Systems", at the International Expert Meeting on Virtual Water Trade, 11–13 December 2002, Delft, the Netherlands.

## REFERENCES

Allan, T. (1998), "Moving Water to Satisfy Uneven Global Needs: 'Trading' Water as an Alternative to Engineering it", *ICID Journal*, Vol. 47, No. 2, pp. 1–8.
*Bangkok Post* (1993), "Kong-Chi-Moon Project", 22 August, p. 6.
Danvivathana, P. (1991), "Statement at Workshop on Lower Mekong Basin International Legal Framework", Bangkok, 20–25 March, LEG/W1/91009, Interim Mekong Committee, Bangkok.

FAO [Food and Agriculture Organization] (2001), "Grave Food Crisis in Afghanistan Could Deepen if Current Situation Deteriorates", *FAO Global Information and Early Warning System on Food And Agriculture – Special Alert No. 318*, Rome, 20 September.

Hori, H. (1993), "Development of the Mekong River Basin – Its Problems and Future Prospects", *Water International*, Vol. 18, pp. 110–115.

JSCE [Japan Society of Civil Engineers] (2002), *Afghanistan Kokudo-Fukkou-Vision-Shian*, Tokyo (in Japanese).

Katsurai, T. (2005), "JBIC's Role in Transboundary River Basin Development and Management – Case Study of Amu Darya River Basin", presentation to Transboundary Impact Assessment Study Group, Tokyo, 14 July.

Kirmani, S. and G. Le Moigne (1997), *Fostering Riparian Cooperation in International River Basins*, World Bank Technical Paper No. 335, Washington, DC: World Bank.

Kitamura, Y. (2005), "Syr Darya gawa ryuuiki ni okeru mizu-seisaku ni kansuru kadai", presentation to Transboundary Impact Assessment Study Group, Tokyo, 14 July (in Japanese).

Lange, K. (2001), "Energy and Environmental Security in Central Asia: The Syr Darya", Corporate Briefing, Center for Strategic and International Studies, Washington DC, 20 February.

Mekong Committee (1975a), *Report of the Second Meeting of the Ad-Hoc Working Group on the Declaration of Principles for Utilization of the Waters of the Lower Mekong Basin*, MKG/R.126, Bangkok: Mekong Committee, p. 1.

——— (1975b), *Joint Declaration of Principles for Utilization of the Waters of the Lower Mekong Basin*, Bangkok: Mekong Committee, pp. 1–14.

Mekong River Commission (1996), "New Era of Mekong Cooperation", *Annual Report 1995*, Bangkok, pp. 5–7.

Mekong Secretariat (1989), *The Mekong Committee – A Historical Account*, Bangkok: Mekong Secretariat, pp. 8–10.

Nakayama, M. (1999) "Aspects behind Differences in Two Agreements Adopted by Riparian Countries of Lower Mekong River Basin", *Journal of Comparative Policy Analysis*, Vol. 1, No. 3, pp. 293–308.

Parnwell, M. J. G. (2005), "The Power to Change: Rebuilding Sustainable Livelihoods in North-East Thailand", *Journal of Transdisciplinary Environmental Studies*, Vol. 4, No. 2.

Tingsanchali, T. and P. R. Singh (1996), "Optimum Water Resources Allocation for Mekong-Chi-Mun Transbasin Irrigation Project Northeast Thailand", *Water International*, Vol. 21, pp. 20–29.

UNEP [United Nations Environment Programme] (2003), *Afghanistan Post-Conflict Environmental Assessment*, Nairobi: UNEP.

Weatherbee, D. E. (1997), "Cooperation and Conflict in the Mekong River Basin", *Studies in Conflicts & Terrorism*, Vol. 20, pp. 167–184.

WFP [World Food Programme] (2005), *Protracted Relief and Recovery Operation – Afghanistan 10427.0*, WFP/EB.2/2005/8-B/1, Rome, 30 September, available at ⟨http://www.wfp.org/operations/current_operations/project_docs/104270. pdf⟩ (accessed 21 November 2007).

World Water Forum (2000), "Interbasin Water Transfer" session report, World Water Forum, The Hague, The Netherlands, 17–22 March.

# Part III

# Opportunities for cooperation

# 10

# Water governance of the Mekong River Basin and Chinese national problems

*Kayo Onishi*

## Introduction: Water governance of the Mekong River Basin

*Background to the water governance of the Mekong River Basin*

Shortly after the withdrawal of France as a colonial hegemon from Indochina in 1954, Mekong development began with the implementation of a study of the Mekong River Basin initiated in 1952 by the Bureau of Flood Control of the United Nations Economic Commission for Asia and the Far East (ECAFE). The study depicted the Mekong's great potential for the multi-purpose development of irrigation, hydropower, navigation and irrigation (UNECAFE 1957). As a consequence, the lower Mekong riparian states – Thailand, Laos, Viet Nam and Myanmar – adopted the ECAFE report in 1957 and the representatives from those countries established the Mekong Committee (MC) by adopting the Statute for the Committee for Coordination of Investigations of the Lower Mekong Basin. Since then, the four lower countries have maintained their cooperation over the development of the basin, which is often referred to by the term "Mekong spirit".

From the early 1990s, however, the media have reported that the exploitation of water upstream by China for hydropower generation and navigation projects has generated a wide range of environmental and social problems in the basin, especially in the lower states.

This chapter focuses on China's domestic aspect to investigate how domestic problems, such as economic, social and security problems,

*International water security: Domestic threats and opportunities, Pachova, Nakayama and Jansky (eds), United Nations University Press, 2008, ISBN 978-92-808-1150-6*

generate *international* problems with regard to transboundary water, in this case the Mekong River Basin. A main concern in this chapter is the international aspect of the problem of domestic security with a specific focus on the transboundary water of the Mekong. In addition, this chapter is also concerned with the question of the manner in which the international environment causes these domestic problems. The chapter then proceeds as follows. First, it provides an overview of the Mekong River Basin and the history of the water governance of the basin. Second, the chapter enumerates some of the real and potential environmental and social problems caused by China in the basin. Third, it sheds light on China's domestic issues, such as minority and economic disparity problems, which are linked to the international aspect of the problem of domestic security, with a specific focus on Yunnan province. Fourth, it clarifies the international environment that leads to China's exploitation of the waters of the Mekong. Finally, the chapter concludes by suggesting that Mekong development is caused by China's internal and external security problems.

Two principal methods are employed in this study of the influence of domestic security problems on the international water issue. First, the study puts together the history of water governance of the Mekong waters until the early 1990s. Second, it posits a framework for analysing international water disputes from both a domestic and an international politics perspective.

## *The Mekong River Basin*

The Mekong River Basin (MRB), the largest international river basin in Southeast Asia, is shared by six riparian states: China, Myanmar, Thailand, Laos, Viet Nam and Cambodia (Figure 10.1). The Mekong River originates in the Himalayan mountain ranges in Tibet and flows through the southern part of China – Yunnan province. It then hits the Myanmar border before entering Laos, and it passes through Thailand and Laos, forming a border between them. When it reaches Cambodia, it connects with the Tonle Sap River (Great Lake) at Phnom Penh. Then the Mekong flows into Viet Nam, and finally discharges into the South China Sea through the Mekong Delta in southern Viet Nam (MRC 2003). Its length is about 4,800 km, half of which flows through China's Yunnan province, and the total area of the basin is about 795,500 km$^2$ (MRC 2003) (Figure 10.2).

In terms of volume, the mean annual discharge of the basin is approximately 47.5 trillion m$^3$. China contributes 16 per cent of the discharge and Myanmar 2 per cent, with the remainder arising from the four countries in the Lower Basin (Table 10.1). The basin has strong seasonality of

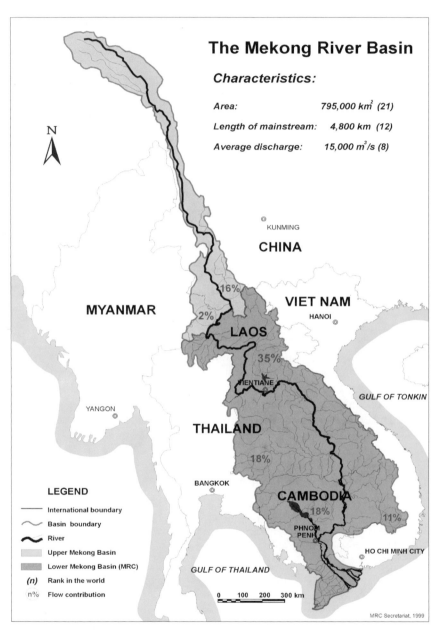

Figure 10.1 The Mekong River Basin.
*Source*: MRC Secretariat 1999.

197

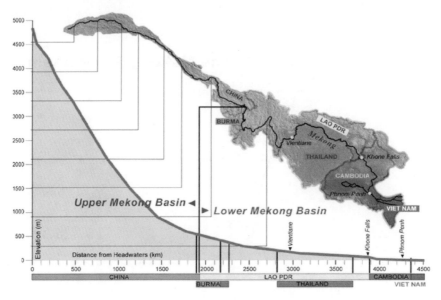

Figure 10.2 Mekong River Basin profile from headwaters to mouth.
*Source*: MRC (2003).

runoff because it is located in a monsoon climate region (Figure 10.3). During the rainy season (from June to October), moisture-laden winds produce large amounts of precipitation; the highest water flow in the Lower Mekong occurs in September and October. During the dry season (from December to May), there is little or no precipitation.

Table 10.1 Approximate distribution of the Mekong River Basin water resources by country

|  | Yunnan | Myanmar | Laos | Thailand | Cambodia | Viet Nam | MRB |
|---|---|---|---|---|---|---|---|
| Catchment area as % of MRB | 22 | 3 | 25 | 23 | 19 | 8 | 100 |
| Average flow (m$^3$/sec) from area | 2,410 | 300 | 5,270 | 2,560 | 2,860 | 1,660 | 15,060 |
| Average flow as % of total | 16 | 2 | 35 | 18 | 18 | 11 | 100 |

*Source*: MRC (2003).

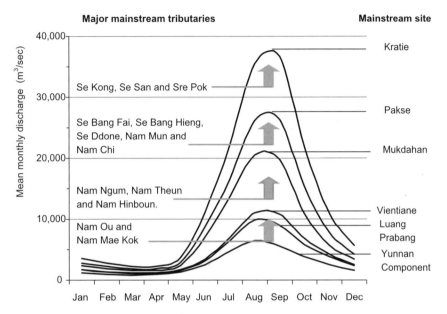

Figure 10.3 Seasonality of runoff in the Mekong River Basin.
*Source*: MRC Secretariat.

## *History of water resources development and the Mekong River Basin organization*

In 1957 the Bureau of Flood Control of the United Nations Economic Commission for Asia and the Far East (ECAFE) reported the great potential for multi-purpose development of irrigation, hydropower, navigation and irrigation (UNECAFE 1957). In the early 1950s the emphasis of the Bureau of Flood Control had shifted from treating flood control as "an isolated subject" to viewing "the wider aspects of multiple-purpose river basin development" of water resources (UNECAFE 1955). Therefore, the Bureau selected the Lower Mekong Basin as a candidate from among other international rivers within ECAFE's jurisdiction, including the Ganges–Brahmaputra and the Indus, to implement this mission (Wightman 1963).

The Lower Mekong riparian states adopted the ECAFE report and in 1957 representatives from Thailand, Laos, Cambodia and Viet Nam established the Mekong Committee (MC) by adopting the Statute for the Committee for Coordination of Investigations of the Lower Mekong Basin. The MC established the Mekong Secretariat in Bangkok as its planning and technical division. The objectives of the MC were (1) data collection, (2) preparation of an overall plan, (3) planning and design of individual projects, (4) maintenance of existing projects, and (5) ancillary work. This led to the start of the development of the Lower Mekong Basin.

In the mid-1960s, the four lower riparian states began to undertake surveys and water-quality sampling in the Mekong Delta, hydraulic modelling studies of the Mekong River levees and resettlement studies, which were supported by the MC (Hori 2000). Although water resources development in the lower basin did not progress as much as expected because the wars in Indochina limited resources, some of the plans were realized: the Nam Pong dam (25,000 kW) and the Nam Pung dam (6,300 kW), located in north-east Thailand, were completed in 1966 and 1965, respectively. The first phase of the Nam Ngum dam (30,000 kW) in Laos was completed in 1972 (Hori 2000).

During the 1970s, the MC issued a 1970 Indicative Basin Plan, including a proposal for 17 mainstream dams. However, internal turmoil in Cambodia impeded its participation in the plan. Consequently, from the early 1970s the MC was virtually unable to function owing to Cambodia's absence from the committee.

In 1978, Thailand, Laos and Cambodia established the Interim Mekong Committee (IMC) in spite of the absence of Cambodia. However, management of the basin cannot be achieved without full membership of the Lower Mekong states. Although the IMC could not undertake comprehensive management of the lower basin without the participation of Cambodia, it carried out hydrological data-gathering, water-quality sampling and flood forecasting and warning.

The third stage of the history of management and governance of the Mekong River Basin commenced in 1995, with the signing of the Agreement on the Cooperation for the Sustainable Development of the Mekong River Basin by the four Lower Basin states: Thailand, Laos, Viet Nam and Cambodia. The signatories at the same time created the Mekong River Commission (MRC). The 1995 Mekong Agreement articulated principles of cooperation and rules for the reasonable and equitable use of the basin's water resources; Article 5 specifies "a reasonable and equitable utilization" of the waters of the basin, providing that any "inter-basin diversion project shall be agreed upon by the Joint Committee through a specific agreement for each project prior to any proposed diversion". The two upstream riparian states, China and Myanmar, did not sign the agreement or join the MRC. However, they did become "dialogue partners", participating in annual meetings with the MRC members.

# Mekong crisis: Internationalization of the domestic problems

These processes of the development and governance of the Mekong River Basin by the four lower riparian states have been often described as "the Mekong spirit", owing to the fact that the MC provided a negotiating forum for these states despite the war (Jacobs 2002). In addition, even though there had been some disputes among the Lower Mekong states – for example, Thailand's plan to divert water to the north-eastern provinces invoked objections by Viet Nam – the ecosystem of the basin remains relatively pristine.

However, from the early 1990s, the basin has been endangered by exploitation of water resources in the upper watershed, which has attracted the attention of academics, journalists and non-governmental organizations (NGOs). Namely, China's exploitation of the upper watershed for hydroelectricity and navigation has raised concerns about negative socioecological impacts on the downstream states. The media have reported, for instance, that "China is building dams on the Mekong, leaving neighbors to worry over the downstream impact" (Crispin 2000); "China has no intention of changing its [dam construction] policy" (BBC News 2004). In academia, John Waterbury (2002) notes that "[t]he People's Republic of China has proceeded unilaterally with hydropower development in the upper reaches of the Mekong without any warning to, let alone an accord with, the downstream riparians". In sum, journalists, academics and NGOs have criticized China as unilaterally exploiting the upper watershed in the basin. And this is precisely the international aspect of the domestic security problems. In the next section, the emphasis will shift to how China has been "generating" international problems by exploiting the waters in the Upper Mekong.

## Hydroelectricity generation projects

China's plan to develop hydropower generation in the Upper Mekong, which is called Lancang-Jiang River ("Turbulent River") in Chinese, began in the late 1980s and was approved by the ministry and the provincial government in 1986 (Yunnan Provincial Electric Power Bureau 1993). Its original scheme was to construct 15 hydroelectricity plants, whose output was supposed to be transmitted to the east coast of China for domestic use (Kunming Hydroelectric Investigation and Design Institute 1985).

The first two hydroelectricity plants are called Manwan (1,500 MW capacity) and Dachaoshan (1,350 MW capacity); the former began construction in 1986, was completed in 1993 and is now operational, and the

● = completed
○ = under construction

Figure 10.4  Hydroelectricity generation projects in China (Yunnan province).
*Source*: He and Chen (2002).

latter began construction in 1997, was completed in 2001 and is now operational. The third and the fourth generations are called Xiaowan (estimated 4,200 MW capacity) and Jinghong (estimated 1,500 MW capacity)
and they are now under construction; a fifth, Nuozhadu, is planned
(MRC 2003) (Figure 10.4 and Table 10.2).
   China's hydroelectricity generation scheme has been deemed unilateral, on the grounds that China did not talk about the scheme and it was

Table 10.2  List of planned and completed hydropower projects on the Mekong in China

| | Installed capacity (MW) | Annual generation (GWh) | Total storage (million m$^3$) | Catchment area (km$^2$) | Average flow (m$^3$/s) | Commissioning |
|---|---|---|---|---|---|---|
| Gongguoqiao | 750 | 4,670 | 510 | 97,300 | 985 | |
| Xiaowan | 4,200 | 18,540 | 15,130 | 113,300 | 1,220 | 2010–12 |
| Manwan | 1,500 | 7,870 | 920 | 114,500 | 1,230 | 1993 |
| Dachaoshan | 1,350 | 7,090 | 880 | 121,000 | 1,230 | 2001 |
| Nuozhadu | 5,500 | 22,670 | 24,670 | 144,700 | 1,750 | |
| Jinghong | 1,500 | 8,470 | 1,040 | 149,100 | 1,840 | 2012–13 |
| Ganlanba | 150 | 1,010 | | 151,800 | 1,880 | |
| Mengson | 600 | 3,740 | | 160,000 | 2,020 | |

*Source*: MRC (2003).

not until the late 1980s that the downstream countries and overseas countries became aware of it (Chapman and He 1996). Whereas all the hydro-electricity plants constructed in Thailand and Laos during the 1960s are on tributaries in their territories, those of China are constructed and planned on the mainstream of the Mekong. Moreover, they might have some negative socio-economic impacts on the downstream states, such as adverse impacts on ecosystems (aquatic life, animals, birds, vegetation), blocking the flow of sediment, and negative impacts owing to changing the river's pattern of flow (MRC 2003), all of which means that China should try to reach a consensus with the affected riparian states.

Therefore, the project has evoked numerous criticisms by academics, journalists and NGOs from outside China. For example, an official of a province of northern Thailand blamed China for the lower water level in Chiang Saen, a port in northern Thailand, attributing the low water level, which caused the stranding of hundreds of boats, to China's dam-building (BBC News 2004). Another example quotes environmentalists and researchers stating that "the most visible threat is posed by the dams", and describes water levels in the Mekong fluctuating by as much as 1 metre per hour, endangering fish habitats, eroding river banks and draining sediment and nutrients from the river (Wain 2004). Furthermore, an international NGO claims that "[t]he dams will be a menace to livelihoods, property, and life in all of the downstream countries", affecting Cambodia and Viet Nam the most (IRN 2001).

However, Chinese academics assert that the only significant change caused by the dams would be in the flow, which might "provide benefits to the downstream states" owing to its increased flow in the dry season and decreased flow in the flood season (He and Chen 2002);

*Navigation project*

Along with the hydroelectricity generation projects, China is implementing a navigation project in the Upper Basin, which is planned to allow free passage of huge shipping in the Upper Basin. The project dates back to as early as 1993 when China expressed an interest in opening a river route from landlocked Yunnan province (MRC 2002). The initial purpose of the project was to remove rapids in the basin. The navigation channel improvement was planned to be 331 km, from boundary mark 243 between China and Myanmar to the Ban Huisai in Laos. Though the Laos and Myanmar governments were the last to agree on the project, the upper riparian states – China, Myanmar, Laos and Thailand – concluded the Upper Lancang–Mekong Commercial Navigation Agreement in 2000. This opened a door for China to export Chinese goods and raw materials along the river.

One of the reasons the navigation project is often depicted as Chinese unilateralism is that China, having engaged in bilateral agreements with the respective riparians before the Navigation Agreement, initiated it without consulting the lowest states. Another reason is that China might not have completed an adequate environmental impact assessment (EIA). A report by an environmental institution in Australia described it as "substantially inadequate" and "fundamentally flawed" (Cocklin and Hain 2001). This report was a response to a request from the MRC to evaluate the navigation project because of the concerns of Laos, Cambodia and Viet Nam about the socio-economic aspects of the EIA China had initiated.

On the other hand, Chinese officials commented that "the implementation of project has no negative impact so far on the surrounding environment" and "navigation channel improvement has greatly boosted the social and economic development of countries along the Mekong River" (Xinmin 2004).

*China's absence from institutional and legal frameworks*

In terms of institutional and legal frameworks, the media and others claim that China is avoiding binding itself to commitment to them.

First, China did not sign the 1995 Agreement because "China fears losing the rights to use the Mekong water if it participates in the Commission" (Sawatsawang 1995).

Secondly, China voted against the 1997 UN Convention on the Law of Non-Navigational Uses of International Watercourses, which specifies the "Obligation Not to Cause Significant Harm" in Article 7. Generally, upstream states do not favour this article (the "no-harm" rule) on the grounds that it protects the established uses of downstream states. China's negative vote should be attributed to its position as an upstream state in ongoing controversies, namely over hydroelectricity generation projects in the Upper Mekong (McCaffrey and Sinjela 1997). In fact, the Chinese representative to the UN General Assembly stated that "the text did not reflect the principle of the territorial sovereignty of a watercourse State. Such a State had indisputable sovereignty over a watercourse which flowed through its territory. There was also an imbalance between the rights and obligations of the upstream and downstream States" (United Nations Press Release 1997).

## China's domestic security issues fostering development of the Mekong

It is clear that the international problem of the endangered Mekong has its roots, by and large, in Chinese domestic problems. Thus, we need to shed light on the Chinese domestic situation to find out why China is pursuing water resources development. What domestic circumstances lie behind this exploitation of water resources by China?

This section begins with a brief overview of Yunnan province and moves on to the national aspect of China's economic development strategy for the western region. It then focuses on China's energy industry reform. I identify these two factors as the national determinants fostering Yunnan's water resources development, especially of hydropower.

### Yunnan province

Yunnan province, located on the south-western frontier of China, shares borders with Myanmar, Laos and Viet Nam. The international border is 4,060 km long. The area of the province is about 394,000 km$^2$. It is a highland province with terraced topographical features stretching from the north-west to the south-east, which result in diverse elevations and climates (UNESCAP n.d.). For several decades, Yunnan province has been economically, politically and culturally backward and isolated in China because of its remoteness from central China.

Yunnan has a population of approximately 42.88 million. The population is ethnically diverse, with minorities accounting for 14.33 million (UNESCAP n.d.).

In terms of its economic condition, total GNP is about US$23,841 million. There is little industrial development. Although Yunnan is abundant in land resources, cultivated land is a small proportion, owing to the steep mountains. The most important industries are wood-processing plants, pulp mills and cement factories. Rice, corn, wheat, rape seed and tea are the most important agricultural products, and tropical crops (e.g. sugar cane), rubber and fruits are produced in the south (Hinton 1998).

### *"Open up the West": Minorities, unity and integrity*

In 1999, the leaders of the Chinese government launched a campaign to "Open up the West" (*xibu da kaifa*), or the "Strategy for Developing the Western Region". The campaign became a mainstay of China's Tenth Five-Year Plan (2001–2005) which makes clear that the focus of national investment policy has now shifted away from the coastal region to the western region. The Tenth Plan aims at (1) construction of "10 big projects" concentrating on transportation infrastructures; (2) transmission of natural gas from the western region to the eastern region; (3) transmission of electricity from the western to the eastern region; (4) diversion of water from the Yangtze River in the south to the northern region.

The western region and the central region comprise 19 provinces and districts, including Yunnan province (Holbig 2004).[1] This region has been economically backward compared with eastern and southern China, which experienced great economic expansion as a result of Deng Xiaoping's "get-rich-first" doctrine, which benefited them from the 1970s. Thus, there is a socio-economic discrepancy between the western, interior region and the eastern, southern region (Table 10.3). As a result, from 1999 onwards, the central government launched a national policy that prioritizes development of the western region: the Western Development Campaign.

The goals of the Western Campaign are, first, to redress the regional economic inequality between the western (and interior) region and the eastern region, and, secondly, to contain ethnic separatism, by maintaining control over the interior region (especially ethnic minority areas), and safeguarding territorial integrity in terms of the state's unity and security (Goodman 2004; Lai 2005). The main features of the campaign were: (1) guaranteeing the supply of natural resources; (2) contributing

Table 10.3 Degree of economic development by the three major regions, 2000

|  | GDP (100 million yuan) | % | Per capita GDP (yuan) | Index |
|---|---|---|---|---|
| Eastern region | 51,631 | 58.8 | 10,103 | 1.00 |
| Central region | 24,207 | 27.5 | 5,459 | 0.54 |
| Western region | 12,003 | 13.7 | 4,172 | 0.41 |

*Source*: Onishi (2001).

Table 10.4  Natural resources in the western region

| Minerals, water and hydropower | Reserves (%) |
| --- | --- |
| Potassium | 97.0 |
| Nickel | 62.0 |
| Natural gas | 58.0 |
| Platinum | 57.0 |
| Coal | 30.0 |
| Petroleum | 23.0 |
| Underground water | 12.5 |
| Hydropower potential | 80.3 |

*Source*: Lai (2005).

to the expansion of domestic demand; (3) protecting the ecological environment; and (4) securing long-term social stability (Onishi 2001). The state has adopted the following measures for the further development of the western region: (1) stepping up fiscal transfers and financial credit supports and increasing investment; (2) launching mammoth infrastructural, environmental, energy and water projects; (3) improving the investment environment by cutting taxes, processes and fees and promulgating favourable policies; (4) attracting foreign investment and expanding external trade (Lai 2005).

The western region comprises a large part of the territory of China and it is abundant in natural resources: large reserves of gas and oil and large rivers (Yangtze, Yellow, Pearl and Lancang rivers) are concentrated in this area (Table 10.4). Thus, these natural resources are to be used in the strategy of economic development of the western region and are to be transmitted to the eastern region.

Furthermore, the western region is home to many ethnic minorities: 52 of the 56 ethnic minorities live in the less-developed western region. Although the western region is home to only 23 per cent of the nation's total population, it accounts for 56 per cent of the nation's ethnic minority populations. It is where ethnic separatism and ethnic tensions are active and acute; indeed, some of the ethnic minority populations have posed a political problem to the Chinese central government that needs to be addressed (Lai 2005). Thus, integrating ethnic minorities and territory into China is an urgent issue to be tackled by central government. As far as Yunnan province is concerned, there are 22 ethnic minorities, such as Yi, Bai, Hani, Tibetan and Mongolian.

Therefore, social harmony, political stability and national security are threatened unless minority nationalities are given better opportunities for economic development (Holbig 2004); it was necessary for the stability and security of the society for the central government to deal with the economic discrepancy between the two regions, to assimilate and integrate ethnic minorities into Great China, and to integrate this resource-rich region. Security concerns are mainly taken care of through infrastructure projects linking the western region to the central and eastern parts of the country (Lai 2005).

Yunnan province has grasped the chance of the Western Development Campaign for its provincial economic development. In 2000, Yunnan province launched a mid-term socio-economic development plan that articulated energy development as one of its priorities (Bi 2005). Concerning hydropower development projects, the western region contains 80 per cent of the nation's potential hydropower (Table 10.4); therefore, hydropower generation development is supported by the Western Development Campaign "to bring resource-rich region into integration". For example, Xiaowan hydropower plant is one of the key projects to be constructed during China's Tenth Five-Year Plan and is an important part of China's strategy for transmitting electricity from the resource-rich western areas to power-short coastal areas such as Guangdong, Jiangsu province and Shanghai Municipality (2001–2005) (Xinhua 2001b).

Furthermore, Yunnan province was identified as the centre of the China–ASEAN Free Trade Area, which central government is encouraging. Yunnan province expects that Yunnan will play a vital role in economic cooperation with ASEAN states with respect to agriculture, energy sources, mineral products and tourism. Yunnan province is building itself into the "large passage, large platform, and large plant" of the China–ASEAN Free Trade Zone (Kong 2004); Yunnan province is expected to develop transportation infrastructure and to be a large import and export hub for the ASEAN states. Since 1998, Yunnan province has invested approximately US$12 million in transportation expansion (Bi 2005). As a result, transport links inside China and to abroad have been established almost completely through road, rail, air and water transportation (see below). As mentioned above, China concluded the Upper Lancang–Mekong Commercial Navigation Agreement in 2000 under which 14 ports of the four signatory states would be opened to ships. China expected that the Lancang–Jiang shipping service would carry 1.5 million tons of cargo and 400,000 passengers (Xinhua 2001a).

In sum, the Western Development Campaign is clearly a domestic aspect of the problems of China's water resources exploitation in the Upper Mekong. In order to reduce the imbalance between two discrete regions and to integrate both a territory with abundant natural resources and ethnic minorities into Great China for security purposes, the Chinese government has encouraged the Western Development Campaign, which supports huge hydropower and navigation projects in Yunnan province.

Thus, the Western Development Campaign is one of the underlying reasons that the Mekong is "endangered".

## Energy industry reform in China: Energy security

Since the 1990s, China has undertaken major energy industry reform that has coincided with the Western Development Campaign. I have identified energy industry reform as the second domestic factor behind Yunnan's water resources development in the Upper Mekong. This subsection gives a brief overview of the underlying energy industry reform, with a specific focus on hydropower development related to Yunnan's water resources exploitation.

In 1998, the Chinese government announced a major structural reform of government institutions and state industries. The objectives were, first, to reduce the cost of government; second, to separate the functions of government and industry; and, third, to increase the effectiveness of government (Andrews-Speed et al. 2000).

The reforms of 1998 had a significant impact on the energy industry. During the late 1980s and early 1990s China faced two major problems: a major increase in generating capacity was required to meet the growing demand; especially in terms of water resources, there was a geographical mismatch between the location of resources and demand – with the hydroelectric potential concentrated in the south-west (Andrews-Speed et al. 2000).

The first step of the reforms was the creation of the State Power Corporation of China (SPCC) and the abolition of the Ministry of Electric Power in 1998. The provincial and lower-level bureaus were reappointed as companies, in an attempt to separate government and enterprise functions in the energy sector (Andrews-Speed et al. 2000). The second step was the dismantling of the SPCC into five power generation corporations – China Guodian Corporation, China Huadian Corporation, China Huaneng Group, China Power Investment Corporation and China Datang Corporation – and into the State Grid Corporation of China (Northeast, Northwest, North China, Central China and three independent provincial power grids) and the China Southern Power Grid Corporation Ltd. Yunnan province has its own independent power supplier and grid (China State Power Information Network n.d.). Each corporation is responsible for the development, investment, construction, operation and management of power sources (China State Power Information Network n.d.). The goals of corporatization were, first, to separate generation from distribution, and, second, to modernize the management of the industry (Magee 2006).

Although decisions on large-scale hydropower projects on transboundary waters require final approval from the State Council (Magee 2006), it can be argued that the provincial-level bureaus and corporations are, to some extent, playing significant roles in the development of water resources. Traditionally, central government has planned, constructed, operated and managed huge hydroelectricity dams. However, with the assent of central government, decentralization for efficiency is in process: to manage the Lancang-Jiang, the Yunnan Huaneng Lancang River Hydropower Company (also called Hydrolancang) was established in 2001 by the SPCC (27 per cent), Yunnan Electric Power Group Company (29 per cent), Yunnan Province Development Investment Company (24 per cent) and Yunnan Hongta Industry Company (20 per cent). The newly organized company is jointly invested in by the Huaneng Group (56 per cent), Yunnan Province Development Investment Company (31.4 per cent) and Yunnan Hongta Industry Company (12.6 per cent).[2]

The first hydropower station (Manwan) was originally a project of the Yunnan government and the Ministry of Water Resources and Electric Power. This was reorganized into a stock company, the Yunnan Manwan Electric Power Generation Company, which then became part of Huaneng's subsidiary, Hydrolancang (Magee 2006). The second dam (Dachaoshan) was built by Yunnan Dachaoshan Hydropower Company, which involves the State Development Investment Company, Yunnan Province Development Investment Company and the Yunnan Electric Power Group Company.

Jinghong dam was originally planned as a joint project with Thailand. In 2000, China and Thailand signed a memorandum for the joint building of the Jinghong power station, which would be funded by a public–private consortium of Sino-Thai partners. A Thai firm, GMS Power (formerly MDX Power), signed an agreement with China's Yunnan Electric Bureau for a hydroelectric project worth US$2 billion. The pact includes a joint venture between Chinese partners and GMS Power, which hold a 70 per cent stake in the venture, with the remaining 30 per cent held by the Yunnan Electricity Generating Authority and the provincial government (Dore and Yu 2004). The Jinghong power station is planned to transmit 1.5 million kW of electricity per year to Thailand by about 2013 and 3 million kW by 2014 (Xinhua 2000). Nuozhadu power station is also planned to be constructed by a Sino-Thai joint venture (Xinhua 2004b).

This energy industry reform represented an adjustment to the increasing demand for energy in China. Thus, the role played by the reformed energy industry in watershed exploitation in the Mekong to secure energy should not be overlooked as a determinant of Yunnan's pursuit of water resources development.

*Domestic security issues: Minorities, energy and economic discrepancy*

In sum, China's water resources exploitation in the Upper Mekong is determined by two domestic conditions: the Western Economic Development Campaign and the energy industry reform. Both factors are the result of China's strategy for domestic security. The socio-economic gap between the two regions and the minority problem are the main security issues for China. At the same time, increasing energy demand should also be a priority security issue in China. These domestic conditions underlie Yunnan's water resources development from a security perspective.

## Mekong regional integration

China's exploitation of water in the upper watershed has not merely in large measure been the product of China's domestic security issues engendered by the national problems; it has also been a product of the internationalization of basin development. This section attempts to describe the effects of the international scale of the Mekong development on China's national problems.

*Yunnan as a "gateway to Southeast Asia"*

While shedding light on Yunnan's economic and political conditions and its economic development policy, we should bear in mind that Yunnan's geopolitical setting plays a vital role in the China–Mekong relationship that is fostering Yunnan's water resources development.

Yunnan province is on the south-western frontier of China and shares borders with Myanmar, Laos and Viet Nam. Historically speaking, because of its geographical position, Yunnan province had been regarded as a "pivot" (Lattimore 1943) between China and the Indochinese countries since Great Power colonial rule. In fact, during the colonial period, the French suzerain power had been anxious to trade with China and aimed to use the Mekong as a trade route to Yunnan, which was a front door to China. However, France abandoned its initial scheme because strong currents and waterfalls hinder free navigation on the Mekong and because navigation of sections south of Phnom Penh by vessels of any size is limited to periods when the water level is at its highest (for about three months of the year). Instead, the French suzerain explored the Red River in northern Viet Nam, which successfully led to the establishment of a trade route with China (Hori 2000). In sum, Yunnan played an important role in linking China and Southeast Asia geopolitically during the colonial period.

Since the victory of the communists in the civil war in China in 1949, the border regions have been closely guarded to prevent outside influences from entering China. However, since the 1980s–1990s, the reopening of border trade has been facilitated, and has become an important source of revenue for local and provincial governments (Kuah 2000). The close regional identification between Yunnan province and Southeast Asia soon re-emerged.

## Mekong regional economic integration

Prior to the collapse of the Soviet Union, the history of the Mekong region had featured deep-seated animosities and rivalries among the states and international and domestic warfare: the Viet Nam war, the China–Viet Nam war, and civil wars and communist victories in Laos, Cambodia and Viet Nam. The region lacked stability and peace, which hindered the economic development of this region.

However, with the end of the Cold War and the signing of the Paris Peace Agreement on Cambodia in 1991, the Indochina region began to recover its relative stability and peace. At the same time, the region has witnessed great regional economic expansion owing to international organizations and international or bilateral donor agencies, which rushed to the region in anticipation of economic development potential.

As a result, a new wave of regionalism among the Mekong riparian states has emerged, and economic links among the various states in the region have been evolving since the early 1990s. With its geographical advantages, Yunnan province, as a part of China, has been incorporated into this regional economic integration. The following institutional frameworks and regimes are promoting economic integration among the Mekong riparians and surrounding states.

### Institutional frameworks promoting economic integration

#### Asian Development Bank–Greater Mekong Subregion
In 1992, the Asian Development Bank (ADB) initiated the Greater Mekong Subregion (GMS). The ADB-GMS comprises all six riparian states: Thailand, Viet Nam, Cambodia, Laos, Myanmar and Yunnan province (China). The aim of the ADB-GMS is to enhance subregional economic cooperation by promoting development thorough closer economic linkages (ADB n.d.).

Since its establishment, ADB-GMS has evolved as the focus of regional development. The ADB launched "Flagship" programmes to pursue its strategic thrust in 2001. The programmes are as follows: North–South Economic Corridor, East–West Economic Corridor, Southern Economic Corridor, Regional Power Interconnection and Trading Arrangements, Facilitating Cross-Border Trade and Investment, Flood Control and Water Resource Management, and so on.

The main projects are infrastructure construction: the North–South Economic Corridor, the East–West Economic Corridor and the Southern Economic Corridor, which link the six riparian states through transportation networks, and the Regional Power Interconnection, which links them through the regional power grid (ADB 2005b,c,d).

### ASEAN Mekong Basin Development Cooperation

In 1995, the Association of Southeast Asian Nations (ASEAN) also initiated a regional development framework for the Mekong River Basin, called the ASEAN Mekong Basin Development Cooperation (AMBDC). The AMBDC encompasses the six riparian states, including China, and other ASEAN countries such as Singapore and Malaysia.

The purpose of the initiative is (i) to enhance economically sound and sustainable development of the Mekong Basin, (ii) to encourage a process of dialogue and common project identification which can result in firm economic partnerships for mutual benefit, and (iii) to strengthen the interconnections and economic linkages between the ASEAN member countries and the Mekong riparian countries.

The main project of the AMBDC is the Singapore–Kunming Rail Link (SKRL), which aims to link China (Kunming, Yunnan) and Singapore by constructing a transnational railway.

### Other frameworks

Other regional frameworks also aim at the regional economic development of the Mekong. They are the Initiative for ASEAN Integration (IAI), the Asian Highway (AH), Human Resources Development at the Enterprise Level, Institutional Capacity Building, Facilitation Measures, Investment Promotion Plan for Private Sector Development in the Greater Mekong Subregion, and the Forum for the Comprehensive Development of Indochina (FCDI).

China puts significant emphasis on these regional frameworks. As China has declared in a state report issued by the State Development and Reform Commission, the Ministry of Foreign Affairs and the Ministry of Finance: "GMS economic cooperation is a very important part of China's diplomatic relations with neighboring countries" (Xinhua 2005b).

The main sectors in which these institutional frameworks are actively working are energy and transportation.

*Energy*

Responding to the increasing demand for energy in this rapidly growing region, energy security is a central issue in regional economic integration in the Mekong region. For economic efficiency, the Mekong riparian states are promoting regional power exchange through the framework of the ADB-GMS. Since 2001, the GMS has facilitated "Regional Power Interconnection and Trading Arrangements" that aim to promote transmission grid interconnection and power development by (a) developing policies and institutions for cross-border power dispatch and trade, and (b) installing grid interconnection infrastructure (ADB 2005b).

The demand for energy in GMS countries paralleled Yunnan's hydropower development as a part of the Western Development Campaign. GMS master plans identify energy sources in Yunnan province (China) as well as in Lao PDR and Myanmar (ADB 2005d). Thus, it is indisputable that, with its tremendous hydropower potential in Yunnan province, China is one of the major energy suppliers in the GMS framework. In 2000, Thailand agreed to purchase electricity from Yunnan: grid connections linking Thai hydropower projects in Yunnan (Jinghong) and connections linking Yunnan and Viet Nam are planned to be implemented from 2012 and 2012–2019, respectively (ADB 2005d). Moreover, at the Second GMS Summit in Kunming in 2005, China emphasized that it is a provider of energy in the Mekong; China declared that it would cooperate with Thailand and Laos to carry out research on the feasibility of Chinese exports of 3 million kW of power to Thailand (ADB 2005a; Xinhua 2005a).

Hence, the ADB frames Yunnan as a supplier of hydropower in the GMS cooperation: in the international environment, Yunnan's hydropower development project integrates with the energy trade in the Mekong region which fosters it.

*Transportation*

Transportation is another priority project in the region to foster economic integration between China and the downstream states. ADB-GMS and AMBDC are vigorously promoting transportation linkages among the Mekong riparian states and surrounding states. Most of the transportation projects include China (Yunnan) as an important stakeholder. China is encouraging this transportation cooperation; it has ratified the agreement on facilitating GMS passenger and cargo transportation and funded the dredging of the river course of the Mekong, and has conducted research on the Pan-Asia railway project (Xinhua 2005b). Two significant factors are driving transportation cooperation between China and the downstream states as well as the ASEAN countries: energy security and the ASEAN–China Free Trade Area Agreement.

From the outset, ADB-GMS has promoted transportation infrastructure linking China and the downstream states. The core project encompasses the Kunming–Chiang Rai–Bangkok route via Lao PDR and Myanmar and the Kunming–Hanoi–Haiphong route. The former connects China to the important sea port of Bangkok in Thailand. The latter connects China to the existing highway running from the northern and southern parts of Viet Nam. In sum, the North–South Economic Corridor is planned to play "a critical role in providing PRC and northern Lao PDR access to important sea ports", requiring "road, rail, water transport, and air transport linkages" (ADB 2005b). In terms of energy security, this transportation cooperation has a significant role: the transportation projects are related to the energy security of China and others because the Mekong is currently utilized as a route for energy, such as oil imports. Although it is not a main route, the Coordination Commission of China, Laos, Myanmar and Thailand for Navigation of Commercial Ships along the Lancang–Mekong agreed that the open water channel of the Lancang would be used to ship oil products and liquefied gas from Thailand to Jinghong in Yunnan in 2004. Since then, around 1,400 tons of diesel engine oil have already been transported from Thailand to Jinghong along the Mekong watercourse (People's Daily 2005).

On the other hand, the Free Trade Agreement between China and ASEAN bolsters the transportation links of the Mekong. At the 2000 ASEAN summit, China and ASEAN leaders agreed to establish the ASEAN–China Free Trade Area (FTA); in 2002, China and ASEAN concluded a Framework Agreement on Comprehensive Economic Co-operation between ASEAN and China. Prior to the establishment of the ASEAN–China FTA, China and Thailand had moved early to reduce taxes on agricultural products. As a result, trade between China and Thailand is growing rapidly, especially between northern Thailand and the south-west frontier of China via road, water and rail; trade through Chiang Rai province – located in northern Thailand along the Mekong River Basin – with China reached 6 billion *baht* (US$153 million) a year in 2004 (Fullbrook 2004). This trade is augmented by ADB-GMS's Kunming–Chiang Rai–Bangkok route. Hence, the China–ASEAN FTA is certainly a determinant of transportation construction between China and the downstream states, which boosts Yunnan's water resources development.

In sum, both the energy security of the various states and the China–ASEAN FTA are boosting transportation cooperation among the Mekong riparian states. Needless to say, this also facilitates Yunnan province's water transportation development as a factor promoting international cooperation.

## Political integration and regional security

This economic integration, at the same time, paralleled ASEAN's efforts to incorporate China into ASEAN's security regime. With little history of regional security cooperation in the Asia-Pacific, the states affected by the Cold War launched a security dialogue in Asia. The ASEAN Regional Forum (ARF) comprises 10 ASEAN members and the Dialogue Partners, which include China. The ARF aims at fostering constructive dialogue and consultation on political and security issues, and making significant contributions to efforts towards confidence-building and preventive diplomacy in the Asia-Pacific Region (ASEAN Regional Forum n.d.).

Since its establishment, the ASEAN members have worked as brokers to bring China, an economic and political superpower, into the system. Owing to negative experiences in the past with China and future uncertainty, the ASEAN states have followed a non-confrontational approach called "constructive engagement" (Antolik 1994).

Thus, regional economic integration in the Mekong functions as a catalyst towards regional security. Regarding the relationship between China and Southeast Asian countries, ASEAN states have tried to incorporate China into the system by taking advantage of the Mekong River Basin development. Therefore, the effort to cooperate over Mekong regional development in the framework of ASEAN is one facet of ASEAN's security strategy aiming at constructive cooperation between China and ASEAN.

## International security issues: Economic integration and regional security

In sum, two international conditions, economic integration in the Mekong region and regional security, determine China's water exploitation in the Upper Mekong. Both factors are the results of international security issues in the region. Hence, China's water resources exploitation in the Upper Mekong has not merely been the product of China's domestic security issues but it also has been a product of internationalization of basin development.

## Towards cooperation

To an extent, the internationalization of water issues has forced China to pay attention to downstream states' reactions and to solicit their acceptance of China's water resources development. Yu Xiaogang, a director of the environmental NGO Green Watershed, has commented that

China's central government has now recognized that China "needs to be accepted as a good neighbour in the Mekong region, and a partner in managing and conserving the numerous benefits that people, economies and societies of region receive from the Mekong river and its tributaries" (Yu 2002).

China, in fact, has been moving recently towards cooperation with the downstream states with regard to uses of water resources in the basin. In 2002, China signed the Agreement on the Provision of Hydrological Information of the Lancang/Mekong River in Flood Season (MRC 2002). In addition, China is a regular "dialogue partner" with the MRC (MRC 2005) and has been involved in the negotiation process for the framework of the MRC, for instance mechanisms such as "Dialogue Meeting", and technical collaboration with two upstream countries in the Water Utilization Programme. Moreover, China has been gradually paying attention to the voices of the downstream states and is open for discussion in multilateral negotiations; for example, at high-level meetings among six riparian states in 2004, China showed its willingness to listen to the downstream states and has been open for discussions. Media reports indicate that Chinese dam development was at the centre of the discussions. Moreover, the Thai natural resources and environment minister and the Cambodian environment minister reported that China gave an increasing sign of cooperation and willingness to discuss environmental problems (*The Nation* 2004).

*Mechanisms of inter-state cooperation*

Why does China have an incentive to cooperate? It is because China finds cooperation with downstream states economically beneficial, as do downstream states themselves. Namely, Yunnan's exploitation of the upper watershed in the Mekong is the result of economic cooperation between China and the downstream states and their "see no evil" development, although it originates with China's unilateral exploitation of water resources for its domestic security: China and the downstream states are avoiding inter-state zero-sum conflict over transboundary water resources in the Mekong by creating a non-zero-sum outcome with the linkage of water resources and non-water resources (Table 10.5).

The mechanism is as follows. In the Mekong River Basin, water resources and non-water resources are interchangeable in terms of their functions. This is in contrast to arid areas, where water resources are scarce (zero-sum resources) and non-interchangeable, thus causing inter-state zero-sum conflicts over the distribution of water resources (Table 10.6). In the Mekong River Basin, thermal power or natural gas power can substitute for hydropower, while highways, railways and airways can

Table 10.5 The nature of water resources and the distribution of benefits by upstream/downstream states and the outcome of conflicts: Arid area and Mekong River Basin (monsoon area)

|  | Nature of water resources | | Distribution of benefits and outcome of conflicts |
|---|---|---|---|
| Arid area (e.g. Middle East) | Scarce (zero-sum) | | Zero-sum |
| Mekong River Basin (monsoon area) | *Dry season* Scarce (zero-sum) | *Flood season* Abundant (positive-sum) | Positive-sum |

Table 10.6 The function of water and non-water resources and their interchangeability

|  | Energy | Transportation |
|---|---|---|
| Water resources | Hydropower | Navigation |
| Non-water resources | Thermal power Natural gas power | Rail, road, air |

substitute for water transportation. Therefore, the general conflicts between upstream and downstream states over shared water resources are being avoided. This situation requires further investigation.

## Conclusion

This chapter has attempted to illustrate how domestic issues, such as economic, social and security problems, give rise to international problems over the Mekong River Basin. Thus, domestic security issues in China are not an isolated phenomenon but are one aspect of an international conflict among the riparian states in the Mekong River Basin. The chapter thus identifies two domestic determinants underlying the geopolitical and geo-economic international setting for the development of Yunnan's water resources in the Upper Mekong watershed: first, in the domestic context, China's Western Regional Development; and, second, energy industry reform. These aspects of Chinese domestic problems are significant factors that encourage Yunnan to foster water resources exploitation of the Mekong. In geopolitical and geo-economic terms, Yunnan's geopolitical ties with China and the downstream states (and ASEAN states) foster economic and political cooperation among the Mekong riparian states; in particular, economic integration in the Mekong region, especially with regard to energy and transportation supported by regional institutions such as ADB-GMS and AMBDC. These regional institutions facilitate cooperation between China and the downstream states (ASEAN states) in regard to the Mekong River Basin. This too fosters the development of Yunnan's water resources.

This chapter can therefore assert that, in international waters, domestic security issues may encourage spill-over effects into the international realm and international problems may also affect the domestic problems countries face. In the case study of the Mekong River Basin, linkages between both the domestic and the international context are important for understanding how the project has developed since its inception.

## Notes

1. The definitions of "western" and "central" region are diverse. According to Holbig (2004), the central region is composed of 8 provincial jurisdictions (Heilongjiang, Jilin, Inner Mongolia, Shanxi, Hunan, Anhui, Jiangxi and Henan) while the western region comprises 10 (Xinjiang, Qinghai, Gansu, Ningxia, Shanghai, Tibet, Yunnan, Sichuan, Chongqing and Guizhou); the "Open up the West" strategy of 1999 referred to western and central China together. On the other hand, according to Lai (2005), the central region comprises 8 provincial jurisdictions (Heilongjiang, Jilin, Shanxi, Hunan, Anhui, Jiangxi, Hubei and Henan) while the western region comprises 12 (Shanxi, Gansu, Qinghai, Ningxia, Xinjiang, Sichuan, Chongqing, Guizhou, Yunnan, Tibet, Guangxi and Inner Mongolia). This categorization is post-1998.
2. Hydrolancang website at ⟨http://www.hnlcj.cn/⟩.

## REFERENCES

Andrews-Speed, Philip, Stephen Dow and Zhiguo Gao (2000), "The Ongoing Reforms to China's Government and State Sector: The Case of the Energy Industry", *Journal of Contemporary China*, Vol. 9, No. 23, pp. 5–20.

Antolik, Michael (1994), "The ASEAN Regional Forum: The Spirit of Constructive Engagement", *Contemporary Southeast Asia*, Vol. 16, No. 2.

ASEAN Regional Forum (n.d.), ⟨http://www.aseanregionalforum.org/AboutUs/tabid/57/Default.aspx⟩ (accessed 22 November 2007).

ADB [Asian Development Bank] (n.d.), "The GMS Program", at ⟨http://www.adb.org/GMS/Program/default.asp⟩ (accessed 17 December 2007).

——— (2005a), "Kunming Declaration: 'A Stronger GMS Partnership for Common Prosperity'", Second Greater Mekong Subregion Summit, Kunming, Yunnan, People's Republic of China, 4–5 July, at ⟨http://www.adb.org/Media/Articles/2005/7879_Greater_Mekong_Subregion_declaration/default.asp⟩ (accessed 22 November 2007).

——— (2005b), "GMS Flagship Initiative: North-South Economic Corridor", 26 June, at ⟨http://www.adb.org/GMS/Projects/1-flagship-summary-north-south.pdf⟩ (accessed 22 November 2007).

——— (2005c), "GMS Flagship Initiative: Southern Economic Corridor", 26 June, at ⟨http://www.adb.org/GMS/Projects/1-flagship-summary-southern.pdf⟩, (accessed 22 November 2007).

——— (2005d), "GMS Flagship Initiative: Regional Power Interconnection and Power Trade Arrangements", 26 June, at ⟨http://www.adb.org/GMS/Projects/1-flagship-summary-power.pdf⟩ (accessed 22 November 2007).

BBC News (2004), "Thais Blame China over Low Mekong", 1 April, at ⟨http://news.bbc.co.uk/2/hi/asia-pacific/3591555.stm⟩ (accessed 22 November 2007).

Bi Shihong (2005), "Development of Yunnan Province" (in Japanese), at ⟨http://www.mekong.ne.jp/ippanreport/bishihong/ronbun200503(1).htm⟩ (accessed 28 August 2006).

Chapman, E. C. and He Daming (1996), "Downstream Implications of China's Dams on the Lancang Jiang (Upper Mekong) and Their Potential Significance for Greater Regional Cooperation, Basin-Wide", at ⟨http://www.anu.edu.au/asianstudies/mekong/dams.html⟩ (accessed November 2005).

China State Power Information Network (n.d.), "Power Reform–Brief Information", at ⟨http://www.sp-china.com/powerReform/bi.html⟩ (accessed 22 November 2007).

Cocklin, C. and M. Hain (2001), "Evaluation of the EIA for the Proposed Upper Navigation Improvement Project. Report Prepared for the Mekong River Commission-Environment Program", Monash Environment Institute, Monash University, Australia, December.

Crispin, Shawn W., et al. (2000), "Choke Point", *Far Eastern Economic Review*, Vol. 163, No. 41, pp. 22–25.

Dore, John and Yu Xiaogan (2004), *Yunnan Hydropower Expansion: Update on China's Energy Industry Reforms and the Nu, Lancang and Jinsha Hydropower Dams*, Working Paper, Chiang Mai University's Unit for Social and Environmental Research, and Green Watershed, Kunming, People's Republic of China, March.

Fullbrook, David (2004), "Bumpy Road to Thai–China Trade Efficiency", *Asia Times Online*, 8 April, at ⟨http://www.atimes.com/atimes/Southeast_Asia/FD08Ae01.html⟩ (accessed 22 November 2007).

Goodman, David S. G. (2004), "The Campaign to 'Open up the West': National, Provincial-level and Local Perspectives", *China Quarterly*, No. 158, pp. 317–334.

He Daming and Chen Lihui (2002), "The Impact of Hydropower Cascade Development in the Lancang-Mekong Basin, Yunnan", *Mekong Update&Dialogue*, Vol. 5, No. 3.

Hinton, Peter (1998), *Resource Management in the Yunnan Mekong Basin*, Working Paper No. 72, National Library of Australia.

Holbig, Heike (2004), "The Emergence of the Campaign to Open up the West: Ideological Formation, Central Decision-making and the Role of the Provinces", *China Quarterly*, pp. 335–358.

Hori, Hiroshi (2000), *The Mekong: Environment and Development*, Tokyo: United Nations University Press.

IRN [International River Network] (2001), *China's Upper Mekong Dams Endanger Millions Downstream*, Briefing Paper 3, October.

Jacobs, Jeffery W. (2002), "The Mekong River Commission: Transboundary Water Resources Planning and Regional Security", *Geographical Journal*, Vol. 168, No. 4, pp. 354–364.

Kong Chuizhu (2004), "Create Yunnan's Characterized Economy by Uniting the East and Developing Southward", Vice Governor of Yunnan Province, November, at ⟨http://www.gxnews.cn/news/20041118/xbltzyyl/153526.htm⟩ (accessed 22 November 2007).

Kuah, Khun Eng (2000), "Negotiating Central, Provincial, and County Policies: Border Trading in South China" in Grant Evans, Christopher Hutton and Khun Eng Kuah, eds, *Where China Meets Southeast Asia: Social and Cultural Change in the Border Regions*, Singapore: Institute of Southeast Asian Studies; Bangkok: White Lotus.

Kunming Hydroelectric Investigation and Design Institute (1985), "Cascade Hydropower Projects on Lancang River In Yunnan Province".

Lai Hongyi (2005), "National Security and Unity, and China's Western Development Program", *Provincial China*, Vol. 8, No. 2, pp. 118–143.

Lattimore, Owen (1943), "Yunnan, Pivot of Southeast Asia", *Foreign Affairs*, No. 21, pp. 476–493.

McCaffrey, S. and C. Sinjela (1997), "The 1997 United Nations Convention on International Watercourses", *American Journal of International Law*, Vol. 92, No. 1, pp. 97–107.

Magee, Darin (2006), "Powershed Politics: Yunnan Hydropower under Great Western Development", *China Quarterly*, pp. 23–41.

MRC [Mekong River Commission] (2002), *Annual Report 2002*, Phnom Penh, Cambodia.

——— (2003), *MRC State of the Basin Report 2003*, June, Phnom Penh, Cambodia.

——— (2005), "Minute: Twenty-First Meeting of the Joint Committee. 24–25 March 2005", Pattaya, Thailand.

Onishi, Yasuo (2001), "Chinese Economy in the 21st Century and the Strategy for Developing the Western Region", in Onishi Yasuo, ed., *China's Western Development Strategy: Issues and Prospects*, IDE Spot Survey, December, Institute of Developing Economies (IDE-JETRO).

*People's Daily* (2001), "Ethnic Minorities Biggest Beneficiaries of West China Development", 3 March, at ⟨http://english.people.com.cn/200103/03/eng20010303_63992.html⟩ (accessed 22 November 2007).

——— (2005), "Lancang-Mekong Waterway, A Channel for Oil Transportation, 14 May, at ⟨http://english.people.com.cn/200505/14/eng20050514_185011.html⟩ (accessed 22 November 2007).

Personal communication (2007), Interview with Programme Officer/Operational Hydrologist, Technical Support Division (TSD), Mekong River Commission Secretariat, via email, May.

Sawatsawang, Nussara (1995), "Mekong Group Incomplete", *Bangkok Post*, 4 April, p. 27.

*The Nation* (2004), "Mekong Meeting: China Lends an Ear to Regional Woes", 20 November.

UNECAFE [United Nations Economic Commission for Asia and the Far East] (1955), *Multiple-Purpose River Basin Development, Part 1. Manual of River Basin Planning*, Flood Control Series No. 7, ST/ECAFE/SER.F/7, New York, 24 January.

―――― (1957), *Development of Water Resources in the Lower Mekong Basin*, Flood Control Series No. 12, E/CN.11/457/ST/ECAFE/SER.F/12, Bangkok, October.

UNESCAP [United Nations Economic and Social Commission for Asia and Pacific] (n.d.), "Status of Population and Family Planning Programme in China by Province. Yunnan: Basic Data", at ⟨http://www.unescap.org/esid/psis/population/database/chinadata/yunnan.htm⟩ (accessed 22 November 2007).

United Nations Press Release (1997), "United Nations General Assembly Plenary-5-Press Release GA/9248 99th Meeting (AM) 21 May 1997", Statement by Gao Feng (China).

Wain, Barry (2004), "River at Risk", *Far Eastern Economic Review*, Vol. 167, No. 34, pp. 48–51.

Waterbury, J. (2002), *The Nile Basin: National Determinants of Collective Action*, New Haven, CT: Yale University Press.

Wightman, D. (1963), *Toward Economic Cooperation in Asia: The United Nations Economic Commission for Asia and the Far East*, New Haven, CT: Yale University Press.

Xinhua News Agency (2000), "China's Thailand Plan for Power Station on Lancang River", Kunming, 7 June.

―――― (2001a), "International Shipping Service on Lancang-Mekong River to Begin in June", Kunming, 10 April.

―――― (2001b), "China Prepares for Gigantic New Power Station", Kunming, 11 April.

―――― (2004a), "China to Build Huge Power Station on Lancang-Mekong River", Kunming, 20 January.

―――― (2004b), "China, Thailand Join Forces on Yunnan Power Projects", Kunming, 17 July.

―――― (2005a), "China Proposes Plan of Power Cooperation in Greater Mekong Subregion", Kunming, 4 July.

―――― (2005b), "China Issues State Report on GMS Cooperation", Kunming, 5 July.

Xinmin, Qiao (2004), "Progress of the Navigation Channel Improvement of The Lancang Mekong River Project", in Mekong River Commission, *Ninth Dialogue Meeting*, 26 August, Vientiane, Lao PDR.

Yu Xiaogang (2002), "Change Flows down the Mekong", *Bangkok Post*, 13 November.

Yunnan Provincial Electric Power Bureau (1993), "Hydroenergy Resources and Development Plan of Middle and Lower Research of the Lancang River in Yunnan Province".

# 11

# Transboundary water issues in the Euphrates–Tigris River Basin: Some methodological approaches and opportunities for cooperation

*Aysegül Kibaroglu, Anthi D. Brouma and Mete Erdem*

## Introduction

This chapter will examine the growing complexity of transboundary water resources management in the Euphrates–Tigris River Basin. Introductory sections discuss the evolution of modernity as it relates to natural resources management, and then analyse "water management paradigms" placed within the modernity framework. We assert in this chapter that these paradigms are predominantly Eurocentric (or Northern). Hence, the use of "environmental security" as the theoretical framework for water analysis may be more appropriate for the parts of the globe (e.g. the Euphrates–Tigris River Basin) that are still struggling to reach modernity. The evolution of the "environmental security" agenda will be described with special reference to the third generation of this school of thought, which asserts that even highly politicized and securitized environmental issues such as the water issue in the Euphrates–Tigris can be approached in a sensible manner where the different phases of the dispute can be analysed by acknowledging the cooperation and collaboration efforts in the basin.

We then analyse the transboundary water issues in the Euphrates–Tigris River Basin, discussing the origins and the evolution of the dispute and major issues of contention. We review the Joint Technical Committee meetings, and suggest a broadening of its agenda. Here, the idea is to tackle the issue of water resources management as part of a larger framework of overall socio-economic development of the region. After

*International water security: Domestic threats and opportunities, Pachova, Nakayama and Jansky (eds), United Nations University Press, 2008, ISBN 978-92-808-1150-6*

showing the limitations and shortcomings of the existing water allocation mechanism, we discuss the merits of the principle of "equitable utilization" and "the needs-based approach" with specific reference to Turkey's Three Stage Plan.

Special reference is made to the regional socio-economic development programme – the Southeastern Anatolia Project (GAP) in Turkey – as a potential role model to collaborate around as well as to the recent rapprochement between GAP's Regional Development Administration (GAP RDA) and the General Organization for Land Development (GOLD) of the Syrian Ministry of Irrigation.

## The emergence of the environmental/water agenda

Until the late 1960s and the development of the environmental movement, international relations suffered from a profound ecological blindness. For as long as nature/environment appeared to be endlessly abundant and perpetually resilient, the study and practice of international relations could proceed as usual. This is no longer the case. With the realization that there are, indeed, limits to growth (Schumacher 1973) and depletion of the world's natural resources is more than an extreme scenario, a new approach is called for. Environmental issues do not recognize conceptual boundaries, nor do they respect state or institutional borders. The complexity of the environmental crisis demands more innovative and receptive insights, interdisciplinary approaches and a combination of different theories in order to tackle it effectively. There is a growing awareness that ecological health must be an essential ingredient in any recipe for (inter)national order. Following the replacement of "certainty" with uncertainty, known as the crisis of modernity (Beck 1992), which was mainly driven by the environmental movement in the 1960s and 1970s, water resources were foregrounded. Although initially perceived like any other environmental issue, in the past two decades water has acquired its own trajectory and currently claims a leading role in the quest for environmental awareness and the eradication of poverty. Its association with modernity also arises from the fact that modernity has mainly been associated with intense industrialization and economic development, which usually sacrifices natural resources on the altar of modernization. Apocalyptic scenarios of water wars,[1] along with the inevitability of water scarcity in some parts of the globe (such as the Middle East and North Africa), have reinforced the view that water is at the heart of current environmental and poverty debates.

## Water management in the age of modernity

"Modernity" refers to a particular constellation of power, knowledge and social practices that first emerged in Europe in the sixteenth and seventeenth centuries. Its forms and structures were subject to several metamorphoses over time, and eventually gained currency so that by the mid-twentieth century they constituted the dominant social order at a global level (Johnston et al. 1991: 388). Modernity is intimately interwoven with the so-called Enlightenment Project. The Enlightenment Project – and thus that of modernity – promised control over nature through science, material abundance through superior technology, and effective government through rational social organization. However, rather than leading to this "promised land", it has brought the globe to the brink of environmental and cultural disaster.[2] The very project of modernity seems to have lost momentum and there is an urgent need to come up with a successor programme. Moreover, the close association of modernity with industrialization[3] is one of the reasons there are thinkers who proclaim the end of modernity. Industrialism, at least as conventionally understood, seems to have exhausted itself, to have reached its limits.

While the modernity project was evolving, challenging itself and developing in the areas where it was conceived, the process of modernization was turning into the main developmental model for the less developed parts of the globe. This process involves social change resulting from the diffusion and adoption of the characteristics of liberal and apparently more advanced societies in societies that are apparently less advanced (Johnston et al. 1991: 392). Its nature is primarily teleological since the proposed model is defined in Eurocentric terms and, thus, the direction of change is more or less predetermined. The main assumption of modernization is that its subject societies have no history, culture or developed set of social or environmental relations, which is a profoundly racist view of the world (Preston 1997: 153–178). The modernity project, commonly identified with the industrial revolution of Western Europe and Northern America, is based on a narrow perspective from the wealthy and economically developed parts of the globe. The question remains: whose modernity are we talking about? The overall modernization project, with its appearance as the ultimate goal toward which all states ought to aspire, is another form of European colonialism. However, this time it has more subtle mechanisms that use the cover of the environmental debate and control over natural resources and it is often referred to as "environmental imperialism or neo-colonialism" (Litfin 1998: 336). In the quest for modernization, development is identified with a very specific model that, more often than not, is not applicable to the developing parts of the world because of the different socio-economic environment. The debate about the diffusion of modernity outside Northern Europe and the United States is ongoing, and the consequences of the overall project (especially the environmental ones) are yet to be seen. In that viewpoint the crisis of modernity has also been identified with the crisis of development theory and practice in general.

On a practical level, modernization manifests itself through the formation and institutionalization of the nation-state as the dominant state structure, the implementation and prevalence of capitalism in the economic arena, and finally the introduction and establishment of liberal democracy in the political sphere. The democratization phase of the neo-liberal project can be seen as a reflexive response to the dangers of mismanaging "labour", which is often referred to as the first failure of capitalism. The reflexive responses to the environmental crisis – the second failure of capitalism – were the result of the reckless use and abuse of too many resources by too many people.

Particularly in "advanced" societies, the trend has been for their citizens to scrutinize science, technology and scientific institutions by making moral claims to rationality that are equal to those of modern science. At the same time, contemporary hazards are seen to be the outcome of human action, principally related to the events of modernization, industrialization, urbanization and globalization (Lupton 1999: 65). One such example is the widespread (almost hysterical) debate about water scarcity and its consequences for the future of the "blue planet". In response, Beck (1992: 14) states that "[r]eflexive modernisation means not less but more modernity, a modernity radicalised against the paths and categories of the classical industrial setting". However, the risk society acknowledges that to continue along the lines of classical industrialization is to run the risk of self-destruction, because nature seems no longer capable of coping with humanity's progress. Giddens (1990: 21) concludes that only societies reflexively capable of modifying their institutions in the face of accelerated social change will be able to confront the future with any confidence and that "the developments considered to be an embodiment of post-modernity are symptoms of the global extension and diffusion of modernity and the associated disintegration or dissolution of the traditional world" (Giddens 1990: 26–29). This pinpoints the heart of the environmental (and water) crisis: the problem is located at the political/ institutional level and is not merely a matter of the abundance and/or scarcity of natural resources. In the same vein, Falkenmark (2001: 539, 543) claims that "it is not the water that is the problem but society's way of using and managing the water. Wise water governance has to be built around the need for societal adaptation to the hydroclimatic constraints

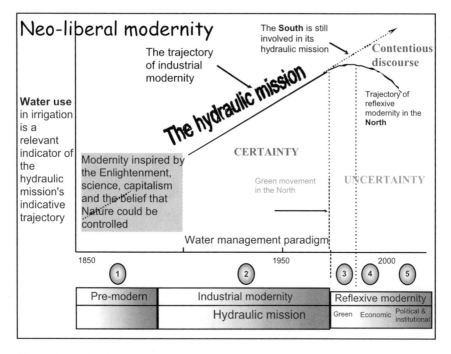

Figure 11.1 The five water management paradigms.
*Source*: Reproduced with permission from Allan (2001).


and strong enough institutions must be developed, capable of supporting unpopular decisions".

*The five water management paradigms*

The different phases of modernity through the discourse on natural re-sources are concisely and comprehensively represented with regard to water in Figure 11.1 (from Allan 2001: 326). Allan identifies five water management paradigms, which accord with the teleological neo-liberal project since the mid-ninetieth century.

The first water paradigm is associated with pre-modern communities, which have limited technical or organizational capacity. The second par-adigm refers to communities that have entered the phase of industrial modernity, where the ideas of the Enlightenment, science and logic underpin the certainties of the neo-liberal project. Industrial modernity has often been identified with what is referred to as the "hydraulic mis-sion" of the mid-twentieth century.[4] "Hydraulic mission" is the vision and political ecology to which the industrialized economies were dedicated from the end of the nineteenth century until the 1970s. This mission was first and most fully implemented in the United States and then emulated in a very different polity by the former Soviet Union. However, the mission was successfully questioned by the environmental movement and consideration for the environment, along with sustainability principles, affected the water sector by the mid-1970s in the North. The industrial modernity phase was followed by the phase of reflexive modernity, which incorporates all the alternatives to water management put forward after the modernity project was declared problematic.

Within the phase of late modernity we can identify three water paradigms: the green, the economic and the political/institutional. The green paradigm denotes the change in water allocation and management priorities that was inspired by the environmental awareness of the green movement; thus, the hydraulic mission ceased to be the paradigmatic resource policy and, as a consequence, allocations of water for the environment increased in the neo-liberal North and semi-arid areas while allocations to agriculture were reduced. The economic paradigm was inspired by economists who began to draw the attention of water users in the North to the economic value of water and its importance as a scarce economic input. These ideas gained currency in the early 1990s. There has been an attempt to export them to the South via such agencies as the World Bank and through such institutions as the United Nations Conference on Environment and Development and the World Water Council. The economic and environmental phases are still in progress. Allan argues that a new paradigm emerged in the late 1990s around what has become known as integrated water resources allocation and management (IWRAM).[5] This approach demands more than the mere recognition of the environmental and economic value of water and the planning of engineering and economic interventions. The paradigm is inspired by the notion that water allocation and management are primarily political processes and, thus, require a holistic approach and unprecedented levels of stakeholder participation and political cooperation.

Figure 11.1 shows that the different paradigms do not function in isolation; quite the opposite in fact, as they seem to complement and to grow out of one another. Elements from different approaches are incorporated into the last paradigm, which seems more capable of responding to the needs of effective water management. Referring to the fifth paradigm and stressing the importance of political and institutional elements does not mean that no attention is paid to economic or environmental aspects. Although the distinction between modern and post-modern is still debatable, the elements that derive from modernity cannot be disregarded or rejected since it would be too laborious a task to define post-modernity without modernity. There exists a level of conceptual linearity between the two.

A limitation of the diagram is its assumption that there is only one route to environmental awareness and environmental respect, which passes through the different phases of modernity and through the modernization procedure as such. Most developing countries aspire to the hydraulic mission because they see it as a reliable path to economic development and they are reluctant to recognize the environmental dangers of this aspiration. Hence the river basin that is examined in this chapter: the Euphrates–Tigris River Basin, which has three riparian countries that are basically still in the industrial modernity phase. Nevertheless, Turkey's Southeastern Anatolia Project (GAP) – a multisectoral and integrated regional water-based development project with a sustainable human development approach – is introduced as a unique effort to bring the water management practices in the region much closer to the fifth paradigm by showing how the integrated management of water resources and water-related services can help to reduce poverty in the contexts of public health, land use, food production, livelihoods, industrial development, urban planning and environmental protection.

In the same way that the failure of modernization has shown that there might be more than one route towards development, there could also be more than one path towards environmental awareness. The narrative of the five water paradigms makes use of a theory that is predominantly Eurocentric (or Northern). Hence, below we discuss the use of "environmental security" as a theoretical framework for water analysis, which we deem more appropriate for the parts of the globe that are still struggling to reach modernity.

## Water and environmental security

The universality of environmental problems and the crisis of nation-statism in the developed North, along with a discourse on (post)modernity that scrutinized everything, question the utility of national borders as well as the very concept of sovereignty. This questioning of sovereignty extends to the use and the right of use of natural resources. As Tuchman Mathews (1989: 162) argues: "Global development now suggests the need for another analogous, broadening definition of national security to include resource, environmental and demographic issues."

As a result, the notion of security (both collective and individual) acquired a new perspective and a broader definition in which its military and political aspects are coupled with economic, social and environmental elements. Each factor defines a focal point within the security problematique and a way of ordering priorities, but all are woven together in a strong web of linkages. Buzan (1991, 1994) and Buzan et al. (1998) provide a comprehensive analysis and explanation of these five distinct sectors: the military concerns the two-level interplay of the armed offensive and defensive capabilities of states and states' perceptions of each other's intentions; the political involves the organizational stability of states, systems of government and the ideologies that give them legitimacy; the economic considers the access to resources, finance and markets that is necessary to sustain acceptable levels of welfare and state power; the societal is about sustainability within acceptable conditions for the evolution of traditional patterns of language, culture, religion, national identity and custom; finally, the environmental incorporates the maintenance of the local and the planetary biosphere as the essential support system on which all other human enterprises depend.

A review of the interface between environment and security by Ronnfeldt (1997: 473–482) presents a chronological trajectory of the research on environment and security in a concise and innovative way. He refers to this analysis as the three generations of environment and security research. The first generation, covering the early 1980s, mainly criticizes the conventional concept of security and calls for a wider approach that incorporates environmental issues into the security agenda. The second generation, starting in the early 1990s, comprises primarily the work of Homer-Dixon (1991) and the Toronto Group. Through the examination of 12 different case studies using a key model in which environmental scarcity (water scarcity being part of it) is the independent variable and conflict the dependent variable, the Toronto Group reached the conclusion that scarcity of renewable resources is never the sole cause of conflict, but it can contribute to these disruptions when it interacts with economic, political and social factors.[6] Finally, the third generation constitutes a critique of the Toronto Group and focuses on the need to expand the independent variables so as to include other material and socio-political variables. It also emphasizes that environmental scarcity is a transboundary issue and that states are not the only actors involved in the interaction; it thus calls for a multi-actor approach. The third generation also argues that when cases of conflict are examined the observer is likely to find confirmation of whatever is being sought. For example, when looking at highly popularized and extensively examined cases such as the waters of the Nile, the Tigris and Euphrates or the Jordan River, one usually focuses on the tension among the riparian states and the different phases the dispute has been through, without sufficiently acknowledging or publicizing examples of cooperation and collaboration. An illustrative example of the latter is the Joint Communiqué signed in August 2001 by the Regional Development Administration of the Southeastern Anatolia Project in Turkey (GAP RDA) and the General Organization for Land Development (GOLD) of the Syrian Ministry of Irrigation, with the purpose of organizing common training programmes, drafting and carrying out joint projects and realizing exchange programmes and partnerships. In such cases, even though water issues are highly politicized and securitized, at the same time they constitute an element of cooperation based on their indisputable value to humans and human welfare; and this is precisely the merit of environmental security.

From a different perspective, environmental security has been heavily criticized because of the security element it entails. Foremost is the view that any form of securitization is an attempt by undemocratic or unpopular regimes to gain or maintain political power. Securitization can potentially enhance nationalistic feelings and promote disparities between neighbouring states, especially when it comes to a vital resource such as water (Bulloch and Darwish 1993; Gleick 1993). There is also the difficulty that people have in identifying the environment as a "security" issue because it does not fall within the conventional understanding of the concept (Brock 1991). Valid as these points are, they have inherent weaknesses. On the water wars hypothesis, there is a plethora of scholars arguing for the opposite case (Deudney 1999: 187–219; Solomon and Turton 2000; Allan 2002), and since a water war, as such, has never actually occurred, the case supporting the war scenario is rapidly losing credibility.

This chapter argues that the discipline of environmental security constitutes a particularly fertile ground for an analysis of water issues that follows the logic and suggestions of the fifth water paradigm. Environmental security has five attributes that enable it to avoid the conceptual mistakes of military security:

(i)   The word "security" provides a way of linking together many areas of theory and promotes not only multidisciplinarity but also interdisciplinarity, since it allows the fusing of different theoretical approaches. Security studies constitutes an inclusive discipline owing to its recent wider agenda and thus does not put constraints on the qualitative and quantitative use of theoretical approaches. Essentially, when tackling the question of "how" when dealing with water resource problems, the answer may come from any intellectual field and any discipline as long as it responds to the new need.[7]

(ii)  The word "security" itself is a powerful tool in claiming priority when it comes to competition for national and international attention. Securitizing (and thus further politicizing) an issue such as water resources is not essentially a negative policy. Such a method assigns the necessary significance to the issue at stake, the problem becomes crystal clear for all the involved stakeholders and the related institutions are forced to respond instantly. Security attributes a greater sense of urgency and elevates water issues to the realm of "high politics". It is the case that in crisis situations a "window of opportunity" is opened for new policies to be initiated and implemented with a good chance of remaining in force after the end of the crisis.[8]

(iii) It is a multi-level approach that facilitates the involvement of all levels of social and political interaction. So, the stakeholders can simultaneously come from the international as well as the national, regional and local levels. To the question of "where" the interaction takes place, the answer is at all levels, both separately and together, if that is necessary. This minimizes the distance between the various actors and transforms all the involved parties into participants.

(iv) It is a multi-centred/multi-actor approach that promotes the participation of all the different actors that may be involved in a case. So, to the question of "who" is involved, the answer may include international agencies, states, bureaucracies, non-governmental organizations and governmental institutions, as well as small groups of people and individuals.

(v) Finally, even though the word "security" suffers from immediate identification with military action, it can also disconnect itself from that connotation and move beyond it. The same occurred with the word "development", which managed to endure and establish itself despite its initial negative conceptualization as a new word for colonization (Sachs 1992).

The analysis of the three generations of environment and security research echoes the five water management paradigms. Both refer to the chronological development or modification of theoretical approaches in order to respond to new needs. Both reflect the conspicuous influence of the environmental movement and the ways in which concepts such as water management or security change over time. The important point to extract from the above analyses is that neither water management nor security can be viewed solely through the lens of a single discipline. For effective understanding it is essential to include all the different aspects of human interaction: social, economic, political, military and environmental. The five sectors are like the five fingers of the hand; although different, all are essential for the harmonic operation of the whole. The weakness of the Toronto Group in Ronnfeldt's analysis, for example, was its limited inclusion of socio-political parameters. As regards water analysis, the weakness has so far been the inability to link the various influencing factors in a comprehensive manner. This is what Falkenmark calls "water blindness" (Falkenmark 2001: 542) and it stems from the negligible attention paid to water as the key link between social and economic development and the maintenance of environmental services.

Human dependence on water is not a mere technical issue, but involves a particularly complex set of interactions and interrelations. Falkenmark calls for a new ethics of hydro-solidarity, which can be established by making water everybody's business while at the same time enhancing participation at all levels of discussion and decision-making. In this way cooperation is facilitated and agreements become easier to achieve. This is within environmental security's problematique and is especially the case when referring to water resources at the international level. Scores of rivers cross state boundaries, and their development requires inter-state cooperation (Ohlsson 1995). This is where the IWRAM is called upon to provide a holistic perspective and offer a valid alternative to the water crisis by combining elements from different paradigms in order to search for a case-by-case optimum proposition.

The following sections will examine the water dispute in the Euphrates–Tigris River Basin. We adopt a broad and holistic approach by proposing that equitable usage and socio-economic development should be considered simultaneously, and cooperation in the region should be based on wider development concepts.

## The water question in the Euphrates–Tigris River Basin

### Mismatch between water demand and supply

The Euphrates and Tigris River Basin has three major riparians: Turkey, Syria and Iraq.[9] Both the Euphrates and the Tigris originate in Turkey, scarcely 30 kilometres from each other. The two rivers constitute a single river basin through their confluence near the Gulf to form the Shatt-al-Arab waterway in Iraq. These twin rivers, like all other rivers in the Middle East, have extremely high seasonal and multi-annual variance in their flow. Variation in the flow of both rivers had ranged from conditions of severe drought to destructive flooding before upstream reservoirs were built (in Turkey) that are capable of smoothing out such variances and providing a dependable year-round flow downstream. For millennia only natural conditions had an impact on the availability of water to the three riparians. Since the 1960s, however, Turkey, Syria and Iraq have invested in large-scale water development projects, the largest of which is Turkey's Southeastern Anatolia Project (whose Turkish acronym is GAP). As a result of these supply-led developments, the water demands of the riparians exceed the actual amount of water that can be supplied by the Euphrates–Tigris river system. Hence, unsatisfied demand for more water is exacerbating tensions in the relations of the riparians with each other.

Table 11.1 The water potential of the Euphrates Basin and the consumption projections of the riparian states (billion m³/year)

|         | Turkey | Syria  | Iraq   | Total  |
|---------|--------|--------|--------|--------|
| Supply  | 28.922 | 3.213  | 0.000  | 32.136 |
| Demand  | 18.500 | 11.500 | 23.000 | 53.000 |

Riparians tend not to agree on how much water there is, on when it is available, or on how much each riparian needs or is likely to need. The annual mean discharge (natural flow) of the Euphrates is 32 billion m³/year and the annual mean discharge of the Tigris is 52 billion m³/year (see the supply row in Tables 11.1 and 11.2). Consumption demand from the Euphrates is projected for the year 2040, which is theoretically when the development schemes will be fully implemented by the three riparians on their respective sections of the river (Belül 1996). The most important result from these tables is that the total demand of the three riparians far exceeds supply.

These tables exclude data relating to supply and demand by other downstream riparians such as Iran, whose supply amounts to 9 per cent (4.689 billion m³/year) whereas it makes no demand on the waters of the Euphrates. The tables nonetheless show mismatches between supply (average discharge) and demand in the Euphrates–Tigris River Basin. Moreover, the 2040 consumption targets in both tables are calculated by each riparian, and thus are likely to be very subjective and exaggerated. Further, the natural flows of both rivers (supply) passing from Turkey to Syria and from Syria to Iraq do change as a result of irrigation and energy projects that the riparians have already initiated. The rapidly increasing populations of these countries and the importance given to agricultural development and to food production necessitate further utilization of these rivers. The major problem, however, arises from the fact that the projected water demands of the riparians for the future exceed the actual amount of water that can be supplied by the Tigris and the Euphrates rivers.

Table 11.2 The water potential of the Tigris Basin and the consumption projections of the riparian states (billion m³/year)

|         | Turkey | Syria | Iraq   | Total  |
|---------|--------|-------|--------|--------|
| Supply  | 20.840 | 0.000 | 26.571 | 52.100 |
| Demand  | 6.500  | 3.000 | 41.800 | 51.300 |

## Water negotiations

Since the early 1960s there had been attempts to foster dialogue and information exchange in the region through a series of technical water negotiations.[10] Here we provide highlights from these negotiation processes. One can observe that the riparians maintained inflexible positions that hardly changed during the course of the negotiations over three decades until the suspension of the negotiations in the early 1990s. Thus, Iraq as a downstream riparian was keen to preserve in perpetuity its historic usage and showed great anxiety about the progress of water development projects in Turkey and Syria. Iraq (later joined by Syria in the early 1980s) kept insisting on the immediate conclusion of sharing agreements. Yet Turkey, as a new user, had argued for the necessity of its planned measures and suggested a joint study to ascertain the irrigation needs of the riparians before any basin-wide allocation was agreed in the river basin.

The three riparians entered a new phase of their relationship over water when Turkey decided to construct the Keban dam on the Euphrates. The downstream riparians, particularly Iraq, insisted on guaranteed flows (350 $m^3$/sec at minimum) to be released by Turkey during the impounding period. Hence, a first meeting was held in June 1964 involving Turkish and Iraqi experts. The Turkish delegation asserted that it was impossible to reach a single and final formula for the pattern of water to be released from the Keban dam reservoir before impounding by the dam. According to the Turkish delegation, this pattern depended upon the natural conditions that prevailed during the filling and on the exact evaluation of the concerned countries' needs. At the end of the negotiations, Turkey guaranteed to undertake all necessary measures to maintain a discharge of 350 $m^3$/sec immediately downstream from the dam, provided that the natural flow of the river was adequate to supply this discharge. This was confirmed to Syria and Iraq the same year. Moreover, during this meeting, Turkey proposed to establish a Joint Technical Committee (JTC), which would inspect each river at its source to determine its average yearly discharge. The JTC would determine the irrigation needs of the three countries through joint field studies and would be authorized, by calculating the needs of the riparians for present and future projects, to prepare a statement of main principles and procedures in order to facilitate an agreement on water rights.

Following this first technical meeting between Turkey and Iraq, a few more ad hoc meetings were held in the region. The most notable of these meetings was the first tripartite negotiation held in Baghdad in 1965. At that meeting, the three delegations exchanged technical data with regard to the Haditha, Tabqa and Keban dams. The delegations then moved on to discuss the question of setting up a Joint Technical Committee. The Iraqi delegation submitted a draft agreement, which covered, among others things, the issue of forming a permanent JTC to be entrusted with supervising the implementation of the agreement. The Turkish delegation strongly rejected the Iraqi draft agreement, and stated that the JTC could be authorized only to coordinate current and future projects in the river basin. In line with the Turkish proposal, Syria suggested it would be convenient to include among the functions of the JTC a study of the water requirements of the irrigable lands in the three countries, and subsequently to examine the possibility of covering possible shortages of water supplied by the Euphrates by diverting a part of the Tigris River's water to the Euphrates. Iraq strongly opposed this proposal and insisted on negotiating only over the waters of the Euphrates.

During the course of the 1970s, delegations from the three countries gathered on several occasions to exchange information about the technical issues pertaining to the Keban, Tabqa and Habbaniye reservoirs. No agreement was achieved at the end of numerous technical meetings, and Turkey and Syria went their own ways in determining impounding programmes for the two reservoirs.

## Setting up the Joint Technical Committee

In the early 1980s, the imminent use of the Euphrates and Tigris by Turkey created new demands for cooperation. Because the issues involved in water development schemes along the Tigris and Euphrates are so complex and far-reaching, the three riparians had to find ways of structuring the dialogue among them. This time Iraq took the initiative for the formation of a permanent Joint Technical Committee. At the end of the first meeting of the Joint Economic Commission between Turkey and Iraq in 1980, a new JTC was established to discuss and finalize the water issue among the riparians. Syria joined the JTC in 1983, and Turkey, Syria and Iraq held 16 meetings up to 1993.

The essential mandate given to the JTC was defined as determining the methods and procedures that would lead to a definition of the reasonable and appropriate amounts of water that each country would need from both rivers. The major items on the agenda of the JTC were the exchange of hydrological and meteorological data and information on the Euphrates–Tigris Basin, the sharing of information on progress in the construction of dams and irrigation schemes in the three riparian countries, and the discussion of initial plans for filling the Karakaya and Atatürk reservoirs.

However, after the 16 meetings, the JTC was unable to fulfil its objectives and the talks became deadlocked and failed to produce even outlines of its meetings. The major issues that led to the deadlock were related to both the subject and the object of the negotiations: whether the Euphrates and the Tigris should be considered as a single system or whether the discussions could be limited to the Euphrates. The wording of the final objective of the JTC (i.e. agreeing on a common terminology) was also problematic: should it be to formulate a proposal for the "sharing" of "international rivers", or to achieve a trilateral regime for determining the "utilization of transboundary watercourses"? Iraq and Syria consider the Euphrates to be an international river and insisted on an immediate sharing agreement under which the waters of the Euphrates would be shared on the basis of each country's stated water needs. Turkey, in contrast, regards the Euphrates and the Tigris as forming a single transboundary river basin where the waters should be allocated according to objective needs.

The role of the Joint Technical Committee should not be underestimated. Although its meetings were infrequent and appear to have made little substantive progress on the question of water allocation, they were a useful channel for communication. However, the JTC meetings were not able to keep going and produce fruitful outcomes to foster broader cooperation in the region. Even though the JTC originated from the Joint Economic Commission, it had focused solely on water issues, whereas its ultimate aim of ensuring cooperation and coordinated management of water resources in the region could not be fulfilled with such a restricted approach in which the riparians had insisted on their water rights.

The mandate of the JTC could be expanded and diversified so that it could act with a broader agenda and the parties could tackle water resources management as part of a larger framework of the overall socio-economic development of the river basin, thereby demonstrating a new potential framework for water-based cooperation.

Aware that sustained cooperation in the region requires a development focus, a permanent institution and a forum for legal and institutional dialogue, the JTC could be designed to provide a platform for discussions on water-related multisectoral development issues along with the establishment of the principles of the equitable usage of waters.

### Episodes of water crisis in the Euphrates–Tigris River Basin

The technical meetings did not fulfil the expressed aim of coordinating the water development and usage patterns of the three riparians. Hence, a number of crises occurred in the region during the 1970s, 1980s and 1990s.

Turkey started impounding the Keban reservoir in February 1974 at the same time that Syria had almost finalized construction of the Tabqa dam. No agreement was achieved at the end of numerous technical meetings, and Turkey and Syria went their own ways in determining impounding programmes for the two reservoirs. The dams were completed in a period of continuous and particularly dry weather, and the impounding of both reservoirs escalated into a crisis in the spring of 1975 (Kut 1993). Iraq accused Syria of reducing the river's flow to intolerably low levels, while Syria placed the blame on Turkey. The Iraqi government was not satisfied with the Syrian response and mounting frustration resulted in mutual threats, bringing the parties to the brink of armed hostilities. A war over water was averted when Saudi Arabia undertook mediation that resulted in extra amounts of water being released from Syria to Iraq.

A major crisis among the riparians of the Euphrates–Tigris River Basin occurred in the early 1990s during the impounding of the Atatürk dam on the Euphrates in Turkey. Turkey had previously decided to fill the reservoir over a period of one month. The month selected for this purpose was January, when there would be no demand for irrigated agriculture – the major user of the river water. Turkey had notified its downstream neighbours by November 1989 of the impending event. In its note, Turkey explained the technical reasons and provided a detailed programme for making up for the losses. Turkey released twice the usual amount for two months prior to the impoundment and sent delegations to Middle Eastern countries to explain the need for the impoundment and the measures taken. On 13 January 1990, Turkey temporarily interrupted the flow of the Euphrates River in order to fill the reservoir; it finished the work in three weeks as opposed to the one month initially planned and opened the gates. However, the Syrian and the Iraqi governments officially protested to Turkey and subsequently called for an agreement to share the waters of the Euphrates as well as for a reduction in the impounding period.

Another crisis occurred in 1996 after Turkey started construction of the Birecik, an afterbay dam on the Euphrates River. The dam is designed to regulate the water level of the Euphrates during the generation of hydroelectricity at the Atatürk dam during peak hours when the downstream flow reaches its maximum. Both Syria and Iraq sent official notes to the Turkish government in December 1995 and January 1996 indicating their objection to the construction of the Birecik dam on the grounds that the dam would affect the quantity and quality of waters flowing to Syria and Iraq.

## Divisive water treaties in the Euphrates–Tigris River Basin

### The Protocol of 1987 between Turkey and Syria

The Turkish–Syrian Joint Economic Commission meeting on 17 July 1987 had an important outcome in terms of the negotiations over the water issue. The Protocol of Economic Cooperation signed by Turkey and Syria at the end of the meeting included provisions for water. It is important to note that the Protocol was regarded as a temporary arrangement. It includes several articles pertaining to the water issue. The text of Article 6 of the Protocol reads as follows: "During the filling up period of the Atatürk dam reservoir and until the final allocation of the waters of Euphrates among the three riparian countries the Turkish side undertakes to release a yearly average of more than 500 m$^3$/sec at the Turkish–Syrian border and in cases where monthly flow falls below the level of 500 m$^3$/sec, the Turkish side agrees to make up the difference during the following month." As a basis for comparison, the long-term average flow of the Euphrates is approximately 1,000 m$^3$/sec at the Turkish–Syrian border.

*Water allocation agreement between Syria and Iraq: The Protocol of 1990*

Syria and Iraq perceived the interruption to the flow of the Euphrates caused by the impounding of the Atatürk dam as the first of many such interruptions that would result from the projects envisaged within the framework of GAP. Hence, the thirteenth meeting of the Joint Technical Committee, held in Baghdad on 16 April 1990, provided the occasion for a bilateral accord between Syria and Iraq, according to which 58 per cent of the Euphrates waters coming from Turkey would be released to Iraq by Syria.

These bilateral accords were interim measures, which were largely products of the then-prevailing political atmosphere in the basin, and they have not served to achieve the goal of efficient and equitable allocation and management of the water resources in the Euphrates–Tigris River Basin.

## An innovative cooperation initiative: The Three Stage Plan

During the above negotiations it emerged that the water potential was unable to meet the declared demands of the three riparians. And, more importantly, there were uncertainties and inadequacies relating to the data on water and land resources. In response to Syrian and Iraqi demands for the formulation of urgent "sharing arrangements" according to criteria that they put forward, Turkey proposed a Three Stage Plan for Optimum, Equitable and Reasonable Utilization of the Transboundary Watercourses of the Tigris-Euphrates Basin.

As a result of his empirical work on water negotiations in various transboundary river basins, Wolf concludes that in almost all of the disputes that have been resolved, particularly over arid or exotic streams, the paradigms used for negotiations have not been "rights based" at all

– in terms either of relative hydrography or specifically of the chronology of use; rather they have been "needs based". "Needs" can be defined by one or a combination of the following: irrigable land, population or the requirements of a specific project or a sector (Wolf 1999).

The Three Stage Plan was drafted with a needs-based approach. It encompasses joint inventory studies of the land and water resources of the region and estimation of the water needs of the competing sectors in the region, agriculture in particular. This, then, will provide the basis for an optimum allocation of the available water to the determined needs.

The creators of the Plan asserted that, by quantifying needs, the water issue would become more manageable. With the Plan, Turkey calls for the establishment of a joint body for collecting, handling and exchanging data on water and land resources so that annual and seasonal variations can be incorporated in the estimates made to determine allocations. In this respect, data-sharing would facilitate the negotiation process and foster the creation of many cooperative structures. Hence, data-gathering through joint efforts would enable the riparians to become accustomed to cooperation and to proceed with discussions over the allocation of water. In addition to reaching a set of agreed criteria in data-sharing, negotiations could move on to talks on the coordination of projects and the creation of joint projects.

The Plan is evolutionary and forward looking in nature. It could be revised according to prevailing conditions and developed further through an interdisciplinary dialogue with the inclusion of the relevant stakeholders. In the conduct of international relations, law can function as a useful tool for dispute avoidance and settlement to alleviate and manage water shortages by way of an international legal order, which would ensure that conflicting riparian interests are reconciled in order to achieve equitable access to water resources and to maintain peace and security (McCaffrey 1997: 52). Hence, given the likelihood of international water disputes, there is a need for an appropriate legal response. The main role of international law is to provide the necessary framework for establishing a legal order in which the rights and obligations of riparian states can be duly ascertained, in particular if and when the parties concerned fail to reach an agreement, as is the case with the Euphrates and Tigris rivers. We therefore suggest that, in implementing the Three Stage Plan, the following customary norms of international water law could be instrumental in achieving the fair allocation of water.

*Equitable utilization*

As seen in the case of the Euphrates and Tigris rivers, where there is a shortage of water available to meet competing demands, there is also a need for some sort of adjustments to be made, on the basis of equity, to accommodate the respective water needs of the co-riparian states. The principle of equitable and reasonable utilization determines the riparian rights to water with a view to arriving at an equitable resolution of a conflict of uses. In so doing, it entitles "each basin state, within its own territory, to a reasonable and equitable share in the beneficial uses of the waters of an international drainage basin" (ILA 1966: 484). Derived from the theory of limited territorial sovereignty, this substantive principle has gained considerable support in state practice, international treaties and judicial decisions.[11] Its customary status has more recently been confirmed by the International Court of Justice in the *Gabčíkovo-Nagymaros* case,[12] with particular reference to Article 5 of the UN Convention on the Law of the Non-Navigational Uses of International Watercourses.[13] Although it rests on the principle of "equality of rights", equitable utilization should not be confused with an "equal division" of waters[14] but should be taken to mean that "all states riparian to an international waterway stand on a par with each other" (Lipper 1967). Having said that, its generality does not allow a precise formulation of equitable and reasonable use, although such flexibility is considered a strength in its application to a wide range of international watercourses, and thus determination is to be made on a case-by-case basis, which, as Birnie and Boyle point out, "turns on a balancing of relevant factors and must be responsive to the circumstances of individual cases" (Birnie and Boyle 2002: 303). Both Article 5 of the 1966 ILA Helsinki Rules and Article 6 of the 1997 UN International Watercourses Convention provide a useful list of all relevant factors and circumstances to be taken into account in each particular case when determining the meaning of what an equitable and reasonable entitlement might be.[15]

In the current controversy surrounding the utilization of the Euphrates and Tigris rivers, Turkey has adopted the doctrine of equitable and reasonable utilization as part of general international law for transboundary water allocation in its proposal for the Three Stage Plan (*Perceptions* 1996). The plan aims to determine the equitable and reasonable uses of Turkey, Syria and Iraq within a technical framework of common criteria, based on riparian interests, to allocate the available water to the needs of each party in a mutually satisfactory way.[16] However, the implementation of such an elaborate plan calls for a whole set of considerations – closely associated with the notion of uses being beneficial, efficient, historical, acquired, existing or contemplated – to be viewed in relation to their harmful consequences, an issue that essentially bears on compatibility with another principle, harmless use.

*Harmless use*

Article 7 of the 1997 UN International Watercourses Convention contains an obligation on a state, in utilizing an international watercourse in its territory, not to cause significant harm to other watercourse states. As a particular expression of a general obligation on a state not to cause harm to another state, there is little doubt about the customary authority that it enjoys in state practice, a number of international treaties and instruments, adjudicative decisions, and the writings of commentators (Schwebel 1982). Nevertheless, it is uncertain whether it originated in the Roman maxim *sic utere tuo ut alienum non laedas* ("so use your own property that you do not injure another's") or in another general principle of international law such as the principle of abuse of rights or of good neighbourliness (Caflisch 1993; Lammers 1984). No matter where it came from, the sovereign equality of states is its very foundation and a handful of cases have endorsed it: the best-known and most widely accepted version of the "no significant harm" principle within the environmental context finds expression in Principle 21 of the 1972 Stockholm Declaration (UNCHE 1972) and then in Principle 2 of the 1992 Rio Declaration (UNCED 1992). More recently, the International Court of Justice's decision in the *Gabčíkovo-Nagymaros* case applied the principle to the area of international watercourses.[17] Notwithstanding its customary status, the apparent simplicity of the no-harm principle is deceptive owing to ambiguity over the applicable threshold of harm and the required standard of conduct involved in its actual application to a concrete water dispute, both of which pose especially difficult problems in relation to equitable utilization.

In the Euphrates and Tigris rivers controversy, the lower riparian states Syria and Iraq have, in a nutshell, accused Turkey of causing harm to their existing and future water uses by reducing the available water resources with the construction of new dams as part of the ongoing GAP scheme. Invoking the no-harm principle despite the recognition of each riparian's right to equitable use suggests that these substantive principles of water apportionment have come into conflict in this dispute, and they take the view that significant harm cannot be deemed either equitable or reasonable. This is tantamount to claiming that the no-harm principle prevails over equitable and reasonable utilization in circumstances where there is not enough water to meet the demands of all riparian states, a claim that has not only been vehemently challenged by Turkey but also been a source of great disagreement in international watercourses law.

*The general obligation to cooperate*

The Three Stage Plan encompasses the emerging principle of institutionalized cooperation for an integrated approach to sustainable development in the region. Article 8 of the UN International Watercourses Convention formulates it as a general obligation on watercourse states to "cooperate on the basis of sovereign equality, territorial integrity, mutual benefit and good faith in order to attain optimal utilization and adequate protection of an international watercourse".[18] Although the supporting evidence cited in treaty practice and the practice of states was significant (McCaffrey 1987), it was seen as a practical necessity rather than a customary legal requirement for the implementation of the principle of equitable and reasonable utilization as well as for the proper functioning of other pertinent procedural requirements in part 3 of the Convention.[19] To be sure, the goal of "optimal utilization and adequate protection of an international watercourse" that the article sets is a novel one and represents the progressive development of international law. It attempts to extend the idea of sustainable development to the field of international watercourses and can duly be linked to the integrated approach adopted by Turkey in its Three Stage Plan through the emerging notion of coordinated management.

*Institutionalized cooperation for coordinated management and optimum development*

The major difficulty with the application of equitable and reasonable utilization, which is not capable of a precise definition, arises from the highly complex process of a balancing of interests subject to the relevant factors and circumstances of each particular case, which requires greater cooperation in practice. However, Birnie and Boyle aptly suggest that because, despite an acute need, in certain cases "third-party settlement has not been widely used in river disputes and comparable judicial elaboration is lacking, [t]he better solution ... is probably some form of common management designed to achieve equitable and optimum use of the watercourse system" (Birnie and Boyle 2002: 303). Their observation resonates closely with the sentiment behind Turkey's Three Stage Plan, which followed somewhat difficult and fruitless negotiations with Syria and Iraq, in order to facilitate "a positive atmosphere which will be conducive to the cooperative use of not only water, but also other natural resources, for mutual benefit" in as much as "to promote confidence between the states of the region" (*Perceptions* 1996).

# Recent developments and prospects for cooperation in the Euphrates–Tigris River Basin

The Three Stage Plan was coolly received by Iraq and Syria. Nonetheless, with its needs-based approach, which is conducive to cooperation, and its particular emphasis on a legal settlement, the Plan will retain its innovative status in transboundary water coordination. Indeed, establishing coordinated regional action in the Euphrates–Tigris River Basin presents a great challenge. However, there remain many opportunities in the region for initiating innovative actions in transboundary water management coordination.

Hence, the GAP RDA took some useful steps in 2001 to initiate contacts with Syria by sending a delegation to that country in response to an invitation by the General Organization for Land Development (GOLD) of the Syrian Ministry of Irrigation. Following this mission, a Syrian delegation headed by the Minister of Irrigation paid a visit to Turkey. As a result of these bilateral relations, a Joint Communiqué was signed between GOLD and the GAP RDA on 23 August 2001. This agreement envisions the cooperation of the two sides in such areas as training, study missions, technology exchange and joint projects. The agreement aims further to improve relations between the two countries, through the training of staff from both countries and by hosting Syrian specialists in Turkey for training activities. Once such training is institutionalized, courses are planned either in Syria or in Turkey for other Arab-speaking countries as well. In fact, further steps have already been taken, and a technical team from Syria has been invited to the region to discuss the principles of implementation. This agreement between GAP and GOLD also includes provisions on "twin protection areas" – one from each country – to be studied, planned and implemented as a Twin Development Project in both countries. In June 2002 the GAP minister visited Syria with a delegation from GAP RDA. Talks were held regarding GAP–GOLD cooperation and an implementation document was signed that defines the principles of implementation of the cooperation envisioned in the Joint Communiqué. This document identifies the projects, training programmes and activities to be conducted by the two parties. A Syrian delegation headed by the Syrian Irrigation Minister later returned this visit, attending the inauguration of the wastewater treatment plant built by GAP RDA on the Turkish side of the border and visiting project-related sites in GAP.

The GAP–GOLD Protocol comprises a limited range of essential but effective activities to create a coordination mechanism between these two government agencies. The overall goal of this agreement and its subsequent implementation protocol (2002) is to provide sustainable utilization of the region's land and water resources and to deal with water management within the larger picture of overall socio-economic development and integration of the underdeveloped regions in Turkey and Syria.

The agreement is in large degree drafted with the basic objective of establishing a dialogue between the two countries and strengthening interriparian engagement by building "intergovernmental networks" that would serve to open up new opportunities for achieving win–win solutions.

Through these recent promising developments between Turkey and Syria, GAP, which once constituted a bone of contention in regional politics, is becoming a source of gradual cooperation for development-related activities. The next section briefly presents GAP as a unique water-based development endeavour in the region. This section is intended to provide insights for future cooperative initiatives geared to specific goals of development and of poverty reduction related to wider socio-economic development.

## GAP: A paradigm shift in water resources development

GAP was conceived and implemented as a means of integrating water resources development with overall human development in a backward region of Turkey. The project area lies in south-eastern Turkey, covering nine provinces corresponding to approximately 10 per cent of Turkey's total population and an equivalent surface area. The project area includes the watersheds of the lower Euphrates and Tigris rivers and the upper Mesopotamian plains. GAP's water resources development programme involves 13 groups of irrigation and energy projects, 7 of which are on the Euphrates River and 6 on the Tigris. The project includes 22 dams, 19 hydropower plants, and irrigation networks in the Euphrates and Tigris river basins to irrigate 1.7 million hectares of land. The total cost of the project is estimated as US$32 billion, US$16 billion of which has already been invested.

As an integrated regional development project based on the concept of sustainability, GAP covers investments in such fields as urban and rural infrastructure, agriculture, transportation, industry, education, health, housing and tourism, as well as dams, power plants and irrigation schemes on the Euphrates and Tigris rivers. This massive push for development places special emphasis on and prioritizes the economic, social and cultural advancement and well-being of the country in general and of the people of the region in particular. The basic objectives of GAP are: to remove interregional disparities in the country by alleviating conditions of abject poverty and raising income levels and living standards in the region; to enhance productivity and employment opportunities in rural areas; and to improve the population-absorbing capacity of larger cities.

As GAP has shifted over the years from an infrastructure development project into a project that coordinates social, cultural, economic and environmental efforts, its changes have followed the changes in global thinking about development. In recent years there has been an increased focus on reducing poverty as a key responsibility of government for development. International conferences such as the 1992 United Nations Conference on Environment and Development in Rio de Janeiro and the 1995 World Summit for Social Development in Copenhagen have put forward ideas about sustainability, gender equity, encouraging grassroots involvement, protecting the environment, and so on. These initiatives were reinforced at the UN Millennium General Assembly when the Millennium Development Goal of halving the proportion of the world's population living in extreme poverty by 2015 was agreed by all member countries of the United Nations. Other goals and targets specific to water and poverty were agreed at the Millennium Assembly and at the World Summit on Sustainable Development in 2002.

These international attempts have generated some consensus about the priorities for development – reaching the poorest, targeting marginalized groups, involving target groups at all stages in the project cycle – which has led to the adoption of policies in support of sustainable development in countries in both the North and the South. GAP has attempted to incorporate these ideas into its activities, and has learned first hand about the tension between how development should look and how it is actually carried out.

Water-based development is a catalyst for economic, social and environmental changes. In GAP, water resources development has enabled human-centred development in the shape of agricultural and other rural development, economic development and entrepreneur support projects, gender equality projects, participatory resettlement, and other activities that are based on the concepts of participation, equity and environmental and social sustainability. GAP is defined as a sustainable human development project, in which water resources development is not an end in itself. It is, in fact, a means to an end, which is to alleviate poverty, to improve the quality of life and to maintain the integrity of the environment and ecosystems.

The concept of sustainability is very relevant to any analysis of water policy. Hence, in the case of GAP, the notion of sustainability is captured in the larger context of the sustainability of society and the economy as well as the environmental services provided by water in the region. Sustainable human development, as applied by GAP for south-eastern Anatolia, encompasses such goals as reaching the poorest, gender equity, capacity-building for local institutions and environmental protection. It is from this philosophy that GAP derives its human-centred focus, using the momentum gained from hydropower and irrigation infrastructure projects to bring opportunities for more sustainable livelihoods to as many in the GAP region as possible.

The main components of sustainability for GAP are: social sustainability, physical and spatial sustainability, environmental sustainability, and economic and agricultural sustainability. In accordance with the sustainable development approach of GAP, special programmes and projects have been initiated to emphasize the human dimension of development through project implementation concerned with basic social services (education, health, housing), gender equity, urban management, irrigation facilities, agricultural and environmental sustainability, institutional and community capacity-building, and public participation.

The case of GAP illustrates that, in the field of water development and management, the three countries are able to exploit potential areas for cooperation by benefiting from the experience and practices of one another, and develop these into common practice.

## Conclusion: Broadening the cooperation agendas

Fruitless negotiations over water allocation and related disputes over water rights in the Euphrates–Tigris River Basin demonstrate that there is a need to create new cooperative frameworks that enable cooperation and development to be linked. Water disputes in the region clearly stem from the mismatch between demand and supply, coupled with the uncoordinated nature of water development projects. Satisfactory solutions to this problem are often premised on coordinated regional action. Hence, it is high time we examined the factors that prevent conflict from occurring, even when the stakes are high concerning water allocation. As recommended in this study, reconsidering a revised version of the Three Stage Plan would enable the parties to determine their objective needs. It would be better for discussions over water needs to take place within the Joint Technical Committee. With its expanded agenda, equitable usage could be determined along with the handling of water-related multisectoral development issues such as infrastructure (energy, telecommunications, transport), agriculture, trade, industry, and health and environmental issues.

Based on the status of relations between the riparians of the Euphrates–Tigris system and recent political developments in Syria, along with projections with respect to Iraq in the new era, one can predict better cooperation and more productive conditions that will make use of the existing mechanisms and modalities, namely the recent collaboration between GAP and GOLD. Transboundary water coordination in the region should be based on sustainability captured in a larger context, just as it has been implemented in GAP.

There is a need to overcome the linear development path of modernity and move beyond it. There are alternatives to the modernization process, as the theoretical discussion on environmental security suggested. The fifth water paradigm aimed at demonstrating that there may be more than one route to sustainable development. This flexibility is one of the pivotal advantages of environmental security's framework because it offers a wide range of qualitative and quantitative choices in approaches and implementation policies. It could be fruitful to let the individual states form their own development model based on their own social capital, knowledge and institutional resources. At the same time, globalization ensures the diffusion of common values and ideas, promotes the exchange of new knowledge and places the water resources discourse within the wider development debate. Hence, we suggest that cooperation in the region needs to be based on wider development concepts; cooperative processes need to be geared to specific goals of development and poverty reduction related to wider socio-economic development.

## Notes

1. Though wars over water do not have any historical basis; see Solomon and Turton (2000).
2. The Spirit of Enlightenment, which is responsible for the social, intellectual and material progress of the West, has always contained within it the seeds of a regression to primitive, unenlightened forms; this is the *dialectic* of the Enlightenment and it manifested itself through the domination of Europe by fascism. See Cahoone (1988: 182).
3. Kumar (1997: 83) claims that "[i]t is difficult to conceive of the modern world without conjuring up steel, steam and speed".
4. For more on the hydraulic mission and how it was conceived and first implemented in the United States, see Reisner (1993).
5. IWRAM information comes from personal communications with Professor J. A. Allan.
6. In 1994 Homer-Dixon revised the original hypotheses to include more variables and asserted that scarcities of cropland, water, forests and fish are of immediate concern. See Homer-Dixon (1994: 39).
7. There is challenging research in progress regarding the applicability of complexity theory to the social sciences. For more on the project, see ⟨http://www.psych.lse.ac.uk/complexity/⟩ (accessed 23 November 2007).
8. In India, the drought of November 2002 led the central government to commit itself to creating a national inter-basin water transfer network, whose implementation would continue even after the emergency period is over (*Times of India*, November 2002).
9. Some of the discussion in this section is drawn from Kibaroglu (2002).
10. Some of the discussion in this section is drawn from Kibaroglu and Unver (2000: 311–330).
11. For a detailed examination see McCaffrey (1986: 103–133).
12. *Case Concerning Gabčíkovo-Nagymaros Project (Hungary/Slovakia)*, Judgment of 25 September 1997, *International Law Materials*, Vol. 37, 1998, p. 162.
13. *International Law Materials*, Vol. 36, 1997, p. 700; Also Article 2(2) of the 1992 UN Economic Commission for Europe Helsinki Convention on the Protection and Use of Transboundary Watercourses and Lakes, *International Law Materials*, Vol. 31, 1992, p. 1312.

14. For the legal positions of Syria and Iraq, see Turkish Ministry of Foreign Affairs (1996).
15. See ILA (1966) and note 13.
16. For the implementation of equitable utilization in law, see Fuentes (1997).
17. *Case Concerning Gabčíkovo-Nagymaros Project (Hungary/Slovakia)*, Judgment of 25 September 1997, *International Law Materials*, Vol. 37, 1998, p. 162.
18. *International Law Materials*, Vol. 36, 1997, p. 700; see also Article 2(2) of the 1992 UN Economic Commission for Europe Helsinki Convention on the Protection and Use of Transboundary Watercourses and Lakes, *International Law Materials*, Vol. 31, 1992, p. 1312.
19. For similar reasoning, see Schachter (1977: 69).

## REFERENCES

Allan, J. A. (2001), *The Middle East Water Question: Hydropolitics and the Global Economy*, London: I. B. Tauris.
——— (2002), "Hydro-Peace in the Middle East: Why No Water Wars? A Case-Study of the Jordan River Basin", SOAS/King's Water Issues Group, Occasional Paper No. 45.
Beck, U. (1992), *Risk Society: Towards a New Modernity*, London: Sage (translated by Mark Ritter).
Belül, M. L. (1996), "Hydropolitics of the Euphrates-Tigris Basin", MSc thesis submitted to the Graduate School of Natural and Applied Sciences, Middle East Technical University, June.
Birnie, P. and A. Boyle (2002), *International Law and the Environment*, 2nd edn, Oxford: Oxford University Press.
Brock, L. (1991), "Peace through Parks: The Environment on the Peace Research Agenda", *Journal of Peace Research*, Vol. 28, No. 4, pp. 407–423.
Bulloch, J. and A. Darwish (1993), *Water Wars: Coming Conflicts in the Middle East*, London: Victor Gollancz.
Buzan, B. (1991), *People, States and Fear: An Agenda for International Security Studies in the Post-Cold War Era*, Hemel Hempstead: Harvester-Wheatsheaf.
——— (1994), "New Patterns of Global Security in the 21st Century", in Olson W. Clinton, *The Theory and Practice of International Relations*, 9th edn, Upper Saddle River, NJ: Prentice Hall.
Buzan, B., Ole Waever and Jaap de Wilde (1998), *Security: A New Framework for Analysis*, Boulder, CO: Lynne Rienner.
Caflisch, L. (1993), "The Law of International Waterways and Its Sources", in J. Macdonald, ed., *Essays in Honour of Wang Tieya*, The Hague: Martinus Nijhoff.
Cahoone, L. E. (1988), *The Dilemma of Modernity: Philosophy, Culture and Anti-Culture*, New York: State University of New York Press.
Deudney, D. H. (1999), "Environmental Security: A Critique", in D. H. Deudney and R. A. Matthew, eds, *Contested Grounds: Security and Conflict in the New Environmental Politics*, New York: State University of New York.
Falkenmark, M. (2001), "The Greatest Water Problem: The Inability to Link Environmental Security, Water Security and Food Security", *Water Resources Development*, Vol. 17, No. 4, pp. 539–554.

Fuentes, X. (1997), "The Criteria for the Equitable Utilization of International Rivers", *British Yearbook of International Law*, Vol. 67, pp. 337–412.

Giddens, A. (1990), *The Consequences of Modernity*, London: Polity Press.

Gleick, P. (1993), "Water and Conflict: Fresh Water Resources and International Security", *International Security*, Vol. 18, No. 1, pp. 79–112.

Homer-Dixon, T. (1991), "Environmental Changes as Causes of Acute Conflict", *International Security*, Vol. 16, No. 2.

—— (1994), "Environmental Scarcities and Violent Conflict", *International Security*, Vol. 19, No. 1.

ILA [International Law Association] (1966), *Report of the Fifty-Second Conference, Helsinki, 1966*, London: ILA.

Johnston, R. J., D. Gregory and D. M. Smith, eds (1991), *The Dictionary of Human Geography*, Oxford: Blackwell (first published in 1981).

Kibaroglu, A. (2002), *Building a Regime for the Waters of the Euphrates-Tigris River Basin*, The Hague: Kluwer Law International.

Kibaroglu, A. and O. Unver (2000), "An Institutional Framework for Facilitating Cooperation in the Euphrates-Tigris River Basin", *International Negotiation: A Journal of Theory and Practice*, Vol. 5, No. 2, pp. 311–330.

Kumar, K. (1997), *From the Post-Industrial to the Post-Modern Society*, Oxford: Blackwell Publishers.

Kut, G. (1993), "Burning Waters: The Hydropolitics of the Euphrates and Tigris", *New Perspectives on Turkey*, Vol. 9, No. 5.

Lammers, J. G. (1984), *Pollution of International Watercourses: A Search for Substantive Rules and Principles of Law*, The Hague: Martinus Nijhoff.

Lipper, J. (1967), "Equitable Utilisation", in A. H. Garretson, R. D. Hayton and C. J. Olmstead, eds, *The Law of International Drainage Basins*, Dobbs Ferry, NY: Oceana, pp. 15–88.

Litfin, K. T. (1998), *The Greening of Sovereignty in World Politics*, Cambridge, MA: MIT Press.

Lupton, D. (1999), *Risk*, London: Routledge.

McCaffrey, S. (1986), "Second Report on the Law of the Non-Navigational Uses of International Watercourses", *Yearbook of the International Law Commission*, Vol. 2, Pt. 1.

—— (1987), "Third Report on the Law of the Non-Navigational Uses of International Watercourses", *Yearbook of the International Law Commission*, Vol. 2, Pt. 2, pp. 24–28.

—— (1997), "Water Scarcity: Institutional and Legal Responses", in Edward H. P. Brams, Esther J. De Haan, André Nollkeamper and Jan Rinzema, eds, *The Scarcity of Water: Emerging Legal and Policy Responses*, London: Kluwer Law International, pp. 43–58.

Ohlsson, L. (1995), *Hydropolitics: Conflicts over Water as a Development Constraint*, London: Zed Books.

*Perceptions: Journal of International Affairs* (1996), Vol. 1, No. 2, p. 13.

Preston, P. W. (1997), *Development Theory: An Introduction*, Oxford: Blackwell Publishers.

Reisner, M. (1993), *Cadillac Desert*, New York: Penguin Books.

Ronnfeldt, C. F. (1997), "Three Generations of Environment and Security", *Journal of Peace Research*, Vol. 34, No. 3, pp. 473–482.

Sachs, W. (1992), *The Development Dictionary: A Guide to Knowledge as Power*, London: Zed Books.

Schachter, O. (1977), *Sharing the World's Resources*, New York: Columbia University Press.

Schumacher, E. F. (1973), *Small Is Beautiful: A Study of Economics as if People Mattered*, London: Blond & Briggs.

Schwebel, S. (1982), "Third Report on the Law of the Non-Navigational Uses of International Watercourses", *Yearbook of the International Law Commission*, Vol. 2, Pt. 1.

Solomon, H. and A. Turton, eds (2000), *Water Wars: Enduring Myth or Impending Reality?*, Umhlanga Rocks: Accord.

Tuchman Mathews, J. (1989), "Redefining Security", *Foreign Affairs*, Vol. 68, No. 2, pp. 162–177.

Turkish Ministry of Foreign Affairs (1996), "Water Issues between Turkey, Syria and Iraq", *Perceptions: Journal of International Affairs*, Vol. 1, No. 2.

UNCED [United Nations Conference on Environment and Development] (1992), *Rio Declaration on Environment and Development*, reproduced in *International Legal Materials*, Vol. 31, 1992, p. 874.

UNCHE [United Nations Conference on the Human Environment] (1972), *Stockholm Declaration on the Human Environment*, adopted by UN General Assembly Resolution 2998 of 15 December 1972, UN Doc.A/CONF.48/14, reproduced in *International Legal Materials*, Vol. 11, 1972, p. 1416.

Unver, O., R. K. Gupta and A. Kibaroglu, eds (2003), *Water Development and Poverty Reduction*, The Hague: Kluwer Academic.

Wolf, A. T. (1999), "Criteria for Equitable Allocations: The Heart of International Water Conflict", *Natural Resources Forum*, Vol. 23, No. 3, p. 30.

# 12

# The politics of security in the Okavango River Basin: From civil war to saving wetlands (1975–2002) – a preliminary security impact assessment

*Jeroen F. Warner and Richard Meissner*

## Introduction

The Okavango Delta is a near-pristine wetland in a semi-arid region. Sustainable development entails a compromise between the ecosystem's integrity and the economic well-being of future generations – safeguarding the economic, environmental and cultural values of the Okavango area. The current consensus in the international water world is that a catchment such as the Okavango is best managed in an integrated manner, in which hydrological boundaries rather than administrative boundaries are respected (Wester and Warner 2002). However, the clash between securitized environmental and economic values of water conflict, and, indeed, interventions (projects) in the Okavango Delta, has given rise to conflicts between states and interest groups as well as to minor inter-state disputes.

The Okavango case is hardly unique. Other projects in the region (Epupa and the Lesotho Highlands Water Project) have provoked similar standoffs, particularly between interest groups and governments. We therefore propose a way of understanding how and why such projects elicit such strong responses and if these can be modified to attenuate existing and future disputes. In so doing, the case study provides building blocks and empirical testing material for a security impact assessment (SIA) for new projects. Our approach will be "strategic constructivism", which is a shorthand phrase to express the assumption that people have perceptions, theories and stories about security. These aspects are used in a goal-oriented manner, in which the goal may not be security itself but

*International water security: Domestic threats and opportunities*, Pachova, Nakayama and Jansky (eds), United Nations University Press, 2008, ISBN 978-92-808-1150-6

where "security" opens a space for urgency that might otherwise have remained closed.

Buzan et al. (1998) have called attention to the experiential fact that the domain of security presents special possibilities for and limits to moving the goal posts by calling on existential threats. Likewise in the field of political ecology, Lees (2001) has shown how threats of crisis proportions have special purchase on the intended audience, legitimizing extraordinary measures. Invoking a danger to life and limb, or, by extension, vital symbols of identity and religion or similarly sacrosanct values, can release special economic, social and political capital.

In this chapter, we introduce the idea of security impact assessment. After describing the theoretical tools, we first make an inventory of the hydropolitical (security) positions, roles and strategies of the riparian countries, including securitizing moves. The problem to be addressed is: to what extent do internal security issues endanger or promote the sustainable use of the water resources of the Okavango River? The hypothesis is that internal security issues will have a negative impact on the sustainable development of the water resources of the Okavango River. The supposition is that more sustainable management of the Okavango can be addressed by better communication and information-sharing between the actors involved in the hydropolitics of the Okavango River Basin. These actors include both state and non-state entities, such as governments, interest groups, non-governmental organizations (NGOs) and members of the epistemic community. The chapter roughly covers the period 1975–2002 – starting with Angola's independence in 1975 and ending with the death of the rebel leader Jonas Savimbi in 2002. Angola is the uppermost riparian in the river basin and therefore a pivotal state in its hydropolitical configuration.

Finally, we explore why it could be a sensible idea to institutionalize such a dialogue between proponents and opponents, initiators and implementers, beneficiaries and adversaries, as a mode of alternative dispute resolution. South Africa's National Water Act (Act No. 36 of 1998) contains strong elements of this in its creation of Catchment Management Agencies. It would be commendable to consider the establishment of a multi-stakeholder forum at the international level.

## Conceptual development

### Transboundary water systems are part of a regional security complex

The Okavango Delta is part of an international river system. The International Law Commission (ILC) of the United Nations (UN) defines an international river as a waterway of which parts are situated in a number of states (McCaffrey 1995: 89). This means that a plethora of actors from these basin states may be involved in the security and risk perceptions concerning transboundary rivers.

A transboundary river is part of a regional security complex, defined by hydrological interdependence (Lindholm 1995). Buzan (1991) makes a valid point in stating that a transboundary river in itself does not necessarily form a regional complex, because water is often not the mainstay of a country's security. However, if we realize that water conflicts are very often only the focus of a wider-ranging conflict, we can indicate that transboundary rivers do involve security and risk concerns for both the environment and humans. For instance, a large dam project can have both environmental and human security impacts and opportunities: contributing to global warming[1] but at the same time providing much-needed water resources to society and the environment (Scudder 1997).

A regional security community is interdependent, a key condition for any multi-stakeholder resource negotiation (Röling 1994). As we shall show below, regional security hinges on different domains and levels – a project in one area has ramifications across borders and social boundaries.

## Projects redistribute risk and security

What is security? Literally, *s(in)e cura* means a state of living without care or concern. Security, then, is a psychological state. Usefully, the German word *Sicherheit* denotes certainty, safety and security, all of which, as Bauman (1999) notes, are under threat in the modern world. It is important to be aware of these connotations because people especially dread uncertainty and, although uncertainty is endemic to complex water systems such as a delta, we shall argue that information and knowledge exchange can go some way to alleviating the sense of insecurity.

Any water project inevitably redistributes (in)security. Changes resulting from developmental interventions may unduly expose some domestic or foreign groups to hazard and exclude actors from security benefits. Rather than concentrate upon the function of undifferentiated nation-states, we need to reflect as much as possible on *all* of the groups who gain or lose (Linklater and MacMillan 1995: 9–10).

A key step therefore is to make an inventory of actors' security position vis-à-vis the water resource (in which, as we shall see, "position" can relate both to physical location and to discursive stance) and how the project changes this position. This is to recognize the damage that can be done by (any) sudden change in security positions, and to consider the risk excesses (security deficits) to be attended to. Nonetheless, it is neither fair nor correct to treat all stakeholders in water interventions as losers or fragile "eggshells". Some are, in fact, clear or unexpected winners; others may be offered a package that improves their prospects for a better future. Although an intervention may present a crisis, change does not have to spell disaster for all. Depending on their resilience, actor groups may find opportunity and gain in change. Indeed, several of us court risk (mountaineers, stockbrokers, etc.) because the opportunity it provides outweighs the potential losses. To give a fairer hearing to both the pluses and minuses we need to consider both opportunities (+) and threats (−) resulting from the intervention, in keeping with the two sides of risk.

Unlike risk, however, which can have positive connotations of adventurousness (risk-taking), *insecurity* is intuitively bad. Security discourse is therefore almost inherently conservative, aimed at retaining a certain status quo. Any change or disturbance of the safe stasis may therefore be perceived as risky.

This is important to note because the study of security is related only to the "danger" side of risk, whereas projects bring opportunities as well. Because different types of security are at stake, a negotiation process may take place in which one type of security is traded off for another – ample financial compensation may make up for the loss of one's land. Often projects involve some kind of security (risk) exchange or swap, which we can make explicit in an SIA (to be discussed later in the chapter).

In economic terms, we may say that security demand is matched by security supply. Demand in the "risk market" is met by actors offering to absorb risk (the insurance industry) or to provide protection from hazard (civil engineers) or risk-free profit on investment (economic security), since providing this good endows them with economic, social or political clout, status and power. This aspect is important, because suppliers of security can be expected to seek out a problem and a clientele for their "security solution". Their problematization of a situation will point to a particular type of solution, a proposal for a particular social arrangement – which represents a claim to provide agency and a claim to scarce resources to enable the solution. Thus, the motives for initiating a project may be ulterior, beyond the stated benefits of the project itself.

In this respect, Leiss and Chociolko's (1994) claim that each actor seeks to offload risk on others is flawed. Risk offload would mean an endless shifting back and forth of risks. The recognition of "positive insecurity" and "security supply" seeks to restore the balance.

## A strategic constructivist approach

The above has indicated the possibility of strategic manoeuvring in the "security market" for water projects. This is made possible by the nature of risk and security and is about what *might* happen and who or what will do the damage – for good or for bad.

Furthermore, there is a lack of universally agreed certainty both about the "facts" and about the values at stake. Although scientists still have a duty to bring in the best evidence they can, they cannot expect to convince their audience but will need to engage with other perspectives and incommensurable values (Espeland 1998). Such problems cannot be solved by expertise and rule-making but need to be negotiated between stakeholders. The combination of pervasive uncertainty and value differentiation involved in both the water management and the security domains undoubtedly creates "intractable" (or "wicked" – Rittel and Webber 1973) problems – problems that cannot be addressed solely on technical and scientific grounds and are burdened by protracted conflict and ineffective outcomes.

In "intractable problems", uncertainty and incompatible value orientations tend to prevent rapid closure through an "objectified" (expert) security discourse leading to one best approach. The issue is so close to the hearts and minds of important interested parties that the stakeholders in security, once they become "aware" of the risk and insecurity, form opinions about whether their current and expected levels of security are high enough.

In constructivist terms (Berger and Luckmann 1966), there is no single best approach to security. We do not claim a position of total relativism ("strong constructivism"), such as when enemy tanks are at your door or a flood washes your house away. There are few basic "facts" to haggle over. We shall take a "weak constructivist" approach (e.g. Tansey 2004) that maintains that a great deal, but not all, of reality is constructed in the eye of the beholder.[2]

Security, then, is a perception, a gut feeling rather than a fact out there. Short of psychometric research, there is no way of knowing how (in)secure people "really" feel. We can only analyse their utterances about the issue. Risk perception and risk representation are not the same thing. Those who speak in the public arena – politicians, interest groups, NGOs, media commentators, etc. – tend to be aware of how a message comes across, and therefore are less likely to speak from an emotion of fear like ordinary citizens do. They are more likely to reflect on the effects of their representation. In fact, the professed sense of risk, insecurity and vulnerability may or may not be different from the experienced, but unexpressed, sense of risk.

From a political science approach, we allow for the possibility that people express their views on risk not out of the blue but for a purpose, that is, with strategic (instrumental) goal rationality. That assumption opens important alternative avenues for understanding discourse. With garbage-can theory in the back of our minds we can see that means and ends are frequently reversed: a "solution" is there and a problem needs to be found to legitimize and enable the solution. Just as military interventions are often legitimized by winning coalitions of (spurious or real) arguments such as hegemonic aspirations, access to resources, humanitarian considerations and personal advancement (Jaap de Wilde, personal communication, 2003), building a dam can be legitimized by security arguments but informed by other considerations – employment, technological challenge, symbolic national pride, etc. We thus surmise that a security claim can be a means as well as an end.

This may or may not always be a conscious strategy. We just note that the definition and language of "security", with its powerful connotation of survival, can be fungible, that is, it can be instrumentalized to meet a set of (ulterior) goals. One powerful use of security language is to provide closure in a protracted debate.

## Securitization and TINA-izations

We have already broached the possibility that stakeholders use language to improve their security position. This has an important consequence for understanding debates on security.

First, it is often observed that political actors make moves for closure by foreclosing alternatives. Most famously, UK Prime Minister Thatcher used to say "There Is No Alternative" (TINA), ignoring the fact that, *strictu sensu*, there always is an alternative (as noted by Beer 1987). Premature closure of project alternatives means that the area of freedom for negotiations is reduced and thus the conflict potential is enlarged. (Of course, if closure never happens, the process also is mired.) We shall coin the phrase "TINA-ization" to denote an attempt to provide a shortcut to rapid decision-making, shutting out time- and energy-consuming competition and democratic debate.

A particular form of TINA-ization is securitization. As Barry Buzan, Ole Waever and Jaap de Wilde (1998) have shown, actors in fact use language to move a project from the realm of everyday political negotiation to the realm of non-negotiable absolutes of life and death (security) issues. Such securitizations (Buzan et al. 1998), where we run up against (discursive) absolutes, impose serious limits on a process of negotiation.

To analyse the value and impact of those strategies we shall take a strategic constructivist approach – accepting that actors ultimately construct security but that these constructions may be conscious, goal-serving strategies rather than mechanistic outcomes of social processes. We argue that "facts out there" are not necessarily decisive for the political outcome; a strong example was the Brent Spar furore in 1995, in which

Greenpeace won the day despite the superior information provided by Shell (Szerszynski 2002).

The security speech act of "securitization" is a claim that an extraordinary threat legitimizes extraordinary measures, elevating a non-security issue to a security issue. In light of the key political science question "who gets what, where and how", we may ask whether securitization plays a role in the process of accessing such resources. From both sides, these arguments are more than anything aimed at enhancing or undermining the legitimacy of the project. We may feel justified in discounting the inevitable amplification and dramatization of both (security) costs and benefits in the heat of the debate, but not in overlooking this eminently political aspect.

Because all is fair in political struggle, one often cannot tell whether securitization is a genuine cry of despair or a cunning strategy. In the struggle for funds and attention, stakeholder groups can pose as beneficiaries or as victims, or may be hijacked as such when outsider groups depict them as vulnerable, either to the supposed malady (the flood) or to the side-effects of the remedy (the project). Buzan et al. (1998) in fact claim that securitization strategies are deliberate strategies to manage the risk perceptions of intended audiences in order to justify policies, by representing risks as mortal dangers or as acceptable and even useful discomforts.

A securitizing move may take the form of the accusation of "under-securitization" (the wilful neglect of an extraordinary pressing threat), which is presented as a "fact" by those who seek to voice concern about an absence of securitization (Buzan et al. 1998). In the strategic constructivist approach, we can highlight the different motives for and interests in calling attention to a shortage of securitization (raising the alarm). People problematize the (imputed) sense of *se-cura*, where a state of "living without a care" becomes "careless living". Deliberate under-securitization no doubt happens, for (institutional) survival or other reasons, but it is more interesting to understand why certain issues become securitized whereas others remain unsecuritized.

A security claim cannot fall out of the clear blue sky. Security claims are constructed on a body of knowledge – whether intuitive fear or scientific knowledge – that provides an *attribution* of who or what is the threat, who or what is being threatened, how grave the danger is and who should remedy it (Buzan et al. 1998). Because certainty is an important aspect of security, the accuracy and transparency of information about risks would seem to be paramount. Yet, in their need to connect cause and effect, people are quite willing to fill in the blanks, so that the validity of the information turns out not to be a necessary requirement. The lack of certainty also gives rise to opposing risk stories (attributions), paving the way for politicization.

Below we explore what the factors in the "happy landing" of the risk story may be.

## Who can speak of security?

A speech act is not really performed unless its audience responds in the intended way. In the well-known Westphalian model, the state is the sole arbiter of security. It is hegemonic in the international arena and sovereign in the protection of its citizens by virtue of its rightful monopoly of the means of violence. However, as new types of security have come on the scene, together with new referents for security as well as actors (private and civil society) who claim to be able to provide security (Gleditsch 1998), this provides new audiences and new "selling points" for securitization.

Because, to our knowledge, there is no theory of appropriateness, we shall provisionally mark the territory. How "appropriate" a security claim is to the intended audience depends on the legitimacy of the sender (e.g. power position, social status) and the message, and how it resonates with the fears and concerns of that audience. Apart from that, the key condition for the appropriateness of securitization is *urgency* (Buzan et al. 1998). As a proxy, we propose that "urgency" has four key elements: time, scale, existentiality (evidenced in a discourse of "survival" and "annihilation") and affinity.

For the scale element, Buzan's five-by-five grid is useful in categorizing the level of risks and securitizations (see Figure 12.1).[3] As for time and existentiality, a "clear and present" threat commands more "resonance" with the intended audience than a "creeping catastrophe". Thus, the inundation of an island now commands greater urgency than a secular process, and the debate about climate change necessarily has a lower political urgency than a debate about al-Qaeda. This by no means makes sea-level rise a lesser evil, but it has the benefit of making it more negotiable, whereas talks on terrorism easily reach a point of no return, demanding or killing off legitimacy for the project. Finally, affinity (cuddlability) makes children and seals so much more successful than amoebas and ozone layers as "securitizable" goods.

Not everybody's claim is accorded equal value. Of the many people making security claims, it is in the world of experts that the *hegemonic* security discourse tends to originate – military experts in the case of conflict, water experts in the domain of threats such as flood, drought, pollution and integrated water resources management. The water balance,

| Level of risk | Type of securitization | | | | |
|---|---|---|---|---|---|
| | Military | Economic | Environmental | Societal | Political |
| International system | | | | | |
| Macro region | | | | | |
| Unit (state) | | | | | |
| Local | | | | | |
| Individual | | | | | |

Figure 12.1 Security diagram.
*Source*: Based on Buzan et al. (1998).
*Note*: This 25-area model is employed to categorize and structure the debate. It provides multiple domains and levels of security. Any water project crosscuts these levels and domains.

hydrographs and flood contours produced by the hydrological community provide the starting points for any discussion about "objective/ objectified" flood security. This may well be at odds with the (less scientifically validated) "subjective securities" of other security claimers.

The present analysis concentrates on people's (discursive) security strategies around a water project. Conflicts easily arise over the (re)distribution of security positions that necessarily follows from major changes in the management of a water resource – whether these are autonomous processes (climate change, population pressure) or planned (interventions, new rules and regulations). Water projects are bound to entail differential costs and benefits for different stakeholders. As a result, water projects change stakeholders' security positions. They create facts because they are not always well anticipated. The analysis starts from this assumption.

## Towards a security impact assessment

So far, we have postulated that actors' security positions and perceptions are affected by project interventions, and that there are suppliers of and customers for security. The supply of water security became a problematic issue in the course of the 1980s and 1990s. Controversies over water projects have caused those who supply or facilitate the goods and skills and design the works – donors, engineers, consultants, NGOs and interest groups – to reflect not just on technical indicators such as efficiency and reliability, but also on the consequences of interventions, on socio-political equitability issues. A lack of perceived legitimacy (to be justified in playing one's role and matching the means to the ends) can kill a technically and economically sound project.

There is, however, no coherent framework for project assessment in security terms. In evaluating public works projects, "value-for-money" or benefit–cost analyses are still the norm. Yet the values involved in pushing through (or resisting) a project are quite often non-economic. In the Netherlands, "insecurity" itself is often enough to justify a project almost irrespective of costs. The environmental movement, on the other hand, could score victories by stopping projects by invoking environmental values over economic considerations. Political motives such as national pride or reputation or cultural motives such as archaeological heritage can be said to "securitize" an issue. It is, then, important to consider the project's socio-political environment and the psychological forces at play before embarking on a major water project. Later, we shall argue that such an assessment should take place with the participation of a diversity of stakeholders, to arrive at a multifaceted picture of gains and losses.

In any such area, some actors ("security suppliers") may be called in because they are prepared to take or shoulder certain risks or are able to improve security. Other actors will force themselves into the debate by insisting that certain types of security should be provided or guaranteed ("security claimants/demand"). In each grid area, there will be risk ceilings (security thresholds) that may not be breached on pain of project abandonment, for example excessive vulnerability to terrorist attacks or the exit of crucial stakeholders who find their basic values compromised beyond redemption. Acceptance will be possible only through remedial measures, a trade-off in which one type of security is sacrificed for another type of security, such as economic compensation for physical harm. In addition to scoring risks in terms of their magnitude and impact in a risk index (Venter 1998), we could therefore have different alternative arrangements for risk alleviation.

As we have seen, such swaps are difficult to make where securitizing moves have taken place. For such cases, de-securitizing strategies need to be developed, which may involve a re-politicization of issues. Finding alternatives where there is "no alternative" can create new areas of freedom for negotiating win–win situations.

Below, we shall make a preliminary analysis of the controversies over the development of the Okavango River system with the help of the above concepts. After a physical description of the actors and factors impinging on the development of the delta, we will make an inventory of the relevant security positions and securitizations.[4]

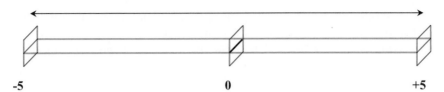

Figure 12.2 The security impact assessment scale.

We devise a scale to determine the security impacts of the issues identified. This scale is structured in such a way as to indicate whether an issue has a positive (+) or a negative (−) impact on the water resources of the Okavango River Basin (see Figures 12.2 and 12.3). The scale is compatible with the risks (both positive and negative) that might affect (positively or negatively) the water resources development trajectory of the Okavango River. An issue with the most positive impact is scored as +5. An issue with the most negative impact is scored as −5. An issue that could go either way (positive or negative) is scored as 0. The arrow indicates that the security issue can move along the scale according to changes in the political situation, time and the level of salience. Thus, the security issues within a river basin are not fixed according to level, time and scale but are dynamic. Riparian position (upper/lower, etc.) and the discursive attitude of the actors towards the water resources of the Okavango will also be scored by using the scale.

## The Okavango River Basin

The Okavango River rises in central Angola (where it is known as the Cubango) on the Bié plateau south of Nova Lisboa and east of Huambo. It flows south-eastwards for 650 kilometres (km) before forming the border between Angola and Namibia for 400 km. It dissects the Caprivi Strip, crosses Namibia and enters Botswana. It then flows for 100 km before it "fans" out to form the Okavango Delta. The delta lends the river a unique characteristic. The Okavango is an endoric river system, with its

Figure 12.3 The position of the Okavango Basin on the SIA scale.

outflow not into the sea but into an inland delta (Meissner 1998a: 70; Ashton 2000a: 94, 2003: 165).

The river has a total length of 1,727 km, with a mean annual run-off (MAR) of between 10.0 and 11.6 billion m$^3$. Some experts note that the Okavango River has surplus water resources of high quality (Conley 1995: 7) owing to a low intensity of utilization.

The main tributary of the Okavango River is the perennial Cuito River, whose source is also on the Bié plateau. Another tributary of the Okavango is the ephemeral Omuramba-Omatako River. This river does not contribute any significant water to the Okavango's flow, except during seasons of very high rainfall. The Nata River joins the system from Zimbabwe and flows into the Makgadikgadi Pans. However, because it does not contribute water to the Okavango, it is not considered part of the Okavango system. Based on this, Zimbabwe does not form part of the water political situation of the Okavango River Basin. Three riparian states therefore share the Okavango River: Angola, Botswana and Namibia (Heyns 1995: 9, 2003: 16; Ashton 2000b: 80, 2000a: 94).

## The state actors: Internal security issues

From the physical description of the Okavango River Basin three state actors are identified – Angola, Botswana and Namibia. Because of their dependence, to a lesser or greater extent, on the river's water resources, these actors will securitize the Okavango, depending on prevailing internal security issues. This will, furthermore, be influenced by the riparian's geopolitical position in the river basin.

Within and crosscutting this hydropolitical configuration of actors, subnational and transnational actors have an impact on the Okavango politics: interest groups and the scientific (epistemic) community. This section of the chapter scrutinizes the internal security issues of the states sharing the river.

### Angola

#### The economy

In 2000, the World Bank estimated the gross national income (GNI) per capita of Angola at US$1,180, and the Angolan economy was ranked 181st out of 208 economies. Comparing these figures with those for South Africa (the regional economic powerhouse in the Southern African Development Community region) clarifies Angola's economic capacity. In 2000, the World Bank estimated South Africa's GNI per capita at

US$9,160, and its economy was ranked 72nd in the world (World Bank 2000a). This indicates to what extent the development of the Angolan economy was hindered owing to years of civil war, despite its huge natural resource base (consisting of oil, diamonds, arable land and water).

Angola is a potentially wealthy country. It is expected that oil production will increase from around 900,000 barrels/day (b/d) at present, to 1.4 million b/d by 2005 and to nearly 2 million b/d by 2007. Offshore oil production dominates the economy, contributing 60 per cent to the gross domestic product (GDP) (World Bank 2000b). Therefore, to facilitate economic development through increased oil production, Angola might start looking at its surface water resources to supply bulk water to its expanding economy. The Okavango River might be one of these water resources.

*The civil war*

One of the outstanding features of Angolan domestic politics was the civil war (from 1975 to 2002). This violent event had a profound impact on Angola's political situation. The war broke out after Portugal relinquished its African colonies following the Lisbon coup d'état of April 1974. Portugal withdrew from Angola in 1975 and left behind a Marxist dictatorship. Yet this new government was a complete failure because it could not foster political stability and economic growth. The civil war broke out when the União Nacional para a Independência Total de Angola (UNITA) tried to get rid of the one-party government system that took power after the Portuguese withdrawal (Calvocoressi 1987: 196; Huntington 1993: 57–58; Kirsten and Bester 1997: 51; Davenport and Saunders 2000: 527).

The conflict between the Movimento Popular de Libertação de Angola (MPLA) and UNITA ended after the killing of the UNITA leader, Jonas Savimbi, on 22 February 2002 (Pearce et al. 2002; Meissner 2002: 100), but political and socio-economic problems remain that need to be tackled by the political leadership.

The civil war has led to the squandering of human, natural, financial and institutional resources. After the Cold War, the MPLA leadership became openly bureaucratic and corrupt, losing its moral claim to be the leader of the struggle for independence. The corruption of the state bureaucracy is still rampant and there is a blurring between governance and business on the part of the political elite (Campbell 2000: 162–163; Cilliers 2000: 11). It is for this reason that Angola has a weak power political position within the Okavango River Basin, because it does not have the second-order resources of Botswana and Namibia for water resources development. However, this might change, especially after the end of the civil war.

*The future*

A number of security aspects can be isolated that will have an impact on Angola's political future, namely:

- The end of the long civil war appears to be final, despite logistical difficulties that have delayed the process of integrating UNITA rebels into the regular government forces and food shortages that pose the risk of unrest at demobilization camps. In August 2002, UNITA announced its transformation from a military force to a political party.
- That the civil war is over does not mean that its risks have completely abated, although they were significantly reduced. The ending of the fighting will bring its own risks, especially in the near future. According to Political Risk Services (PRS 2003a): "The most significant of these is the danger that the end of the war will unleash pent-up hostility over the misdistribution of the country's wealth and the corruption that permeates all layers of government."
- If the government hopes to finance investments in infrastructure and social services – water included – a lending arrangement with the International Monetary Fund (IMF) will be required. This will be needed to dampen social discontent. If this scenario plays out, the IMF will demand from the government that it take steps to improve the transparency of government accounts, especially the payments received from oil companies (PRS 2003a).

Thus, the security issue is shifting from the military to the economic domain. This is likely to increase the pressure on the environmental resource (the Okavango River), jeopardizing the integrity of the resource (environmental security).

*Probable use of the Okavango's water resources by Angola*

Angola is the upstream riparian in the Okavango River Basin. Post-war reconstruction in Angola is likely to see a rapid acceleration in the demand for water upstream in the basin. About 140,000 people live in the Cuando-Cubango province, most of whom engage in subsistence agriculture. According to the United Nations Development Programme (UNDP), "current use of the basin's water resources is limited to water supplies to small regional centers and some small scale floodplain irrigation". Moreover, since independence, there have been no sizeable developments and investments in the headwaters of the Cubango and Cuito rivers. A 1995 provincial rehabilitation plan indicated that the development of Cuando-Cubango province would require considerable investment in water supply, sanitation, agriculture and transportation. These plans are still to be undertaken and could have severe potential consequences for the two downstream riparians. The Angolan Minister of

Energy and Water, Botelho de Vasconcelos, has stated that his country is considering the development of agricultural zones in south-eastern Cuando-Cubango province, using water from the Okavango River for irrigation (Porto and Clover 2003: 76; Turton et al. 2002; Heyns 2003: 17).

There is therefore uncertainty about Angola's plans to utilize the Okavango River as a source of water for either domestic or agricultural purposes. However, according to Porto and Clover (2003: 76), "Largely as a result of this last phase of the war [during 2001 and early 2002], there are now 66,431 confirmed internally displaced peoples (IDPs) and 204,024 unconfirmed IDPs in the Province ... These waves of de-population and displacement in the Province of Cuando Cubango have the potential to affect the hydro-environmental integrity of the source [of the Okavango River]."

To tackle the current socio-economic situation, the provincial government has identified seven priorities under a Provincial Emergency Plan of Action. Three of the priorities hold direct implications for the utilization of the water resources of the Okavango River:

- Agriculture and food security – to improve food security by distributing land and providing agricultural inputs and technical support, and the promotion of reforestation initiatives in resettlement areas. *Reforestation poses an additional demand on the resource, owing to the environmental water demand of trees.*
- Water and sanitation – improvement of sanitation facilities by the construction of pit latrines in areas with high concentrations of IDPs and the conducting of awareness and information campaigns on safe water and excrement disposal (this could lead to groundwater pollution seeping back into the river system).
- Resettlement – support the resettlement of 4,000 families and establish a reception area for new IDPs arriving in Cuito Cuanavale (Porto and Clover 2003: 76).

The other four priorities are: health and nutrition; education; protection of IDPs; and de-mining actions. These priorities are associated with the development priorities in Cuando-Cubango province as peace is re-established (Porto and Clover 2003: 76).

## Botswana

### The economy

Botswana's GDP is about US$4,318 million and between 1990 and 1995 the GNI grew at 4.2 per cent. Between 1997 and 2000 GDP grew by 7 per cent; and this is for a country that was classified as one of the six poorest countries in the world at independence in 1966. So poor was Botswana that it received grants from the UK government to cover its government expenditures (Handley 1997: 24; Fidzani 1998: 232; Meissner 1998a: 74).

By 1976, this had changed significantly. Botswana had uncovered some extensive sources of natural resource wealth. The most important of these were diamonds, copper and coal deposits. Today, Botswana is one of the top seven diamond producers in the world (Fidzani 1998: 233).

Because of the discovery of diamonds, Botswana adopted a trickle-down approach to development. The government got rapid and large returns from its intensive capital investments in mining and reinvested those returns in improving the living standards of those who do not benefit directly from the mining sector. This strategy resulted in an economy that is too dependent on the mining sector and on imported foodstuffs, leading to neglect of the agricultural sector (Fidzani 1998: 233). However, Botswana achieves huge savings in water resources through the importation of virtual water. This has a positive impact on the water resources base of the country, in that less water is consumed by the agricultural sector.

*The delta as a Ramsar site and a prime tourist attraction*

The government of Botswana acceded to the Ramsar Convention on Wetlands on 4 April 1997, and the Okavango Delta was listed as a Ramsar Site of International Importance (Ramsar Convention on Wetlands 1999). In accordance with Article 3 of the Convention, Botswana is required to promote the conservation and wise use of the delta. To this end, the country, under the leadership of the National Conservation Strategy Agency, has embarked on a management plan for the entire delta. According to Pinheiro et al. (2003: 111):

> The need for the plan was necessitated by the fact that existing land use patterns for different areas are often guided by somewhat conflicting guidelines, and these need to be integrated in a single overall planning framework. The long-term goal of the management plan is to provide an integrated resource management for the Okavango Delta that will ensure its long-term conservation and provide benefits for the present and future well being of the people, through sustainable use of its natural resources.

The delta is not only a Ramsar site but also an important source of foreign revenue. The near-pristine delta is a big tourist attraction. Over the years, the tourism industry has grown significantly, and the delta has been one of Botswana's prime destinations. The Botswana government makes every effort to keep the delta a prime tourist site. To this end, the government has opted for a low-volume/high-cost tourism policy (Pinheiro et al. 2003: 110), which has lessened the impact of people on the environmental integrity of the delta.

Nonetheless, the Okavango Delta's water resources represent a valuable resource to meet a number of needs. Yet the delta is far from any human settlements of significant size. This means that no notable water abstractions have been implemented by Botswana, apart from the local use of water by communities situated in and around the delta (Pinheiro et al. 2003: 110).

## HIV/AIDS

Botswana had one of the healthiest populations on the African continent until the onset of the HIV/AIDS epidemic. HIV/AIDS is a growing problem that has begun to damage the economy and the people. The Botswanas' average life expectancy dropped from more than 60 years to 47 years in 1999. Official reports indicate that 25 per cent of adults are infected with HIV/AIDS, but as many as one-third of the sexually active population may be infected (PRS 2003b: 61).

We can thus say that economic expansion is matched by a prioritization of environmental security, which will support economic security in another form as eco-tourism brings economic benefits. The overlay of HIV/AIDS affects the human security of people.

## Developments in Botswana's section of the Okavango system

According to Heyns (2003: 17), "no major development of the water resources of the Okavango River or the delta have taken place in Botswana, except for the Mopopi Dam, which was built to supply water to the Orapa diamond mine and was created by using the basin of the Putimolonwane pan and constructing earth embankments around it to impound more water". This dam is situated at the southern end of the delta and is supplied by water pumped from the Boteti River, which flows out of the delta. Nonetheless, this system has been replaced with groundwater owing to the weak flow of the Boteti from the delta (Heyns 2003: 17).

In the early 1990s, Botswana planned the Southern Okavango Integrated Water Development Plan (SOIWDP). It was temporarily shelved in 1992, even before the World Conservation Union (IUCN) published its draft review report on the project in October 1992. This was after the Botswana government was criticized by interest groups for planning to implement the project (Neme 1997; Meissner 1998a: 93; Heyns 2003: 17).

In theory, because the delta is entirely in Botswana, the country can do as it pleases with it. However, national and international pressures from interest groups influence its management. Botswana is now presenting itself as a socially and environmentally responsible actor, liaising with IUCN on wetland conservation and promoting another, less tangible type of security: a positive reputation.

## Namibia

### The economy

The Namibian economy relies heavily on the extraction and processing of minerals, processed fish and other manufactures for export. The country is the fifth-largest producer of uranium in the world and an important source of gem-quality diamonds. Namibia also has one of the richest potential fisheries in the world. Furthermore, real GDP growth averaged 5 per cent from 1990 to 1993, although it slowed to an average of 3 per cent during the period 1994–2001 (World Bank 2000c).

The largest contributor to GDP is government service, accounting for one-quarter. This is followed by primary sector activities, such as mining, large-scale commercial livestock farming and fishing. Mining contributes one-tenth to GDP. Namibia has a large natural resources base, good infrastructure and access to regional and international markets. These factors bode well for the development of a more diversified economy (EIU 2002).

### Water as a scarce resource

Although Namibia is endowed with a large natural resources base, water is extremely scarce. "Owing to low rainfall, rapid water evaporation caused by high temperatures, and the absence of perennial rivers except along the northern and southern borders, Namibia is highly susceptible to drought, and water supplies to the expanding populations in the main towns are coming under increasing pressure" since independence (EIU 2002).

Extraction of groundwater resources is increasingly exceeding aquifer replenishment because of recurrent drought and rising demand. Demand in Windhoek has increased substantially owing to population growth. Water-saving measures have had a limited impact in this urban centre. The state-owned water company, NamWater, is implementing progressive tariff increases in an attempt to achieve full cost recovery on new water-supply projects. The innovative Windhoek wastewater reclamation plant is being upgraded to increase the supply of potable water. Supplies to Walvis Bay and the central coastal area are also under pressure. Falling water levels in local aquifers are the main reasons (EIU 2002).

Namibia's Second National Development Plan (NDP2), which covers the period up to the year 2006, makes clear reference to the central role of water in Namibia's development plans. The NDP2 is an indication of the necessity to align the activities of all government departments that influence the country's water resources with this strategic objective (Republic of Namibia 2001; Ashton and Neal 2003: 41).

Namibia seems bent on a "hydraulic mission", a water-fuelled economic development plan to escape from drought and underdevelopment. This is coupled, to a certain extent, with water demand management, as the upgrading of Windhoek's wastewater reclamation plant indicates. Because economic resource development is equated with security, the integrity of the resource may be less of a concern.

## HIV/AIDS

According to the Economist Intelligence Unit (EIU 2002), HIV/AIDS has overtaken tuberculosis as the major killer disease in Namibia. Moreover, and according to the Joint United Nations Programme on HIV/ AIDS (UNAIDS), 22.5 per cent of the population were infected with HIV at end-2001 and 13,000 people died from AIDS in 2000. The number of so-called AIDS orphans was an estimated 47,000 at the end of 2001. It is estimated that, by 2021, AIDS will cut average life expectancy to 47 years for males and 54 years for females, from 59 and 66 years respectively in 2001 (UNAIDS 2002).

## A concise hydropolitical history

So far, consideration has been given to the individual actor's relation to the water resource. In this part of the chapter, the hydropolitical history of water resources development and cooperation in the basin is sketched (see Table 12.1).

From Table 12.1 it is evident that it was not only states that played a role in the hydropolitical history of the Okavango River. Non-state actors were also involved. In the following section, we scrutinize more closely the role and involvement of interest groups as well as the epistemic community's role.

## Non-state actors in the water politics of the Okavango River Basin

Over the past decade the number of actors involved in the water politics of the Okavango River Basin has increased substantially. This section will look at the involvement of interest groups and the epistemic community in the water politics of the Okavango River Basin. Although water politics is a transnational matter, interest groups operate as linkage actors, connecting domestic security issues (mainly water resources projects) with the international political domain. The interest groups are mainly concerned with the environmental integrity of the delta should any upstream developments take place in future.

## Interest groups

### The Southern Okavango Integrated Water Development Plan

In 1992 Botswana shelved the SOIWDP, which planned to use part of the river's water resources for urban and mining water needs (Heyns 2003: 17).

The role and involvement of interest groups lobbying against this project were an important factor in its being "temporarily shelved". The people of the delta opposed it, contending it would ruin their livelihoods because the project might adversely affect the delta. The international environmental lobby also condemned the project, particularly Greenpeace, which started a campaign against Botswana's diamond industry (a portion of the delta's water was used to supply water to the Orapa diamond mine in the north of the country) (Neme 1997; Meissner 1998b: 30, 1998c: 20).

### Phase 5 of the Eastern National Water Carrier (ENWC)

In the mid-1990s, interest groups again played a role when the Namibian government planned to implement Phase 5 of the ENWC. Presently, the project's purpose is to divert water from the upper catchment of the Omatako River and the Karstveld aquifer for domestic and industrial consumption in the Windhoek–Okahandja–Karibib complex in the Swakop River catchment in central Namibia (Meissner 1998a: 88; Heyns 2003: 17). The extension was planned as a result of a severe region-wide drought. In 1995, with the end of the drought, it remained dry in Namibia. It was for this reason that Namibia planned to implement Phase 5 (Swatuk 1996: 19; Meissner 1998a: 88).

Namibia's plans led to a low-level dispute with Botswana. The media and interest groups were quick to brand the dispute a "water war" (Meissner 1998c: 20). Was it in fact a water war or were the (national and international) interest groups only attempting to create a "water war" discourse to further their arguments against Phase 5? Looking at the definition of "conflict", "armed conflict" and a "water war" will shed more light on the question.

The Africa Bureau of the United States Agency for International Development (USAID) defines a conflict as "a struggle over values or claims to status, power (i.e., through the politicization of identity) and scarce resources (for example land, water, natural resources, minerals, and food), among two or more parties that perceive incompatible interests or express hostile attitudes" (USAID n.d.). An armed conflict (war) takes place when two actors "engage in hostilities and military operations, usually for some political purpose" (Viotti and Kauppi 1999: 499). Meissner (1998c: 20) and Turton (2000: 112) note that a "water war" can

Table 12.1 A concise hydropolitical history of the Okavango River Basin

| Year/period | Event | Rationale of water-related plans, policies or projects | Implementation of water-related plans, policies or projects (Yes/No) |
|---|---|---|---|
| 1908 | Proposed development, by the UK government, of Ngamiland by using the Okavango Delta's water for irrigation. | Agricultural development of the region | No |
| 1918 | Professor Ernest Schwarz's proposed grand plan to alter the climate of Southern Africa by using the Okavango's water to turn Makgadikgadi Pan into a vast lake | Meteorological manipulation to make the region suitable for agriculture | No |
| 1949 | Proposed plan to construct a barrage at the delta's inlet | To tap the delta's agricultural potential | No |
| 1956 | Reconnaissance mission to look for a suitable dam site along the Okavango River | To construct a hydroelectric and irrigation project | No |
| 1964 | Treaty between Portugal and South Africa | Regarding rivers of joint interest, which included the Cuvelai, Okavango, Limpopo, Maputo and Incomati rivers | Yes |
| 1966 | Botswana gains independence from the United Kingdom | – | – |
| 1975 | Water master plan for Namibia by South Africa | To implement the Eastern National Water Carrier | Yes |
| 1975 | Angola becomes independent | – | – |
| 1976 | Symposium organized by the Botswana Society | To look into how the delta's environment would be affected by development plans. | Yes – the symposium concluded that the resource potential of the delta should be exploited in an integrated manner |

| Date | Event | Purpose | |
|---|---|---|---|
| 1990 | Namibian independence from South Africa | – | – |
| 18 September 1990 | Treaty between Angola and Namibia | To establish a Joint Commission of Cooperation (JCC) regarding general cooperation between the two countries | Yes |
| 13 November 1990 | Treaty between Botswana and Namibia | To establish a Joint Permanent Water Commission (JPWC) covering aspects regarding the Chobe–Linyanti river system and operating separately from OKACOM | Yes |
| 1992 | Botswana shelves the Southern Okavango Integrated Water Development Plan | Opposition from interest groups was too strong | Yes |
| 15 September 1994 | Establishment of the Permanent Okavango River Basin Water Commission (OKACOM) | Multilateral legal forum between Angola, Botswana and Namibia for the development of the Okavango River | Yes |
| Mid-1990s | Namibia announces plans to extend the Eastern National Water Carrier from Tsumeb to Rundu on the banks of the Okavango River | To deliver more water to the central region of the country, because of a severe drought | No |
| 2002 | Namibia announces plans to develop the Popa Falls hydroelectric installation | To produce electricity for ever-increasing energy demand in Namibia and elsewhere | Uncertain |

*Sources:* Schwarz (1921: 166–181); Meissner (1998a: 85, 86); Turton et al. (2002); Wellington (1949: 566–567); Smit (1991: 166, 167–168, 172); DWA (1974); Stern and Lau (1990: 75–76); Heyns (1995: 10); Ohlsson (1995: 60); Treaty (1994); CSIR (1997: 13–16); Treaty (1990); Ramberg (1997); Ashton (2000a: 82); NamPower (n.d.).

mean one of two things. First, it is when water is used as a weapon, either to bring about destruction or to deny a population access to it, by targeting water installations such as dams or by shutting off water supplies. Secondly, water resources can be the direct cause of conflict between two states – defined as a true water war.

Seen thus, there was no question of a "water war" between Namibia and Botswana, because the two countries did not engage each other militarily over the Okavango's water resources. The interest groups created a *discourse* of war, because war is one of the most undesirable situations to which human beings can be exposed in the modern world. By creating a "war" discourse, the interest groups painted a stronger and more negative image of the project and indicated the threat it poses to the Okavango Delta. This was an attempt to raise the issue to a higher level on the national (Botswana and Namibia), regional and global agendas. Had they succeeded, it would have assisted their "crusade" against the ENWC.

Thus, not only states were involved in the low-level dispute. Interest groups, from Botswana, Namibia and abroad, lobbied the Namibian government not to implement Phase 5. In 1997 it rained over large parts of Namibia, ending the drought. This prompted the Namibian government temporarily to shelve Phase 5 of the ENWC. However, the need to complete Phase 5 can be delayed only until 2009 (Meissner 1998b: 31; Pinheiro et al. 2003: 8).

*The Popa Falls hydroelectric installation*

The Okavango River was yet again a target for development in 2002/2003. This time it concerned the 1969 plan to produce hydroelectricity at the Popa Falls in the Cavango region of Namibia (DWA and Hydroconsults 1969; NamPower n.d.).

The plan is to construct a hydroelectric installation on the Okavango River for the production of 20 MW of electricity. A low-level weir that allows for no water abstraction but constant intake levels will produce the electricity. This system will release adequate water to maintain the flow of the falls, while diverting water from the diversion weir into a channel towards the hydropower station. The project's pre-feasibility study (for which permission was granted by the Okavango River Basin Water Commission – OKACOM) was completed in November 2003 (Terblancé 2002; NamPower n.d., 2003). The hydropower installation would be able to provide electricity to south-eastern Angola, north-western Botswana and southern Zambia, and would lead to the extension of NamPower's (Namibia's electricity utility) electricity grid (Terblancé 2002; Maletsky 2003b).

The project has not yet been implemented and it has already attracted criticism from both the epistemic community and interest groups. Geologists monitoring the development of the proposed project have expressed "grave concern". The geologists, under the leadership of Professor Terence McCarthy of the University of Witwatersrand in South Africa, said the most significant impact would be the impoundment of river sediment by the weir. "Approximately 100,000 cubic metres of sand are brought into the panhandle portion of the Okavango swamps each year. This sediment is vital to the functioning of the ecosystem", McCarthy said. The sediment forces constantly change, resulting in continuous ecosystem renewal within the delta (Maletsky 2003a).

A number of public meetings in Namibia and Botswana were organized in February 2003 to gauge public opinion concerning the project. In Botswana, participants at one of the meetings in Gabarone rejected the plan. Fears, mainly from proprietors of safari companies, were expressed that the installation would destroy the delta. Residents of Maun also said that they would not allow the Namibian government to continue with the project. They are dependent on the Okavango Delta as a source of revenue because Maun is the base for safari operators, hotels and lodges. Residents stated that plants and animals would die if the project were implemented. The livelihood of people living around the delta would therefore end (Terblancé 2003; Maletsky 2003a; Retief 2003) according to them. The same fears as were expressed over the SOIWDP and the ENWC were raised, and again it was interest groups in Botswana that most vociferously opposed the proposed project.

Because of the aversion towards the project, NamPower's general manager, John Langford, indicated that it would not continue with the project if there "are some concerns that we [NamPower] cannot mitigate ... We will be transparent and if this project is not feasible we will look at other options." Moreover, OKACOM also has to approve the project. At the time of writing OKACOM has not yet given its approval (Maletsky 2003a). There is therefore at this stage uncertainty regarding the implementation of the proposed project.

## The epistemic community's role

The role of the epistemic community has already been touched upon to a certain extent in the previous section. Here we will look more into the community's role in the hydropolitics of the Okavango River. Again, as in the case of interest groups, the epistemic community acts as a link between internal security matters and the international domain.

Regarding this, the community may be important as an information broker. Information itself may be withheld or even classified (securitized), invoking national security. We have seen that "security" can be a strategic construct and that non-military reasoning can inspire securitization. A plethora of reasons can underlie the non-sharing of information, from a desire to monopolize strategic knowledge, to a sense of vulnerability down to sheer embarrassment because the information is incomplete, ill understood, disorganized or inaccessible, which can breed distrust and hostility.

Reasonably impartial knowledge brokers can help take the sting out of information deadlock or fill knowledge gaps. Indeed, during the past decade the epistemic community has started to become increasingly involved in matters concerning the Okavango River Basin. This is not to say that previously there was no interest, but the frequency of the involvement increased significantly during the 1990s, owing to the water discourse putting more focus on the river basin as a potential source of conflict and cooperation and because of the unique natural characteristics of this aquatic system (the delta's Ramsar site status and its being seen as one of Africa's last "untouched wildernesses") (Meissner 1998a: 99).

So-called multi-stakeholder platforms (MSPs) that bring conflicting parties and neutral knowledge facilitators around the table can function as forums for defusing conflict and facilitate constructive negotiation and joint learning (Röling and Woodhill 2001; Warner 2006). So-called "water governance games" are role-playing MSPs in which actors (preferably those involved in or close to the conflict) play each other's role; they can thus simulate actor responses to intervention and crisis scenarios (Baraglio Granja and Warner 2006). This facilitates an analysis of security positions and how they are affected by change – a participatory security impact assessment. A precondition for this is that actors recognize their interdependence in both the problem and the solution (Röling and Woodhill 2001).

A number of studies have been conducted on the socio-economic and natural conditions of the Okavango River Basin. We will briefly focus on two such projects – the Green Cross International (GCI) Water for Peace Okavango Project and the Water and Ecosystem Resources in Regional Development (WERRD) project.

## The GCI project

The GCI's Water for Peace project consists of a number of scientists from a wide range of academic disciplines, from the natural to the social sciences. The project is an initiative implemented in conjunction with the "From Potential Conflict to Cooperation Potential" project of the United Nations Educational, Scientific and Cultural Organization (UNESCO). The GCI project's main rationale is the building and strengthening of OKACOM. The crucial factor "in ensuring sustainable and equitable water resources sharing is the level of cohesion within OKACOM. This will contribute to the social integration of a marginalized state such as Angola, as well as allowing civil-society to engage with the respective governments, through the commission" (Turton and Earle 2003: 2).

## The WERRD project

The WERRD project, under the auspices of Linköping University in Sweden, is running parallel with the GCI's project but has dissimilar objectives. This project also consists of scientists from the natural to the social sciences. WERRD's general objective "is to increase the understanding of the pre-condition for improved livelihoods for people living in different parts of the Okavango river basin without compromising essential environmental concerns, and to elevate relevant policies concerning land and water. Apart from policies within national entities, the attempts to formulate and assist in the execution of basin-wide policies are of key interest" (Lundqvist 2002: 1).

These projects, and the involvement of the epistemic community through them, is an indication of an attempt to present a balanced view to prevent resource conflict, build grassroots diplomatic contacts and strengthen cooperation within an international river basin. Interest groups and governments are usually at loggerheads over the sustainable utilization of an international river basin's water resources. The GCI and WERRD projects may contribute to a more stable political environment. In such an environment governments and civil society actors can engage each other through meaningful dialogue and come to an understanding regarding the environment and the security issues at stake. The epistemic community can therefore act as a stabilizing agent through the scientific validation of certain securitized issues and as an initiator of dialogues between stakeholders. It is also a linkage agent, connecting the internal and external political milieus of the Okavango River Basin.

## Conclusion

A number of internal security aspects of the basin countries play a role in the development of the Okavango River. In Angola, the end of the civil war, the resettlement of IDPs and their reintegration into the Angolan economy through agriculture, and the rehabilitation of the Angolan economy are high on the security agenda. Botswana, on the other hand, is concerned with the "pristine" quality of the Okavango Delta as a tourist and Ramsar site. For Namibia, sustained socio-economic development through the implementation of water resources management projects tops the agenda. Thus, different security issues and constructions (in different security domains) are at stake within the Okavango River Basin and have an impact on its hydropolitics.

In Table 12.2 the actors and the securitized objects within the Okavango River are identified. Although we have assigned values on the basis of the above analysis, such an analysis should preferably be carried out together with the conflicting parties or with actors able to

Table 12.2  A security impact assessment of the Okavango River Basin

| Actor | Geopolitical position | Power political position | Securitized object |
|---|---|---|---|
| Angola | Upstream −2 | Weak economy, because of civil war, but has potential to become stronger −3 | Water for post-civil war rehabilitation −3 |
| Namibia | Mid-riparian −1 | Strong economy and HIV/AIDS epidemic +3 | Water for socio-economic development −2 |
| Botswana | Downstream riparian +1 | Strong economy and HIV/AIDS epidemic +3 | Water for tourism in the delta +4 |
| Interest groups | Internal and external to the basin +4 | Can be influential in the policy processes of the Okavango River Basin 0 | The entire Okavango River Basin and especially the Okavango Delta +5 |
| Epistemic community | Internal and external to the basin +4 | Can be influential in the policy processes of the Okavango River Basin +1 | The entire Okavango River Basin +4 |

represent them credibly, of course in much more detail. The method recognizes that both state and non-state actors have the ability to (counter-)securitize issues in the basin.

In addition to incompatible core values, both groups can be at logger-heads over facts. Where both values and facts are at stake, a joint learning multi-stakeholder process with experts and lay people would be in order to get a handle on the matter (Verhallen et al. 2007). By providing verifiable information, the epistemic community can take the lead in de-securitizing issues from this environment (though, we hasten to say, this role does not have to be limited to this community). It is also well placed to take a "holistic" (integrated, basin-wide) view of the area.[5]

From Table 12.2 it is clear that different security issues are important in the context of different political and socio-economic environments. The scoring of these issues on the SIA scale also varies according to the type of actor, the milieu, the geopolitical and power political positions, and the securitized object (presented as a Buzan diagram – securitizable issues organized by domain – in Table 12.3).

The general conclusion to be drawn is that most of the security issues can be rated as positive for sustainable management of the water system.

Table 12.3 The Buzan model applied to the Okavango case: Securitizable issues by domain

| Level | Type of security | | | | |
| --- | --- | --- | --- | --- | --- |
| | Physical | Economic | Ecological | Cultural | Political |
| International | | | Threatened integrity of Ramsar site (Botswana, international interest groups) | | |
| Regional | Threat to peaceful coexistence | | | | Reputation of OKACOM |
| National | Civil war; HIV/AIDS; hydraulic mission, socio-economic development, and the Ramsar site | National socio-economic development (Namibia, Angola, Botswana) | Drought (Namibia and Botswana) | Threatened identity (community groups); internally displaced persons (Angola) | Water resources development policies |

Only one is neutral: the role and impact of interest groups on the policy processes of the Okavango River Basin. The only negative aspects are Botswana's geopolitical position in the basin and Angola's weakened economy.

This generally positive outlook should be viewed with caution. Internal security issues inform the regulations and policies by which the three riparian countries manage their water resources. These regulations and policies are quite divergent, making it difficult to come up with a comprehensive plan to manage the water resources of the Okavango River. This could lead to the unsustainable development of the Okavango River by each of the riparians. There is, therefore, an endangering element inherent in the internal security issues as regards sustainable development. However, there are three balancing factors in this regard.

The first is the role and involvement of interest groups. Although environmental interest groups have the ability to develop a "water war" discourse, it is their efforts to "save" the delta that have truly raised awareness of the area throughout the world. This has directly led to the second element – the role and involvement of the epistemic community as a stabilizing dialogue initiator and linkage agent. The epistemic community is therefore a go-between between non-state entities and OKACOM – the third balancing factor. Having the necessary information from non-state entities and the epistemic community, OKACOM can make informed decisions regarding the sustainable development of the Okavango River Basin. Thus, although internal and transnational security issues have the potential to endanger the sustainable development of the Okavango River Basin, a number of actors (interest groups, the epistemic community, and OKACOM) can mitigate this danger through dialogue and an informed understanding of these issues.

It should be noted that the SIA scale is based on our subjective observation of the actors, environments and security issues operating within the Okavango River Basin. Other observers, using a more refined methodology, might come to a different conclusion than ours, which is only tentative and subject to change over time. What is important though is that the basis for a model for the analysis of security issues has been introduced to the water discourse. We hope that the instrument will kick off a more participatory approach to water management and security issues.

## Notes

1. An argument made by environmental interest groups to highlight the negative implications of large dams.

2. Cultural studies of risk, with landmark publications by Holling (1978) and Douglas and Wildawsky (1982), suggest that risk perception correlates with the degree of social organization and the links between rules and solidarity ("group" and "grid"). In the case of great *uncertainty*, different "stories" about how a mishap emerged, based on competing cultural knowledge systems, can take on great significance. Because they need to support their way of life against others, different groups will construct the world such that their world view best supports their way of organizing. This leads to "contradictory certitudes", that is, each group is certain of certain things but the certainties clash with those held by the other groups (Thompson 1989).

3. It is helpful in this respect to follow Venter's (1998) identification of macro and micro political risks, the former affecting the whole system, the latter only a sector or industry.

4. Note that such an assessment may be based not only on the current opinion of stakeholders but also on reasoning to predict what people might think in the future. The latter has the advantage that the stakeholders can less easily try to manipulate the outcome if they are aware of the research aim. Since we are interested in predicting strategies and the underlying opinions of stakeholders, it is important to compare the prevailing perceptions even if they are illogical from the perspective of the researcher.

5. We should of course not be naive about the impartiality of the epistemic community – research is being paid for and sometimes pressure is applied by paymasters to come up with a particular view. A diversity of views, as represented in Multi-Stakeholder Platforms, seems the best guarantee to overcome such bias.

## REFERENCES

Ashton, Peter (2000a), "Southern African Water Conflicts: Are They Inevitable or Preventable?", in Hussein Solomon and Anthony Turton, eds, *Water Wars: Enduring Myth or Impending Reality*, Africa Dialogue Monograph Series No. 2, Durban: African Centre for the Constructive Resolution of Disputes.

——— (2000b), "Southern Africa Water Conflicts: Are They Inevitable or Are They Preventable?", in Green Cross International, *Water for Peace in the Middle East and Southern Africa*, Geneva: GCI.

——— (2003), "The Search for an Equitable Basis for Water Sharing in the Okavango River Basin", in Mikiyasu Nakayama, ed., *International Waters in Southern Africa*, Tokyo: United Nations University Press.

Ashton, Peter and Marian Neal (2003), "An Overview of Key Strategic Issues in the Okavango Basin", in Anthony R. Turton, Peter Ashton and Eugene Cloete, eds, *Transboundary Rivers, Sovereignty and Development: Hydropolitical Drivers in the Okavango River Basin*, Pretoria and Geneva: African Water Issues Research Unit (AWIRU) and Green Cross International.

Baraglio Granja, Sandra Inês and Jeroen Warner (2006), "A Construção de Jogos de Negociação para Bacias Hidrográficas: Ampliando Práticas de Gestão", paper presented at the X Coloquio Internacional Sobre Poder Local, Salvador, Bahia, 11–13 December.

Bauman, Zygmunt (1999), *In Search of Politics*, Chicago: Stanford University Press.

Beer, Stafford (1987), "Foreword (Metacomment)", in John P. van Gigch, *Decision Making about Decision Making: Metamodels and Metasystems*, Cambridge, MA: Abacus Press.

Berger, Peter L. and Thomas Luckmann (1966), *The Social Construction of Reality: A Treatise in the Sociology of Knowledge*, Garden City, NY: Anchor Books.

Buzan, B. (1991), *People, States, and Fear*, New York: Harvester Wheatsheaf.

Buzan, Barry, Ole Waever and Jaap de Wilde (1998), *Security: A New Framework for Analysis*, London: Lynne Rienner Publishers.

Calvocoressi, Peter (1987), *World Politics Since 1945*, London: Longman.

Campbell, Horace G. (2000), "Militarism, Warfare, and the Search for Peace in Angola", in York Bradshaw and Stephen N. Ndegwa, eds, *The Uncertain Promise of Southern Africa*, Bloomington: Indiana University Press.

Cilliers, Jakkie (2000), "Resource Wars – A New Type of Insurgency", in Jakkie Cilliers and Christian Dietrich, eds, *Angola's War Economy: The Role of Oil and Diamonds*, Pretoria: Institute for Security Studies.

Conley, Allan (1995), "A Synoptic View of Water Resources in Southern Africa", paper presented at the Southern Africa Foundation for the Economic Research on Integrated Development of Regional Water Resources Conference, Nyanga, Zimbabwe, November, unpublished.

CSIR [Council for Scientific and Industrial Research] (1997), *An Assessment of the Potential Downstream Impacts in Namibia and Botswana of the Okavango River – Grootfontein Pipeline Link to the Eastern National Water Carrier in Namibia: Initial Environmental Evaluation Report*, Contract Report to Water Transfer Consultants, Windhoek, Namibia, by the Division of Water, Environment and Forestry Technology, CSIR, Report No. ENV/P/C 97120.

Davenport, Rodney H. and Christopher Saunders (2000), *South Africa: A Modern History*, Houndmills and New York: Macmillan Press and St Martin's Press.

Douglas, Mary and Aaron Wildawsky (1982), *Risk and Culture*, Berkeley: University of California Press.

DWA [Department of Water Affairs] South West Africa Branch (1974), *Water Resource Development in South West Africa with Special Reference to the Utilisation of Surplus Water Sources within the Country as an Alternative to the Utilisation of the Northern Border Rivers*, Windhoek: Department of Water Affairs, South West Africa Branch.

DWA South West Africa Branch and Hydroconsults (1969), *Okavango River Project Popa Falls Hydro Power Scheme: Preliminary Feasibility Study*, Windhoek: Department of Water Affairs, South West Africa Branch.

EIU [Economist Intelligence Unit] (2002), *Country Profile Namibia*, New York: Economist Intelligence Unit.

Espeland, Wendy N. (1998), *The Struggle for Water: Politics, Rationality, and Identity in the American Southwest*, Chicago: Chicago Series in Law and Society.

Fidzani, Happy (1998), "Land Reform and Primitive Accumulation: A Closer Look at the Botswana Tribal Grazing Land Policy", in Wayne A. Edge and Mogopodi H. Lekorwe, eds, *Botswana: Politics and Society*, Pretoria: J. L van Schaik Publishers.

Gleditsch, Nils P. (1998), "Armed Conflict and the Environment: A Critique of the Literature", *Journal of Peace Research*, Vol. 35, No. 3.

Handley, Antoinette (1997), "South and Southern Africa", in *South African Yearbook of International Affairs, 1997*, Johannesburg: South African Institute of International Affairs.

Heyns, Piet (1995), "Existing and Planned Water Development Projects on International Rivers within the SADC Region", paper presented at the Conference of SADC Ministers Responsible for Water Resources Management, Pretoria, 23–24 November, unpublished.

———— (2003), "Water-Resources Management in Southern Africa", in Mikiyasu Nakayama, ed., *International Waters in Southern Africa*, Tokyo: United Nations University Press.

Holling, C. S., ed. (1978), *Adaptive Environmental Assessment and Management*, New York: John Wiley.

Huntington, Samuel P. (1993), "The Clash of Civilizations", *Foreign Affairs*, Vol. 72.

Kirsten, Johann and Marius Bester (1997), "Political-Constitutional Change in Angola and Mozambique since Independence: A Comparative Perspective", *Politieia*, Vol. 16, No. 2.

Lees, Susan (2001), "Kicking off the *Kaiko*; Instability, Opportunism and Crisis in Ecological Anthropology", in Ellen Messer and Michael Lambek, *Ecology and the Sacred: Engaging the Anthropology of Roy. A. Rappaport*, Ann Arbor: University of Michigan Press, pp. 49–64.

Leiss, William and Christina Chociolko (1994), *Risk and Responsibility*, Montreal: McGill University Press.

Lindholm, Helena (1995), "Water and the Arab-Israeli Conflict", in Leif Ohlsson, ed., *Hydropolitics: Conflicts over Water as a Development Constraint*, Dhaka: University Press.

Linklater, Andrew and J. MacMillan, eds (1995), *Boundaries in Question: New Directions in International Relations*, London: Frances Pinter.

Lundqvist, Jan (2002), *Water and Ecosystem Resources in Regional Development – Balancing Societal Needs and Wants and Natural Resources Systems Sustainability in International River Basin System – Technical Annex*, Linköping, Sweden.

McCaffrey, S. (1995). "The International Law Commission Adopts Draft Articles on International Watercourses", *American Journal of International Law*, Vol. 89.

Maletsky, Christoff (2003a), "Impact of Popa Scheme Could Be Felt for 'Several Centuries'", *The Namibian*, 10 January.

———— (2003b), "Popa Hydropower Plants Get Cold Shoulder in Botswana", *The Namibian*, 18 February.

Meissner, Richard (1998a), "Water as a Source of Political Conflict and Cooperation: A Comparative Analysis of the Situation in the Middle East and Southern Africa" (in Afrikaans), MA dissertation, Department of Political Studies, Rand Afrikaans University (RAU), Johannesburg, South Africa.

———— (1998b), "Piping Water from the Okavango River to Namibia – The Role of Communities and Pressure Groups in Water Politics", *Global Dialogue*, Vol. 3, No. 2.

———— (1998c), "Water Wars – Myth or Reality?", *SAIIA Review*, Vol. 6, No. 1.

———— (2002), "Regional Food Security: Using the Concept of Virtual Water", *African Security Review*, Vol. 11, No. 3.

NamPower (n.d.), "Popa Falls", at ⟨http://www.nampower.com.na/2005/pages/popa-reports.asp⟩ (accessed 27 November 2007).

——— (2003), "Popa Falls Power Project to Be Investigated", Windhoek, Nam-Power.
Neme, Laurel A. (1997), "The Power of a Few: Bureaucratic Decision-making in the Okavango Delta", *Journal of Modern African Studies*, Vol. 35, No. 1.
Ohlsson, Leif (1995), *Water and Security in Southern Africa*, Publications on Water Resources No. 1, Stockholm: SIDA, Department for Natural Resources and the Environment.
Pearce, Justin, Ranjeni Munusamy and Sechaba ka Nkosi (2002), "Savimbi's Last Hours", *Sunday Times*, 24 February, p. 1.
Pinheiro, Isidro M. G., Gabaake Gabaake and Piet Heyns (2003), "Co-operation in the Okavango River Basin: The OKACOM Perspective", paper presented at Workshop 1 of the Okavango Pilot Project in Maun, Botswana, 9–11 September.
Porto, Joao G. and Jenny Clover (2003), "The Peace Dividend in Angola: Strategic Implications for the Okavango Basin Cooperation", paper presented at Workshop 1 of the Okavango Pilot Project in Maun, Botswana, 9–11 September.
PRS [Political Risk Services] (2003a), *Angola*, East Syracuse: PRS Group Inc.
——— (2003b), *Botswana*, East Syracuse: PRS Group Inc.
Ramberg, Lars (1997), "A Pipeline from the Okavango River?", *Ambio*, Vol. 26, No. 2.
Ramsar Convention on Wetlands (1999), "A Framework for International Cooperation for the Management of the Okavango Basin and Delta", Ramsar COP7 DOC. 20.5, paper presented to the 7th Meeting of the Conference of Contracting Parties to the Convention on Wetlands, San Jose, Costa Rica, 10–18 May.
Republic of Namibia (2001), *Second National Development Plan (NDP2), 2001/02–2005/06*, Windhoek: National Planning Commission.
Retief, Christo (2003), "Popa trek vuur uit Botswana", *Die Republikein*, 21 February.
Rittel, Horst and Melvin Webber (1973), "Dilemmas in a General Theory of Planning", in *Policy Sciences*, Vol. 4, pp. 155–169, Amsterdam: Elsevier Scientific Publishing Company.
Röling, Niels (1994), "Platforms for Decision-making about Ecosystems", in Louise Fresco, Leo Stroosnijder, Johan Bouma and Herman van Keulen, eds, *The Future of the Land. Mobilising and Integrating Knowledge for Land Use Options*, Chichester: Wiley and Sons, pp. 385–395.
Röling, Niels and Jim Woodhill (2001), "From Paradigms to Practice: Foundations, Principles and Elements for Dialogue on Water, Food and Environment", background document for the Workshop on National and Basin Dialogue Development, Bonn, 1–2 December.
Schwarz, Ernest H. L. (1921), "The Control of Climate by Lakes", *Geographical Journal*, Vol. 57.
Scudder, Thayer (1997), "Resettlement", in Asit K. Biswas, ed., *Environmental Planning, Management and Development*, New York: McGraw-Hill.
Smit, Pierre (1991), "The Kavango Area: Resources, Population and Development" (in Afrikaans), MSc dissertation, Department of Geography, University of Stellenbosch.

Stern, Christel and Brigitte Lau (1990), *Namibian Water Resources and Their Management: A Preliminary History*, Windhoek: National Archives of Namibia.

Swatuk, Larry A. (1996), "Power and Water: The Coming Order in Southern Africa", *Southern African Perspectives*, No. 58.

Szerszynski, Bronislaw (2002), "Ecological Rites: Ritual Action in Environmental Protest Events", *Theory, Culture and Society*, Vol. 19, No. 33, pp. 51–69.

Tansey, James (2004), "Risk as Politics, Culture as Power", *Sustainable Development Research*, Vol. 7, No. 1, pp. 17–32.

Terblancé, Niël (2002), "Popa-krag 'n werklikheid", *Die Republikein*, 18 December.

———— (2003), "Waterkrag by Popa-valle weer onder soeklig", *Die Republikein*, 7 February.

Thompson, Michael (1989), "From Myths as Falsehoods to Myths as Repositories of Experience and Wisdom", commentary to John J. Metz, "Himalayan Political Economy: More Myths in the Closet", *Mountain Research and Development*, Vol. 9, No. 2.

Treaty (1990), "Agreement between the Government of the Republic of Botswana and the Government of the Republic of Namibia on the Establishment of a Joint Permanent Water Commission".

———— (1994), "Agreement between the Government of the Republic of Angola, the Republic of Botswana and the Republic of Namibia on the Establishment of a Permanent Okavango River Basin Water Commission (OKACOM)".

Turton, Anthony R. (2000), "Water Wars in Southern Africa: Challenging Conventional Wisdom", in Green Cross International, ed., *Water for Peace in the Middle East and Southern Africa*, Geneva: GCI.

———— (2003), "The Evolution of Water Management Institutions in Selected Southern African International River Basins", in Cecilia Tortajada, Ole Unver and Asit K. Biswas, eds, *Water and Regional Development*, London: Oxford University Press.

Turton, Anthony and Anton Earle (2003), "Project Report April 2002–March 2003", in *Green Cross International Okavango Project: A Component of the GCI Water for Peace Project*, Geneva: GCI.

Turton, Anthony R., Petrus Brynard and Richard Meissner (2002), "Four Strategic Policy Issues for Consideration by the Permanent Okavango River Basin Water Commission (OKACOM)", paper presented at the Workshop for Water and Ecosystem Resources in Regional Development (WERRD), in conjunction with the 3rd WATERNET/WARFSA Symposium on Water Demand Management for Sustainable Use of Water Resources, IWRM, Dar es Salaam, 30–31 October, unpublished.

UNAIDS [Joint United Nations Programme on HIV/AIDS] (2002), *Epidemiological Fact Sheets on HIV/AIDS and Sexually Transmitted Infections: Namibia*, New York: United Nations.

USAID [United States Agency for International Development] (n.d.), "Conflict Management", at ⟨http://www.usaid.gov/locations/sub-saharan_africa/sectors/cm/index.html⟩ (accessed 27 November 2007).

Venter, Albert J. (1998), "An Assessment of the Micro-Political Risks: Reasoned Decision-Making as a Management Tool", *Politeia*, Vol. 17, No. 2.

Verhallen, Annemiek, Jeroen Warner and Leo Santbergen (2007), "Towards Evaluating MSPs for Integrated Catchment Management", in Jeroen Warner, ed., *Multi-Stakeholder Platforms for Integrated Water Management*, Aldershot: Ashgate, pp. 259–273.

Viotti, P. R. and M. V. Kauppi (1999), *International Relations Theory: Realism, Pluralism and Beyond*, Needham Heights: Allyn & Bacon.

Warner, Jeroen F. (2006), "More Sustainable Participation? Multi-Stakeholder Platforms for Integrated Catchment Management", *International Journal of Water Resources Development*, Vol. 22, No. 1, pp. 15–35.

Wellington, James H. (1949), "Zambezi-Okavango Development Projects", *Geographical Review*, Vol. 39.

Wester, Philippus and Jeroen Warner (2002), "River Basin Management Reconsidered", in A. Turton and R. Henwood, eds, *Hydropolitics in the Developing World: A Southern African Perspective*, Pretoria, South Africa: African Water Issues Research Unit, pp. 61–71.

World Bank (2000a), *GNI per Capita 2000, Atlas Method and PPP*, Washington DC: World Bank.

―――― (2000b), *Countries: Angola*, Washington DC: World Bank.

―――― (2000c), *Countries: Namibia*, Washington DC: World Bank.

# Part IV

## Conclusions

# 13

# National sovereignty and human security: Changing realities and concepts in international water management

*Nevelina I. Pachova, Mikiyasu Nakayama and Libor Jansky*

The past several decades have brought about important changes in the theory and practice of international relations. Most notable among them have been the widespread recognition of human security as the ultimate goal, justifying the existence of states, and the multiplication of actors, both in the domestic and in the international arena, allegedly safe-guarding human security from state failures. Water security, i.e. all aspects of human security pertaining to the use and management of water, has thus become a key objective of a range of governmental and non-governmental agencies across the spectrum of governance levels and integrated water resources management is increasingly seen as the means for ensuring it.

In the case of international waters, i.e. waters shared by two or more states, inter-state cooperation in water management has been traditionally seen and interpreted as infringing the sovereignty of riparian states. The changing security paradigm and the associated changes in both domestic political systems and inter-state relations, however, require that international water management and the challenges for ensuring international water security be re-examined from a new perspective, namely one that recognizes state sovereignty as a means for ensuring human security rather than as a goal in itself.

In democratic states, sovereignty, i.e. the exclusive right to exercise supreme political authority over a geographical region, a group of people or oneself, is held by the people. They can exercise their power through different mechanisms, e.g. directly, through popular assemblies, or more

*International water security: Domestic threats and opportunities, Pachova, Nakayama and Jansky (eds), United Nations University Press, 2008, ISBN 978-92-808-1150-6*

commonly indirectly, through elected representatives and civil rights movements aimed at redressing political misrepresentations of social preferences and human security goals. The rise of democratization in the post–Cold War era has thus allegedly given an increasing number of people in different states across the globe an important role to play in determining what national sovereignty means.

At the same time, the processes of globalization have been changing the decision-making context for both private and public agents and agencies over recent decades. The expansion of information and communication technologies and of international trade has enhanced the opportunities for independent learning and action. Meanwhile, the growing economic, political and social integration and interdependence of states have considerably reduced their capacity to act recklessly, both domestically and internationally.

How these processes have changed the power balances and the relationships among actors in international water management and the implications of the evolution of the concepts of sovereignty and security for the search for effective, equitable and sustainable approaches to ensuring international water security are questions open to debate. The collection of studies included in this volume broach some of them, with a particular focus on recent changes in domestic security considerations and concerns and the challenges and opportunities for international water security arising from them.

## Understanding change: New perceptions of root causes and new drivers of international water security threats

Understanding how domestic factors and processes have interplayed with key actors in shaping their strategies and influencing international water management decision-making in the past can serve as a starting point for assessing the changes that have taken place over recent decades. For that purpose, however, past water management cases need to be re-examined through the lens of human security rather than state sovereignty, as commonly done in the past. The set of historical case studies from Africa, Asia and Europe included in this collection attempt to do that.

The findings from the examined cases confirm the well-established understanding of the critical importance of national economic development considerations as a driving force for domestic decisions on international water management, in a complex context of domestic and international political incentives and constraints. But they go beyond that recognition to highlight the fact that state agencies have been the most prominent decision makers in international water management cases in the past. Furthermore, their decisions have often been based upon unsustainable and inequitable economic policies, inter-institutional competition and political power games, which have commonly distorted domestic water needs and the options available for addressing them. This has often led governments into hasty commitments to joint water development schemes and has delayed urgently needed international water developments, thus posing an array of water and human security threats in international river basins in the past.

Domestic power relations and the policies that maintain them undoubtedly continue to influence international water management and security today. Furthermore, they continue to be disguised as physical and demographic realities, which are treated as given, rather than as the results of state policies that are subject to change. The current rise of population concentrations along the banks of the Nile River in Sudan, which threatens to strain riparian relations with Egypt, is a clear illustration of this point. The in-depth analysis of the root causes of the problem at hand highlights refugee flows from regions torn by civil war and inequitable economic development and water management policies as the driving forces that need to be addressed if water and human security in the region are to be ensured and maintained. The study demonstrates the multi-level causes of international water security threats and the need to recognize and address them correspondingly.

The democratization wave that has taken place over recent decades seems to have brought about a set of changes that could facilitate the development of the necessary multi-level integrated responses to international water security threats in some parts of the world. With the increasing recognition of civil rights and the voice of people in policy-making concerning their well-being, environmental and social activist groups have begun to command the power to check distorted political and economic motifs and redress injustices in cost–benefit sharing and security trade-offs from large-scale water development works. The Lesotho Highlands Water Project and the Gabčíkovo-Nagymaros project illustrate some of the alternative uses to which the rising power of domestic social and environmental movements can be put in the course of implementation of state-supported international water management projects and schemes that fail to address the social and environmental security threats they create.

Civil society checks on political distortions of domestic security concerns, however, have their limitations, both in light of the extent and scope of the new power of domestic publics and in terms of their capacities to appreciate and use it wisely. Post factum adjustments to water management schemes may not be able to address all relevant security concerns and redress irreversible consequences. At the same time, social and environmental causes can be easily kidnapped in support of political interests and goals, which in turn can politicize international water management projects, endangering international security and peace. This is a particularly potent threat in multi-ethnic societies changing at different paces, as demonstrated by the Gabčíkovo-Nagymaros water management case. Maintaining the right balance is most often a question of adaptive learning, yet what exactly this means and how it can be stimulated and enhanced are questions open to research.

Furthermore, authoritarian and semi-authoritarian states continue to exist alongside democratizing ones, and the inability of often the most vulnerable societal groups to protect both themselves and their rights needs to be taken into account when discussing international water security. The rising leverage of civil society groups in one state may threaten the livelihoods and security of marginalized social groups in another, even when no outright threat from a political conflict between the two states exists. The Salween case between Thailand and Myanmar and on-going and planned upstream water developments in the broader Mekong region discussed in the book are good illustrations of this point. They highlight emerging obligations of both domestic societies and the international community to monitor threats not only to peace but to human security and to employ their increased leverage over the domestic policies of states to ensure that appropriate compensation is integrated in all water development schemes, be they unilateral or jointly agreed.

New and promising tools for monitoring emerging threats and mechanisms for involving all relevant stakeholders in the search for effective, equitable and sustainable measures for preventing and addressing international water security threats are already being developed and explored.

## Responding to change: Engaging the challenges

Traditionally, international treaties have been the basic tools for ensuring international water security. History indicates that they provide useful frameworks and guarantees for sovereign states to support the undertaking of needed international water developments. Treaties, however, are most often drafted as static political responses to dynamically changing economic priorities, social preferences and related water needs. The growing rates of change in all spheres of life in the context of the processes of democratization and globalization, as well as the rapidly changing physical needs in the context of global climate change, are increasingly raising doubts about the adequacy and sufficiency of international treaties for ensuring international water security.

Treaties take time to negotiate. Meanwhile urgent water security needs often remain unaddressed. Furthermore, even once signed, treaties are liable to be broken under the pressures of change and related legitimacy concerns. When drafted with sufficient flexibility in mind, they may fail to provide meaningful guidance for avoiding international water management disputes and water security threats. Maximizing the benefits that treaties provide in light of the changing water security contexts and threats is essential for responding to security threats more adequately. Exclusive reliance on treaties to solve the existing and emerging water security problems we face, however, is hard to justify in light of the multi-level causes of security threats, which require appropriate responses at the level at which they emerge.

In the context of the growing recognition that one-time fixes cannot provide the necessary security guarantees, significant hopes have been placed in institutions as promising mechanisms for mediating conflicts arising from dynamically changing water security considerations and for developing adaptive responses to emerging security threats. Institutions, however, are costly and hard to maintain. Furthermore, their functionality is vulnerable to the very changes they are intended to tackle and cope with, as indicated by the history and current state of the Lake Chad and Mekong Basin commissions discussed in the book. The interlinking of the interests of regional agencies with semi-overlapping mandates in the context of the increasing recognition of the benefits from regional security cooperation and trade could provide alternative forums for discussing and addressing international water management issues and concerns, even when river basin commissions fail to do so, as indicated by the Mekong River Basin case. Although this is a potentially useful fall-back option, it is one that should be treated with caution, particularly when promoted by a regional hegemon.

Ultimately, institutions are as good as the rules and tools through which they function, and, even more so, as good as the people running them. In this regard both research and development agencies have an important role to play in enhancing individual and institutional capacities. The integration of new concepts, such as the concept of virtual water, in standard water management decision-making practices could help enhance institutional capacities to serve as adaptive agents. The concept of virtual water could serve as an innovative diagnostic tool for monitoring security threats, particularly ones associated with changes in domestic water demands, as suggested in the book. Furthermore, it could help to identify alternatives to the traditional engineering-based solutions to domestic water needs and to estimate the sufficiency of the benefits from international trade for meeting water security needs.

Similarly, the security impact assessment (SIA) concept proposed in the book and applied to the Okavango River Basin could provide a useful tool for responding to some of the emerging water security issues mentioned above. The increased number of stakeholders involved in international water management poses the challenge of integrating and balancing a wide range of diverse interests, perceptions and goals. The SIA could help cope with this issue by providing a framework for recognizing and accounting for security trade-offs arising from water development projects for all relevant stakeholders. The concepts of virtual water and SIA, however, are still primarily discussed in scientific research. The further development and adaptation of these and other relevant tools for practical use in international water management are a challenge waiting to be recognized and taken up jointly by water management scientists and practitioners.

The international development community could help support such efforts through or alongside traditional development cooperation initiatives. Collaborative research, capacity-building and information exchange in the framework of broader development cooperation projects could, as suggested in the Tigris–Euphrates case discussed in the book, provide short-term solutions to the urgent water security needs faced by the inhabitants of conflict-torn international water basins, while supporting the development of a sound basis of joint experience, shared knowledge and trust, which are essential in the search for long-term international water security.

Indeed, neither development cooperation nor any one of the proposed tools is a panacea for the problem at hand. However, their application could help enhance the understanding we currently have and highlight critical gaps that need to be filled, thus bringing us a step closer to adaptive water management.

## Bridging existing gaps: Recommendations for future research

Indeed, the changing realities and concepts in international water management over recent decades have already given rise to a range of new questions for further thought and research, as discussed in the case studies presented in the book. Issue- and case-specific recommendations have been made by the authors of the individual chapters and have been expanded upon above. At a broader scale, the collection of studies highlights the multifaceted and multi-level nature of both old and emerging international water security threats. The rise of a host of new domestic and international actors in international water management entails the possibility of finding the appropriate responses to the multi-level causes of international water security threats. It also entails a major new challenge, namely that of bringing about the realization across the various actors involved that new rights entail new responsibilities and that each stakeholder has to act in cognizance of that fact if effective, equitable and sustainable solutions to international water security are to be found.

The book has been primarily based on case studies of individual international water management cases and disputes. Although useful, this perspective is insufficient to capture all relevant aspects of the multifaceted changes that are taking place. Comparative analysis of relevant cases could help fill some of the current knowledge gaps. So could a more extensive and geographically representative selection of cases (which was not the objective of this book).

Furthermore, whereas the focus of the book has fallen on changes taking place at the domestic level, the strategies of domestic actors are inevitably developed in the framework of a complex set of international incentives and constraints. As highlighted in several places in the book, the same changes that have brought about the multiplication of domestic actors in international water management have also increased the number and leverage of international actors. In the context of the reduced power of states and the rise of the power of domestic actors, many of whom are yet to become aware of the new responsibilities that their new freedom and rights entail, the importance of international agents and agencies in maintaining an adequate balance between the interests and objectives of all relevant stakeholders involved in light of the goal of human security has also increased. How capable, effective and efficient they are in coping with their changing tasks in the context of the changing realities and concepts discussed in this book are questions that require further exploration and research.

# Index